To Les Du

Fr: R.S.

Thanks for your assistance

Hope this is usefull

WORLD
RESOURCE MANAGEMENT

J. Edwin Becht   *The University of Texas of the Permian Basin*

L. D. Belzung   *University of Arkansas*

As man is forced to depend increasingly on distant water sources, with some large cities relying on water pumped and channeled over 500 miles, a capability to measure water reserves and flow is essential to allocate and time the arrival of adequate quantities. Technologies to do this with uncanny accuracy (within .10 percent) for streams of even Columbia River volumes have been developed. Photograph shows release of Columbia River water reserves. Photograph courtesy of Westinghouse Electric Company, 1973.

PRENTICE-HALL, INC., ENGLEWOOD CLIFFS, NEW JERSEY

WORLD
RESOURCE MANAGEMENT

KEY TO CIVILIZATIONS
AND SOCIAL ACHIEVEMENT

Library of Congress Cataloging in Publication Data

Becht, J Edwin, 1918-
  World resource management.
  Includes bibliographies and index.
  1. Natural resources.   2. Power resources.
3. Human ecology.   I. Belzung, L. D., joint author.
II. Title.
HC55.B43   333.7   75-5742
ISBN 0-13-968107-8

This book is dedicated to DORENE and WANDA,
both *special* names with *special* meanings.

WORLD RESOURCE MANAGEMENT
J. Edwin Becht and L. D. Belzung

Printed in the United States of America.

10 9 8 7 6 5 4 3 2

PRENTICE-HALL INTERNATIONAL, INC., London
PRENTICE-HALL OF AUSTRALIA, PTY. LTD., Sydney
PRENTICE-HALL OF CANADA, LTD., Toronto
PRENTICE-HALL OF INDIA PRIVATE LIMITED, New Delhi
PRENTICE-HALL OF JAPAN, INC., Tokyo
PRENTICE-HALL OF SOUTHEAST ASIA (PTE.) LTD., Singapore

CONTENTS

PREFACE

Resources and their development are everyone's business. In effect, everyone expresses himself in favor of resource development because, in the course of each day, he is sustained and otherwise benefited from material comforts that can be derived only by the alteration of nature. Clearly, man cannot leave nature alone. Unaltered and untended, Mother Earth simply will not support today's population—much less tomorrow's. Man not only must add to existing resource features, but also must build new ones. For example, dams must be available to store, retain and redistribute water, and even to furnish water for cooling, navigation, and energy generation. Even so, because of man's ability to alter nature and, in too many instances, his crassness in doing so (i.e., his garbage, his pollution and pollutants), environmentally we have reached a crisis level. In short, man now must give first consideration in resource development to what his works will do to the earth's ongoing capability to sustain this *and* succeeding generations.

Even though the United States is well along in the changeover from a "products" economy to a "processing and service" economy, this does not mean that resources have become less necessary. Rather, it suggests the magnitude and diversity of activities that now rest on the base of physical resources—manufacturing, transportation, marketing, government, education, national defense, the arts, and many other aspects of modern society. Physical resources—land and its products such as timber, crops and livestock; water; mineral fuels; metals, and other nonfuel minerals—are still the indispensable bases on which civilizations are built.

Also, social achievement within any country, whether advanced or relatively backward, is dependent to a large extent on the development of resources in that country. As new resources are created, or new sources of existing resources are found and developed, a parallel refinement in marketing, management, technology, communication, and the sciences, may be observed.

Decision makers, scientists, and individual citizens must be continually aware of the broad spectrum of resources; they must recognize the impact and how it affects their community, state, and nation, as well as their own specific fields of interest. Indeed, the entire anti-poverty struggle is but a major national effort to provide the physical allocation of the country's resources so as to satisfy better the wants of its citizens. Similarly, wars and threats of wars, world trade and world corporations are but further attempts to turn the world's natural materials into resouces.

Nor are these resources-oriented problems new. A millennium before the steam engine made possible the Industrial Revolution, man's agriculture was the chief "alterer" of the environment. Plato observed and reported that deforestation and overgrazing produced soil erosion and ruination. Lack of regard for environmental factors helped destroy great civilizations of the Middle East, in the Tigris and Euphrates Valleys, and in Jordan. Their demise is history. To the deforestation and overgrazing of the past, man today has added air pollutants at levels which inhibit photosynthesis; he has introduced oxygen-using chemical agents into the lakes, streams and aquifers; he has released insecticides, herbicides, and radiation; and he has covered millions of acres of garbage, spoil banks, and mining gangue.

Thus, man's transformation of the earth is not new. Rather, it is the history of civilization. What is new about man's abuse of the land is the increased velocity of change which encompasses both the mass that is being altered and the speed with which man is changing nature. Unless *every resource development* project—old, as well as new—is weighed, and every *resource-using* activity is evaluated in terms of how such developments and activities will (in balance) aid or limit this planet's capacity to support life, and unless action is taken accordingly, current incapacitating blights will overwhelm civilizations of today, as well as those of tomorrow. Significantly, *resources* have become major issues of public policy. Indeed, President Nixon's domestic message to the Congress called for consolidation of what are now widespread, diluted, and diverse functions of government, dealing with many and varied facets of physical resources, into one federal department: The Department of Natural Resources.

Resource-related matters are being dealt with currently one by one as a series of unrelated, separate crises. Now, although not in general agreement, the public is aroused, indignant, and demanding that something be done. Seemingly too few citizens are even aware that conservationists long have been waving "red flags"—danger ahead. But the public, preoccupied with both material wants and mobility needs, has been too busy to heed warnings until today's series of crises swept over the land. Now, immediate action is demanded to correct situations that man has taken hundreds of years to foster.

Rather than crisis by crisis solutions, as this country has been attempting, what is needed is a wider appreciation and understanding of "resources" and "resource relations," especially as resources relate to cultures, technologies, economies, geographies, and social goals and values. Hopefully, in time, such appreciations and understandings will lead to forms of civilizations that will conform more nearly with the resource parameters of this planet.

Admittedly, resources are more problems of politics than of technology. Also, resource problems are more political than economic. Although the economic aspects of conservation apply to all "facets of resource development," strong conservations translated into political/economic actions will deliver major shocks, and result in long-lasting changes in life styles and standards. Even so, if politics are favorable, the economy can adjust, and science and technology already have many feasible answers. The key to sound resource management is everyone's business; and, especially in the United States, sound resource management is irrevocably locked in politics. The *key* is political action.

Thus, the chief purpose of this resources program is to bring together those appreciations and understandings of resources, especially as these relate to cultures, technologies, civilizations, and social achievements, that might help all men accept ways of life more consonant with the resource parameters of this planet.

ONE

BASIC NATURE
OF RESOURCES

INDISPENSABILITY OF RESOURCES

The United States and the world are deeply involved in the changeover from a "products" economy to a "processing and service" economy. But this transition does not mean that resources have become less vital; rather it suggests the magnitude and diversity of activities now demanding resources and that ultimately rest on a base of physical resources. Such activities include manufacturing, transportation, marketing, government, education, national defense, the arts, and many other aspects of modern society. Physical resources—land and its products like timber, crops, and livestock; water; the mineral fuels; and metals and other nonfuel minerals—are still the indispensable bases on which civilization is built. These are the *basic resources.*

Social achievement within any country, whether advanced or relatively backward, is dependent to a great extent on the development of the basic resources in that country or by that country through international trade. As new resources are created, understood, and developed, parallel refinements in such other fields as marketing, management, technology, communication, and even mathematics may be observed.[1]

---

[1] See Chapter Four.

Every person, whether as private citizen, businessman, politician, or soldier, should be aware always of the broad impact of resources on the community, state, and nation, as well as on his specific fields of interest. The U.S. antipoverty struggle, the world-corporation movement, and other efforts to satisfy the wants [2] of man are just as dependent on the proper physical distribution of resources as are hot and cold wars.

THE BASIC THEME

Inherent in the basic theme of this text—that resource mobilization and resource systems are indispensable to the advancing of civilizations and to the achieving of social progress—is the idea that every generation has had its problems; and every generation has had its optimists (and to be sure its opportunists), holding out their promises of success. Usually the major national and international goals set by men for themselves, individually or collectively, have been either to provide security and comfort (whether here on earth or in the hereafter) or to seek free choices and/or knowledge. True, for certain individuals, excitement and danger are sought and become an end in and of themselves, but for the group (especially the nation as a whole) this has not been the usual, acceptable behavior pattern.

Even though man's goals have been expressed in many different ways at different times in history,[3] and have been embodied as preambles to some of his major documents,[4] these goals have dealt to some degree with his material wealth, or his ability to guarantee himself certain rights and freedoms which, in turn, are necessarily supported by the material means of providing for police or inhibitory safeguards. These same materials are prerequisite to all goals mentioned above, excepting those that are purely religious in nature and that give considerations to a life after death. These materials, then, are the basic resources which require mobilization.

But man's ability to attain his goals and to perform those things which he considers of value is not entirely dependent on his own or national basic resources. Also affecting his level of accomplishment are certain moral-psychological factors which shape his intentions and, thus, the ultimate uses of his physical resources. However, historically, man has required

---

[2] Erich W. Zimmermann, *World Resources and Industries* (New York: Harper and Brothers Publishers, 1951), pp. 7 and 13.

[3] "Peace in Our Time," "Save the World for Democracy," "Prosperity Around the Corner," "A Chicken in Every Pot," "The Great Society," "The New Frontier," "The Square Deal," "The New Deal," "To Each in Accordance With His Labor,' "The Four Freedoms," and so on.

[4] For example, The Preamble to the Constitution of the United States and the Magna Charta.

access to basic resources to wax opulent, even if this access had to be won by force of arms.

Fortunate have been those nations with territory rich in easily developed basic resources in sufficient volume to provide comfort and security for their citizens—*although security has never lasted indefinitely for nations* —and to sustain, temporarily at least, the luxury of individual freedoms. For most countries a secure existence free from apprehension is a possibility only after the people have first endured a long struggle to mobilize basic resources and have then developed a capability to utilize these resources. Where man has appeared to be content, nature has been at least permissive, if not bountiful. So, for the most part, access to basic resources is prerequisite to satisfactory living patterns which minimize insecurity, hunger, and suffering. Individual "happiness" cannot be construed as necessarily dependent on basic resources; but man's goals can be attained only to the degree that he has access to basic resources which can provide him with mobility and physical comfort.

Characteristically, man's avenues for obtaining and harnessing basic resources are:

1. Economic
2. Political
3. Moral-psychological
4. Military/police

Usually used in combinations or sequence, these are the avenues by which man discovers, seeks out, or obtains the basic resources suggested and determined by his objectives—recognizing in turn that these objectives are shaped by controlling individual and social values.

Whatever the objectives of man, a geographical region [5] is still his arena. And according to geographers, a given region holds but eight categories of basic resources [6] (nine, if one adds a category for natural radiation). These eight categories are:

1. Terrain features	5. Natural vegetation
2. Location and spatial relations	6. Native animal life
3. Climate (and weather)	7. Water bodies
4. Soils	8. Economic minerals

---

[5] Any area defined for a purpose: i.e., political, land, soil-type, terrain, climate.

[6] Vernor C. Finch, Glenn T. Trewartha, Arthur H. Robinson, and Edwin H. Hammond, *Elements of Geography* (New York: McGraw-Hill Book Company, Inc., 1957), p. vii.

To repeat, these are the categories of basic resources to be found in any region; they are the building blocks upon which man creates his economy, practices much of his politics, and structures his police and military forces; they are the physical forces to which he attempts to apply moral-psychological factors, which are then strongly influenced and molded by the degree to which these basic resources may or may not be available.

That regions are unequally or dissimilarly endowed is axiomatic and well understood. The effects of these differences, both short- and long-range, are less well understood, as are the dynamics of regional comparisons, especially in light of changes in the relative availability of resources. They are obscure because of discoveries, technological change, depletion, the principle of increasing costs, pollution, territorial shifts, or changes in transportation and mobility. All or any of these conditions may alter man's needs or wants and, in turn, dictate his economic, political, and police-military actions. They usually reflect, and are reflected in, man's moral-psychological fiber.

CHARACTERISTICS OF THE BASIC RESOURCE MOBILIZATION PROCESS

Historically, decisions as to where certain types of economic activities take place nearly always reflect the mix or combination of basic resources that prevail in a given area. Differences in basic resources occur in every region, if for no other reason than that location and corresponding spatial relations vary from place to place, and consequently, the relative merits of one area over others have been important reasons for area specialization. Especially in primitive societies man's activities reflected the basic resources of his environment. In time, expanded transportation and communication facilities have resulted in new human wants and goals that call for basic resources from ever-widening geographic areas, until today competition for these basic resources is interwoven in virtually all that man does, including his economic activities, political action, ideologies, concern for the individual and for collective security, and in the exercise of his territorial imperative.[7]

Man's relations with basic resources is made more complex because resources differ in kind, amount, and quality from region to region; also, basic resources available to man are constantly evolving from kaleidoscopic combinations of what formerly was "neutral matter,"[8] and are tempered

[7] Robert Ardrey, *The Territorial Imperative* (New York: Atheneum Publishing Company, 1966).

[8] Zimmermann, *World Resources;* he called it "neutral stuff."

by existing cultures which, in turn, cause men to covet the potentially "basic-resource-rich" territories. Behind all these forces or pressures is the awesome immensity of man's insatiable appetite for basic resources, and the desire to have them readily available in the future—first highlighted in a scholarly way by the "President's Materials Policy Commission," perhaps more commonly known as the Paley Report.[9] The report warned that the United States had entered into a new era—new in that the country could no longer consider itself among the self-sufficient nations in terms of the basic resources required by day-to-day consumer demands. The isolationist argument could no longer be sustained, even though the 1970s have seen many unreasoning Americans lean further toward isolationist views. Beyond a doubt, the United States had become a have-not nation—especially in the fulcrum area of minerals. Before it could guarantee the technology to develop otherwise potentially favorable and secondary basic resources of land, soils, and climates, the United States would need key minerals from other lands. That this problem is far from solved even today is clear in statements by government officials.[10]

As long as three decades ago, the United States recognized that its soil resource was being seriously eroded, and within the past *two decades water pollution and air pollution have posed equally challenging crises.* They are crises that will have to be dealt with if the United States is to continue long to serve her own citizens, let alone remain as a force, hopefully for good, within the world's family of nations. Man is, indeed, at one of the resource crossroads which, although a relatively new experience for the United States, promises to become a recurring one as more and more problems develop in terms of basic resources.

How to Organize to Deal with Resource Mobilization Problems

Under the free enterprise system in western culture, no principles historically are more sacred than those contending that basic resources should

---

9 United States President's Materials Policy Commission, *Resources for Freedom; A Report to the President* (Washington, D.C.: Government Printing Office, 1952), I-V. The committee chairman was William S. Paley, chairman of the Columbia Broadcasting System.

10 Dr. Walter R. Hibbard, Jr., Director of U. S. Bureau of Mines, *Macomb Daily Journal,* February 28, 1968, p. 1, warned that the United States, alone, used more minerals during the past thirty years than the rest of the world did in all of recorded history, and he predicted that the nation's mineral consumption would double by the year 1980.

be allocated in the market place. But prices administered by government bodies on minerals and on certain agricultural products, and government controls placed on land-use or water-use, have long applied to these basic resources and have been accepted for certain commodities or for certain areas. Now, with deterioration of even those resources which were once considered in plentiful supply, and for still other basic resources, the "feast-or-famine" type problems are all the more complicated because they are combined with geometrically increasing demands and secular inflationary trends. In response to the impact of all these developments and forces, there have been, at least in the United States, congressional and executive attempts to organize an administration of resources at the Cabinet level. As far back as 1967, a federal "Department of Natural Resources" was being discussed.[11] It proposed to redesignate the Department of the Interior as the Department of Natural Resources [12] with a Secretary of Natural Resources and Under Secretaries for lands and for water. The new department would have included controls, functions, and activities of the Department of the Interior, the Forest Service, Rivers and Harbors flood control, civil works functions of the Corps of Engineers, National Oceanographic Data Center activities, the Sea Grant program, Air Pollution Control functions, Solid Waste Disposal functions, and Federal Power Act activities.

The 1967 congressional effort was not approved, and later proposals by the Nixon Administration, somewhat different, but similar in intent, fared no better; this country's bureaucratic system is strongly entrenched and any proposals that threaten to alter job-descriptions in the public sector generally meet with intense resistance, as these did.

However, this issue is very much with us, and some version of the plan to organize and administer physical resources at the Cabinet level is perhaps inevitable (e.g., during 1974 the United States and most other oil-importing nations established energy czars). Thus, the significance and timeliness of considering the entire field of basic resources at this particular time in the history of the United States is well established.

---

[11] Refer to Senate Document No. S886, February 7, 1967. President Nixon's 1971 version would have abolished seven of the twelve cabinet level departments and consolidated them along functional lines in four new super-departments. The Departments of State, Treasury, Defense, and Justice would have remained unchanged, while the other new bodies would have been the Departments of Natural Resources, Human Resources, Economic Affairs, and Community Development.

[12] Chapter Two of this book points out that resources are not "natural" and should be called resources, basic resources, or physical resources (if one wishes to distinguish them from human resources and capital resources); most specialists in the field no longer call them *natural* resources, but many laymen (and congressmen) still do!

In the United States today, individuals, corporations, and the nation collectively are concerned with basic resource problems because they have witnessed the destruction, for practical and expedient use, of vast areas of their land. And the nation has experienced the *exhaustion* of what once was considered to be *inexhaustible* mineral resources. Today the people are busily determining the nature and extent of the authority of individuals, corporations, states, and the federal government in an effort to see what conservation measures can be applied and how they can be enforced in the future. In this study, initial emphasis will be placed on the United States; and, once basic resource problems within this nation are visualized, then, perhaps, it will be meaningful to turn to other societies and cultures that have quite different goals and values. Before this can be undertaken, a greater knowledge of comparative basic resource mobilization systems must be acquired.

In fact, comparative studies of basic resource mobilization systems form one of the great frontiers that needs to be explored more diligently and understood more fully in the world today—whether these systems relate to *military and police activities,* as in Korea, Vietnam, or the Middle East; whether to *political action,* as in North Africa or Eastern Europe, or, even closer to home, the conservationists (such as the Sierra Club); or whether to *economic penetration,* such as Japan's investments in Alaska or The Netherlands, and the United States' investments in Venezuela. And a comparative study of basic resource mobilization systems, worldwide, should benefit the United States by offering suggestions about how this country can improve its own system of garnering basic resources to meet its population wants and needs now and in the future. Less directly, and in perhaps the longer run, a study would help in understanding the United States' need to trade with other countries. But most importantly, such considerations would lead to an understanding of basic resources and their attendant mobilization problems.

The ultimate goal of such a study should be to reach a degree, or a point in time, when fair, meaningful allocation of priorities can be established. A list of some of the areas that must be better understood before such allocation can be established includes the following basic resource problem areas:

1. Exploration
2. Measurement and Inventory
3. Rights

4. Timing of Exploitation
5. Production Levels
6. Exhaustibility
7. Ubiquitous Occurrence
8. Localized Occurrence
9. General Occurrence
10. Fair Price
11. Degree of Competition
12. Work Levels and Working Conditions
13. Subsidies
14. Protective Tariffs
15. Import Quotas
16. Quality
17. Abusive Trade Practices
18. Engineering Problems
19. Physical Distribution or Collection Problems
20. Social Pressures
21. Desirable Levels of Basic Resource Balance
22. Source of Authority
23. Ownership

THE INDIVIDUAL, THE BUSINESS COMMUNITY, AND BASIC RESOURCE MOBILIZATION

It is both intriguing and essential to consider three different points of view concerning the status of basic resource mobilization in the United States and in the world today. At one extreme are the so-called *preservationists* who argue that society and the individual are largely the pawns of business exploiters, cheap sophisticated hucksters, seeking to gain profit at the expense of most of the population. It seems that many preservationists would, if they could, reverse world events to the point where most of the land would be returned to its primitive state. Because they realize, for the most part, that this would be impossible, they argue for the setting aside of large tracts of land, including everything of value on or under it, to be held in a "natural state" for posterity. At the other pole are to be found the opportunists—the *exploitationists*—who are still spoiling the land without taking adequate measures to insure clean waters, clean air and return of the land to a potentially useful condition. Somewhere in between are the *conservationists,* who argue for the wise use of all basic resources. Conservationists want the resources used, but used wisely.[13]

The conservationist, however, is faced with so many alternatives that he has difficulty making a rational decision regarding even such basic questions as the establishment of acceptable levels of pollution (where pollution may be necessary technically to fulfill other essential needs and wants). At present, then, problems exist in which the basic resource that is finally mobilized may not be, in the long run, the best resource utilization for man. But it is to be hoped that, with the recording of experience and further study in the future, mankind will make ever wiser decisions toward the establishment of basic resource mobilization priorities. Certainly there are many cases where basic resource decisions are based on the individual's own experiences and may or may not best serve a nation of people. For example, consider the deplorable state of Lake Erie's polluted waters, and keep in mind that, as badly as people may want the water "cleaned up," the iron, steel, and refining industries on Lake Erie's south shores are important factors in the mobilization of basic resources to satisfy mankind's basic needs and wants. It can be argued, with merit, that these facets of the economy actually serve more individuals than do clean sand dunes and beaches, and even clear water. So the pollution of Lake Erie was not considered a serious national problem as long as only unsoiled beaches and recreation facilities were involved; but now that an abundant supply of clean water is essential for drinking purposes and for industrial use, a much wider base of concern has developed; it now is evident that the numbers of people affected may be greater than those who benefited from low-cost iron and steel, and thus the issue is now raised. The necessity, then, is for individuals, corporations, and the nation to devise a fair, authoritative system of establishing and enforcing basic resource mobilization priorities as a stark reality. A basic priority already appears to be emerging: that is, water is more important to more people than cheap iron and steel. Similarly, clean air may become more important on the "scale of priorities" than the industries which are causing the air pollution. Just as with the production of low-cost iron and steel, clean air and clean water may be purchased on our crowded planet only at a price. The roles of the individual, the corporation, and state

---

[13] "Wise use" is a term that varies, of course, with time, technology, scientific knowledge and goals of a society. Wise use of a forest might be the clearing of land to build a city or freeway, or surface restructuring and subsequent forest management on land (as a park) after minerals are removed, if that is deemed the best possible use from society's view; but currently it would not be blind designation of huge tracts to be left untouched by human hand simply so that posterity can have it, or (at the other extreme) the degradation of land for commercial purposes with consequent erosion and accompanying air and water pollution.

and national governments toward these ends are now in the process of being established. Before the many requisite roles can be determined and basic resource mobilization priorities established, broader understandings and acceptances of inherent principles will be necessary. This text will attempt to treat both areas of consideration.

The Battleground—Individual Interest and National Survival

Before basic resources are mobilized, there are several questions which should be raised. Is the result good for the individual? Is it good for society? Will it enhance the economy of the nation and the political effectiveness directed at national security? And will it add to the moral-psychological prestige of this nation by making it possible to influence the future of mankind, hopefully for the good?

In federal, state, and local legislative and regulatory chambers throughout the nation, there is an increasing degree of interest and activity dealing with basic resource mobilization. This legislative activity doubtlessly will have a significant impact on the entire nation, including individuals, the entire business community, and governmental establishment at all levels. If the legislative enthusiasm for improvement of the environment subsides before the end of this decade, this nation will be in irreparable trouble.

A mounting concern for the general well-being of the individual within his regional and national environments has reached an almost frantic level in some areas, and this critical attention is direly needed. It has become increasingly clear to many persons that, rather than our taking an individual or limited (by area) view of basic resources mobilization problems, organizations above the state level are needed to examine nationwide problems. Some interstate agreements such as the Ohio River Valley compact already have proven to have merit. Still, because of the vast scope of basic resource problems and the attendant costs, it now appears to be time for government action on the national scale.

Government proposals at the national level are the apparent result of a groundswell of sentiment devoted to the individual's health, happiness, and his right to be heard. Such actions contain warnings for business and for those individuals who have enjoyed relatively low-cost material benefits from mining, farming, or manufacturing activities without fully considering the social cost of their pollution or exploitation. Technological developments are responsible for many of this nation's environmental problems, and technology must be relied upon, at a cost, to solve many of them. In all fairness, it should be pointed out that business reaction to better resource utilization has been "reluctantly" favorable and the response generally rather good, when one considers the capital outlays involved. For example, many industries are installing pollution abatement equipment and expending large sums of money in research, seeking technical solutions to their disposal and exploitation problems. Still, new laws probably are needed and new legislation undoubtedly must provide additional incentives for polluters and exploiters to find solutions to many resource-use problems in the decades immediately ahead. No doubt there will be a greater reliance on legal measures. Incentives to industry can range from subsidies (financial or research-and-development aid) to penalties for the offenders.

Legal measures understandably constitute a highly sensitive area to individuals interested in basic resources. This is because, all too often, the adoption of legal measures reduces flexibility and responsiveness to future problems which are bound to result as a hierarchy of priorities emerges, putting some business firms and individuals on the defensive. These firms and individuals, long inured by the impersonal nature of today's automated society, are for the first time finding that the specific source of their particular pollution is being sought out and exposed to public opinion. And public opinion is crying out against what is considered the imposition of big business's impact on the general environment. What has been until now a growing abyss between the producer of basic resources and the individual citizen—primarily owing to the mechanical, impersonal nature of today's mass production techniques and the vastness of the production system—is now lessening. An information void, caused by a lack of personal knowledge of what it has taken to produce basic resources, is now being filled, and the real expense of "low-cost production" is being weighed against the higher costs of other aspects of basic resource mobilization. Whatever the causes, individual and governmental interests in basic resource mobilization are receiving more attention today in terms of money, news space, and serious concern than ever before. The 1970s will be recorded as the decade that saved this nation's environment, if public opinion does not tire of the subject and divert its attention to other problems.

There is an urgent need for the means to harness, on the one hand, and to respond to, on the other, the wants, needs, and aspirations of individuals within our society. The immediate concern is to establish communication channels from individuals to the government, from the government to business concerns, and from business concerns back to the individual, with the goal of measuring individual interest, prejudices, and attitudes. Ever more government legislation and regulatory activity are based on the questions, "Is good for the individual, is it good for the nation, and does it enhance the nation's position in relation to other countries and its own survival?" When answers to such queries are considered in subsequent action, the result should be the establishment of a society in which basic resource mobilization more nearly reflects the middle ground of the conservationist.

This would arrest the fears of the preservationists and hinder the exploitation by the inconsiderate. There should be a middle ground—there has to be. If not, it may be that the people cannot afford the real cost of those basic resources that will be needed to satisfy all of the declared needs and wants of the growing population. Why, then, mobilize basic resources if no feasible, equitable allocation system can be devised which, at the same time, can pay the "real cost" of attendant pollution or exploitation problems?

Government and Basic Resources

It is especially important that the general population has a knowledge of the relation between government and basic resource mobilization. More and more, government agencies are expected to maintain an orderly environment within which citizens can live in comfort and security. Examples of such government activities include the provision of machinery for enforcing copyrights, the establishment and enforcement of pollution levels, allocations of basic resources, research into substitutes for basic resources, exploration, inventory, and priorities.

SOCIAL ISSUES IN BASIC RESOURCE ANALYSIS

Introduction

A study of basic resources mobilization must inherently present a broad spectrum of analysis and opinion concerning the techniques, methods, and policies regarding basic resource mobilization and allocation within the United States economic system and society at large. The purpose of this introductory section of the text is to draw attention to the broad range of difficult analytical problems generally neglected and often misunderstood concerning any consideration of how this nation, its corporations, and individuals garner the basic materials for all of their activities. Each of these social issues is presented in this introductory chapter as a part of the total perspective discussed throughout the book. It is intended that the text be a survey of issues important, not in the past, but now and in the future. These issues will in themselves be studied for their own sake, entirely apart from any other consideration than that of those problems attendant on the mobilization of basic resources. The social issues related to basic resources have been chosen to illustrate the many social dimensions of basic resource mobilization and to provide examples of the types of analysis and study-approaches which will be required to understand attendant problems. Also, the examples selected (they are illustrative, not all-inclusive) reflect an effort to consider the social role of basic resources primarily, but not exclusively, in the United States and other leading countries.

As noted, any consideration of basic resources from the social viewpoint necessarily involves property rights, land use, and extraction problems, including exploration and the buying, selling, and trading of these basic resources. All of these activities combined are social in nature and constitute important facets of the total social milieu. The implications permeate the entire social structure. Many of the social issues to be considered relative to basic resources deal with such concepts as fairness (including fair competition), equitable resource allocation, and the welfare of consumers. Basic resources are therefore primary considerations of economists, political scientists, geographers, sociologists, military leaders, industrial and commercial managers, and others who would understand the moral-psychological issues involved with the ownership of wealth.

Individuals and Social Goals and Values

Our serious concern in relating social objectives or issues to basic resource mobilization stems from the fact that Americans, as individuals, are not satisfied limiting themselves to the problem of simply producing materials, per se, today and tomorrow, but rather, are primarily and basically interested in what these resources mean to their society as a whole, and what can be achieved for mankind if such resources are properly used. A major change to be considered in the study of basic resource mobilization is the reorientation of U.S. business from primary concentration on production to primary emphasis on market considerations. In this regard, it should be understood that through the 1920s business in the United States considered mass production to be all-important. Much of this production took place as a direct outgrowth of resource discoveries and the availability of resources, and illustrations of this will be provided throughout the text. Suffice it here to point out that the basic resources for this mass production came from the vast agricultural yields from freshly converted forests and grasslands, or the abundant minerals easily seen or located from the surface. The primary objective of profit-oriented businesses throughout this period was to increase their own share of the ultimate consumer's money.[14] Considerations of real needs or wants by the consumer were secondary to that of converting into goods, as quickly as possible, easily obtainable basic resources. Following the late 1930s, and particularly in the post-World-War-II era, the primary goals of business were to meet customer wants and needs, as well as to help attain regional and national goals. The results of this reorientation of goals on the part of business management have by no means disappeared, but there is now

---

[14] There are always exceptions to any generalities such as those given here (and some particular business may object to such characterization); but there is considerable literature to support these observations.

a greater concern about making the basic resource mobilization effort more nearly reflect the ultimate goals of the nation's overall policies and the wishes and needs of all of its individuals. The significance of this change in regard to basic resource mobilization is that some of the basic resource lands have been withdrawn from productivity, some mines have been closed or abandoned, and there is a constant search for more specific minerals, including beneficiation of ores, if necessary. Technological assistance will speed this process in the future; with new technology and a changing economic condition, some abandoned marginal mines were even reopened in the mid-1970s. Much of this shift in mobilization is a reflection of individual and collective goals and of value changes, so that now business and government are particularly interested in the quality, variety, and degree of satisfaction obtained by the ultimate consumer or user of basic resources.

Considering social needs and wants, in respect to basic resource mobilization, one finds that the problem is determining how individuals and their nations, with self-centered objectives, can be convinced that there are broader objectives than their own direct wants and profits. Whether this can be attained through a broader acceptance of religious principles, moral precepts, or education remains to be seen. That man has learned he can lay waste to vast areas of his planet to such a degree that his fellow men are uncomfortable is evidenced in such monstrous destruction as that along some shores of the Great Lakes; in the Ducktown, Tenn., copper area; in the strip mines of Ohio, Indiana, and Illinois; and in the polluted air of Los Angeles and other cities. It is now evident that certain restrictive controls, already practiced on a minor scale, must be imposed both locally and nationally in far greater degrees in the future.

Furthermore, consideration by society of basic resource mobilization must take into consideration several levels.

The first level is that of the individual—perhaps the owner or a stockholder or someone who is in a position to exploit a portion of the air or land-surface to benefit himself at the expense of his fellow man. Usually, the primary consideration is to maximize his profits. Admittedly, there are a few exceptional individuals who have willingly contributed to mankind by opening their land to public use or by donating a rare metal for defense purposes, or perhaps for further study.

The second level is that of the large firm which exploits basic resources as a secondary objective, the primary objective being the control of markets. At this level, considerable political pressure is organized in the form of lobbying for tariffs or foreign quotas, or for limitations on the importation of an ore or some other raw material. Favorable tax laws or other advantages which would help control or attain the ultimate goal of broad markets also may be sought.

The third level is that of national interests: the consideration of the wants and goals of an entire people, present and future. The responsibility here is to equalize differences between the weak and the strong, to provide for national security, to preserve law and order, and to maintain a vibrant economy. At this level, it is difficult to determine where the keystone interests really lie. A single key metal, if lacking, might spell disaster for a whole economy—it could be pitchblende, or tin or babbitt, or one of the other alloys. There could be a lack of fertile ground, the absence of a favorable climate, or any one of the aforementioned eight basic resource types. In terms of basic resource mobilization, then, it becomes a matter of national interest and, therefore, policy to develop in balance and harmony all basic resources needed by a complex society. This is a prerequisite if individuals or corporations within that nation are to be provided security, and if, in turn, their freedoms are to be developed and maintained. National needs (in this case, energy) prompted the President to veto early in 1975 tough legislation regulating strip mining of coal, but there can be no doubt that the nation will control such activity in the future.

Need for Universal Values

Any attempt to establish priorities for basic resources and their mobilization must first include the attainment of universal values that can be applied as a prerequisite to such an establishment of priorities.

For example, the south shores of Lake Michigan were once an important recreation area; clean water and unspoiled sand invited the surrounding population, and even tourists, to enjoy this area as a recreational attraction. Inexorably industry (chiefly refineries and steel mills) moved into the area, usurping the recreational aspects and replacing them with deadly fumes, noxious chemicals, and other pollutants, changing the entire landuse of the area. Which group has a priority on these resources? Is it the man who wants to use the area for relaxation and sport or is it the man who benefits from low-cost iron and steel? The matter is not a simple one because, when one considers the importance of the metal and the number of people who have benefited from low-cost iron and steel, in terms of increased food production, comfortable homes, and other satisfactions, then a valid argument for either extreme point of view can be made. And, as mentioned, this is essentially the argument between the preservationist on the one hand and the exploiter on the other, with perhaps the conservationist in the middle advocating, or at least seeking, ways in which both the iron and steel production and the recreational value of the area can be maintained. Future generations will need both; it is not a question of "either-or."

The first step that must be taken in order to make a comprehensive study of basic resource mobilization would be determination of the universal values sought by man. Although some of these universals may be in direct conflict, they need not have less value in ultimately deriving a hierarchy of priorities. In the absence of true universals, only generalizations limited by experience, points of view, and selfish interests can be substituted. Even the consideration of these differences and conflicts has merit because specific differences can be identified from such a comparison. Measurements of these differences may be followed by evaluations of the positions and it is to be hoped a consensus gained. Without consensus, wise arbitration or compromise also may be of use. Many factors enter into such a consideration, making it very difficult to arrive at an order of priorities for land-use or basic resource development. The obstacles to establishment of priorities in regard to basic resource development include a lack of scientific knowledge of broad areas of resources, a general lack of understanding by the population at large, the various ramifications and kaleidoscopic nature of resources, and the broad failure to comprehend and accept basic resources as the foundation which they are for social institutions and social good. These matters become even more critical if they are considered in terms of different cultures, social systems, economic approaches, and ideologies. In this regard, of singular importance is the fact that, before one considers basic resource mobilization problems worldwide, he must first be prepared to deal with them effectively at home. To date here in the United States, it has been *assumed* that decision-makers in government bureaus or business enterprises have understood the problems, from their own points of view at least, and have made decisions beyond the ability of most other individuals. But they have not, and the situation becomes clearer when the complexities of resource allocations are considered.

BASIC RESOURCE ALLOCATION

For society the primary goal of all basic resource production is consumption. Basic resources are produced to satisfy man's needs and wants. Under any ideology or economic structure, the problem of how to allocate resources, once they have been mobilized, is a perplexing one still to be solved in nearly all economies. In the struggle between free enterprise economies of the United States, Western Europe, and Japan, and the more authoritative, directive, type economies of the U.S.S.R. and China, the alternatives, for the United States, appear to be between use of the principle of consumer choice or of bureaucratic directive, and strong arguments can be made for either.

There is probably no principle more important to the present-day structure of U.S. industry than that of free enterprise. Under the free enterprise system, basic resources are expected to be allocated in the market place, and the key to the system is the marketing pattern. Within the U.S. marketing system, goods, including basic resources, are produced and distributed as determined in the market place by the vote of the consumer. It is the dollar which enfranchises and gives the consumer the right to decide how resources are to be allocated. Indeed, the right of resource allocation is so vital in the United States that it is doubtful whether this nation could maintain freedoms for its individuals if the control of basic resources were taken out of the market place entirely and placed in the hands of an overriding bureaucratic organization that would dictate all allocations. The inherent danger that such a bureaucratic system threatens to the freedom of the individual is clear. For example, if control of basic resources allocation is taken from the people, on the assumption that the consumer is not sufficiently wise to deal with basic resource productivity in the best interests of himself and the nation, then the question can be raised as to how the same individuals can be sufficiently astute to select a government which would use its strong bureaucratic authority with wisdom and fairness. Who will awaken public opinion to the perils to individual freedoms through such a sequence of events? Toward this end, for example, many business firms (businessmen) are concerning themselves with the problem of values in the total scheme of basic resource allocations.

From the view of satisfying man's wants and needs, which, incidentally, is the end purpose of all production, basic resources are extremely difficult to control, primarily because of localized occurrence and ownership laws and policies. That is, many raw materials (basic resources) are not now equally available to each individual, and, from time to time, state and federal governments have found it necessary to step in and interfere with the basic rights of individual freedom. With nearly all basic resources, the individual has enjoyed the right in the past to try his hand at their production and distribution, only to find that government allocations, price controls, or some other administrative price measures had to be invoked because there were not enough resources to go around at some particular time.

In addition, for many basic resources, the individual has no alternative but to buy those which are available, and in the case of some minerals, such as manganese, which is controlled by a relatively few nations, he has not been free to buy and sell as though there were a large variety of goods available in the market place.

Like other freedoms, freedoms of the market place sometimes have been abused. There have been sellers who sought to exploit the buyer simply because there were no alternative sources of particular raw materials. Therefore, price controls and other government regulatory steps have been taken to assure an equitable distribution—copper is a good example. As already stated, there are responsible people in government circles and in business who doubt the ability of consumers to manage the purchase and disposition of copper wisely; this scarce commodity has been wasted at times in the opinion of some, and there have been adequate grounds for charges of exploitation of the areas that possessed this basic raw material.

The availability, ownership, occurrence, substitute possibilities, and other factors of basic resources vary so greatly that, as each resource class is introduced, the inherent problems of marketing this new group produce a different set of patterns which must be understood before the inherent problems of the basic resource, itself, can be understood. This fact certainly reveals one of the failures of the American market system, which, if it is performing efficiently, does two things to the public in a democracy: it informs and it persuades. However, basic resources are so submerged in the production pattern of an economy that the ultimate consumer is too far removed from this operation either to understand it or, in many instances, even to care about understanding it. The public often has not been informed of some of the problems inherent in obtaining the basic resources upon which this nation's vast material wealth is dependent. And in a dynamic consumption economy, such as exists in the United States, where tremendous volumes of basic resources are involved, damage (irreparable in some cases) can occur before the public is aware of the ultimate cost to society. This, then, forms the background of the conservation movement that first took formal shape around the turn of the century under Theodore Roosevelt, and that is discussed in great detail in Chapter Two.

National, corporate, or individual objectives must always be determined and understood before resources can be properly allocated. It is fitting to ask what any particular action at the national, corporate, or individual level seeks to achieve; certainly, in this case, actions should be interpreted in terms of a goal. Yet it has been common practice for the nation, large corporations, and individuals to operate for years and even decades without any clear statement of objectives. Not only are national, regional, and state objectives not understood, but they differ greatly, depending on regional viewpoints, political viewpoints, and the like. It is generally understood that national efforts and policies have tried to create conditions in which individual citizens could make a profit. However, in the United States, most firms and individuals have been allowed to make profits only under certain constraints, either self-imposed or nationally imposed. Some individuals and firms are conscious of the social effects of their activities and have not, by conscious policy, willfully abused or destroyed resources. Others, such as coal companies, have literally turned whole counties upside down and abandoned them as a problem for posterity. Thus, a statement of the nation's objective for its corporations and individuals is complicated by many considerations. Is a national goal of allowing businessmen to maximize profits a short-range goal or a long-range goal? What degree of risk should be assumed? Should certain moral and personal constraints be applied? An understanding of a national, corporate, or individual objective can be undertaken only after there is an assessment of both basic resources and opportunities to gain basic resources.

Assessing Basic Resources

What a nation, corporation, or individual can attempt to do depends upon the basic resources it has available, and whether these resources should be so expended must be weighed in the light of gains to be achieved. Top planners at all levels may have brilliant ideas about what goals should be implemented and what courses should be followed; but, if a nation or its components lack the basic resources to accomplish such goals, it may be foolish to try. Also, goals that would enhance the people of a nation, but which would require far more money or human resources than that nation has or can get for effective development of her basic resources, are best left to others to develop, or, perhaps, should be postponed for a period of time. Many nations, firms, or people have inflated ideas of their own capabilities, and they base their goals more on their own notions that they want to be, or should be, more efficient, progressive, and imaginative than their rivals. These notions seem about as prevalent in poorer nations as in prosperous nations. All of these factors combine to emphasize a vital point: that national, corporate, or individual goals must be undertaken only after there is an assessment of what basic resources are available. The purpose of assessing a nation's, or a firm's, or an individual's basic resources and opportunities is to insure the undertaking of only those projects which can be fulfilled within the capabilities of those who are expending time and effort to develop them. The idea of resource assessment is not a simple one. Each cultural complex interprets basic resources differently.[15]

Erich Zimmermann pointed out that resources in relation to technology, resources in relation to social structure, and resources and the interpretation of habitat are three such different viewpoints in the assessment of basic resources. Others involve progressively wider ranges of sub-

---

[15] Ian Burton and Robert W. Kates, *Readings in Resource Management and Conservation* (Chicago: The University of Chicago Press, 1960), pp. 1–10, states ". . . it has been necessary to tie across cultural comparison of the interpretation of natural resources to several rather arbitrarily selected reference points."

ject matter and vary greatly from place to place. It is a truism that every nation must assess its basic resources in light of its own environment and its will to survive, and the level of material wealth which the people of a nation wish to attain becomes a part of the assessment. Each of these basic resources becomes an important part of this book on basic resource mobilization.

Techniques Relative to Population and
Population Growth

Adding further to the complexities of basic resource mobilization studies is the conflicting manner in which man looks at population and population growth. Genesis' injunction advises man to increase and multiply. Until recently, in most of the world, and particularly in the United States, expanding populations were equated with economic progress.[16] This equation is meaningful only so long as basic resources can be mobilized in a geometric progression to match the population growth. Where this has not been feasible—in countries like India, for example—then the population expansion is not generally equated with economic progress. If only the United States is considered, basic resource assessments and forecasts that are founded on past population projections may come in for some very serious reassessment as birth control measures and abortion provisions become more effective and slow the growth rate, or even result in a decreasing population. For example, the U.S. birth rate, following two decades of a virtual "population explosion," proved to be at an all-time low in the late 1960s and early 1970s. Even if the population growth rates remain high, man is optimistically confident, almost certain, that advances in technology will enhance the extraction, and broaden the use, of basic resources and their products so that man can look ahead to adequate supplies. There is no doubt that technology has already played a major role in developing and locating basic resources, and most people [17] are confident that technology will do so in the future with increasing effectiveness.

As man faces international struggles, and as he labors here at home to solve his poverty and to overcome problems inherited from pollutions of his own making, it is no wonder that many conservationists state that man is now at the resource crossroads. The next chapters attempt to

---

[16] Many U.S. cities are beginning to realize now that population growth and industrial growth require a drain on physical and capital resources that is greater than the benefits derived.

[17] This includes the authors, who are optimists and hold no doubts about either man's ability to adapt to change when absolutely necessary or his capacity to solve problems when "the chips are down"; doomsday adherents will disagree with this faith in mankind, of course.

portray this junction as mankind faces up to the basic resource mobilization decisions confronting all of mankind. What direction should man take as he searches for an assured flow of basic resources which will satisfy his needs and wants?

SELECTED BIBLIOGRAPHY

BARNETT, HAROLD J., and CHANDLER MORSE, *Scarcity and Growth; The Economics of Natural Resource Availability* (Resources for the Future, Inc.). Baltimore: The Johns Hopkins Press, 1963.

BROWN, HARRISON SCOTT, JAMES BONNER, and JOHN WEIR, *The Next Hundred Years: Man's Natural and Technological Resources.* New York: The Viking Press, 1957.

CLEPPER, HENRY EDWARD (ed.), *Origins of American Conservation.* New York: The Ronald Press Company, 1966.

Committee on Resources and Man, the Division of Earth Sciences, National Academy of Sciences—National Research Council, *Resources and Man: A Study and Recommendations.* San Francisco: W. H. Freeman and Company, 1969.

DETWYLER, THOMAS R., *Man's Impact on Environment.* New York: McGraw-Hill Book Company, Inc., 1971.

JARRETT, HENRY, *Perspectives on Conservation: Essays on America's Natural Resources.* Baltimore: The Johns Hopkins Press, 1958.

KNEESE, ALLEN, ROBERT V. AYRES, and RALPH C. D'ARGE, *Economics and the Environment: A Materials Balance Approach* (Resources for the Future, Inc.). Baltimore: The Johns Hopkins Press, 1970.

LANDSBERG, HANS H., LEON L. FISCHMAN AND JOSEPH L. FISHER, *Resources in America's Future; Patterns of Requirements and Availabilities.* (Resources for the Future, Inc.). Baltimore: The Johns Hopkins Press, 1963.

MURDOCH, WILLIAM W. (ed.), *Environment, Resources and Society.* Stamford, Conn.: Sinauer Associates, Inc., 1971.

UDALL, STEWART L., *The Quiet Crisis.* New York: Holt, Rinehart and Winston, 1963.

RIDKER, RONALD G. (ed.), *Population, Resources, and the Environment* (Commission on Population Growth and the American Future). Washington, D.C.: Government Printing Office, 1972.

RIENOW, ROBERT, and LEONA TRAIN RIENOW, *Moment in the Sun; A Report on the Deteriorating Quality of the American Environment.* New York: Dial Press, 1967.

United States President's Materials Policy Commission, *Resources for Freedom; A Report to the President.* Washington, D.C.: Government Printing Office, 1952.

TWO

MAN AT THE
RESOURCE CROSSROADS

Whenever anyone encounters the term "resources" in this resource-conscious nation, he generally feels that he knows exactly what the word denotes; he refers repeatedly to "natural" resources and is confident that he is well enough versed on the subject to discuss it at length. Yet, the concept is neither simple nor "cut and dried."

NATURE OF RESOURCES

Part of the misunderstanding that has developed among the general public stems from the fact that resources is a *dynamic* concept that is operating within a *closed* system. The misunderstanding is further aggravated by the fact that the term "resources" is neither easy to define nor easy to delimit in scope. As discussed more fully later, the word refers to a *function,* rather than to a thing or substance;[1] it is a means to an end, and as that end or goal changes, resources may change with it.

---

[1] Some economists now distinguish physical resources from human resources and capital resources (the old "land, labor, and capital" factors of production approach). Such a distinction is arbitrary, and certainly physical resources cannot be discussed apart from their relation to labor and capital; but inasmuch as the discussion here concentrates mostly on what the economists term "physical resources," the reference to "things or substances" is appropriate. Geographers have long distinguished between physical and cultural features. See Chapter One.

FIGURE 1. While the Apollo 8 spacecraft crewmen described the earth as a "jewel in the heavens," it is nevertheless a closed system with finite limits. This is the closed system that is nature—a system isolated by "universal space." The view includes almost all of the Western Hemisphere, from the mouth of the St. Lawrence River to Tierra del Fuego at the southern tip of South America. Courtesy National Aeronautics and Space Administration.

The closed-system concept refers to the planet earth, on which nature has set the outer limits. The earth holds only certain limited quantities of water, land, and other basic materials, although man may not know all the exact limitations at this time. This is the closed system that is nature. However, within this system, resources change—and mobilization techniques change—as new cultural patterns evolve. Something that was not considered a resource a few decades ago may be very valuable today (e.g., magnesium, taconite),[2] and something that is no longer vital may have been a necessary resource in yesteryears (firewood, whale oil, etc.).

---

[2] A British firm is paying housewives 12 cents a pound for the dust they sweep up in vacuum cleaners. The firm purifies the dust and makes it into vaccines for those who are allergic to dust (*Arkansas Gazette,* December 25, 1969, p. 10B); this makes vacuum cleaner dust a *resource,* when so used, because it has a function.

A dictionary definition of the word is rather inadequate for purposes of this discussion. The word's etymology apparently originated from Latin *resurgere,* to rise again; to Old French *resourdre,* to relive (literally, to rise again), and then to *ressource,* relief or resource; and finally to modern French, with the same word and meaning. The word is variously defined as "a new or a reserve source of supply or support," "available means," "something to which one has recourse in difficulty," or "an ability to meet and handle a situation." For the purposes of resource discussion, one can read more into those definitions than he can get out of them. First, all of the definitions presuppose the existence of a person, and, second, all suggest that resources are a means to attaining a goal.

Some writers maintain that physical resources are materials from which goods and services are produced; but that is far too narrow a concept. The word "resource" does not refer to the thing or substance, but rather to the function which that thing or substance performs or participates in to reach a goal or purpose. Oil is not ipso facto a resource. It was not a resource to early man, for he had no use for it; and it was only a very minor resource to the American Indians, who dabbed it on open cuts on horses to repel flies until the wound could heal. But, in today's society, oil serves as an important resource, and one that requires careful national mobilization, because it fulfills various important functions—as energy or lubricant for machinery and as raw material for man-made products. In each case, it serves a functional purpose. If the day comes when other substances can achieve these goals more efficiently, and oil no longer performs a function, oil will cease to be a resource (and will no longer need to be mobilized as it is now through economic, political and-or military-police action).

Resources Are Not Natural

There are countless resources on earth, but no *natural* resources. This may sound like a dogmatic statement, but it is valid reasoning if the functional approach to the subject is employed.

What does one mean when he uses the term "natural" to modify the word "resource"? Does he mean that the resource comes *from nature* or that it is *naturally* a resource? In either case, the definition is incorrect. Everything on earth comes from nature, or via nature from a diety; nature was here first. Today, the term "man-made" is applied to many things, from fats and fibers to a living something in a test tube; but somewhere along the line, a substance was taken from nature to start the process. So "natural," meaning "from nature," has no distinguishing meaning.

To say that certain substances are *naturally* resources is equally erroneous. If they are natural resources—with this connotation—then they always *were* resources, from the time that this planet began; always *are* resources, and are valuable even when lying in their natural habitat; and always *will be,* until the earth becomes extinct. Even air was not a resource until it served a function for man, animal, or plant life (and man is concerned with the last two only because they serve man's needs).

Were the Appalachian mountains, rich in coal, a resource in Colonial times, when people considered them only an obstacle to westward movement? Were mountains of stone a resource to early man before he had a need for the stone and learned to quarry it? Were the soils of the Great Plains grasslands a resource to American pioneers, who could not cut the grass roots with their wooden plows and, instead, had to clear forests to grow their crops? Or, was the soil along the Columbia River a resource before the Grand Coulee Dam made irrigation possible? In each case, the answer is "no"—they were not resources, and certainly not "natural" resources. The newest dictionaries have more than two dozen definitions of "natural," and none of them can be applied universally to the word "resource."

Some readers will wonder why all the "fuss" over a term, when it seems to be only a problem of semantics. They feel that everyone knows what is meant by the term "natural" resource and that no harm is done. However, such a heroic assumption overlooks an inherent danger. Reference to oil, for example, as a "natural" resource affects the public's thinking concerning use and conservation of this resource, and also influences attitudes toward the petroleum industry and its profits and taxation. Many individuals believe that since mankind had nothing to do with placing oil under their land, it thus should be utilized by the individual as he pleases. This thinking has led to tremendous physical and economic waste related to this resource in the United States. Other people feel that the domestic supply of oil is very limited, and that this nation should save its reserves by importing foreign crude oil for its needs; these people overlook the fact that many years ago, America used up its known reserves of the past, and the supply that is being consumed today is available only because of the techniques and know-how that the industry developed to find more oil. Those who argued for consumption of foreign oil (rather than dependence on domestic reserves) lost much of their appeal after the Arab embargo in 1973–74 almost paralyzed the world's industrial nations. Some segments of the American economy object to the resource industries—those which produce oil, sulfur, steel, aluminum, copper, etc.—

because they are monopolistic or oligopolistic and profitable. Yet, these industries have been among the nation's leaders in research and development, and such costly research was undertaken only because the capital was accumulated and the profits and incentives were sufficient to encourage development of new products. Some state severance tax laws were initially levied, and later increased, because the lawmakers believed that the resource industries were depleting a "heritage of the people." [3] Undiscovered oil in the ground is cheap and useless; it is the cost of finding it, producing it, and refining it that makes oil costly; and, more importantly, it is the *function* that oil serves which gives it value. Resources are not natural; they never were, and they never will be!

The foregoing functional concept is the approach taken by resource economists today as they stand at the crossroads to future economic development and recognize the need to mobilize their basic and other resources. A glance back into history shows that this stage of theoretical development was reached at the end of a long, winding road of economic thought which meandered down wrong turns from time to time as man attempted to fulfill the goals set by his society.

THE FUNCTIONAL CONCEPT EVOLVES

Resource use certainly is not new in the world, but resource consciousness and proper resource mobilization and utilization are relatively modern in thought and in deed. The next chapter will discuss the functional concept of resources, as viewed today by resource economists; but, first, the reader needs some background to see how the world has arrived at a crossroads, with one route pointing toward greater social achievement and the other leading to further degradation of the planet earth.

Earliest man had very limited resources, few in number. He worried about food, water, shelter, clothing and weapons, and inasmuch as all of these were means to an end—his survival—they were his resources. However, he apparently gave little thought to their conservation in today's meaning of the word (at least, this is what has been concluded from un-

---

[3] One of the earlier recorded statements to this effect was made by the Minnesota Tax Commission in 1920, when it said of iron ore: ". . . its presence in the ground not being the result of the expenditure of capital or labor, is a natural heritage of all the people, and as such, the people are justified in appropriating to their use, in some form of taxation, some considerable part of the value arising from its exploitation." [*Seventh Biennial Report of the Minnesota Tax Commission* (Minneapolis, Minn.: Syndicate Printing Company, 1920), pp. 27–28.] More recently, a widely known economist said that "high taxes on destructible resources are advocated on the ground that they are a common heritage and can be taxed but once." [H. M. Groves, *Financing Government* (New York: Henry Holt and Company, 1950), p. 337.]

recorded history). When earliest man used up what he had at hand, he moved on until he found more—or he perished.

Gradually, man became more settled into small groups. In their primitive cultural patterns, some bands wandered about in search of necessary "resources," while others later set up normal patterns of existence (distinguished by food production, rather than food gathering); they followed their herds of domesticated animals into the highlands for part of the year and into the lowlands at other times. These nomadic herders also supplemented their diets by hunting and gathering the fruits of nature. Such people developed their own social controls, with various tribal taboos and acceptable patterns of behavior. With some apparent exceptions, history tells us, these people still gave little or no thought to conservation or mobilization of their resources.

As societies stabilized through historical time, some people in the group became rulers, while others became ruled; privileged individuals had considerable freedom, but the great majority were slaves, serfs, or subjects, depending upon the era in which they lived. Because the resources were those of a predominantly agrarian society and still few in number during this period of kings and subjects, lords and serfs, only a relatively few people pondered over their country's resources to any extent, and their outlook was generally selfish, with little consideration given to the society's future.

To jump in time again, one finds that early theorists argued for the absolutism of the State (the national government). In the early seventeenth century, Thomas Hobbs (1588–1679) denied that freedom of choice should prevail and claimed that the State was all-important. William Petty (1623–1687) emphasized the importance of gold, silver, and jewels—all resources—but he *also* urged the scientific development of other resources and said that labor and land were more important resources than treasure: "Labour is the Father and active principle of Wealth, as Lands are the Mother." [4] Then came John Locke (1632–1704) as an economist of the transition from mercantilism to the classics (the classical period generally is considered as that era that ushered in the Industrial Revolution). Locke turned the thinking of his time toward laissez-faire theory as he came under the liberalizing influence that was being felt in England, and the realization of self-interest as the motive force of conduct is inherent in Locke's entire political philosophy.[5] His philosophy was a symptom of the decline of state power, which commercial capital had created in an earlier period in its war against feudalism.

---

[4] "Treatise on Taxes and Contributions," Chap. iv, *The Economic Writings of Sir William Petty* (ed. C. H. Hull), I, 1899, p. 68.

[5] Eric Roll, *A History of Economic Thought,* 3rd ed. (Englewood Cliffs, N.J.: Prentice-Hall, Inc., 1956), p. 91.

Then came a new era of social development, especially in the areas where the white man lived. The discoveries and inventions that followed inauguration of this era brought on the Industrial Revolution (though it was more an evolution than a revolution), and the feudal system gave way to laissez faire in the eighteenth century. Social controls became relaxed, and the rights and powers of the individual became paramount. This brought about a tremendous burst of individual effort, and under the free enterprise system that developed, individual energies and drives surged ahead into new opportunities, but there still was no thought to either conserving or mobilizing and fully utilizing basic resources.

One can readily see what this emphasis on self-interest led to in practice. For example, a man could fell all the trees in a forest that belonged to him, because the trees were his, and his alone; no outsider had any right to fret about the consequences, such as soil erosion, dust storms, or downstream pollution from the bare land's eroding silt. Or, if this thinking were imposed upon today's world and a man wanted to recover all the oil from under his land, society would have no license to concern itself with conserving the basic resource for a future generation, and no complaint if the individual dumped his excess oil on the ground and polluted down-stream waters of a nearby river. The laissez-faire philosophy could tolerate no restraints upon the individual and *his* "rights."

There were many other writers who dealt with political philosophy in the years that followed, and they were not all economists, but Adam Smith (1723–1790)—and the Physiocrats before him—usually is cited as the champion of individual rights in his time. Adam Smith's writings brought amazingly rapid and complete acceptance in the late 1700s, and the impact of his *Wealth of Nations* upon businessmen and politicians, alike, was extremely significant. He formulated the first systematic statement of the harmony of social interests—the belief in the necessary harmony between individual and group interests—and he presented it at a time when people were willing to listen.[6] Smith believed that a society is made up of individuals, each of whom knows what is best for him; therefore, if each person does what he can do best, then the society must be functioning at its optimal level. Society, as a unit, thus should not exercise any control over conservation of its resources, full utilization of those resources, or the proper allocation of them; the individual, led by the "invisible hand" of self-interest and the profit motive, will bring this about automatically:

---

[6] It is interesting to note that virtually every widely known writer of the past was preceded by other writers who expressed similar ideas; but certain authors have become famous because they wrote at a particular time in history when people were sympathetic and ready to listen.

He [the individual] generally, indeed, neither intends to promote the public interest, nor knows how much he is promoting it. By preferring the support of domestic to that of foreign industry, he intends only his own security; and by directing that industry in such a manner as its produce may be of the greatest value, he intends only his own gain, and he is in this, as in many other cases, led by an invisible hand to promote an end which was no part of his intention. Nor is it always the worse for the society that it was no part of it. I have never known much good done by those who affected to trade for the public good.[7]

Theorists of the 1800s were concerned mostly with scarcities of various resources. Of the many writers of that time, three "name-brand" classical economists stand out in their predictions that resource scarcity eventually would lead to diminishing social returns and then a slowing and, finally, a halting of economic growth. It was this pessimistic premise that gave classical economics the reputation of being the "dismal science." However, certain premises held by certain "hippie cultists" of today give a resurgence and eerie credence to these predictions.[8]

Thomas Malthus (1766–1834) and David Ricardo (1772–1823) developed their scarcity doctrine in the first quarter of the nineteenth century, and John Stuart Mill (1806–1873) elaborated upon their doctrines later.

The Malthusian variation of the scarcity doctrine held that there was an absolute limit to the stock of agricultural land, and once this limit was reached, there would be diminishing return of agricultural products per capita. He believed that the population would double its size every 25 years—or increase in a geometrical ratio (1, 2, 4, 8, 16, 32, 64, 128, 256)—while the food supply could increase at no more than an arithmetical ratio (1, 2, 3, 4, 5, 6, 7, 8, 9). Thus, the population would continually press upon the available food supply and would be kept in check by it—another way of saying that a resource scarcity would impair economic growth. Ricardo's views toward agricultural land were somewhat similar, except that he believed that the most productive land in the world was already in use in his time and that the population would have to resort to successively poorer grades of land to survive. His same reasoning also was applicable to mines. The Industrial Revolution had already started by the time that both men wrote, but neither allowed for the

---

[7] Adam Smith, *An Inquiry into the Nature and Causes of the Wealth of Nations* (ed. Edwin Cannan), Vol. I, Book IV, Chap. xi (London: Methuen & Co., Ltd., 1922), p. 421.

[8] "Hippie cultists" is, of course, a generality that could include even some respected economists today—especially when they express views as citizens, rather than in their professional capacities.

dynamic nature of technological development and changing institutional patterns.[9]

Both Malthus and Ricardo recognized on a limited scale the fact that resource availability is a determining factor in economic development, but both men held firmly to the laissez-faire doctrine that governmental restrictions on the individual should be kept at a bare minimum. John Stuart Mill (1806–1873) reflected some change that was beginning to become evident in laissez-faire thinking during the third quarter of the nineteenth century. Mill still held firmly to the concept of minimum government interference ("Laissez-faire, in short, should be the general practice: every departure from it, unless required by some great good, is a certain evil.") but he proceeded to list so many exceptions that the rule was almost vitiated.[10]

Karl Marx (1818–1883) came on the scene and decried the capitalist system with its laissez-faire doctrine, and while many later economists owe a great deal to his pioneering studies, the capitalistic world was not willing to listen to this revolutionary. However, theory was changing in a changing world, and shortly before the twentieth century opened, Alfred Marshall (1842–1924) reversed the pattern and broke with the laissez-faire school. Marshall refused "to leap the yawning gap between the individual and society," and recognized that society's common good was not assured by the relentless pursuit of individual interest. He refused to admit that there was a necessary harmony between individual and group interests, as Smith and later theorists had professed, and advocated instead that public policy was required to safeguard public interests.

Marshall's position was upheld by other leading theorists who followed. Arthur Pigou, with his classic *Economics of Welfare* (1920), and Cambridge economists in England were joined by their American contemporaries in asking how the total welfare of the people in a community can be maximized. Finally, one of Marshall's students, John Maynard Keynes, came to the forefront to illustrate how public policy might be formulated to increase a nation's economic welfare.

Keynes, with his *General Theory* [11] and other writings, did more than anyone else to swing the focus of economics from concern with an economy's specific units and a detailed consideration of the behavior of

---

[9] Thomas Robert Malthus, *First Essays on Population, 1798* (facsimile reprint with notes by James Bonar, revised, New York: St. Martin's Press, 1966); David Ricardo, *The Principles of Political Economy and Taxation* (New York: E. P. Dutton & Co., Inc., 1911).

[10] John Stuart Mill, *Principles of Political Economy* (ed. John Lubbock, London: George Routledge and Sons, Ltd., 1891), pp. 609 and 614–28. His *Principles* was published first in 1848 and went through six revisions, the last in 1871.

[11] John Maynard Keynes, *The General Theory of Employment, Interest and Money* (New York: Harcourt, Brace and Company, Inc., 1936).

these individual units (microeconomics) to concern with either the economy as a whole or with the basic subdivisions or aggregates (macroeconomics). The difference between these approaches may not seem important to the reader initially, but the new concentration upon the entire society and its basic resources was a major shift in theory. Keynes was highly concerned with the proper allocation of a nation's resources—human, capital, and physical resources.

It was about this time, in the early 1930s, that physical resource theory was born as an academic discipline separate from economics. A gap was bridged between the economist's *theory* of resource use and the economic geographer's *reality* concerning the physical basis on which an economic structure rests. The designer of that "bridge" was Erich Zimmermann, with his mammoth *World Resources and Industries.*[12] While both Keynes and Zimmermann had earlier writings, Zimmermann's major work (in 1933) predated Keynes' masterpiece by three years. A growing concern over mobilization and conservation of national resources in the United States made Zimmermann's work particularly timely. Again, it was a case of both men having written a significant work at a time that the public was willing to listen; the United States—indeed, the world—was in the grips of the Great Depression, and everyone was looking for some advice that would help ease the troubled times. Despite critics, both men's works have withstood the test of time.

Zimmermann's massive book (832 pages) is still the bible of the resource theorist and, while much has occurred and conditions have changed since completion of the book, many of the concepts set forth by this "grandfather of resources" are still valid and undoubtedly always will be. Important to the present discussion is one point which Dr. Zimmermann brought out clearly in class lectures of his later years. This concept, which he called a "dichotomy of interests," refers to a basic distinction which exists between private business and society in the area of resource development. Zimmermann maintained that business has a short-run view, or microeconomic approach; it is market-oriented and commodity-conscious. The businessman, logically, is profit-oriented and wants to produce his resources quickly to regain his capital investment in a short-run period. While the corporation has an indefinite existence and therefore a somewhat longer viewpoint than the proprietorship, the corporation still cannot profitably put much weight upon the welfare of future generations of a nation. Society, on the other hand, has a long-run, macroeconomic approach and must look to the welfare of future generations, as well as that of today's people.

---

[12] Erich W. Zimmermann, *World Resources and Industries* (New York: Harper & Brothers, Publishers, 1933). His revised edition, which perfected and updated some of his ideas, was published in 1951.

The Great Depression of the early 1930s became a real touchstone for this dichotomy of interests throughout much of the world, and the American people and their leaders revealed a growing resource consciousness. Earlier, Theodore Roosevelt had appealed for a conservation policy and an end to the mad rush of resource squander; but it was not until Franklin Delano Roosevelt's New Deal Era that the American public was willing to listen and act, and his deep concern over wise utilization of both physical and human resources bore fruit. Possibly the most important legacy of the New Deal Era was the American public's awareness that fundamental social assets lie outside the concern of private business—a recognition that gave reality to the faintly heard warnings of theorists since Alfred Marshall's early break with "harmonics"—the idea that individual and group interests were in harmony.

World War II, with its total mobilization of resources for survival, contributed even further to resource consciousness in many parts of the world, and particularly in the United States. Concern might have subsided in the post-war era had not the nation moved into an extended "cold war" period, with interspersed local hot wars in Korea and Vietnam. But wars—both hot and cold—are only a part of the cause for growing resource consciousness. The "space age," with its race to the moon and beyond, and earthly problems such as air and water pollution and burgeoning populations and their accompanying problems are another part of world concern over basic [13] resource mobilization and utilization.

The following case study of America's conservation movement during the past century will serve to illustrate graphically how the nation's thinking has changed through the years—from unawareness, to indifference, to concern for wise use of basic resources.

THREE APPROACHES TO RESOURCE UTILIZATION

Throughout American history, there have been three main schools of thought concerning resource utilization. These approaches can be identified as those of exploitation, preservation, and conservation.

Exploitation

One segment of the American society believes that conservation will come about as a natural by-product of the normal operation of a price

---

[13] The reader is reminded that the term "basic resources," as noted on the first page of the first chapter, is used to describe those physical resources—land, water, mineral fuels, metals, and other nonfuel minerals—that are the indispensable bases on which civilization is built.

economy. This view, which reached its peak in the late 1700s, but is still heard today, is that competition will force optimum utilization of resources inasmuch as the individual or firm who squanders resources will have greater costs and will be forced out of business; the more efficient entrepreneurs who remain in business will set the pattern of prices. History has not borne out this laissez-faire approach. Those who could skim the cream of the land—"get in," make a profit, and "get out"—found the process most profitable, ignored waste, and moved on to other endeavors. This idea that what is good for an individual or a single corporation is good for the country still prevails in some parts of the economy; but history has shown that the profit-motive does not protect society's well-being. The result is exploitation of basic resources.

Preservation

Another segment of the American economy believes that the nation should use its own physical resources as little as possible. This group wants to preserve its domestic resources—hoard them even—for future generations. For example: save natural gas and use more plentiful coal for space-heating and cooking; conserve domestic petroleum and import foreign crude oil; or save local sources of metals and minerals and depend upon supplies from abroad. This approach is, of course, unrealistic. It fails to recognize the dynamic nature of basic resources. Society might hoard a valuable resource today, only to find that future generations had developed a more efficient substitute and that what had been a resource was no longer a necessity and, therefore, no longer a resource. Applying this reasoning to the past, one finds that firewood, whale oil, and natural nitrate deposits, once vital resources to man, are relatively insignificant in today's industrialized society. But an even more important point should be considered: it is only through the *mobilization* and *utilization* of man's resources to attain goals and reach objectives that man has the incentive to find more sources of them. Petroleum will serve as an example. In 1900, the United States proved reserves were less than 3 billion barrels, while today they total more than 30 billion barrels. If, during this century, the nation had hoarded those reserves of 1900, there would have been no incentive to probe for more domestic oil, and today a 3-billion-barrel reserve would last less than one year at current rates of domestic consumption (compared with about 10 years of reserves now available).[14] Furthermore, the nation would have

---

[14] Figures based on American Petroleum Institute, *Petroleum Facts and Figures* (New York: American Petroleum Institute, for selected years). This is without Alaska's North Slope oil potential, which is a resource only as it becomes available to the market place.

lacked sufficient domestic sources to improve substantially its standard of living and to fight two World Wars, and it would have had no incentive to develop the technological changes, such as slim-hole drilling, multiple-completions, secondary recovery, ad infinitum, that it now has. There would have been no inducement to develop the vast domestic oil shale deposits (1.1 trillion barrels potential) and Athabasca tar sands (300 billion barrels potential) in Canada—or search for petroleum in the Arctic reaches of Alaska (10 billion barrels potential). It is impossible to imagine at what stage of infancy the oil industry would have remained. America is at its present level of petroleum technology only because it used what it had in the past, while mobilizing its search for additional supplies and developing efficient methods of utilization and conservation. All of these arguments against the preservation approach to resource use help support a third, more realistic, way of viewing the problem.

Conservation

A third school of thought believes that the nation should use its resources as it needs them; it should use them wisely—without waste or folly—but *use* them.[15] This is conservation, but it goes beyond that, for such an approach also recognizes the need for occasional manipulation of the normal process of the economy in anticipation of resource shortages. Such is part of the continuous mobilization process that is necessary for the assurance of adequate basic resources. This may require some control by society, through one of its governing bodies, of either the production, processing, or consumption of the resources. America has gone the full gamut from unawareness of its resources, to the laissez-faire-type exploitation approach, to preservation, to conservation. Because of its significance in this nation's resource development, the conservation movement makes a good case study.

THE AMERICAN CONSERVATION MOVEMENT

The American conservation movement showed hardly any "movement" in the beginning. The early colonists, who had been confined mostly to the Atlantic seaboard because of mountain barriers, hostile Indians, and

---

[15] The term "wise use" is a subjective evaluation that depends on the state of technology and the goals of a particular society at a particular time; but the term can be as definite as the economists' "optimum allocation of resources" (what is optimum depends upon one's assumptions). National parks may be considered as a form of conservation if society decides that the esthetic beauty of such "natural" environment is the optimum use that can be obtained from such areas.

French and British colonial policy, began their westward movement in the late 1700s. Settlers found the basic resources of their time abundant (logs for cabins, rich soil for crops, and animals for meat) and reports from the South and West indicated that good land was limitless. Two main shortages, capital and labor, faced the frontier people; consequently, they exploited the land to obtain capital, and they substituted work-saving devices to meet the labor shortage. The young states even used land as gold, providing the means of education, erection of churches, compensation for damages, rewards for military service, and financing for roads, canals, and railroads.

As the years passed, the industrializing East required one group of resources, while the frontier West had another set: those of an agrarian society. Though some people in the East began developing a conscience of conservation, the free-enterprising farmers of the West did not; they were too busy trying to stay alive "today" to think about tomorrow, much less a future generation! To the frontiersman, wise use of resources meant balancing them against other factors of production, and the capital and labor shortages of his time led to wasteful use of basic resources. Besides, the West was thought to be inexhaustible in resources until the late 1800s, and such thinking was reflected in both customs and laws.

Then scientific men in the East slowly began a conservation movement. As early as the 1850s, two eastern professors were lecturing about conserving the land,[16] and a career diplomat in government published a book in 1863, calling for conservation on a national scale.[17]

In the years that followed, there was some teaching and writing on the subject of conservation, but the Congress seemed to show no awareness of the mounting problem of basic resource waste. Various congressional acts, including the Homestead Act of 1862, Mineral Lands Act of 1872, and Timber and Stone Act of 1878, mostly transferred basic resources to private hands. The apparent objective was to create a nation of small farmers; none of the acts carried a national land policy or provisions for protecting society's interests. Finally, an Irrigation Division was added to the U.S. Geological Survey in 1888 and Congress permitted the Secretary of the Interior to take lands from private hands and set them aside for future irrigation purposes; later the Forest Reserve Act of 1891 authorized the president to withdraw areas of public domain as forest reserves. But still the movement progressed slowly.

As Americans look back, they find that the conservation leaders of the formative years of the movement included Thomas Jefferson (who dis-

---

[16] Louis Agassiz at Harvard and Arnold Guyot at Princeton. This discussion of the early movement is based in part on Guy-Harold Smith, *Conservation of Natural Resources* (New York: John Wiley & Sons, 1950), pp. 4–6.

[17] George P. Marsh, *Man and Nature*, later revised and called *The Earth as Modified by Human Action* (New York: n.p., 1907).

patched the explorers Lewis and Clark), Henry Thoreau, George Perkins Marsh, Carl Schurz, John Wesley Powell, John Muir, Frederick Law Olmsted, Gifford Pinchot, Theodore Roosevelt, Herbert Hoover and Franklin Delano Roosevelt.[18]

Theodore Roosevelt was the first president to emphasize the interlocking character of the nation's problem of resources; he noted that proper control and use of waterways would conserve other basic resources, including coal, iron, soil, and forests. He formed the National Conservation Commission in 1909; later expanded it to include all governors; then all countries that were interested; and a conservation meeting was held at the Hague. However, the popular appeal of conservation subsided after Theodore Roosevelt's administration for several reasons: some of the leaders left public office; too much emphasis had been directed to pending shortages and the shortages did not seem to develop (vast new petroleum discoveries helped to negate the feeling); a conflict in ideologies (private gain vs. society's future) developed in the nation; and World War I diverted America's attention to other problems.

Herbert Hoover, first as secretary of commerce and later as president, used less dramatic but more realistic and enduring means of getting the conservation program back on the right track after the war ended. Among his many accomplishments were creation of the Colorado River Compact and the reclamation project that came to bear his name (the Hoover Dam), completion of the Mississippi-Ohio System, signing of the Great Lakes-St. Lawrence Seaway Treaty, a joint agreement on U.S.-Canadian fisheries control, further pollution abatement along the Middle Atlantic Coast, and stoppage of the leasing and sale of government-owned oil lands. He also inaugurated national planning, rather than politically induced planning, and initiated numerous measures that were completed during later presidential administrations.

Franklin Delano Roosevelt was a most conservation-minded president, and he was able to accomplish substantially more than Hoover because public reaction to conservation was far more sympathetic during the depression days of his New Deal. He emphasized both physical and human resources. Most notable among his accomplishments were the Civilian Conservation Corps, which put a half-million young men to work improving forests, fighting fires and performing flood-control work; his Soil Conservation Act, which set up demonstration areas in almost every state, gave government aid to soil conservation associations, and induced farmers to use better cropping plans and farming methods; his Taylor Grazing Control Act, which created an agency to form, manage, and supervise grazing dis-

---

[18] For a discussion of these men and their importance, see Stewart L. Udall, *The Quiet Crisis* (New York: Holt, Rinehart and Winston, 1963).

tricts in the public domain; his Resettlement Administration, which purchased land too poor to furnish farmers a living, turned it into forests, wildlife sanctuaries, and recreation areas, and moved dispossessed people to other areas; and his National Resources Planning Board, which published an eleven-volume resource inventory of the United States. He made great strides in mobilizing the nation's basic resources.

World War II was a total war that required total resource utilization for the United States, and thoughts of conservation were neglected for its duration. However, while the peace-time goals and methods were interrupted by the war, it was a period of planning that paid off in the postwar years. Since 1945 the nation has seen unusually rapid change taking place. Alternate periods of peace, cold wars, and hot local wars have demanded a continuous military concern over resource availability, while the nation's spreading cities, growing industry, and expanding and shifting population have caused great civilian concern. As the nation has moved into the "space age," its populace has become continually more resource conscious and has put ever-increasing pressure on federal, state, and local governments to protect the social welfare. While air and water pollution abatement and an energy crisis gained the greatest share of public attention in the early 1970s, other problems of resource mobilization (such as mercury poisoning) are far from being ignored. These problems will be discussed in greater detail in succeeding chapters.

Research and development related to exploration of outer space is exceeding only somewhat that related to inner space—the ocean depths— and both are of incalculable value to future mobilization of resources. Multispectral photographs (four synchronized cameras with a complicated series of film and filter combinations to study the earth from outer space) and Earth Resources Observation Systems (EROS) that, among other things, search for new mineral and metal deposits are just two examples; others include research in the life sciences, discoveries of new metals and materials, new techniques, and space-age benefits in the fields of weather, oceanography, forestry, agriculture, geography, medicine, cartography and hydrology, communications, navigation, and transportation.

But, with the space-age research and development, there also is arising a more fundamental shift in the basic philosophy behind technological progress. The broader question of how a nation should use its technology in a period of environmental deterioration is gaining momentum and altering goals—and such changing goals in turn affect resource mobilization. In the 1960s, there was a prevailing assumption that if something could be built, or if enough pressure could be exerted for it to be built, it would be done. The 1970s, instead, are witnessing more attention to the *impact* of new technological discoveries on the physical aspects of nature, and environmental impact studies often must be part of a final decision. This presumably will improve man's environment,[19] rather than often damaging it, and will make the 1980s a better decade in which to live.

SELECTED BIBLIOGRAPHY

BARBER, WILLIAM J., *A History of Economic Thought*. Baltimore: Penguin Books, Inc., 1967.

COYLE, DAVID CUSHMAN, *Conservation: An American Story of Conflict and Accomplishment*, New Brunswick, N.J.: Rutgers University Press, 1957.

DARLING, FRANK F., and JOHN P. MILTON (eds.), *Future Environments of North America* (Conference convened by the Conservation Foundation, April, 1965). Garden City, N.Y.: The Natural History Press, 1966.

GHERITY, JAMES A. (ed.), *Economic Thought: A Historical Anthology*. New York: Random House, 1965.

HAMILTON, DAVID, *Evolutionary Economics: A Study of Change in Economic Thought*. Albuquerque, N.M.: University of New Mexico Press, 1970.

HARRIS, SEYMOUR EDWIN (ed.), *The New Economics: Keynes' Influence on Theory and Public Policy*. New York: Alfred A. Knopf, 1947.

KURIHARA, KENNETH K. (ed.), *Post-Keynesian Economics*. New Brunswick, N.J.: Rutgers University Press, 1954.

LEVY, LESTER S., and ROY J. SAMPSON, *American Economic Development; Growth of the U.S. in the Western World*. Boston: Allyn and Bacon, Inc., 1962.

MARINE, GENE, *America the Raped; The Engineering Mentality and the Devastation of a Continent*. New York: Simon and Schuster, 1969.

MARTINDALE, DON (ed.), *Functionalism in the Social Sciences: The Strength and Limits of Functionalism in Anthropology, Economics, Political Sciences, and Sociology*. Philadelphia: The American Academy of Political and Social Science, 1965.

NEWMAN, PHILIP C., ARTHUR D. GAYER, and MILTON H. SPENCER (eds.), *Source Readings in Economic Thought*. New York: W. W. Norton & Company, Inc., 1954.

NICHOLSON, MAX, *The Environmental Revolution: A Guide for the New Masters of the World*. New York: McGraw-Hill Book Company, Inc., 1970.

ROLL, ERIC, *A History of Economic Thought* (3rd ed.). Englewood Cliffs, N.J.: Prentice-Hall, Inc., 1956.

---

[19] There is always the inherent danger, of course, that vested interest groups and environmental extremists who want no change at all will abuse a nation's checks and balances (such as lengthy struggles through the courts over technicalities) and prevent society's collective wishes from being carried out for some time.

VAN DYNE, GEORGE M. (ed.), *The Ecosystem Concept in Natural Resource Management.* New York: Academic Press, 1969.

ZIMMERMANN, ERICH W., *World Resources and Industries.* New York: Harper & Brothers, Publishers, 1951.

ZURHORST, CHARLES, *The Conservation Fraud.* New York: Cowles Book Company, Inc., 1970.

THREE

FUNCTIONAL CONCEPT
OF RESOURCES

The reader may be in something of a quandary at this point. He has been told not only that there are no "natural" resources and that the world has far more resources today than at any time in history, but also that the substances found in nature (e.g., oil, coal, timber) are resources not because of what they *are,* but because of the function that they perform. This information may be disturbing to him because in most cases it reverses a pattern of thinking formulated in early school years and indelibly impressed upon him. Perhaps this chapter will alter his view from the traditional concept of resources to the functional, a necessary shift if the United States is to gain public support for its continuing effort to mobilize and use its basic and nonbasic resources properly.

If substances used from nature are not "natural" resources, what are they? Increasingly, the literature in this field refers to these substances simply as resources. This, admittedly, is a very broad term that includes human and capital resources as well; so one may prefer to use the term "physical resources," or be more specific and divide them into separate categories such as mineral resources, metal resources, or timber resources. Also, the eight fundamental categories listed in Chapter One can be called basic resources.

The doctrine of acquired resources is a functional or operational approach. Dictionaries define a "function" as, paraphrased here in one way, an action for which something is especially fitted or used, or for which something exists; also, it is something that is dependent on and varies with another. The word "functional" is defined as being designed or developed chiefly from the viewpoint of *use*. Both terms embrace the important distinction of use, and they include the idea of being *dependent on* and *varying with* something else. This approach precisely describes the doctrine of acquired resources, for all resources are used by man, are dependent on existence in nature and on man's needs, and vary with his culture and its goals.

A TRIPART INTERACTION

A thing or substance becomes a resource through the tripart interaction of nature, man, and culture.[1] All three must perform their respective roles before a resource can be created.

Nature, the first occupant of our globe, created countless substances through various processes. Such matter came into existence through an evolutionary process; nature did not place any particular value on it and did not designate any particular use for it.

Man plays a vital role in resource development because he *utilizes* nature's creations and transforms them into products that satisfy his wants and needs. Man has risen above the other animals on this earth because of his superior endowments—a tool-holding thumb, larger and more flexible brain, erect posture, and flexible vocal cord—a combination which no other animal can match. But, far more importantly, man has individually determined techniques,[2] can invent and turn those inventions into innovations, can comprehend cause-and-effect so that science and technology are possible, and can communicate his actions in writing so that future inhabitants of our globe will know what has gone before them and will not need to "start over from scratch." Accumulative knowledge is prerequisite to resource development (and it, too, must be mobilized, just as physical resources must be).

---

[1] This approach to resource creation was developed by Erich W. Zimmermann, who, before his death, taught many years at The University of Texas, Austin, and who has continued to teach through his bible of the trade, *World Resources and Industries* (New York: Harper & Brothers, Publishers, 1951). His ideas, naturally, were drawn partly from the writings of others.

[2] Other living creatures alter their environment; beavers erect dams, bees build hives, birds make nests, ants construct colonies, and spiders spin webs, but their techniques are genus determined, rather than individually determined as is the case for man.

Culture, the third factor in the tripart interaction of resource creation, involves all the changes in environment that take place as man works with nature. Culture includes man's wants and desires, skills and know-how, implements and handicrafts, science and technology, arts and institutions, language and religious beliefs—the list is long. Man has basic (animal) wants such as food, air, water, shelter, and protective devices, but all of his additional wants can be considered cultural needs and desires.

The individual roles played by nature, man, and culture are considered in greater detail in the next three sections of this chapter.

NATURE AND RESOURCES

The planet earth's closed-system concept concerning resources was discussed in the previous chapter. In this closed system nature has established the outer limits by creating definite quantities of the various substances found on earth.[3] However, culture alters resource patterns and the availability of resources within such a closed system.

Is nature bountiful or is it niggardly? Writers of the past have taken both viewpoints and, depending upon their assumptions, have found justification for both approaches. The Physiocrats, eighteenth century French political philosophers, considered nature very bountiful. Their view was that all surplus (and thus profits) in the world resulted from the fact that nature works without reward; man must be paid, but nature works free, and as nature does all the work, man takes the fruits of such work for himself.[4] Their theory, of course, did not go beyond agriculture, which they considered the source of all wealth, and they regarded its surplus as a gift, attributable not to the productivity of labor, but to the productivity of nature. David Ricardo, on the other hand, said in the early nineteenth century that nature is stingy in what it gives away free. He referred to the "original and indestructible powers of the soil," [5] and supported the theme that the quantity of land could never change. In Ricardo's day, the term

---

[3] As man travels to the moon and the stars beyond, theorists may find it necessary to expand this "outer limits" concept to the universe, for it is possible that man may someday bring valuable substances back to earth from elsewhere. The economics of the situation at the time will dictate whether this is feasible.

[4] The most notable Physiocrats were Francois Quesnay (1694–1774), Pierre-Paul Mercier de la Riviere (1720–1793), and Anne Robert Jacques Turgot (1727–1781). For discussion of these men's views, see Philip C. Newman, Arthur D. Gayer, and Milton H. Spencer, *Source Readings in Economic Thought* (New York: W. W. Norton & Company, Inc., 1954); and Eric Roll, *A History of Economic Thought* (Englewood Cliffs, N.J.: Prentice-Hall, Inc., 1956).

[5] David Ricardo, *Principles of Political Economy and Taxation,* E. C. K. Gonner edition (London: George Bell & Sons, 1891), pp. 44f.

"land" meant soil, since the world was mostly agrarian with very little industrializing yet underway. But later economists extended the definition of land to include all things coming directly from nature: urban land, as well as agricultural land, minerals, timber, and other raw materials that are a part of industrial production processes. This is an unfortunate and confusing choice of terms for the person who studies economics, because he must continually shift his thinking from the layman's definition of land to that of the economist—as in land, labor and capital, the three factors of production.

If Ricardo's concept of land is interpreted to mean the closed system that is nature, then land is fixed and never changing; but if the influence of culture is applied to the concept, then land is limitless, dynamic, and always changing. For example, if technology (tools, machines, fertilizers, know-how, etc.) is added to poor land, this basic resource can be improved greatly; and if the land ever becomes incapable of producing adequate food, as Thomas Malthus believed it would, then man will turn increasingly to the sea (land, to today's economist) and harvest it for more food. If some raw materials come to be in short supply, substitutes can be found, and so on through a long list of dynamic possibilities as resources change and new ones are mobilized by the nation.

Whether nature is bountiful or niggardly is a question of emphasis and of the historical period. When the world population was much smaller than it is now, everyone had access to the abundant supply of rich soil for farming, waterfalls for energy, and, of course, pure air and fresh water for sustaining life. But as populations increased and expanded their resource bases, scarcities began to develop and nature seemed quite stingy. Culture, however, can reverse such a pattern, and technological development can make available plentiful resources—by transforming into resources today those substances that were not resources yesterday!

Ricardo and many theorists since his time have believed that the quantity of resources could never be increased. Even today, this anxiety prevails among many Americans, and there is widespread fear that the United States is rapidly using up its resources—that when a tree is cut, a barrel of oil is used, or a ton of coal is burned, it is gone forever and is one less unit remaining in the world storehouse of resources. Even in the post-World-War-II years, a President's Materials Policy Commission (generally called the Paley Commission after its chairman) began its five-volume report by stating:

> In area after area the same pattern is discernible: soaring demands, shrinking resources, the consequent pressure toward rising real costs, the risk of wartime shortages, the ultimate threat of an arrest or decline in the

standard of living. . . . A ton of ore removed from the earth is a ton gone forever; each barrel of oil used up means one less remaining.[6]

Such reasoning is illogical and erroneous; based upon it, Americans would have to support the position that the more resources they use today, the fewer they will have tomorrow, and the fewer consumed now, the more available for consumption in the future. By this reasoning, since the world has been using resources at an ever-increasing rate for almost 2,000 years A.D., one would have to conclude that the world in year 1 A.D., with a much smaller world population, had far more abundant resources and therefore a higher standard of living than it could ever expect to have again. Today, of course, the world in general and the industrialized nations in particular are living better and are enjoying far more abundant resources than ever before in history, despite the fact that population has increased manyfold and most known resource reserves of the past have been consumed or dissipated. The fallacy of the traditional view of resources is that it considers such resources to be "natural," rather than a function of man's needs and so man-made.

MAN AND RESOURCES

Man is the second factor in the tripart interaction which brings about resource development. To understand man's place, one must view him in a dual role: man the animal, and man the human.

Early man was an animal, with only an animal's basic wants: air, water, nourishment, and a place to sleep. For food, he ate other wild animals and wild plants; for rest, he slept on the ground, or in caves if he needed protection from the natural elements. And like other animals, he was plagued by the negative forces of nature: hostile elements, exposure, wild beasts, poisons, and diseases. Changes in this animal-man were slow and genus (group) determined, and were wrought as a function of environmental pressures. His change, as with that of other animals, was through the natural selection of the evolutionary process, with survival possible only for those who had the characteristics that best fitted the environment of a particular area. For this animal-man, nature was very niggardly, and his survival "hung in the balance" for centuries.

Once this animal-man started modifying his environment on an individual basis, culture began to evolve. As he started using weapons (first wielding sticks and rocks and later binding them together to form a third

---

[6] Resources for Freedom, *A Report to the President by the President's Materials Policy Commission* (Washington, D.C.: Government Printing Office, 1952), I, pp. 1 and 5.

weapon, the hatchet), and as he began to make his own crude shelter, the human-man arose. If there had not developed *man, the culture builder,* man, the animal may well have become as extinct as the dinosaur.

From the dawn of man, the culture builder, some 5000 centuries ago, the human population began to increase, slowly at first, then more rapidly, and today at such an accelerating rate that some writers fear that the Malthusian projection of a geometric progression is conservative.

How many people are there in the world? Almost any figure that could be listed would be outdated within a short time, but demographers estimate that the earth's population is more than 3½ billion and well on its way toward the 4 billion mark. To understand a figure like 3 billion, do this: take the current year, multiply that by the number of days in a year, that by the number of hours in a day, that by the number of minutes in an hour, and that figure by three.[7] In other words, there is presently about one person for every 20 seconds that have elapsed since the birth of Christianity. As the world population reaches 4 billion, it will be the equivalent of one person for every 15 seconds since the birth of Christ.

But such figures of population prolificacy are quite recent in history; for most of man's existence, there were never more than 100 million people on earth. There were only 250 million when Christianity was born, and only 500 million by the year 1500. The upsweep in population began about 1650, and the real increase came after 1900.

Only two basic influences could have brought about the rise in population: an increase in birth rates or a decrease in death rates (or a combination of both). Mankind is not particularly more prolific now than formerly (although medical developments have made it possible for some women to become fertile who otherwise could not have borne children); but the death rates, especially in the developing countries, have declined drastically, and the mere fact that more of the population have stayed alive longer has resulted in more people bearing additional offspring. Prehistoric man lived only about 18 years; the life span of the Romans and Greeks averaged about 33 years; Americans lived about 50 years before 1900; and today the peoples born in advanced nations are expected to live more than 80 years. Prior to 1650, starvation, disease, war, and a high rate of infanticide kept the population in check. All of these "controls" have changed in varying degrees in different parts of the world; medical advances (sanitation, drugs, new medical techniques) have lengthened life-spans and reduced infant mortality; agricultural innovations, better transportation, and improved food preservation have allevi-

---

[7] This illustration was used, in a somewhat different form, by John W. Alexander, *Economic Geography* (Englewood Cliffs, N.J.: Prentice-Hall, Inc., 1963), pp. 17–18.

ated starvation; and wars have been less deadly (the long religious wars killed a far larger *percentage* of the world population than more recent wars have).

Population Size and Distribution

The current world population of nearly 4 billion persons would be no cause for concern if it were not for the growth trends and the distribution of those people. Joseph L. Fisher has illustrated the relation of a population of 3 billion (the number when his book was published) to the size of the earth by pointing out that if a cube-shaped box were built so as to allow each person a standing space of 6 × 2 × 1 feet, the entire world population would fit into a box that measured only five-eighths of a mile on each side.[8] Fisher carried the example to one further extreme by suggesting that if such a box were pushed over the edge of the Grand Canyon in Arizona, and someone stood on the canyon rim and looked down on it, the box would appear very small.

The current population would be a quite acceptable size if it were "properly" distributed over the earth.[9] But it is not. Only one-fourth of the earth's surface is land; but three-fourths of the landed surface is either void of population or has a very low population density.[10] Some 30 percent of the world population lives in eastern Asia (e.g., China, Japan, Korea, Vietnam, the Philippines); southern Asia has another 25 percent (e.g., India, Pakistan, Indonesia, Thailand, Burma); Europe is third with another 25 percent of the world total; then the numbers drop rapidly, with North America fourth at only 8 percent.

The reader should not jump to the conclusion that the number of people in an area is the main cause of a high or low level of living. New York's Manhattan Island and Holland have high population concentrations and high standards of living; eastern China and parts of India have similar high concentrations and poor living conditions. New Guinea and Switzerland have about the same number of persons per arable acre of land, and other comparisons could include Korea and the United Kingdom, Vietnam and West Germany, or Indonesia and Norway. It is the mobilization and proper utilization of resources that make the important difference.

The world population is currently growing about 2 percent annually

---

[8] Joseph L. Fisher, *Annual Report, Resources for the Future* (Washington, D.C.: Resources for the Future, Inc., 1963), p. 1.

[9] "Proper" in relation to resource development, not distributed *evenly* necessarily.

[10] These include Africa-Asia, Siberia, Eurasia, northern portions of North America, the Amazon Basin, Oceania, Southwest Africa, and southern South America.

(and adding about 70 million persons a year), and such a rate of growth, if it continues, will double the population every 37 years or so.[11] From time to time various writers present their calculations of what the world population will be in 50, 100, or 500 years from now if current trends go unchecked. Such projections range from barely tolerable conditions to a complete lack of space for human survival. This would be the case *if current trends go unchecked,* but it is inconceivable that they will continue unrestrained. As with resources, which are dynamic and vary with changing conditions, so population trends will change, too.

Various projects have stemmed from work of the prestigious Club of Rome, an international group of industrialists, scientists, educators, and economists who have taken a "doomsday" approach to the world situation and concluded that the world will bring about its own end in some 100 years.[12] For example, some researchers at a widely known American university attempted to make a computer behave like the world—and feeding in information on population, agricultural production, "natural" resources, industrial production, and pollution, reached the inevitable mathematical conclusion that current trends of growth will use up all available food, water, air, and resources sometime in the 2000s. By these projections reductions in population growth patterns and resource consumption can only delay the doom, and nothing short of a reversal of man's progress can prevent the inevitable catastrophe; even zero population growth will not alter the inevitable! Aside from the researchers' faulty assumptions that technology changes slowly, that materials will be recycled at a rather low rate, and that substitution of less scarce resources for more scarce ones is not too practical, they treat resources as a static phenomenon (with fixed "known reserves," and current prices, for example). Their entire approach to resources is contrary to the basic philosophy of this book, which is in full agreement with Erich Zimmermann's often-quoted statement that "re-

---

[11] Just how dramatic a purely arithmetic approach can be is illustrated by Philip M. Hauser, *Science,* CXXXI (June 3, 1960), No. 3414, pp. 1641–47. He notes that just 100 persons multiplying at 1 percent per year for the 5000 years of human history would have produced a current population of 2.7 billion persons per square foot of land surface on the earth.

[12] D. H. Meadows, D. L. Meadows, J. Randers, and W. W. Behrens III, *The Limits of Growth,* A Potomac Associates Book (New York: Universe Books, 1972); for a computer model, see Jay W. Forrester, *World 2 Model* (Cambridge, Mass.: Wright-Allen Press, Inc., 1971), translated from Dynamo language to FORTRAN IV by W. E. Schiesser, Computing Center, Lehigh University, Bethlehem, Penn. For critiques of the approach taken in *The Limits of Growth,* see U.S. Department of Health, Education, and Welfare, *The Implications for Government Action of the Limits of Growth* (Washington, D.C.: Government Printing Office, 1973); Allen Kneese and Ronald Ridker, "Predicament of Mankind," *The Washington Post,* March 2, 1972; Peter Passell, Marc Roberts and Leonard Ross, *The New York Times Book Review,* April 2, 1972; Carl Kaysen, "The Computer that Printed Out WOLF," *Foreign Affairs,* July, 1972.

sources are not, they become." As for world population trends, the third quarter of the twentieth century has been a time for concern, but not alarm. Some parts of the world are already overpopulated, even with few people per square mile or per acre of arable land, and this is the subject of the next section of this chapter. But it is folly for researchers to try to look ahead farther than they can see; there are too many variables, not the least of which include the unusual capacity of man and his institutions to react to new problems in rare and constructive ways.

Problems Caused by Overpopulation

Some areas of the world are already overpopulated in the sense that existing resources of the areas are inadequate to provide a satisfactory level of existence for the population, even when measured by very basic ideas of human dignity and wants. The National Academy of Sciences has said that the basic standard of living for human beings the world over should be able to provide at least "adequate food, good health, literacy, education, and gainful employment." [13]

Problems caused by overpopulation would form an endless list, but the most obvious ones include the following:

1. Inadequate food supplies cause starvation for many and malnutrition and premature death for others.
2. Health standards are low and disease is widespread.
3. Physical resources available to each person in the area are limited and cannot be increased if rising populations keep pressing upon them.
4. It is difficult for an overcrowded country to produce a margin of goods and services over and above what is needed to keep the population alive.
5. New capital formation, required to build industries and produce tools, is drastically limited.
6. Children must seek employment before they are sufficiently educated and trained; and, as economic writers have noted for two centuries, this hinders specialization, which could greatly increase productivity of the labor force.
7. Ambitions are limited to scraping together only enough necessities to meet immediate needs; this psychological factor has an important influence upon the economic development of a nation.
8. Science and technology develop far slower because of the foregoing reasons (poor health, inadequate resources, insufficient education and skills, lack of ambition, and low capital accumulation).
9. Good soil, adequate water, and a scarcity of other basic resources come into short supply and pollution of air and water becomes a problem.

---

[13] National Academy of Sciences, op. cit., p. 1.

10. Space is inadequate for the physical and psychological well-being of the people; in all biological observations, the amount and quality of available space ultimately limits the indefinite multiplication of any species.

It was stated earlier that there are encouraging signs of a reversal in the current trend of a rising world population. Any certainty of this is premature, but widespread public concern, together with scientific developments in the area of birth control, might lead one to optimism. In the early 1800s, Thomas Malthus' *Essay on the Principle of Population* described only two main checks on population growth: positive action such as starvation, disease, war and infanticide; and preventive action such as late marriage and abstention. Americans today, led by a natural interest in methods of birth control, generally are somewhat familiar with the growing array of preventive techniques, ranging from the rhythm method to various external, intrauterine, and oral contraceptive devices. But the reader may not be aware that induced abortion, legal or illegal, is the most important single limitation on births throughout many countries of the world.

CULTURE AND RESOURCES

Culture, the third aspect of resource development, is a key ingredient as man works his wonders on nature. In geologic time, culture is a latecomer on the scene, being preceded first by nature and then by man; but culture is no less important because of this. Man is a culture-builder, and without enlightenment that culture brings, he would still be existing among the lower forms of animal life—or he might not be in existence at all! It bears repeating that nature sets the outer limits of the world, and culture is continually changing the world within those limits.

To understand the part that culture plays, one must visualize it in a dual role. Culture, which is the sum of the attainments and activities of man, includes all the modifications that it has imposed on nature—tangible modifications such as canals, railroads, dams, machines, agricultural terracing, fertilizers, hybrid seeds, domesticated animals—the list is long. But it also includes all the modifications that it has made on man—intangibles such as human attitudes, man's relations to other men, mores, education and knowledge, training and skills, health—the list is equally long.

The part that culture plays in resource development may be summarized as:

I. Culture and nature
    A. Culture permits man to duplicate and extend nature by:
        1. Copying nature
        2. Improving nature
        3. Creating substances not available in nature

    B.   Culture helps correct resistances in nature by:
         1.   Enabling man to produce more
         2.   Alleviating seasonal limitations
         3.   Moving products from a place of production to place of need

II.   Culture and man
    A.   Culture improves man's abilities
    B.   It contributes to man's continued existence
    C.   It helps man to live with his fellow man

III.   Culture, the equalizer
    A.   Culture comes to the rescue if nature is in short supply
    B.   Culture comes to the rescue if man (labor) is in short supply

The remainder of this section will analyze each point in the order presented in the foregoing outline.

Culture and Nature

One of man's greatest attributes has been his cultural ability to duplicate substances found in nature and to extend and improve upon what nature has to offer. Man, working through his culture, copies nature in many ways. He has learned to make plastics look like wood in fine furniture (only the termites can tell for sure) and like metal in innumerable objects from automobiles to toys; to obtain nitrates from the air rather than depending upon limited and sometimes inaccessible deposits found in the ground (e.g., Chile); to make synthetic rubber to replace less-available natural rubber; and to synthesize drugs and chemicals in order to reduce the cost and increase the quantities available.

Man also has utilized his culture to improve nature, either to ameliorate its resistances or alleviate its deficiencies. He can eliminate the problem of rust and corrosion in steel; concentrate drugs and vitamins in far more potent doses than are found in nature; produce synthetic rubber that resists deterioration from chemicals, oils, and the like; manufacture saccharin and other nonfattening sugar substitutes; treat foodstuffs with chemicals and radiation to reduce spoilage; and even buffer his aspirin. American women also have learned to use synthetic materials to alter their "natural endowments" to an acceptable standard that their culture has come to expect.

Many substances not available in nature are now created by man— again with knowledge, tools, and techniques that are a part of his culture. These include dacron, orlon, polyethylene, and many other plastics and synthetics, fissionable energy, and fusionable energy.[14]

---

[14] Fusion, the energy that perpetuates the sun, is still a source of the future, insofar as man's ability to produce it on a sustained basis with a net energy output; the hydrogen bomb is not a sustained yield.

Through the years, man's culture has enabled him to correct resistances that occurred in nature. He has domesticated animals and crossbred them so that they can resist climatic conditions dissimilar to their native environment (the hot tropics and the cold north) and can produce more beef or pork—or turkeys with larger breasts and drumsticks—and increase production (more milk or larger eggs). He has developed hybrid seeds that grow disease-resistant plants, larger crops, or crops that mature more quickly in areas with short growing seasons. He can convert poor soil into rich land by applying fertilizers and conditioners, and he can persuade dry lands to produce fertile crops by using irrigation and removing salt from the land (as he has done in the Imperial Valley). But culture's influence goes beyond that, for man's railroads have transformed into granaries the once almost uninhabitable plains and prairies of the central United States and of areas in Russia, Argentina, Canada, and elsewhere.

Culture also has helped correct nature's seasonal limitations on crop production so that weather problems are offset by new hybrids that bear earlier in the year—or later, if necessary; mechanization sometimes makes it practicable to grow successive crops in a single season, whereas slower hand planting and hand harvesting would have permitted time for only one crop. The widespread use of warehouses, silos or elevators, and refrigerators, freezers or freeze-drying processes (all products of culture) make it feasible for man to store crops all year long; while refrigeration plus rapid transportation enables an American living anywhere in the country to eat fragile and perishable products such as tomatoes or lettuce, no matter how far he lives from where they are grown. In the nonagricultural sector air-conditioning and central heat have made new areas of the world habitable year-round.

Culture also has made it possible for man to move products from one area to another area on earth to fulfill a specific need or to utilize a good to the fullest extent. For example, food is transported to people who live in the cities, so that man no longer must live on the soil and be self-sufficient. Planes, railroads, ships, and motor vehicles also convey people from place to place, and this high degree of mobility creates a much stronger society. Plants and animals have found new homes—cotton plants were introduced into Japan from their native location, cattle with superior qualities came to America from France and India, Brazilian rubber was taken to the Middle East, American wheat to Canada, Mexican wheat to Indonesia, white potatoes from the Andes to northern Europe, and so on. Cotton came originally from the Caribbean, corn from Central America, soybeans from Manchuria, alfalfa from Asia, and quinine from the Andes. In fact, most of the important crops and animals in South America—sugar cane, coffee, wheat, rice, linseed, hogs, sheep, and cattle—are foreign in their origin.

Many imperfections in man are ameliorated with the aid of his culture. His abilities are improved with education, training, and the learning of new techniques and skills; and his physical defects (resistances) are corrected with eyeglasses, microscopes, radar, sonar, hearing aids, weightlifts, and telescopes. His chances for continued existence are furthered by medicines, better sanitation, health services and health standards (e.g., pure food and drug laws), storm warnings, and other forms of protection (fire, police, armed forces, etc.).

Culture also benefits man as he tries to live with his fellow man; these cultural aids include various forms of government; the church; penal and moral codes; the institutions of marriage and private property; communes; associations for labor and for trades; and time, places, and means for recreation.

Culture, the Equalizer

Wherever mankind encounters a dearth of nature's gifts, culture comes to the rescue; and wherever man (labor) is in short supply, again culture steps in to bridge the gap—culture being the great equalizer in the tripart interaction.

There are many examples of how a meager nature can be bolstered through cultural aids. As mentioned before, culture furnishes fertilizers for poor soil, irrigation systems for dry land, terracing for rice-growing, hybrid seeds and tree-grafting to improve crops; it provides devices to save fuel where the supply is short and to conserve ores and minerals where they are scarce. For example, the Bessemer converter consumes less fuel than previously used furnaces; the hydrogenation process made oil-like products from coal when Europe had a shortage of petroleum (Hitler fought World War II on synthetic rubber and oil made from coal); natural gas can be derived from coal; American techniques made it possible to process low-grade taconite in locales where rich iron-ore deposits were depleted; France developed rayon when it had difficulty obtaining sufficient quantities of cotton and silk; the European countries turned to small cars and motor scooters because fuel was too scarce and expensive to use in larger vehicles.

If man (the labor force) is in short supply, culture again mitigates the problem. Mechanical devices use inanimate energy to replace muscle energy, thus reducing labor and-or time (which indirectly saves man-hours). In America, of the countless labor-saving devices developed, a list of the most valuable would surely include the McCormick reaper, the sewing machine, typewriter, calculator, power loom, linotype, and machinery used in the cotton gin and in textile spinning. Fast transportation, instant communication, data processing, and scientific management techniques are other examples of culture's coming to the rescue.

The reader who is knowledgeable in economics will note some similarity between the term "culture," as used here, and "capital," as used by the economist in the factors of production: land, labor, and capital. To the economist capital serves to supplement land or labor, whichever is in short supply. While there is some similarity between the economist's *land, labor,* and *capital,* and the resource theorist's *nature, man,* and *culture,* obviously the latter approach is far more inclusive; culture, for example, embraces many more concepts than does the term capital.

Cultural Differences

Up to this point, the discussion has dealt with culture as if it were a worldwide unit, and of course it is not. The earth is not even seriously approaching a one-world concept in theory, much less in reality. Cultures vary from the degenerate nomad to the affluent U.S. city dweller, from the hand-laboring Indian to the mechanized Swiss, from tribes of the Pacific islands to the societies of advanced industrial nations, from areas with population bursts to those practicing birth control or with high abortion rates, from subsistence agriculture to commercial farming, from nations with widespread disease and malnutrition to those with high public health standards, or from donkey carts and elephants to jets and missiles, from the cowboy economies to the space-capsule economies. The cultural gaps between extremes are gradually narrowing as rapid transportation and communications cause cultures to become cross-fertilized; but the abyss will close very slowly and very painfully for cultures that resist change.[15]

The most important differences among nations of the world are cultural differences. Man is common to all nations. The color of his skin may vary, he may have larger or smaller hands, or he may stand tall or short; but his more significant characteristics in education, abilities, skills, drives, values, adaptability, temperament, way of life, and the like—are culturally determined. Nature also is present in all nations. Climates, soils, vegetation, and minerals may vary; but the *use* that man makes of them is decided by

---

[15] The reference here is to closing *cultural* gaps; economic gaps (e.g., per capita income and gross national product) are actually widening in many cases between advanced and less-developed countries. In the previous sentence, reference to "cowboy economies" denotes frontier-type societies, whose varieties of resoruces are limited in number, but are treated as if they were inexhaustible. The United States has reached the technological "spaceman economy" but is moving now toward the self-contained "space capsule economy."

his culture. If man wishes, he can overcome some resistances of nature. He *can* make the desert arable (turn the Colorado Desert into the Imperial Valley or the Arctic wastelands into habitable military bases), refrigerate his surroundings, transplant vegetation and animals, or improve the soil, and he opts through his culture (his needs and goals) the neutral materials in nature which will become resources. One nation may have coal, while another country has no coal but has pitchblende or intense solar radiation; the fact that coal was an important source of energy a century ago, while the others were not, was a culturally determined matter, not a decision of nature. Thus, the important differences among nations of the world clearly are not variations in man or nature, but in culture.

There are so many ways in which cultures can vary; only a few can be provided here for illustrative purposes.

Forms of government may vary, ranging from dictatorships to democracies, and the latter may be weak democracies or strong democracies. The United States has a strong democracy, with federal and-or state governmental agencies supervising or regulating most major economic activities and intervening when basic resources are threatened (e.g., air and water pollution or the energy crisis of the early 1970s).

Dominant religions in nations differ, with various ones opposing birth control and abortion, the eating of certain foods (such as pork), the destruction of animals, the use of medicine—or even the operation of businesses on Sunday (or on Saturday, for another religion). These differences have an important direct or indirect impact upon a nation's economic fiber. For example, pork comes from an animal that is a scavenger by nature, easy to raise in areas dominated by Jewish and Moslem religions, where feed is scarce and the people badly need protein in their diet. In India and surrounding areas, where much of the population believes in reincarnation, cattle can tromp unmolested through the grain fields that are badly needed by starving people in the region. Moslems in Saudi Arabia must spend five one-hour periods of prayer each day, and American oil companies have been required by law to release their local employees at least two times a day for such purpose. And, during the month of Ramadan (the ninth month of the Muhammadan year, observed with fasting daily from dawn to sunset) the people in Saudi Arabia customarily work only four hours a day. Among other religions the Protestant Reformation was conducive to economic development, as was the Puritan belief in working and saving, and achieving spiritual satisfaction through work. Some religions preach salvation through work, which includes the earning of money; others preach salvation hereafter, which brings about satisfaction with one's economic lot here on earth.

Some cultures work all through the day, while others take a siesta and then work into the night. Perhaps this practice came about because of climatic conditions (heat) originally; but it is basically a cultural pattern now, and it is not found universally within the same latitudes around the world. The *mañana* attitude that often accompanies the siesta custom affects entrepreneurship and resource utilization. Significance of the "time factor" is another variation; in Brazil, for example, a bus trip from the south to the northeast can last a week or two, while a long-distance telephone call can take days to complete.

The female's place in society differs among nations. Woman is basically a servant to man in some areas, such as in parts of the Orient, and even has to appear veiled in public in certain eastern countries. In the United States women are approaching equality with men (with women constituting more than one-third of the labor force in the 1970s) and contributing to the nation's productivity. The female has achieved equality, for the most part, in Russia and China. Women working alongside men affects a nation's productive and consumptive levels. It also affects the pattern of dress; women who work around machinery must wear tighter clothes and have shorter or confined hair—just as men had to give up ruffled shirt fronts and cuffs when the Industrial Revolution changed their work patterns—and the resulting dress styles have their own economic impact. In most cultures, the father is the head of the household; but others have the mother as the stronger force in the family (this is generally true among Southern Blacks in the United States, for example). On the other hand, and in a different vein, Germans refer to their Fatherland, while Americans think of their Mother Country, where their forefathers survived with the help of Mother Nature.

Mores differ greatly among nations of the world, too. What is right in one country is wrong in another; cartels are illegal in the United States, but are acceptable contractual agreements enforceable in the courts of Europe. The French and Italians pinch women in public as a compliment; but, at the other extreme, many East Pakistanian marriages were nullified by the simple act of enemy soldiers having raped Pakistanian wives during the brief 1971 conflict with India. Swedes often consider a wife and a mistress—or a husband and a boyfriend—as an accepted way of life, while other nationalities object to such pluralistic practice. Some cultures endorse polygamy, while others insist on monogamy. Some people consider population control a moral question; others do not. In some cultures, the elite do not engage in any work that might "dirty their hands," while other cultures feel that "hard work never hurt anybody" and even a millionaire may become virtually a slave to his job. Of course, mores are interwoven with traditions and customs in many cases, and all of these have at least an indirect effect on resource utilization, attitudes, and adaptation to technological change.

The concept of personal property offers another example of cultural differences around the world. The American owns all minerals under his land (unless he has chosen to deed them to someone else), and this has led to enormous physical and economic waste in regard to minerals; in past decades every individual who had oil under his land had the right to produce it, even if it meant a well located every 50 feet in areas of small-tract drilling. In most other countries the central government owns all subsurface minerals and can dictate production patterns; with today's knowledge of oil reservoir management, that can mean that wells are located many miles apart. Another personal property example is the widespread practice of subdivision of land through inheritance, a pattern found in much of the Orient and parts of Europe, as well. Eventually, a man may find that he owns 50 or 60 small plots of land, scattered over an area of several miles and all too small to use modern machinery on them; and because of ancestor worship, he will not sell the inheritance so that large plots of land can be formed and worked economically.

Examples of cultural differences around the world are virtually endless. However, one of the most perplexing problems arises when one society attempts to impose its culture upon another society. This is especially true if the attempted change is imposed too rapidly and severely, whether it is the English colonial policy of early days; the Japanese invasion of Pacific islands in World War II; Russian dominance of neighboring nations since that war; or American economic aid and capitalist influence in Puerto Rico, South America, Africa, India, or Southeast Asia. And the painful problems are not limited to the intermingling of cultures between nations; they can occur within a nation, as in America when the urbanite tries to dictate to the rural areas or the North wants to change the cultural patterns of the South, or university students want to change the patterns of professors and administrators on campuses. It may be only fair to acknowledge that a few anthropologists disagree that rapid change is necessarily disturbing to a society—a position contrary to that taken here.

A nation should not strive to remake other nations into its own image; and such an effort becomes an impossible task when attempted in a short period of time. If culture is a derivative of man and nature, and the significant variations in the two among nations are cultural differences, then it is the cultures that must be modified if improvements are to be made in either man or nature. And changes in culture come about very slowly. This "cultural lag" was recognized by Karl Marx, who wrote in the middle 1800s about the fact that technological change is dynamic and very rapid, but cultures resist change as long as they can.

To illustrate this point, one can hypothesize the introduction of a relatively simple product of technology (a modern American repeating rifle, for example) to a tribe of uncivilized natives somewhere in a jungle. It would take the natives less than an hour to learn to *fire* the rifle and thus make use of this technological change. But, how many years would it take their culture to adjust to this technology, to devise the regulations for control and self-protection found in advanced countries? To wit, that the native is not permitted to carry the weapon concealed, must dismantle it when carrying it in public, can legally kill only wild game with it (and then only during certain hunting seasons), and must not shoot it in the village or at another member of his tribe—unless that individual is committing adultery with his wife! Culture changes very slowly, as the Americans found when they furnished tractors and other agricultural advances to agrarian societies of less-developed nations, and then found that the machines rusted in the fields and new production methods went unused, because the culture was not prepared for (or willing to risk) such technological change.[16] Then the Americans attempted to teach other nations of the world the "American way of life" and ran into resistance when the established cultural patterns of those nations would not accommodate the change rapidly enough. Finally, many people have come to realize that change in less-developed nations must be gradual and the teaching must be done carefully with a "soft sell" approach.[17]

RESOURCES OVERCOME RESISTANCES

Just as man uses his culture to turn "stuff" found in nature into resources, he then employs his resources to overcome the resistances— referred to by geographers variously as hazards, constraints, obstacles, or handicaps—found in nature, man, and culture.

Some writers have called resistances the opposite of resources;[18] this gives an inaccurate verbal picture, for one then tends to visualize resources and resistances as counterparts, equated to supply and demand, profit and loss, or assets and liabilities. Resources and resistances do not

---

[16] Walter Krause, *Economic Development* (Belmont, Calif.: Wadsworth Publishing Company, 1961), pp. 53–54; Benjamin Higgins, *Economic Development* (New York: W. W. Norton & Company, 1968), p. 202.

[17] This view is not shared universally, especially by some anthropologists who have studied areas after their cultures underwent a major and massive shock from outside forces. Margaret Mead studied the Manus islanders after their society leaped 2,000 years during 10 years of occupation of the island by American troops in World War II, and she concluded that rapid change is not necessarily painful. However, complete domination of a small island by a massive outside force is quite different from the impact that an advanced nation can afford to superimpose on an underdeveloped nation, where the scale of influence is far less.

[18] This type description can be found in numerous texts. Even Zimmermann, op. cit., pp. 18–19, and Henry L. Hunker (ed.), *Erich W. Zimmermann's Introduction to World Resources* (New York: Harper & Row, Publishers, 1964), pp. 26–27, can lead the reader to this conclusion.

necessarily have an equal impact (as supply and demand tend to have)[19] or a balancing effect (as with the other pairs of terms). An elementary, but more realistic, analogy for comparison would be a person's pulling up the covers when he is cold; he is using something developed through his culture (the blanket) to overcome nature's resistance (the cold).

Nature poses many constraints and offers resistances to man's activities. For example, there are natural disasters such as floods and droughts, tornadoes and hurricanes, land slides and earthquakes—all resistances which man tries to overcome by such culturally developed techniques as advanced warnings and predetermined precautionary moves. There are problems of insects and disease, which he overcomes with insecticides and herbicides or sanitation and public health. There is friction, and lubricants (a resource) mitigate this. Even distance is a resistance of nature that must be overcome, and man, through his culture, has developed energy-driven machines to help him; he has automobiles, ships, and planes to overcome horizontal distances, and he uses elevators and escalators to offset the resistance of vertical distances.

Most readers will think of resistances in terms of nature alone; but such obstacles occur in man and culture as well.

Man's resistances include physical limitations on his lifting power, his vision, and his hearing abilities—all of which culture has overcome with various devices. Culture also has tried to offset man's natural tendency toward human frictions and greed: it has police forces, courts, and social organizations. Ignorance is overcome by schools and other forms of training, and man's innate feeling of insecurity is alleviated by pension plans, social security, and government health plans in advanced countries or the rearing of many children to care for aged parents in underdeveloped areas.

And culture has its resistances, too. A tendency toward overpopulation is a cultural problem,[20] as is cultural lag and institutional backwardness—ancestor worship, the family concept, religion, women's place in society, differing mores, and even the concept of personal property. All of these can hamper full utilization of resources and culture attempts to mitigate them in various ways, including education and even laws. Resistance to change, racial conflicts, class struggles, and wars are forms of cultural resistances, to list but a few examples.

Wherever conditions unfavorable to man's happiness or well-being are found, resources generally are developed to overcome these conditions. If such resources have not been sought and utilized to date, there is little

---

[19] Alfred Marshall described supply as "the other blade of a pair of scissors" with demand.

[20] The sex urge may be a part of nature; but the reproduction of children today is a product of culture, whereby mates are brought together through societal patterns.

doubt that they will be some day, for the very fact that something is considered a resource means that there is a need for its function. The reader is reminded that the term *resource,* as used in this text, does not really refer to a thing or substance, but rather to the function which that thing or substance performs to reach a goal or purpose.

RESOURCE CREATION AND DESTRUCTION

The doctrine of acquired resources allows for both the creation of resources and their destruction. Under the functional approach resources are means to ends; consequently, as the ends or goals become modified or are changed altogether, new resources are brought into being, while some existing resources are no longer required and, thus, cease to be resources. They are, in effect, destroyed as resources.

Creation

Examples of resource creation are as numerous as the cultural changes that have taken place since the dawn of the human race. They can be as basic as the terracing of wasteland to form paddies for the rice cultures or the introduction of irrigation in desert or steppe areas. They also can result from new processes, techniques, or innovations. The space age has necessitated the creation of new materials: metals and other substances that were not needed in an earlier era. Mechanization of agriculture made it possible to grow wheat in Canada, where the time consumed in planting, growing, and harvesting could not exceed the nation's short growing season. The vulcanization process, discovered by accident in 1839 by Charles Goodyear, created a resource of the rubber tree in the Amazon region of Brazil and, later, elsewhere in the world. Deposits of iron ore in the Minas Gerais area of Brazil were known for many years, but they were inaccessible and thus not a resource—until domestic needs and World War II requirements, plus modern transportation, sanitation, and other cultural changes such as legislation and development of foreign markets, made it possible to recover the ore economically; as the goals changed (as a need became evident), a basic resource was created.

When new products are created, resources can be unearthed in the process; for example, molybdenum became valuable for hardening steel, and widespread use of aluminum required the development of bauxite and cryolite deposits. New processes create resources, as occurred with the Athabasca tar sands of Canada and the once useless oil-saturated shale deposits in Wyoming, Colorado, and New Mexico. The seas and oceans contain every known mineral in solution, but thus far man produces little more than salt, bromine, and magnesium from them; someday he will obtain countless benefits from this vast reserve source (the oceans, of course, have long been a resource in such important roles as a means of transportation and a source of food). Chapter Five contains a detailed discussion of the sea as a basic resource.

The Imperial Valley of California is a good example of resource creation. This area, about the size of Rhode Island, is located between the Mojave Desert and the Mexican border, and was known as the Colorado Desert in 1900. But today the Imperial Valley produces about one-third of the nation's winter carrot and cabbage crops, harvests enormous quantities of winter lettuce, and raises some of the best cattle and longest-staple cotton found anywhere. All these and other valuable agricultural products are produced there despite the fact that there are practically 365 days of sunshine a year; the temperature reaches 120 degrees in the shade; and soil temperature often climbs to 160 degrees in the summer. The secret lies in the irrigation furnished by more than 1,700 miles of canals running from the higher elevations of the Colorado River. Rainfall averages less than 3 inches a year, and the farmers confess they would prefer that it never rain because a shower makes the fields too muddy to work, interrupts tight planting schedules, washes insecticides off the plants, and sucks plant-damaging salt to the surface. Salt is a major problem in any area as arid as the Imperial Valley. In areas of normal rainfall, salt, which is found in most rocks and minerals, is washed down the rivers or carried underground to the ocean; but where climates are dry, rainfall dissolves the salt and then draws it to the surface as the moisture evaporates. The once-fertile Tigris-Euphrates Valley virtually died of "salt poisoning," as did large areas of North Africa, Asia, and some irrigated parts of Pakistan. The same problem began to occur in the Imperial Valley, and by 1920 some 50,000 acres were abandoned because of salt poisoning. Then the people of the area devised a plan of flushing the salt from the soil by laying long drainage pipes of tile some six feet below the surface. Irrigation waters from the canals then carried the salt down to the drainage system and through the tiles to the nearby Salton Sea. Today much of the abandoned land has been reclaimed and made fertile again. Meanwhile, the Salton Sea, which in 1900 was a bone-dry salt bed known as the Salton Sink, receives some 4 million tons of salt from the land each year. While some people might call the Imperial Valley a valuable "natural" resource, it is entirely man-made with man's knowledge, skill and millions of dollars, and there is nothing "natural" about it!

The taconite deposits of Minnesota serve to illustrate a somewhat different type of resource creation. Northern Minnesota was once the United States' greatest iron-ore producing area, with its open-pit mines of rich ore forming the base for 60 percent of all U.S. iron and steel output. Then, after a century of production, the 110-mile Mesabi Range began to run out of the ore; the mining industry started fading and the area's economy deteriorated. All that remained in the area was grey taconite rock, which was too hard and of too low a grade to be mined profitably. But technology came to the rescue. The steel industry devised a way to "drill" the once useless taconite with jet flames of some 4,300 degrees of heat, and it developed machines to crush the ore, and magnetize and roll the iron content into pea-sized pellets. The end result was a product that was richer per ton than the natural iron ore. Now a group of individual companies, building and expanding billions of dollars worth of taconite-processing plants in the area, are revitalizing the economy of the region, and are proclaiming that they have a 300-year supply of taconite ore, at current rates of iron consumption—another instance of man's culture creating a resource from a once-useless substance found in nature.

Destruction

Just as man and his culture can create resources, so can they destroy them. This destruction can occur through the normal consumption of non-renewable reserves, the loss of resources because of waste and folly, or the abandonment of still other resources as national and world goals change.

Many resources are destroyed through ignorance or folly. This includes loss of good topsoil by erosion or poor cropping methods, pollution of streams and rivers, wasteful flaring of natural gas (burning it in the field, rather than man's properly utilizing it for well pressure or for consumption), and countless other forms of waste. The fact that Americans can expect to develop more resources in the future than they have today does not mean that forests can be squandered with impunity or that fertile land can be permitted to waste away. The real issue is not physical scarcity, but economic scarcity—the rising cost of replacement (though there are some who fear that population expansion will cause actual physical scarcity). Man rarely exhausts completely the contents of a mine, a well, a forest, or a field; costs simply increase until it is no longer economically feasible to continue the operation. This is an economic fact of life that should not be taken lightly, for it makes resource destruction through folly even more costly than it might appear at first glance.

Resources also are destroyed because of changing cultural patterns. A nation's resources change as its aims or goals change, and once-vital resources lose their value. The United States no longer needs pitch for caulking wooden boats, firewood for heating homes and cooking meals, indigo or madder root for dyeing cloth, bayberry bushes for candles, or whale oil for lighting lamps. Americans are no longer dependent upon nitrates from natural deposits in the ground, and some aluminum-making processes can now dispense with Greenland's cryolite. Just as the vulcanization process once created a resource in the Amazon regions of South America, as discussed earlier, the development of synthetic rubber-like products has gradually destroyed natural rubber as a vital resource for many purposes, to the distress of nations that are highly dependent upon the export of this product for their welfare. In a similar manner synthetics have replaced other once-essential materials (nylon for silk in women's hose, polypropylene for hemp in rope and wool in carpets, vinyl for leather in ladies' shoes and handbags, etc.).

Techno-Reserves

There can be no question that, given today's technology, when a barrel of oil is burned for energy, it is gone forever. It can be replaced by more oil; but that particular barrel of hydrocarbon is gone. In the case of iron and aluminum the scrap can be reclaimed and recycled, but oil and coal cannot be reused once these basic resources are burned. This is not to say that the world has fewer known oil reserves now than 100 years ago because of what has been destroyed through use—actually, it has a greater quantity of proven reserves now. Not only is man learning more about how to discover new reserves, but he also knows how to get more oil out of existing sources through proper reservoir management and secondary recovery methods such as repressuring and water-flooding. Also, the supply is "increasing" because of less loss during handling and transport and because nations are developing better techniques of utilization (e.g., more efficient automobiles, space heating units, electric generating systems, steel-mill furnaces). If one barrel of oil will produce five times the utility today than it did a century ago, then nature's storehouse of petroleum, in effect, is increased fivefold. The additional four barrels in this example might be called *techno-reserves,* because it is through man's growing knowledge and technological developments that these "added" reserves are available.[21] Though the original oil deposits of the world have not been augmented by nature in our lifetime,[22] the utility of the original potential reserves is expanded by an enormous amount that can be termed techno-reserves.

Resources can only be fixed under the static conditions of a given

---

[21] "Techno-reserves" seems to be a better term than "techno-resources," inasmuch as it is possible that these substances may cease to be resources some day if we no longer have a need for them. Erich Zimmermann referred to "Phantom Resources," but this term seems to confuse many students of resources.

[22] Geologists estimate that it requires millions of years for nature to produce petroleum from living matter.

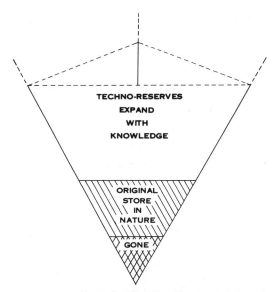

FIGURE 2. Nature has put on earth only limited quantities of all substances. These form the potential reserves, and some of these have been destroyed already through wise use or waste. However, the availability and utility of what remains are increased by man's advancing technology, and the increase can be considered techno-reserves of man's resources.

point in history; over a period of time, they are dynamic and can either increase or decrease—and if history is any indication, they will *increase* tremendously through the development of techno-reserves. Yet man does live within a closed system, and each barrel of oil burned and destroyed is one less in that closed system; one can only hope that it is through wise *use,* and not through folly, that the resource is destroyed.

New Frontiers

Occasionally some writer will hypothesize that as a nation's frontiers disappear, the country matures and slows its economic growth because of a lack of large-scale capital investment opportunities.[23] Such an assumption is not valid in resource theory. Though there may no longer be free land in the West, the American frontiers have not been eliminated; there will always be unexplored fields to offer the thrill of discovery. If a technological

---

[23] This idea is not limited to lesser-known writers; in England, John Maynard Keynes once wondered if the economy had become mature, and in the United States, Professor Alvin H. Hansen was the leading American exponent of the "mature economy thesis." Others have followed.

development or a cultural advance like a dam or canal opens the wastelands of the desert to agriculture, that is a new frontier; if industry develops a machine that makes it possible to grow a crop in a state that never raised that crop before, or if a new grain like light-insensitive triticale is developed, that is a new frontier. Space exploration, data processing, cryogenics, miniaturized circuitry, aquaculture, and oceanography are all new frontiers. So long as man continues to increase his knowledge, and to utilize that new knowledge, there will continue to be new frontiers.

The Institutionalist theory of economic development fits well this approach to growing resource opportunities.[24] Institutionalists believe that technology—the sum of all tools and skills in a society—is highly dynamic and, through time, is continuous, cumulative, and ever-accelerating in its rate of change. Its growth is slowed only by society's institutions—those cultural relations between persons and persons, and between persons and things, that are prescribed by habitual ways of thinking; institutions are static, past binding, past glorifying, and ceremonial. But despite the continuous drag of institutions, technology grows at an ever-increasing rate because it is the combination and recombination of existing tools and techniques (from early times when a caveman bound together a rock and a stick —two existing weapons—to form a new tool, the hatchet). The geometric way that technology increases by combining existing tools to form new ones will be quite evident to those who recognize the many changes that have taken place in the world just in the past one or two decades. This rate of technological change, fantastic as it has been, will be ever-increasing in the future, and with it man's resources will continue to grow and change. A particular culture of the world can make more material progress than another because it has a broader technological base and more flexible institutions, not because its members are generally more intelligent or inherently more gifted.

Arable Land and Cultivability

Culture has an important influence on land utilization among all nations of the world. One technique of describing population densities of various countries is to measure the number of arable acres of land that each has per capita. There was a time when this was considered a good technique for judging a nation's standard of living and for assessing the ability of the

---

[24] Undoubtedly, the late Professor C. E. Ayres was the leading authority (and partial architect) of Institutionalist theory. The brief digest that follows is about as complete as the drawing of a molehill to illustrate what a mountain looks like. The student who is interested in the Institutionalist's interpretation of economic development will do well to read some of Dr. Ayres' published works.

land to support a larger (or perhaps only a smaller) population. Yet, one might well wonder if this is not analogous to "facing up to the problem" by grabbing the bull by the tail. The approach is wrong. Why is one type of land under cultivation in the United States, but the same type is not farmed in China?

There are two main limitations on cultivability of land: first, the physical characteristics—the outer limits set by nature—including temperature, moisture, topography, and type of soil. But if similar land is being used in one nation and not in another, it is because of a more important aspect, the cultural limitations. Why do so-called underdeveloped nations barely manage to feed themselves, while America has produced huge surpluses? Why do the backward nations need 90 percent of their population working in agriculture, while America can support an economy with only 4½ percent of its people in the fields? [25] The answers lie in cultural differences.

The most important difference is the type of energy used in agriculture. The American farmer, using mechanization and inanimate energy, can produce up to 20 times as much product per farmer as can his counterpart in China, India, or Africa, where animate energy of humans and animals is the primary source of power and work. A few men working with farm machinery around the clock (with lights at night) on an American farm can do the job of thousands of men bending over in the fields or walking behind animals and hand plows in a less-developed nation. Furthermore, the American farmer can do his job in a fraction of the time that it takes the nonmechanized man. This speed in planting and harvesting often makes it possible to grow more than one crop, and perhaps as many as three successive crops, within a single growing season in the United States, and it makes agriculture possible in colder climates where shorter growing seasons [26] do not allow enough time to plant, raise, and harvest a crop by hand labor alone.

Mechanization and the use of inanimate energy are the most important cultural differences, but they are not the only ones. Training and skills, institutional patterns, transportation facilities, size of land holdings, and techniques of storing and marketing of crops are others. Undoubtedly the oriental farmer is the world's greatest artisan in *intensive* farming—the ability to obtain the greatest possible productivity from a small area of land —but the American farmer has acquired the training and skill necessary

---

[25] U.S. Bureau of the Census, *Statistical Abstract of the United States: 1972* (Washington, D.C.: Government Printing Office, 1972), p. 584. This percentage has declined each year for decades, and was 10 percent as late as 1957.

[26] A "growing season" is defined as that period of time between the last frost of spring and the first frost of fall. This can vary from a year-round growing season in the tropics to one of only a few weeks in the polar regions.

for *extensive,* large-scale, commercial agriculture. The oriental farmer also is more bound by tradition in his agricultural methods (what the Institutionalists would consider the "drag" of past-binding and past-glorifying institutions), while the American farmer has become accustomed to research and development and is willing to adopt new techniques. Adequate transportation also plays an important role, and a lack of it has left many parts of the world undeveloped entirely or at a mere subsistence level. The railroads are credited with opening the vast granaries in America's central plains years ago, and it is now possible for a farmer living virtually anywhere in the United States to obtain the goods and services he requires and, by the same means of transportation, move his crop to market. There also are other cultural differences such as refrigeration and storage facilities, packaging and marketing techniques, but the size of land holdings should not be overlooked as an important aspect. The American farmer can acquire acreages of land that can be worked easily with mechanized equipment; some giant farms in this country are operated as factories with hundreds of workers and an equivalent amount of farm machinery. But the oriental farmer, who has inherited a small plot of land here, another there, and a few more somewhere down the road, does not have enough area on any one piece of land to justify even a single tractor of the type used in the United States (the Japanese have developed a small mechanical "hand" plow that may help some in fractionated farming).

The type of crops grown is another cultural difference worth noting. The American farmer, noted for his monoculture, can produce large surpluses and make several plantings within a growing season. He can even change crops if market demand shifts. The subsistence farmer tends toward diversity; but he cannot afford the possibility of a crop failure (which would create famine) and must stress the most reliable food products, such as rice. Even so, widespread starvation occurred in 1974–75, when poor weather conditions caused worldwide crop failure, a problem that continues as a threat.

ENERGY AND RAW MATERIALS

Some writers, particularly those in geography and some in economics, consider agriculture and industry simply as two different forms of endeavor that are found in varying degrees of development in most nations. This approach tends to distinguish between a "high" level of agriculture in one nation and a "low" level in another area, "large" (capital intensive) industry one place and "small" industry somewhere else. Such categorizations are quite valid for some purposes; but a somewhat different approach is required if one is to study the roles of agriculture and industry in resource development. This entails an analysis of the types of raw materials and energy that such economic activities employ in their production processes.[27]

As was indicated in the foregoing discussion, energy can be animate or inanimate; but there also is a dichotomy of raw materials: the living and the nonliving. Using these two forms of measurement, one can theoretically align economic activity along an efficiency scale. At the lower extreme is agriculture in its purest, most basic form; it uses the animate energy of human beings and animals, and it depends upon living matter (or that which has lived recently) for its raw materials. At the upper extreme is industry in its purest form; it uses inanimate energy and nonliving matter.[28] Arrayed between these extremes are all the other forms of economic activity, and their particular location on the "scale" is determined by each one's degree of dependence upon one or the other form of energy and raw material. The closer their similarity to pure agriculture, the weaker they are economically; the more they resemble pure industry, the stronger their economic position is. They can be depicted graphically (see Figure 3).

Agriculture in any form, as will be explained later, is generally economically weaker than any type of industry; but there are differing types of agriculture. The small-plot farmer of the orient, planting and harvesting with human labor and animals and using wooden plows, is in the weakest possible economic position. The highly mechanized American commercial farmer, using all the latest mechanical equipment operated on fossil fuels or electricity, is in a much stronger position. An industry that uses a great deal of hand-labor (hand-made appliances, for example) is weaker than one that is automated and computerized; but an industry that uses a great quantity of manpower *and* depends upon agricultural raw materials (lumber, hand-made shoes and laces, or food processing) is still weaker.

Animate v. Inanimate Energy

Why is animate energy less efficient than inanimate energy? First, only about 10 percent of the bodily energy can be used for extra work (for carrying capacity); the remainder must go to keep the body mechanism functioning. Thus, people in a subsistence agriculture must spend all their time raising food for themselves and feed for their animals in order to survive

---

[27] Zimmermann, op. cit., used this approach and called it a "basic dualism"; and the idea also can be found, though not in so many words, in Gunnar Myrdal, *Economic Theory and Under-Developed Regions* (London: Gerald Duckworth & Company, Ltd., 1957), which was published in America under the title *Rich Lands and Poor* (New York: Harper & Brothers, Publishers, 1957).

[28] It is recognized that oil, coal, etc., originally came from living matter but that was millions of years ago, and they are considered nonliving for purposes of this discussion. The uppermost extreme of this scale is only theoretical at this time, since machines also would run machines and no human labor would be present.

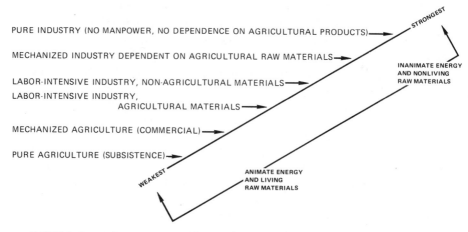

PURE INDUSTRY (NO MANPOWER, NO DEPENDENCE ON AGRICULTURAL PRODUCTS)→

STRONGEST

MECHANIZED INDUSTRY DEPENDENT ON AGRICULTURAL RAW MATERIALS→

INANIMATE ENERGY
AND NONLIVING
RAW MATERIALS

LABOR-INTENSIVE INDUSTRY, NON-AGRICULTURAL MATERIALS→

LABOR-INTENSIVE INDUSTRY,
AGRICULTURAL MATERIALS→

MECHANIZED AGRICULTURE (COMMERCIAL)→

PURE AGRICULTURE (SUBSISTENCE)→

WEAKEST

ANIMATE ENERGY
AND LIVING
RAW MATERIALS

FIGURE 3. Pure industry (using inanimate energy and nonliving raw materials) is the strongest form of economic activity, while pure agriculture (using animate energy and living raw materials) is the weakest; other activities, only a few of which are indicated, fall at intermediate points, depending upon their dependence on the two basic determining factors.

so that they can do the same thing again in the next growing season. They never manage to raise enough surplus crop to climb above this minimum level of living, and surpluses are necessary if capital is to be accumulated for mechanization. To produce more food and feed, they need more workers, and this leads to larger families, but the additional children also require food, and the cycle of drudgery continues. If, by chance, nature is good to the subsistence farmer and his crops yield surpluses, usually the ruling class in control of the country takes the net production in the form of taxes or assessments, or the human and animal population increases (as Malthus believed it would), and the people are right back where they started.

The commercial farmer, using machines that operate on inanimate energy, can produce large surpluses because of the greater efficiency of machinery. Admiral H. G. Rickover described well many years ago what the harnessing of energy meant, when he noted that man's muscle power, rated at only 35 watts continuously, equals about .05 horsepower. He noted that machines in his day were furnishing every American industrial worker with the energy equivalent of 244 men and the average family is supplied with the energy equivalent of 33 faithful household helpers.[29]

[29] H. G. Rickover, rear admiral, U.S. Navy, "Energy Resources and Our Future," presented May 14, 1957, before the Annual Scientific Assembly of the Minnesota Medical Association. Today's automated factories and energy-devouring homes undoubtedly would greatly enlarge the late admiral's estimates.

The humblest American, he said, lives far better than most ancient kings ever dreamed and enjoys the work of more "slaves" than the richest nobles ever owned. One might conceive the human-energy equivalent needed to operate a dishwasher or a clothes drier; but the average family automobile would take the energy of more than 2000 men, and, even more impossible, the human energy needed to propel a space station into earth orbit would be astronomical.

Sheer muscle power, human and animal combined, produces only about 2 or 3 percent of the horsepower-hours of energy used annually in the United States; the remainder comes from mineral and other fuels. Nobody knows exactly what the combined power rating of all existing gasoline, diesel, and jet engines might total in America, but engineers have calculated, as a reasonable guess, that it probably exceeds the total muscle power of all the men who ever lived.[30]

There also are other reasons why animate energy is far inferior to inanimate energy. Man and animal require shelter and time to rest; they get sick and their life-span is relatively short, especially the work years of the subsistence farmer, who usually dies at an early age. Machines require some maintenance, but not much, and they serve far better as "beasts of burden" than does man. The human brain is man's greatest attribute, and for him to use his brawn and not his brain is a tremendous waste and a violation of the economist's "principle of specialization." Yet, the cultural patterns of the less-developed nations resist vigorously any "new" way of doing things—even though they really are not new to the world anymore.

Agriculture and Industry

Even though commercial agriculture is far superior to subsistence farming, the most advanced American farm, operated virtually like a factory with the highest degree of mechanization, is at an inherent disadvantage when compared with an industrialized endeavor. Agriculture is by far the weaker operation, industry the stronger, though technology may minimize agricultural weaknesses in time.

Agriculture is still highly dependent on the weather, soil conditions, water availability, and the biological rhythm of nature. The farmer might mollify somewhat the effects of weather with such advances as hybrid seed or frost-minimizing devices, but an unexpected hail or windstorm or an unseasonable drought can still ruin him; whereas the factory can continue to operate, regardless of the weather, with controlled heat or air condition-

---

[30] *American Petroleum Institute Quarterly,* Centennial Issue (New York: American Petroleum Institute, 1959), pp. 4 and 26.

ing. The farmer can improve his soil at great expense and he can irrigate if necessary, but his irrigation waters are used once and reclaimed by nature, while his industrial counterpart can reuse its water time and again. The farmer is far more limited in his production process because of the difficulty of altering the biological rhythm of animals and plants; nature's gestation periods average, for example, 112 days for hogs and 283 days for cows, and specific time periods are required to grow new crops of grains and productive trees. The factory, on the other hand, merely has to turn a switch on or off to start and stop its production process.[31] Agriculture also must have considerable acreage (hundreds of thousands of acres for wheat, for example), while some types of industry need very little space, possibly drawing their raw materials from the air or from a narrow oil well or a small mine entrance. For agriculture, there also is some limit to the amount of land that can ever become arable, while industry has no conceivable limit, except time, on possible expansion of its tools and sources of energy. The farmer, because of factors already noted, has very limited control over either the quantity or quality of his product—he may have an abundant crop of perfect grain one year and a small crop of diseased or drought-damaged grain the next—while the factory can start and stop its machines virtually at will, and can control quality down to the smallest conceivable tolerances.

From an economic aspect, agriculture also is at a disadvantage. The economist differentiates between many types of market structures, but four principal ones are pure competition, monopolistic competition, oligopoly, and monopoly.[32] If it were not for government control and assistance, agriculture would currently fit most closely the pure competitive structure, in which there are many sellers and buyers in the market; no single seller can control the price because his sales are too small a percent of the total sales, the product is identical or homogeneous, and there is complete freedom of entry into the industry. On the other hand, America's strongest industries fit most closely the oligopolistic structure, in which a small group of sellers dominate the industry in the marketplace, each seller affects the price and behavior of his rivals, the products are differentiated, and entry into the industry is substantially restricted. As economic activity comes closer to purely competitive conditions, the more dependent it is on government to

---

[31] This is true of industries that are not dependent upon agriculture for their raw materials; to the extent that an industry is tied to the farmer, it is weaker than the industry that is not. Even so, an industry that manufactures chairs, for example, can operate overtime if demand increases (and it can obtain the wood); but overtime work is not as effective for a rancher who wants to meet increased demand for beef.

[32] The "market structure" is the competitive relationship among firms of an industry in a market.

alleviate depressed conditions within the industry (the grain or cotton farmer, the lumber industry, or coal mining of a decade ago, for example). Conversely, industries that fall within the oligopolistic market structure (oil, steel, aluminum, tobacco, and rubber, for example) account for most of the nation's research and development, are the least depressed economically, and require government intervention only to safeguard public interest, rather than protect the industry's private well-being.[33] The coal industry has moved toward this stronger market structure in the 1970s as energy companies, mainly large oil companies, gained a dominant role.

From the preceding discussion, one can see why agriculture is harmed the most whenever the business cycle turns downward in the American economy. Not only is that part of agriculture which produces foods hurt as the buying public spends less for what it eats, but the segment that supplies raw materials for industry is drastically affected as the industrialists curtail their output. And the farmers, who can not substantially reduce production (because of high fixed costs, a purely competitive market structure, etc.), must suffer a drastic price reduction on their products; while the oligopolist, who has far greater control over his output, is in a more advantageous position to keep his prices from hitting "rock bottom."

TRADE BETWEEN NATIONS

The discussion of cultural differences between nations plus the varying strengths and weaknesses of subsistence farming, commercial agriculture, and industry should give the reader some insight into the problems that can arise when nations of the world attempt to trade with each other.

Occasionally the idea is expressed that freely moving goods among the various nations of the world would benefit everyone concerned. Usually this idea carries the connotation that all nations are equal in the eyes of the traders, and if the industrialized nations would just consent to trade freely with the less-developed agricultural nations (such as the United States' trading freely with Africa, India, Venezuela, or Brazil) the benefits would be mutual. Everyone concerned should then be able to raise his level of living. If only that reasoning were valid!

This idea is a carry-over from the classical theory of the eighteenth and nineteenth centuries. Adam Smith, in seeking to learn what determined the wealth of nations, found his answer in trade. But his approach was

---

[33] The professional economist will recognize that this discussion is, of necessity, "painted with a mighty broad brush." On the other hand, anyone who has not had a basic course in economics will do well to go to a work such as J. K. Galbraith, *American Capitalism* (London: Hamish Hamilton, Ltd., 1957), if he is interested in exploring this subject in greater depth.

"atomistic," and he saw the world as millions of individuals operating equally in a single world market.

A more realistic approach today is to visualize the trade, not as between individuals, but as between nations; and the level of living is not determined by the quantity of trade, but rather by each nation's basic resource development and level of utilization. The eighteenth century studied individuals; the twentieth century should concentrate on nations.

When this approach is employed, it is found that this is a world of inequality. The industrial nations and the agricultural nations are far from equal. They are at the extreme ends of an economic ladder, with the top rungs occupied by those countries that have large amounts of capital accumulation, a high degree of technological development, widespread use of inanimate energy, and specialization and advanced know-how in the labor force; the bottom rungs are occupied by the "underdeveloped" nations that have little capital, a low grade of technological development, a reliance on animate energy to do their work, and an unskilled, uneducated labor force. Trade among equal nations is mutually beneficial; but when unequals trade, the industrial nations have the advantage—and the rich get richer, while the poor get poorer.[34] The flow of capital is in one direction only, toward the industrial nations, whether their financial centers are in New York, London, Moscow, Paris, or Tokyo. Foreign capital invested in less-developed countries by the private sectors of industrial nations is of little help to the backward area, because the primary reason that a foreign corporation invests in such a country is to return a higher profit (through lower costs) to the stockholders "back home." In the case of Moscow, that "profit" is nonmonetary. Eventually the less-developed nation begins to feel exploited, rightly or wrongly, and its resentment often is followed by strong government control of foreign investments or expropriation of holdings and nationalization of the business activity. If the industrial nation agrees to lend capital to the backward nation, the lending country wants some assurance that its money will be used wisely, and the borrowing nation then tends to feel that a foreign government is intervening in its local affairs. If the industrial nation simply gives large amounts of capital to another nation, resentment grows among taxpayers in the munificent country, while the receivers may feel like pet dogs being fed, and—an even

---

[34] Students who have taken a course in the principles of economics often "jump" to the conclusion that this discussion contradicts the principle of comparative advantage, which states that total output in the world will be maximized when each nation specializes in the lines where it has the greatest comparative advantage or the least comparative disadvantage. To apply the latter principle to the world *today* would be unrealistic and would require embracing the "one world" concept, including such assumptions as no barriers to trade, complete freedom of movement of workers over the globe, a free price system, no feelings of nationalism or independence, and no possibilities of war in any form.

greater tragedy—may not be able to utilize the funds they receive. All of these methods were tried in the post-World-War-II years: the "gift" technique justified to the American voters as an "effort to stem the tide of communism" and by the Russians as an effort to win satellites and "thwart capitalism." A more recent technique tried by the Americans is to help the less-developed nation help itself by gradually altering its cultural patterns. As noted earlier in this chapter, cultural change comes slowly, but it is fundamental to a nation's economic development and, in this regard, economic development is synonymous with resource development.

THE PLIGHT OF LESS-DEVELOPED NATIONS

Trade between advanced countries and less-developed nations, the subject of the previous section, remains one of the more bothersome economic problems in the world today. Except in the skewed situation that has arisen in the 1970s, whereby some less-developed nations have a monopolistic position on a source of energy in what developed as an energy-short world condition, trade between the two extremes (advanced v. underdeveloped nations) usually has found the rich gaining and the poor losing. There would seem to be some merit, therefore, in a brief analysis of the general characteristics of underdeveloped countries as a group.

Any generalization is open to criticism (a statement that is, in itself, a generalization), and the following is no exception. Some readers may feel, for example, that some particular point should be higher up on the list, while others may feel that a topic should be included that is not—and certainly some nation can be found that is an exception to any individual point. And yet, the generalizations do seem justified as a measure of the overall plight of the underdeveloped world. All of these characteristics involve some types of resources: physical, human, or capital.

While the student of geography may, on first impulse, feel that he has no interest in the economic aspects of underdeveloped countries, he will find that they are as fundamental to his understanding of the nations' problems as are the cultural aspects. On the other hand, the student of economics will find the noneconomic aspects equally as vital. Both areas must be understood if one is to grasp the significance of backward nations' resource patterns or, more realistically, the scarcity of basic resources.

Economic Characteristics

All less-developed nations suffer from some degree of poverty, although that is an ambiguous term that is difficult to measure, even in the

GENERAL CHARACTERISTICS
OF UNDERDEVELOPED NATIONS

Economic	Noneconomic [35]
High Level of Poverty	Rapid Population Growth
Inadequate Free Education	Political Instability
Chronic Unemployment and	Restrictive Family Structure
Underemployment	Bound by Tradition (Including Mores
Narrow Occupational Structure	and Ancestor Worship)
Low Health Standards	Discriminatory Class Structure
Regional Extremes	(Including Race, Women's Place)
Absence of Science/Technology	Restraining Religion
Ineffective Monetary and Fiscal	Urban-Rural Cultural Differences
Policy	Small Social Units
Low Volume of Saving	Adverse Cultural Personality
Shortage of Foreign Exchange	Static Institutions and Culture
Limited Markets	Nonuse of Cheap Inanimate Energy
Rigidities of International Tie-Ins	Lack of Resources

United States; but poverty might be considered as that level of living that provides for no more than food, clothing, shelter, and the essentials for health, with no margin for simple "luxuries" such as education, recreation, and preparation for old age, sickness, or loss of income. An economist might characterize the situation as a vicious circle—low real income, which results in low consumption, which in turn gives low incentive for investment, which accounts for low productivity, which is the reason for low real income. The vicious circle could be attacked at some particularly weak point, if it could be identified; but in simplest terms poor countries are poor because they are poor, and all of the foregoing points are so interdependent that it is difficult to ascertain the starting place.

Universal free education is a basic requirement in a country that hopes to progress and develop. It may be that the education in underdeveloped nations should not be of the same type found in advanced nations. Perhaps it should include instruction in only reading, writing, and arithmetic, followed by on-the-job training (rather than education financed by the nation's wealthy, who are more interested in perpetuating the status quo and represent a conflict of interest that actually could carry antisocial values), but there needs to be some form of education to reduce the widespread illiteracy and to give the people basic skills. Skills lead to specialization, a key to higher productivity and mobility. Without general education, entre-

---

[35] Noneconomic, used here as the counterpart of economic, might be called cultural or social aspects by the sociologist, psychologist, psychiatrist, or cultural anthropologist.

preneurship and good management are lacking in what little secondary and tertiary sectors (nonagricultural areas) that have managed to develop in the backward nations.

Unemployment—or, more important, underemployment (part-time work or only a partial effort, etc.)—may be a problem in and of itself, or it may be a symptom of other problems already discussed. Advanced countries have their unemployment problems; but usually they are associated with recessions or depressions, or they are frictional or structural in character.[36] However, underdeveloped countries have a permanent problem; the jobs are not to be had, or the people work only two or three days a week and are not looking for more work (disguised unemployment).[37] Underdeveloped countries also have a serious problem with seasonal unemployment, especially if the jobs are in agriculture or tourist trades, but their structural unemployment is most chronic.

A weak occupational structure in less-developed nations is another handicap, for almost all of the workers are in the primary sector of economic activity (agriculture, forestry, fishing, and the like). Economic development is stimulated if the people can be moved from the primary sector into the higher-productivity secondary sector (such as mining, manufacturing, construction) or the tertiary sector (such as professions, finance, trade, transport, personal services). But such movement usually is hampered by economic and cultural inertia caused by lack of education, ambition or skills, or in high levels of taxation or financial demands by the church. All of the nations have some secondary and tertiary activities; but their dominant economic endeavor usually is traditional agriculture with highly labor-intensive, nonmechanized farming that results in very low productivity per worker. Because of lack of technology and little use of inanimate energy, surpluses are rarely produced, and this means meager profits and savings and, thus, scarce capital accumulation. Since the middle class encompasses so few people in underdeveloped countries, there is little mass demand on the part of consumers and, therefore, no reason for domestic producers to enter the market place on a large scale.

Less-developed nations also characteristically have very low health standards, unless some advanced country has moved in to correct the situation. The poor health conditions may be accounted for by low incomes, crowded living conditions, and poor diets, or they can be due to poor edu-

---

[36] Frictional refers to people who are changing jobs and are temporarily unemployed; structural unemployment occurs when there is a basic change in economic activity, such as a shift to nuclear power from coal for electric generation, and the unemployed coal miners are unqualified to move into jobs in a nuclear plant (this is much oversimplified).

[37] The reason may be cultural (they are satisfied with a subsistence level of living), attitudinal (there is a great deal of disutility to working) or economic (doors have slammed in their faces so often that they quit looking for work).

cation (lack of training in hygiene or a shortage of medically trained personnel) or a scarcity of capital that can go into sanitation and sewage disposal systems.

Regional extremes are very severe in backward countries. Most underdeveloped nations have at least one large city (the capital or an industrial, shipping, or commercial hub); but the gap between the advanced large city and the surrounding poverty-stricken countryside is extreme and, in most cases, is growing worse. An advanced country like the United States usually will pour resources into the development of lagging regions (such as the South or ghetto pockets); but underdeveloped countries with severe poverty areas (such as southern Mexico or northeastern Brazil) cannot afford to do so. These extremely backward areas form a permanent drag on the more advanced segments of the countries that are trying to develop. The resources of these backward regions are little more than those used by primitive societies.

Science and technology are almost absent in underdeveloped countries, unless they have been introduced by some multinational corporation for its own reasons. The lack of these ingredients of growth in backward countries results, again, from poor education and low capital accumulation, from adverse cultural patterns (tradition says to do something one way because the ancestors always did it that way), or from the handicap of surplus labor. Mechanization occurs in a country only when labor is in short supply, not when there are plenty of hands to do the work manually. Again, with science and technology lacking, the utilization of resources are minimal at best.

Fiscal policy, in the sense that government uses its taxing and spending powers consciously to improve economic conditions, is notably ineffective in underdeveloped countries, mostly because the government lacks sufficient funds with which to apply fiscal policy. Its tax base is small and its needs are great. If the government receives funds in the form of aid from advanced countries, pressures to utilize the funds immediately are so great that they can not be hoarded until fiscal conditions call for their use in public investment projects. Of course, inflation is one of the more bothersome economic conditions found in backward nations; if an anti-inflationary fiscal policy could be accompanied by an anti-inflationary monetary policy, some favorable results would be forthcoming. However, monetary policy, as it is understood in advanced countries, is absent as a stabilization device. If one includes in monetary policy all government efforts at increasing or decreasing the money supply through the banking system, the results are more encouraging (this occurred in Indonesia), but the monetary techniques used frequently are very unorthodox, if compared with central bank policies employed in advanced countries.

With all the other economic problems already noted, it is only natural that a major obstacle to development of backward countries is their very low volume of savings. Savings, which generally run less than 5 percent of national income (compared with about 15 percent of the United States), are needed to improve agriculture, buy or build mechanical equipment, create industry, develop transportation, expand education, and even provide for the retirement of people. Without these capital resources, the physical resource base remains very small. Furthermore, what *is* saved usually is put into opportunities in the advanced countries, where there is more political stability and better investment opportunities; those savings that are kept at home (by choice or by force from the government) usually go into the purchase of land, which is considered "safe" and a hedge against chronic inflation.

Some economists would rank shortage of foreign exchange very high among obstacles that hamper less-developed nations. Foreign exchange is necessary to obtain machinery, energy, and technology when capital investment is needed in greater amounts than can be produced domestically (which is always the case); but all of this assumes that the other factors are favorable to induce such investment anyway. Brazil has excellent hydroelectric sites in the south, if it could obtain the equipment from abroad, if there were someone in the area to use the electricity when it is generated, if . . . if. . . .

Limited domestic and foreign markets are a severe handicap to the development of backward nations. The extent of this limitation varies from country to country, but it is characteristically restrictive for all of them. Domestic markets are small because, as explained earlier, there is an almost nonexistent middle class, which customarily would be the large consuming group. As for foreign markets, most underdeveloped countries are one-crop economies; e.g., rubber, rice, sugar, coffee. Some countries specialize in two crops, and a few in slightly more than two; but most produce chiefly one crop for sale abroad. This creates instability, for a change in demand (because of a business downturn or a resource substitute like butyl rubber or beet sugar) in the consuming advanced nation is disastrous for the underdeveloped country. Sometimes the nation is hurt by an oversupply that floods the market. Brazil has had its problems with coffee and Cuba with sugar, and Venezuela could have collapsed under a flood of Middle-East oil in the 1960s if the United States had not made a concerted effort to help.

In line with the problem of limited markets are the characteristic rigidities suffered by underdeveloped countries because of international dependencies. Venezuela sells most of its oil to the United States, Cuba once was tied to U.S. consumers and now is linked to Russia, Brazil's main markets are in the United States (though increasingly Japan and Europe are getting their share), the Middle East sells mostly to Europe and Japan,

Indonesia supplies chiefly Japan and the United States, and so on. The underdeveloped nations become almost "colonies" of the advanced countries, and they suffer virtually a colonial fate. If the backward country nationalizes foreign holdings (as some have been doing), it tends to lose its markets, sources of capital, and protection (which is discussed in Chapter Ten). Another advanced country will move in to fill the vacuum, if only for ideological reasons or to obtain needed raw materials, and the underdeveloped country is back where it started. Furthermore, the advanced nation is interested primarily in development of only a portion of the backward country's economy (e.g., U.S. interests in Malaysian tin production) and will help other economic segments only if there is some "profitable" reason (to help Malaya produce automobiles for sale in U.S. markets would only hurt American manufacturers). And, if the backward nation builds its own industry, it must struggle during the introductory period against competition from advanced-country manufacturers who have reached economies of scale because of size and technology. So the backward countries find themselves in a trade straightjacket that is virtually impossible to break.

Noneconomic Characteristics

Many noneconomic characteristics of underdeveloped countries impose more fundamental handicaps than do economic limitations.

The size and rapid growth trends of a country's population have more of a cultural base than an economic base, though most economists would claim that this falls within their discipline area, and certainly there are tremendous economic implications. Since this subject has been discussed at length in this chapter, suffice it to say that the overall task of economic development is greatly complicated by high rates of population growth; the higher those rates are, the harder it is to launch and sustain development of the nation and its resources. Some 70 percent of the world's population currently lives in the underdeveloped countries (e.g., Asia, Africa, Latin America), and those are the areas where population is growing most rapidly; it is estimated that by the year 2000 Asia will have as many citizens as the entire world did in 1970.

Political instability and weak public administration are commonly found in the less-developed countries. These conditions may result from frequent changes in government (Bolivia had more than 175 revolutions between 1825 and 1950), or they may stem from either external threats of aggression or internal threats of subversion; whatever the causes, the political instability and weak leadership strongly deter development of the nation and its resources. Uncertainties about the future cause wealthy citizens either to invest abroad, where conditions are more stable, or invest domestically in real estate, which is considered safer. Occasionally they will put their money into trade, which is more liquid, but rarely into manufacturing or technology. The instability of underdeveloped countries also discourages foreign capital from entering the backward economy for investment purposes.

One also finds a different family structure in the societies of less-developed countries. Usually, young adults live with either the husband's or wife's parents and contribute earnings to a common family pool; this practice limits mobility, savings, risk-taking, and even wage rates. While young people in advanced countries are very mobile and will move to wherever the job is, their counterparts in underdeveloped nations usually are not willing to move; this makes it difficult for newly developed industries to obtain workers from beyond the immediate vicinity, and this in turn keeps the industries small and wage rates low. Also, the security of the family unit provides less initiative for people to save and acquire assets (which would go into a family pool) and blunts any incentive to take risks in entrepreneurship.

Strong traditions are a distinct obstacle to development in many countries. For example, landholding may carry more prestige than entrepreneurship and the moneyed elite traditionally does not enter industry; educated people may be expected to do only certain types of work and not get their hands dirty; or farmers may not use agricultural methods because they are bound to the time-honored ways of their ancestors. In fact, ancestor worship, itself a tendency to look backward instead of ahead, adds rigidity to a nation's patterns of landholdings, and is the antithesis of research-and-development efforts because it opposes change.

Class structure, including race relations and the position that women hold in society, is another important noneconomic factor in development of a nation. Individual abilities and society's capacity to produce are hampered by closed classes, slavery, nepotism, or discrimination against minorities. These patterns, often based on the status of the individual's family, or his religion, caste, or income, usually lead to the existence of a small upper class and a vast lower class; if there is a middle class at all, it is small and weak, dependent upon the upper class and subservient to it. A very large middle class, as is found in advanced countries, tends to grow by feeding upon itself, increasing its income from commerce and industry and creating demand for better services and products. The role that women play in a society, ranging from seclusion in parts of India to complete equality in China, tends to affect population increases, the proportion of women in the labor force, demands for labor-saving devices in the home, and a host of other economic variables, all requiring additional basic resources.

Religion can influence a society's outlook toward work patterns, eating habits, population control, medical cures, and forms of dress. For example, if Sunday must be a holiday for worship, it is difficult for continuous operations, like a steel mill, to function. Religion exercises control over dietary habits: though grapes thrive in the subtropical climates around the Mediterranean, there are no vineyards in Africa and the Middle East because the Koran forbids wine-drinking; the Buddhist faith (strong in Japan) forbids the killing of animals; and it influences the Chinese, who hate milk, butter, and cheese; Moslems eat meat, but not pork, while Hindus (in India) regard the eating of animal flesh as cannibalism and blasphemy; Judaism objects to pork; only the women drink milk in Tanganyika, while only the men drink it in Uganda; and maize has a religious foundation in the Mexican diet—the Yucatan Indians consider it a reward from the gods for good behavior.

Differences in cultural beliefs, social values, and religious habits exist between urban and rural areas, and the urban cities, which must take the lead in economic development, lack influence in predominately agrarian underdeveloped nations. Even in a country as advanced as the United States, urban areas have only recently wrested control of Congress away from the rural areas, and many state legislatures still are dominated by agricultural segments of the economy. Rural people tend to have a more rigid social life and pattern of values because they are isolated and must fight the demands of nature continually—they are used to communing with nature. On the other hand, city residents have their contacts with fellow human beings and man-made objects, a condition that increases their need for rationality; their life-style breaks down family ties, racial and religious habits, taboos, and class differences. They have a different approach to the environment, the status of women, family sizes, and even morality; if nothing else, the urbanite's almost complete dependence on money gives him a different viewpoint from that of his rural counterpart.

Some social scientists have pointed to the small size of the social unit as an important obstacle to economic development of backward nations. In many villages, interest in the affairs of other families extends little more than 150 yards (or less), compared with ties that tend to be regional in Italy, Spain, or Greece, national in the United States or Switzerland, and increasingly continental in some parts of Europe. The social unit must be at least national in scope if a country is to develop evenly economically and make rational use of its resources (or create the ones it needs). In less-developed areas, where nepotism is common (only the family and close friends can be trusted, for one might lose all his assets to a stranger), there are severe handicaps to national development. Of course, many other factors also limit the size of the social unit, including language barriers, poor communication and transportation systems, obstructive topography, inadequate education, and narrow marketing techniques.

Some sociologists and social-psychologists have claimed that the cultural "personality" of a nation is a factor in its development or lack of development. A country's national character, which is "handed down" to children by parents during the child-raising process, may instill a desire to work and achieve or it may discourage ambitions and competitive spirit. Some people have an instilled desire for cooperation (New Zealanders and Danes), while others grow up with almost a lust for competition (England and the United States). And, such "generalizations" could be continued: Germans have a compulsive urge to work, French are individualists, and most Latin Americans are temperamentally explosive. In underdeveloped countries, a desire to work, achieve, compete, or improve conditions usually is lacking.

Cultural lag and static institutional patterns, discussed earlier in this chapter, are stressed by some social scientists, especially the so-called "institutional economists," as a severe handicap to development and full resource utilization. Certain societal institutions outlive their usefulness; but they have such strong holds on the nation's culture that they are extremely difficult to change or modify. While technology (such as tools, machines, communication techniques) is very dynamic in nature, a society's institutions (governments, laws, the church, mores, traditions, etc.) are very slow to change. In fact, the change may occur only after a bloody revolution—conflicts like the overthrow of feudalism, the American Revolution, the French Revolution, the Russian campaign against a czarist government, or the many juntas in underdeveloped countries. On the other hand, change may be traumatic, but more peaceful—the Cultural Revolution in China and the attempted abolition of racial discrimination in the United States. It may even be legal and relatively free from violence—the election of a communist president in Chile (although his later ouster was violent), the nationalization of basic economic activity in England or expropriation of foreign holdings in Mexico, Libya, Algeria, Nigeria, or Zambia. Latin American members of the so-called Andrean Code (Peru, Ecuador, Bolivia, Chile, and Venezuela) are gaining state control over their minerals peacefully through a gradual forced majority ownership by the government. Institutional lag takes many other forms, too, such as government corruption, a tax squeeze on citizens, land tenure, village organization, and economic production, distribution, and consumption.

The utilization of cheap inanimate energy is an essential ingredient in the development of any backward country. This subject has already been discussed at length in this chapter. The root of this problem lies far more in the cultural bases of a country than in the localized occurrence of minerals in nature. For example, advanced countries have found vast inanimate sources of energy in underdeveloped countries—lignite and some coal in Brazil, oil in the Middle East and Indonesian Islands (on land and offshore), pitchblende in Africa, and natural gas in Algeria, to list just a few cases. And, of course, such flow-type energy sources as the sun and tides are still untapped in all parts of the world. So the basis of this problem lies in lack of utilization of cheap inanimate energy in under-developed countries, not in a lack of its occurrence.

The final characteristic, the "lack of resources in underdeveloped countries," probably is the most important point of the entire list and it needs considerable analysis. It is put at the end, not as a measure of its significance, but rather because it demands more elaboration than do the other points. Again, the answer lies in the nations' cultural patterns, not in the erroneous assumption that the backward countries were "short changed" by nature. Two recognized authorities in the areas of economic development, Walter Krause and Benjamin Higgins, both seem to take the latter approach in their widely used textbooks. Dr. Krause says:

> . . . known resources per person—including mineral and forest wealth—are far greater in some countries than in others. The situation can be summed up by saying that the blessings of nature are not evenly distributed throughout the world.[38]

And, Dr. Higgins says:

> The most advanced countries have been in some sense "rich" in natural resources, not only in having "a lot" of resources but also in having varied resources. . . . On the other hand, no country dependent on a single natural resource—the oil countries and Chile being obvious examples—has yet become highly developed.[39]

Such statements give the despairing feeling that the backward nations simply got a "raw deal" from nature; they are victims of their unfortunate location. Much of the problem of these countries stems from man's idea that resources are "natural"; the blame should fall on man and his culture in those underdeveloped countries, not on nature.

In the advanced countries the inhabitants *used* what they had on hand and, thus, the things found in nature *became* resources; they found a way to use natural gas, and it became a resource because of that use. The fact that underdeveloped countries do not have these same "things" in as diverse a quantity is unfortunate (for then they might borrow technology from advanced nations, if the culture would permit), but that really is beside the point. If the currently underdeveloped countries' culture and other noneconomic factors had been such that they could have utilized what they *did* have in nature, those things would have *become* resources

---

[38] Walter Krause, *Economic Development* (Belmont, Calif.: Wadsworth Publishing Company, 1961), p. 47.

[39] Benjamin Higgins, *Economic Development* (New York: W. W. Norton & Company, Inc., 1968), p. 218.

and the nations would now be highly "gifted" in resources. For example, many underdeveloped countries are in the tropics, where sunlight is intense; if the cultural and other conditions (like capital accumulation, the state of the arts) in those countries had been such that utilization of solar energy were now at a highly developed state, those tropical nations would be far more advanced, whereas middle-latitude nations in North America and Europe would be in a less favorable position. The same can be said for wind power for Pacific islands, or ocean power (tidal or thermal differences of the seas) for the high-latitude nations. In other words, the mere existence of matter within their boundaries did not *make* the advanced nations what they became; the nations took *things* found in nature and *made* them into resources, and only then did those resources become the indispensable bases of further civilization and social achievement in those nations that used them.

It is true that, when underdeveloped countries are *dependent* on a single commodity like oil or copper, they *are* at a disadvantage in today's world. But they are at a disadvantage because they are tied to a particular advanced nation's need for what is a vital resource to *its* inhabitants and, when the advanced country's need fluctuates, the supplying nation is affected because of the tie. Oil or copper is not a resource created by the particular underdeveloped nation (it uses very little of the product domestically, and the commodity is a local resource only to the extent it is used locally); rather, it is a case where that backward nation is only supplying something that is a vital resource to the advanced country.

Overview of Underdevelopment

This discussion of underdeveloped countries of the world has attempted to cover as briefly as possible the many factors that help explain why those areas have remained backward. About one-half of the factors are economic in nature, while the others are based on cultural and social characteristics of the regions. All of the points are generalizations and exceptions can be found for any single factor.

This text has stressed mainly the resources of advanced nations of the world, rather than those of underdeveloped countries. The reason is quite simple: underdeveloped nations have very limited physical resources of their own; mostly their resources are those of an agrarian society—scarce in size and variety. Most of the countries have one or two major cities, but the remaining areas are still close to the primitive agricultural stage found a century ago in currently advanced countries.

When one thinks of oil in Venezuela or the Middle East, iron ore in Brazil, copper in Chile, tin in Malaysia, or pitchblende in Africa, he should not think of those as major resources of the particular countries. They are resources to these countries *only* to the extent that they are utilized domestically—and that extent is very meager in most cases. Actually the under-developed countries are only the beneficiaries of localized occurrence (discussed in Chapter Four) and are chiefly supplying what are *resources* to the advanced countries that *use* them. And the significance of this pattern of supply and its ramifications are the subjects of Chapter Ten.

THE VARIOUS ROADS AHEAD

Chapter Three has shown how resources result from the tripart interaction of nature, man, and culture. Nature, which was on earth first and provided substances without value or purpose, has set the outer limits to resource development. Man, the culture-builder, has qualities that are superior to those of other animals and is capable of utilizing resources; he will be able to continue doing so if he does not overpopulate the earth (and probably he will not). And culture, the last of the three to appear on earth, involves all the changes that take place in man's environment as he works with nature. Culture, which is highly dynamic within a closed system, helps man duplicate and extend nature, as well as mollify its resistances, and it helps man improve and ensure his own existence on earth; but it also serves as an equalizer whenever nature or man is in short supply.

Also analyzed are how resources are created and destroyed by culture, and how nations advance rapidly or lag behind, depending on their cultural progress and what use they make of energy and raw materials. Finally, the basic differences within nations and among nations were considered, and the implications of these differences were found to have many facets.

Where the nations "go from here" depends upon where they stand culturally at this time. There are many roads ahead, as each country develops from a different cultural base. But the future growth of these disparate political entities will depend upon how they mobilize and utilize basic resources, which are a function of cultural goals; and these goals differ widely over the world. The resources that the nations develop will fall into two broad categories: exhaustible "fund" resources and inexhaustible "flow" resources—the subjects of the remainder of this book.

SELECTED BIBLIOGRAPHY

BAGBY, PHILIP, *Culture and History: Prolegomena to the Comparative Study of Civilizations.* Berkeley and Los Angeles: University of California Press, 1959.

BALDWIN, DAVID A., *Foreign Aid and American Foreign Policy: 1943–62*. Chicago: University of Chicago Press, 1966.

BOSERUP, ESTER, *The Conditions of Agricultural Growth: The Economics of Agrarian Change Under Population Pressure*. Chicago: Aldine Publishing Company, 1965.

BOWERSOX, DONALD J., EDWARD W. SMYKAY, and BERNARD J. LA LONDE. *Physical Distribution Management: Logistics Problems of the Firm*. New York: The Macmillan Company, 1968.

BRACHER, MARJORY LOUISE, *SRO, Overpopulation and You*. Philadelphia: Fortress Press, 1966.

CHAMBERLAIN, NEIL W., *Beyond Malthus: Population and Power*. New York: Basic Books, Inc., Publishers, 1970.

COALE, ANSLEY J., and EDGAR M. HOOVER, *Population Growth and Economic Development in Low Income Countries: A Case Study of India's Prospects*. Princeton, N.J.: Princeton University Press, 1958.

DEMKO, GEORGE J., HAROLD M. ROSE, and GEORGE A. SCHNELL (eds.), *Population Geography: A Reader*. New York: McGraw-Hill Book Company, 1970.

EHRLICH, PAUL R., and ANNE H. EHRLICH, *Population Resources Environment: Issues in Human Ecology*. San Francisco: W. H. Freeman and Company, 1970.

ENKE, STEPHEN, *Economics for Development*. Englewood Cliffs, N.J.: Prentice-Hall, Inc., 1963.

FAYERWEATHER, JOHN, *International Marketing* (2nd ed.). Englewood Cliffs, N.J.: Prentice-Hall, Inc., 1970.

FERGUSON, CHARLES E., *Microeconomic Theory* (rev. ed.). Homewood, Ill.: Richard D. Irwin, Inc., 1969.

FREJKA, TOMAS, *The Future of Population Growth: Alternative Paths to Equilibrium*. New York: John Wiley & Sons, 1973.

GASTON, J. FRANK, and JANE LITTMAN, *Population and Economic Growth*. New York: National Industrial Conference Board, 1966.

GLASS, DAVID V. (ed.), *Introduction to Malthus*. New York: John Wiley & Sons, Inc., 1953.

HAGEN, EVERETT E., *The Power Structure and Economic Development*. New York: Southeast Asia Development Advisory Group, The Asia Society, 1968.

HAUSER, PHILIP M. (ed.), *The Population Dilemma*. Englewood Cliffs, N.J.: Prentice-Hall, Inc., 1963.

HEER, DAVID M., *Society and Population*. Englewood Cliffs, N.J.: Prentice-Hall, Inc., 1968.

HETZLER, STANLEY A., *Technological Growth and Social Change; Achieving Modernization*. New York: Frederick A. Praeger, Publishers, 1969.

HIGGINS, BENJAMIN, *Economic Development*. New York: W. W. Norton & Company, Inc., 1968.

HIGHSMITH, RICHARD M., JR., GRANVILLE JENSEN, and ROBERT D. RUDD, *Conservation in the United States*. Chicago: Rand McNally & Company, 1969.

HILLER, E. T., *The Nature and Basis of Social Order*. New Haven, Conn.: College & University Press, Publishers, 1966.

HLA MYINT, U., *The Economics of the Developing Countries*. New York: Frederick A. Praeger, Publishers, 1965.

KRAUSE, WALTER, *Economic Development*. Belmont, Calif.: Wadsworth Publishing Company, 1961.

MERHAV, MEIR, *Technological Dependence, Monopoly, and Growth*. New York: Pergamon Press, Inc., 1969.

MISHAN, E. J., *Technology and Growth: The Price We Pay*. New York: Frederick A. Praeger, Publishers, 1970.

MONTGOMERY, JOHN D., *Foreign Aid in International Politics*. Englewood Cliffs, N.J.: Prentice-Hall, Inc., 1967.

MÜLLER, KURT, *The Foreign Aid Programs of the Soviet Bloc and Communist China* (translated by Richard H. Weber and Michael Roloff). New York: Walker and Company, 1967.

PETTITT, GEORGE A., *Prisoners of Culture*. New York: Charles Scribner's Sons, 1970.

RYMES, THOMAS K., *On Concepts of Capital and Technical Change*. Cambridge, England: University Press, 1971.

YUDELMAN, MONTAGUE, GAVAN BUTLER, and RANADEV BANERJI, *Technological Change in Agriculture and Employment in Developing Countries*. Paris: Development Centre of the Organization for Economic Co-operation and Development, 1971.

United Nations Conference on Trade and Development, *Towards a New Trade Policy for Development: Report by the Secretary General of the United Nations Conference on Trade and Development*. New York: United Nations, 1964.

WALLACE, ANTHONY F., *Culture and Personality*. New York: Random House, 1961.

WESTWOOD, ANDREW F., *Foreign Aid in a Foreign Policy Framework*. Washington: The Brookings Institute, 1966.

ZIMMERMANN, ERICH, *World Resources and Industries*. New York: Harper & Brothers, Publishers, 1951.

FOUR

CHARACTER OF RESOURCES
AND RESOURCE SYSTEMS

Several variables must be considered in the analysis of availability of basic resources and their use by man.

Basic resources may be grouped into two broad categories: (1) fund resources, for which nature has set an outer limit on the amount available; and (2) flow resources, for which usually there is a continuing, renewable supply in nature, combined with the systems of flow resource mobilization (gathering, processing, and harnessing). This chapter deals primarily with the latter group, but these important flow-type resources and resource systems can be understood better against a brief, initial discussion of the equally important first group—fund resources (which are dealt with extensively in later chapters).

FUND RESOURCES

Resources that are exhaustible over a period of time may be considered fund resources, because the evolutionary processes of nature have placed only a certain quantity or fund of these on earth. Man may not have discovered all of nature's oil and coal reserves, its extensive mineral and metal deposits, or all of its radioactive elements, but he knows that nature has set an outer limit on them. In fact man will never use all of nature's supply because, as he approaches the limits, scarcity will force price up to a point where substitutes will become economically feasible. There are at least three major problems which are especially significant in the concept of fund resources; these are localized occurrence, exhaustibility,[1] and economic costs.

Localized Occurrence

One factor that causes particular consternation to major powers today is that most of the important minerals and other vital resources are found in only limited localities. There are, of course, some resources which are found generally throughout the world: for example, salt, lime, sand and gravel, and feldspar. At the other extreme some substances, such as tungsten, tin, chromite, or pitchblende, are found in only a few spots in the world; and the scarcity of these resources often create political, economic, and military implications, some of which will be discussed in the tenth chapter. Between these extremes are resources that are found in very large quantities on earth (e.g., aluminum, iron, potassium, magnesium, phosphorus, manganese); but abundant concentrations, sufficient for economic recovery with today's state of technology, are limited to a relatively few places on the globe. This is the problem of localized occurrence.

Exhaustibility

Another important factor, as man mobilizes basic resources to satisfy his needs, is the problem of exhaustibility. Some minerals have been found in sufficient quantities to meet past needs, but continued demand (iron ore in the Mesabi Range, coal in England, or diamonds and oil in Arkansas) has emphasized their exhaustible characteristics in the local areas where they initially occurred. This is one reason that some nations (e.g., China and Russia) are reluctant to ship their minerals to "competing" nations.

Economics of Recovery

A third factor influencing man's mobilization of fund resources concerns the economics of his acquiring needed substances in the profit-oriented, price economies of most areas of today's world. Only the deposits

---

[1] The term "exhaustibility" refers here to depletion in a given area; the product (oil, copper, tin, etc.) is still a resource to the user, who obtains it elsewhere. If no more can be obtained elsewhere, the material is, of course, destroyed as a resource.

that can be obtained easily and at (or close to) the least cost for the particular substance tend to be produced. This may not be as important a factor in some nonprofit-oriented nations [2] or whenever military considerations overrule the price aspect in even the free-enterprise countries; but the cost factor dictates availability and consequently utilization in most other cases.

For example, for decades some of the world's most extensive iron ore deposits (estimated at one-fourth of the known reserves and of 50 to 65 percent iron content) were known to exist in the Minas Gerais state of eastern Brazil; but the area lay undeveloped until the demands for iron and steel by the Allies in World War II, by postwar foreign needs (in the United States and elsewhere), and by domestic requirements of the industrializing Brazilian economy justified the expenditure of huge sums of capital for transportation and sanitation facilities to make exploitation of the ores profitable. But Brazil illustrates still another important economic point: quality steel production consumes a combination or system(s) of resources, as does the production of most other finished materials that must be readily available in sufficient quantities along with the basic ore or ingredient. Steel smelting requires both coking coal and iron ore (in approximately a 3 to 1 ratio), and a quirk of nature put the best known coking coal in the northern hemisphere, making it difficult for Brazil to grow into a strong industrial power unless technology could furnish an economic substitute for the blast furnace, which requires coking coal to make good steel.[3]

Sustained-Fund Resources

Two qualifications should be considered regarding fund resources. One is that nature is continually "manufacturing" new deposits of petroleum, coal, soil, and some other fund-types of resources; but the time span is too great relative to man's life span for the fund to change significantly. Pedologists note that it takes thousands of years for rock to evolve into soil, and geologists point out that it requires millions of years to convert living matter into oil or coal.

Another more important qualification is the fact that most metals can be utilized for extended periods (for example, in buildings or bridges) or can be reclaimed and reused time and again in different products. Insofar as the life of a fund resource is extended by reuse, it might be considered a sustained-fund resource.

---

[2] Even these nations must weigh alternative uses of labor and capital; the economist refers to the alternatives as "opportunity costs."

[3] Iron smelting with charcoal produced a good quality product in Brazil, until the problem of providing a steady supply of charcoal became acute because of almost complete depletion of nearby forests.

The world's resources that are inexhaustible (because nature continues to renew the supply) can be considered as flow resources. The sun will continue to furnish various areas of the earth with a regular supply of solar energy and light for plant photosynthesis; the hydrologic cycle will continue to extract water from the oceans and deposit it on the land; plants will continue to convert carbon dioxide into oxygen; waterfalls will flow, forests will grow, tides will rise and fall, and soils will renew their fertility—so long as nature is permitted to function without interference from man.[4]

Pollution—Flow Can Falter

Nature is quite generous to man in many ways: it furnishes him with renewable supplies of many vital resources that he must have to survive. However, that same benevolent nature has certain additional reservations in its generosity and is willing to guarantee the sources only as long as man uses wisely and without abuse what nature supplies. Thus, as was the case for fund resources, an important qualification also must be noted in the case of flow resources.

It is quite possible for man, for all his supposed wisdom, to let either his ignorance of, or his disregard for, the normal functions of nature's biosphere—its atmosphere, hydrosphere and lithosphere—to bring about his own decline. For primitive man, nature was so powerful and dominating that he sincerely respected, and even worshipped, it; but today's technological man, in his industrializing environment, has become so aware of his strengths that he has ignored his weaknesses. He may modify nature, but he cannot crucify it, or it will take revenge; and if man does not use wisely what nature has offered, even the flow resources can stop flowing. When properly managed, the forest can yield an endless supply of products; but indiscriminate exploitation can halt the supply (wood pulp and paper companies have had to spend many millions of dollars replacing the softwood forests of southern Brazil after their virtual destruction by other users). The hydrologic cycle will keep rivers running and hydroelectric sites flowing; but they will cease to flow if irresponsible destruction of forest and vegetation cover permits silt from the land to clog the waters' paths. Nature will replenish the soil fertility; but uncontrolled wind and water erosion will destroy its work.

---

[4] Theoretically, there *is* a limit on flow resources: the sun could cease shining, the tides moving, or the hydrological cycle functioning, but these possibilities are too remote for consideration here; if there is a practical limit on flow resources, however, it is *man's obstruction* of nature's processes (discussed in the next section).

Even the intensity of sunlight, the oxygen in the atmosphere, the temperatures over the earth, and the other climatic forces of nature can cease to be flow resources if abused. Carbon dioxide in the atmosphere increased by about 14 percent during the 100 years between 1860 and 1960, as a result of the widespread burning of fossil fuels,[5] and ecologists fear that a continued reduction in the rate of oxygen regeneration (such as by covering once-green fields with cities and people or by inundating vast areas of the world with man-made lakes)[6] can lead to disaster in time. Other scientists fear that the rising carbon dioxide will keep the earth's heat from escaping into space, and the hotter planet will in time melt polar icecaps and raise the level of the oceans to drown coastal cities. Still others warn that dust from continued nuclear explosions and smog from continued industrialization will block out sunlight, cooling the earth (which has been the trend recently) and aggravating weather conditions.[7] And still others warn that uncontrolled use of man-made pesticides and herbicides will accumulate in sufficient quantities over time to affect adversely the earth's natural vegetation and native fauna, two of man's basic resources. None of these possibilities is intended as a cry of gloom or doom, but only as an observation and a warning that flow resources may cease to flow if current and future generations of mankind abuse and mismanage what nature has supplied.

Resource Systems

Resource systems can be defined as the entirety or wholeness of the dynamic methods, techniques, and movement of goods and peoples underpinning man's garnering or mobilizing of resources. The concept of resource systems implies, or depends on, "systems thinking" or the use of a systems approach. This, in turn, entails consideration of related cybernetics, geographic controls, marketing patterns, and physical distribution patterns.

---

[5] *Time,* May 10, 1968, p. 53.

[6] A proposed damming of the Amazon River, to flood the entire Amazon Basin and give western South American countries water access to the Atlantic, would eliminate vast areas of nature's oxygen-generating vegetation. Alone, the project would have an insignificant impact on nature's balance; but it is the long-term trend, of which this proposal would be a part, that worries environmentalists.

[7] Beginning about 1900, a warming trend was discernible, and by midcentury, some scientists were predicting that the world's climate would average 3.5 degrees Fahrenheit warmer by the year 2000. However, the pattern then reversed and a cooling trend became evident after 1950. Scientists blamed the warming conditions on rising carbon dioxide content in the air, while others had blamed the cooling trend on dust, smoke, and man-made clouds in the air; in reality, both effects may be occurring simultaneously, with one offsetting the other somewhat. See *U.S. News & World Report,* August 19, 1968, p. 61.

Cybernetics deals with the dynamics of an entire system, including its subsystems and the controls which limit or affect the functions of that system. Basic to an understanding of how cybernetics underlies and undergirds "resource systems" is an appreciation of the fact that physical resources (though often local in occurrence) are inherently related regionally and interregionally, at least in terms of residing within boundaries, even if the latter are contested.[8] Where do resources originate? Where do they terminate? What kinds of associated commodities or traffic move with them? At what cost? For what purposes? In brief the parameters of resource systems are regional in character (Figure 4).

The regional-interregional view of resources is a somewhat macroview even though it deals specifically with the ebb and flow of resource materials within and between regions. Thus, the concept is based on geography first, and then on institutions and functions as these operate within, through, and on regional frameworks. An important way to look at resource problems is to consider the reasons behind their ebb and flow.

A second-level approach is possible through a study of the cybernetics involved. What are the signals that trigger the movement of resource materials, especially between regions (compare Figure 4A and Figure 4B)? In terms of resource systems, a region usually is both a producer and consumer of resources. Thus, regions function as markets for resources in that they might be concentrated, stockpiled, sorted, assorted, disseminated, and transported within the boundaries of the regions.

For almost 3500 years geographers have attempted to understand the wholeness of regions. To date these students of geography have found the study of the "total region" to be an elusive and frustrating undertaking. Probably the fact that few, if any, regions are entities within and unto themselves explains the greatest difficulty in geographers' comprehending fully the phenomena. That is, regions are subject to both extra- and intra-cybernations. Similarly, the resources student, dealing with kaleidoscopic spatial relations found operating within a region, has found that his attempts to understand and master the intricacies of his region or sphere of operations usually escaped his efforts to incorporate all of them into his decision-making processes. Today, however, high-speed communications, data processing, and selective computation equipment and techniques, when used in combination with the cybernetics concept, assist the geographer, economist, ecologist, transportationist, and others who need to understand regional aspects of resources. Resource researchers are coming to grips

---

[8] For example, Ecuador's claim of a 200-mile offshore limit, or in any one of numerous border disputes, past, present, or future.

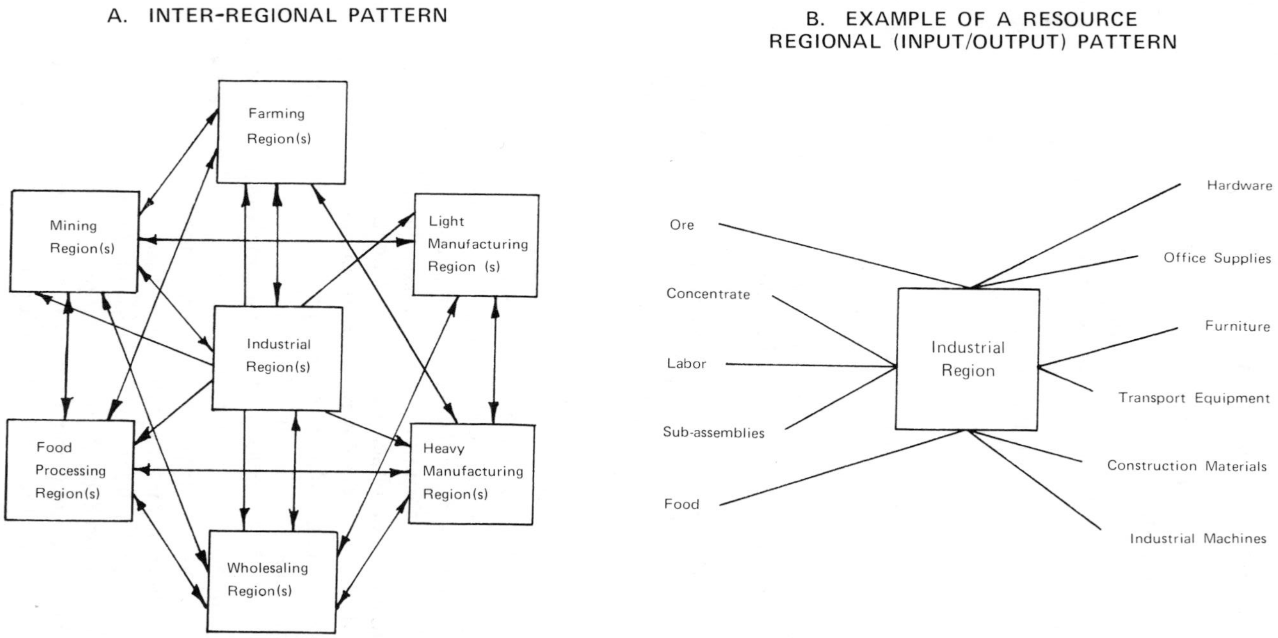

A. INTER-REGIONAL PATTERN

B. EXAMPLE OF A RESOURCE REGIONAL (INPUT/OUTPUT) PATTERN

FIGURE 4. Interregional and regional patterns of resources in motion, or regionality of resources systems.

with many of the multifaceted problems inherent in regional operations as they must be carried out against the complex backdrop of their economic-geographic settings.

It is axiomatic that as long as mankind has wants, and these wants can be filled only from unevenly distributed resources, there will be a continuing need for their transportation. Historically man's wants and the use of resources to fill these wants have been regional in nature. Transportation systems and accompanying communication facilities are the arteries and nerves, respectively, of the regional bodies, sustaining man through his resources. Thus man wants resources, and regional settings are the parameters of any resource system. Decision-making processes that deal with resource systems consequently must incorporate the ebb and flow of man's wants (the market place) with the resources (defined in the broadest sense) available through regional transportation systems (and political or military limits) to meet his wants.

Therefore, the outer limits, or parameters, controlling resource systems are regional in nature. As such, resource controls, more than being merely physical in place and operational in character, are also geographic, economic, military, political, and moral-psychological in nature. To date most resource-oriented work in cybernetics has dealt chiefly with transportation, market, and economic forecasts. Environmental considerations and interregional competition have been omitted in the resource decision-making processes. To illustrate: the Carlsbad, New Mexico, area was famous for its potash mines. The community and its people are now feeling the economic impact of mine-closing because of lower-cost (trainload) rates established from new Canadian potash deposits to major "chemical processing regions" (combined with certain economies of scale and modern loading facilities). Transportation costs made the difference, and the carrier serving Carlsbad can either develop competitive services in respect to cost, or find alternate employment opportunities (to the degree that the community's economic well-being depends on potash); otherwise Carlsbad's economic position will decline. Cybernetics emanate, in this case, from locations nearly 2000 miles distant; the implementation of a unit-train concept in one place has threatened economic ruin in a community thousands of miles away, changing a "resource" *back* into a neutral material if the potash from New Mexico is no longer *used*.

Within the outer limits, or controls, of the region operate all the resource systems devised by man: the major, intermediate, and minor subsystems, which are geographic, economic, ecological, military, political, moral-psychological, logistical and-or operational in character. To date most resource-oriented work in cybernetics has been limited to seasonally related migrations, equipment automation, paper processing, and operational problems. Most data come from wildlife managers, mineral explorers, production schedules, car distributors, and dispatchers. Before a complete system can be "cybernated," far more data will have to be processed, reduced to meaningful quantities or signals, and interjected into the operating and decision-making mechanism of a whole resource system.

Patterns of Regional Physical Controls and Feedback

Within a resource system anything that affects the movement of goods acts as a control on that system. Many controls are obvious and direct; others are extremely subtle and indirect. However, all interact with, or on, the system, and must be considered in the development of a fully cybernated resource system. Admittedly the definition of any system is arbitrary, but only within limits. In the case of the transportation artery and its tributaries, the body accommodated is the geographic region traversed or served by that transport system. And so, as noted, the basic or extreme controls on resource mobilization are, in effect, both physical and cultural.

Geographic Controls

Geographic controls affecting a transportation system also are both physical and cultural in nature. The physical geography controls are eight-fold: (1) climate and weather, (2) soils, (3) natural flora, (4) minerals, (5) water resources, (6) landforms, (7) natural fauna, (8) location and spatial relations. The cultural geography controls (discussed elsewhere throughout the text) are: (1) people, (2) houses and settlements, (3) features of production, (4) features of transportation and telecommunications.

Climate and weather controls need to be read into a cybernated operation because of their impact on both resource generation and operational requirements. Droughts, blizzards, cold fronts, storms, and prevailing winds all play major roles in what is grown, manufactured, or shipped in a region, as well as the work and recreation attractions. Similarly, these elements affect resource mobilization in terms of out-of-pocket costs, disrupted schedules, and rate levels. In extreme cases of natural catastrophes, routes may be damaged or destroyed by water, earthquake, or landslide. These are some of the resistances of nature that are discussed in Chapter Three.

Soil patterns or catenas likewise need to be measured, evaluated, and programmed for productive capacities, for fertilizer requirements, and for actual-versus-potential utilization. In this last connection political programs such as soil banks and crop quota programs and even the erosion rates are sufficiently rapid for one to consider soil as a *dynamic* control affecting resource systems. Regarding soils and other land-use criteria, perhaps the most important input data would be derived from notations of variations from a norm, as registered on charts that show areas within regions according to their land use and yield records, as compared with actual or anticipated production figures.

Similarly, data on forests and woodlot disease, cuttings, plantings, and board-foot estimates could be used to develop regional input values for resource systems. In recent years quantitative techniques have been applied to geomorphological aspects of regions with interesting and valuable implications to man. For example, watershed soil removal, predictions of basic geometry, flooding, fertilizer requirements, and sequential development of terrain [9] all lead to the development of cybernations meaningful to resource development, as well as to business logistic [10] decision processes. Even land fills (and garbage-refuse to fill them, or sewage disposal on agricultural land as is occurring in Illinois and Michigan, is planned for Denver, and proposed for Detroit, Cleveland, Akron, and San Francisco-Sacramento-San Jose), island-forming tides, river improvements, beach changes, and shifting channels are but many kinds of dynamic geomorphic changes that affect resource problems.[11] At the very minimum physical geography shapes the technology of transportation and is, therefore, a cost factor in resource mobilization.[12]

To review, physical geography factors are extremely powerful economic forces shaping the patterns of resource systems.[13] As environmental forces, they are permissive (and cost factors), rather than prohibitive. And, as important as geographic factors might be in shaping resource systems, they are no more important than are business logistic controls.

---

[9] George H. Dury, *Perspectives in Geomorphic Processes* (Commission on College Geography, Resource Paper No. 3, Association of American Geographers, 1969), p. 27.

[10] See footnote 14 for explanation of the term "logistics."

[11] Meigs Field, Chicago; Kennedy Airport, New York; floods in the Midwest; mud slides in Southern California; plus Corps of Engineers harbor improvements and beach construction are additional points illustrating the dynamic nature of geomorphic changes.

[12] For example, development of the *S.S. Manhattan* as a prototype to transport oil from the North Alaska Slope; utilization of this technique has been shelved for the time being, but the technique proved possible.

[13] An important step in this direction was the 1972 completion of a $4.8 million data center at Sioux Falls, S.D., built by the federal government to process information from satellites and planes about earth resources. EROS (Earth Resources Observation Systems) satellites and aircraft can survey the earth's environmental land and water resources, noting changes in availability and problems. Astronauts also spent considerable time in similar photographing operations during the 1973 Skylab project.

Of equal importance with the geographic controls and limitations of a region are the operative business logistics that control a region's resource patterns. The array of business logistical controls is too lengthy to develop completely in this text. Still, a consideration of selected logistical controls provides worthwhile insights into the causes or reasons behind existing resource patterns and will serve to illustrate how such "business controls" act as cybernations often affecting an entire resource system.

The Marketing Pattern of the Firm

From the firm's or shipper's viewpoint, transportation increasingly bridges time and place discrepancies so that orderly production and marketing can take place. An overview of this requirement of business firms must include:

1. Concentration/storing
2. Production
3. Storing/dissemination/timing of deliveries of goods or services
4. Market assorting
5. Market equalization

Resource logistics encompasses all transportation and warehousing activities, including transport, materials handling, storage, and related communications.[14] As plant and warehouse locations affect these activities, their locations are integral to over-all resources logistics planning.

The production management viewpoint dominates in some firms, and, in comparison, the market management aspect of getting and filling orders may suffer; the market management view dominates in other firms, and production inputs suffer, relatively (Figure 5). In the firm that applies a total flow (or total resources logistics) concept, the entire flow of goods is considered as one. This concept includes the input of resources as raw materials, parts and subassemblies, as well as the output of the production or

---

[14] The term "logistics" (the word is derived from "logic" and signifies a logical or systematic approach) was initially used in the military to denote the procurement, maintenance, and transportation of armed forces materiel, facilities, and personnel. The authors have borrowed the term and applied it to resource patterns—the logical flow of a resource from its source to its ultimate function.

A
MENTAL IMAGE OF FIRM VIEWED FROM A
PRODUCTION MANAGEMENT ORIENTATION

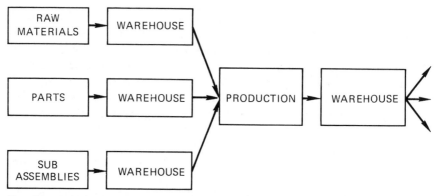

Note: This pattern favors the even flow of goods and materials through production lines (all other factors being equal).

B
MENTAL IMAGE OF FIRM VIEWED FROM
MARKET MANAGEMENT ORIENTATION

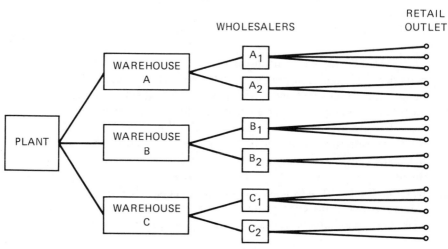

Note: This pattern favors the even flow or timely movement of goods and materials to the customer (all other factors being equal).

FIGURE 5. (A) Mental image of firm viewed from a production management orientation. (B) Mental image of firm viewed from market management orientation.

manufacturing effort. The total view includes resources development, materials handling, packaging, and warehousing (see Figure 6).[15]

In this mental picture of a resources logistics system, many of the stages may not be owned by the firm. Its only control may be as a buyer of services such as basic resource materials, transportation, storage, packaging. Many firms integrate as many of these functions as possible to assure a smooth flow and to control costs (in turn, to optimize profits). Toward this end many firms own and operate their warehouses, trucks, ships, barges, tank cars, gondolas, or whatever. At the same time some firms find that it is more economical to rent, lease, or buy storage, materials handling, and transportation from contract or common carriers or public warehousemen, even though they sometimes lose control over location and give control of goods to a third party for handling or transporting.

Demand for a certain good or service is the strongest factor in the determination of a total business logistic pattern and whether a firm is completely integrated or rents, leases, or buys storage and transportation. All of these are aspects of the firm's total logistical pattern, whether it is in a socialized or a free-enterprise economy. If it is to be competitive (successful), the firm must consider the market place and demand.

Demand of Transport Services for Resources Developed Within a Region

The demand of a resource system's market area depends on its size, shape, and intensity. Size and shape are relatively easy to understand. All other things being equal, the larger the size, the greater the demand; in theory a circle provides the optimum market area from a focal point. However, in practice, Lösch, Isard, Hoover, and others theorize that a polygon—probably a hexagon—is the ideal market area to be served from a point.[16] In the case of a resource system, there would be a whole series of overlapping market areas delimited by the dissemination of flow patterns of a single resource chain. These descriptions of resource market areas may be overgeneralized; but they are useful in picturing the area serviced by a resources chain or routeway system. In any event the intensity of the market is of far greater importance when one analyzes demand.

The resource market area's intensity is a product of three major interacting forces: (1) spirit and educational levels of the people, as determined

---

[15] The business logistics approach, although closely identifying with purchasing, production, and selling, does not include these functions of the firm per se.

[16] August Lösch, *The Economics of Location* (New Haven: University Press, 1952), p. 414–21; Walter Isard, *Location and Space-Economy* (New York: John Wiley and Sons, Inc., 1956), pp. 266–81; and E. M. Hoover, *The Location of Economic Activity* (New York: McGraw-Hill Book Company, Inc., 1948), pp. 50–65 and 219–24.

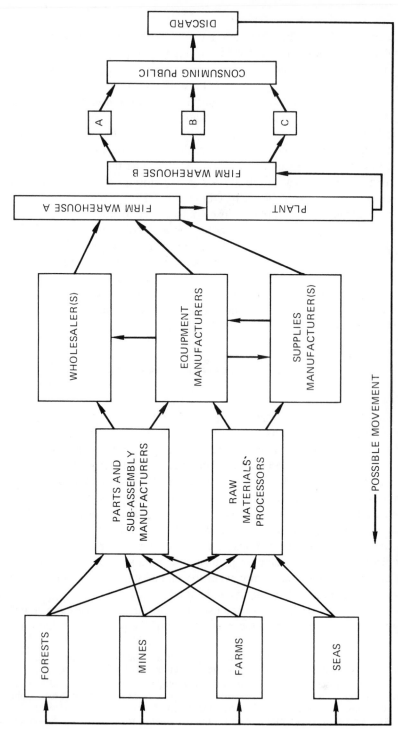

FIGURE 6. Mental image of firm viewed from resource chains or military business logistical systems.

100

by societal values, which in turn decide needs and wants; (2) technology available and skills of the people; (3) basic resource building blocks or nonpolitical geographic controls available within a nation, subpolitical unit, or region.[17]

The degree to which the three interacting forces differ from place to place sets the standard of comparative advantage for a given region and for each of its subregions, as these might be restricted or shaped by time factors and transportation cost. In summary, it might be helpful to note that, according to Greenhut, there are three categories of locational factors to be measured in the determination of an optimum resource development site in a capitalistic economy.[18]

Demand factors include the:

1. Shape of the demand curve
2. Location of competitors
3. Competitiveness of the industry in location and price
4. Significance of proximity and type and speed of service
5. Extent of the market area
6. Relations between personal contacts and sales

The cost factors include the:

1. Cost of land
2. Cost of labor and management
3. Cost of materials and equipment
4. Cost of transportation

The purely personal factors include the extent to which the minimax principle [19] outweighs the quest for maximum profits; this principle includes the:

1. Importance of psychic income (plant size)
2. Environmental preferences
3. Security motive

---

[17] The geographic controls are: (a) a favorable climate, (b) usable terrain, (c) soil type, (d) vegetation stages, (e) ores, (f) water bodies, (g) native fauna, (h) location and spatial relations. These geographic parameters may sound to the economist as if they should be of concern only to the geographer; but each of the eight has enormous economic implications to a region, as is explained in Chapter One.

[18] Melvin Greenhut, *Microeconomics and the Space Economy* (Fair Lawn, N.J.: Scott Foresman and Company, 1963), Chap. v.

[19] The optimum combination of minimum cost and maximum utility or satisfaction.

Resource systems and their various attendant logistical patterns, through many cybernations, tend to touch upon every aspect of an economy. Resource systems tend both to shape the patterns of goods and passengers in motion and, at the same time, to be shaped by them. The most obvious evidence of the pattern produced is transportation routeways—those which seemingly feed on, and are augmented and reinforced by, the very resources which brought them into being in the first place. The sum impact of routeways is found in the fact that they in turn form the framework of towns, cities, and metropolitan conglomerations (the strip cities). Routeways are very much part and parcel of a nation's metropolitan enigma and, as such, are increasingly receiving national attention in the hope that man can alleviate many of his urban, security, and pollution problems. Toward this end, national policies must be established if contributions from fund resources, flow resources, and resource systems are to be mobilized and maximized for the good of the nation.

SELECTED BIBLIOGRAPHY

ALDERSON, WROE, *Dynamic Marketing Behavior,* Chap. III, "Transactions and Transvections." Homewood, Ill.: Richard D. Irwin, Inc., 1965.

BOWERSOX, DONALD J., EDWARD W. SMYKAY, and BERNARD J. LA LONDE, *Physical Distribution Management: Logistics Problems of the Firm.* New York: The Macmillan Company, 1968.

HOOVER, EDGAR M., *An Introduction to Regional Economics.* New York: Alfred A. Knopf, 1971.

MCGUIRE, JOSEPH W., *Theories of Business Behavior.* Englewood Cliffs, N.J.: Prentice-Hall, Inc., 1964.

MINSHULL, ROGER, *Regional Geography; Theory and Practice.* Chicago: Aldine Publishing Company, 1967.

PEGRUM, DUDLEY F., *Transportation: Economics and Public Policy.* Homewood, Ill.: Richard D. Irwin, Inc., 1968.

SPENCER, MILTON H., *Managerial Economics: Text, Problems, and Short Cases* (3rd ed.). Homewood, Ill.: Richard D. Irwin, Inc., 1968.

STANTON, WILLIAM J., *Fundamentals of Marketing* (3rd ed.), Part IV. New York: McGraw-Hill Book Company, 1971.

FIVE

WATER:
THE ESSENTIAL
BUT ABUSED RESOURCE

Nature has furnished the inhabitants of this planet with an abundance of flow resources, and these basic resources can be both renewable and inexhaustible if the normal forces of nature are not too seriously abused.

Some of the flow resources—climate, soil, natural vegetation, and forest resources—are discussed in other chapters. This chapter will consider fresh water and ocean resources. These two basic flow resources are so vital to man's continued existence, and have been so abused by some of the industrialized nations of the world, that their proper management has in some cases become a first order of business. Thus, this chapter focuses attention on the essential water resources, their use and abuse, with emphasis placed on current and prospective conditions in the United States.

FRESH WATER RESOURCES

The planet earth contains the elements of all the water that its inhabitants ever consumed in the past and all the water they could conceivably need in the future. Yet, in this world of plenty, there are vast areas of need.

The study of water requires one to visualize the world of water as a cyclical movement that is constant and unceasing. Most people think of the atmosphere as the focal point or source of this movement: rain falls from the sky and water returns to it by evaporation. But that concept gives an erroneous picture; it is like thinking of an automobile's wheels as the source of its movement.

If, instead, the ocean is taken as the center of the cycle, then a new perspective to the process becomes obvious. The world of water then can be seen as a vast mechanism for distilling water. It is distilled from the great ocean reservoirs and moved over land, with the sun serving as the source of energy for the distillation process and the winds acting as the conveyors. So the sun, which keeps the inhabitants of earth from freezing and which synthesizes their food, also furnishes their water.

Solar energy distills pure water vapor from the undrinkable ocean brine. By the time people drink it, the water has picked up various impurities along the way, but chemically pure water is not necessary for human needs; in fact, pure distilled water tastes flat and insipid, and probably is not as good for human consumption as tap water, which contains minerals that one's body needs.[1]

The horizontal cyclical movement of water, from ocean to land to ocean, has been thought to be both never-ending and unchanging in quantity. There is now on earth approximately the same amount of water as existed at the time of Genesis, and most scientists believe that the world will have about the same amount thousands of years from now.[2] Current evidence indicates that man does not burn water for energy as he does food, except in fairly limited chemical processes, and he does not change it chemically as he does oxygen from the air; he only borrows it for a short time, and over the long run his daily input and output are almost equal.

Yet, unquestionably, water shortages and pollution (thermal, biological, and physical) exist in today's world, and if corrective steps are not taken in the years ahead, the shortages of pure water will become increasingly acute.

REASONS FOR WATER SHORTAGES

Water shortages in varying degrees of severity are relatively commonplace. They result from at least five broad causes:

---

[1] The U.S. Public Health Service Standards says of potable water, "The turbidity shall not exceed 10 p.p.m., color 10 p.p.m., total solids 1,000 p.p.m. and odor and taste shall be absent." (Public Health Reports 61, 1946, pp. 371–84.)

[2] Some water is created by combustion processes and some is decomposed by natural and industrial processes, but this is negligible.

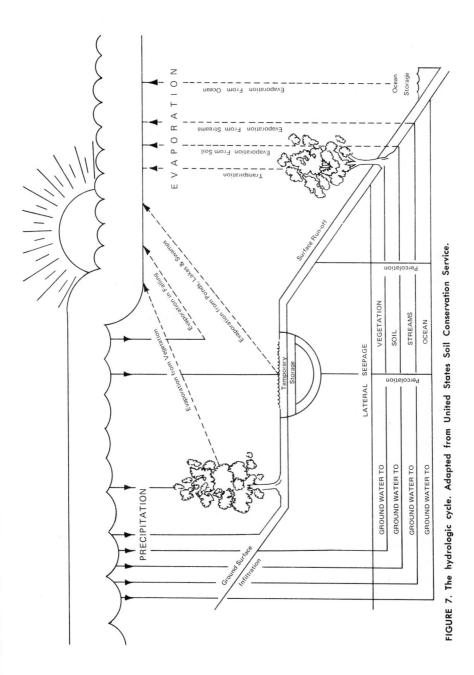

FIGURE 7. The hydrologic cycle. Adapted from United States Soil Conservation Service.

105

Man uses very little of the earth's water at any one time. The oceans cover about three-fourths of the globe, and if all land were leveled uniformly, the earth would be enveloped by a vast body of water two miles deep. If, by some miraculous process, all the vapor were wrung out of the atmosphere, the oceans would rise only one inch: about .001 of 1 percent. In the United States approximately one-fourth of the precipitation returns to the oceans (some three-fourths re-evaporates into the atmosphere to fall again), but of the one-fourth that runs over and under the land surface, only about 15 percent is utilized by the inhabitants. But the distribution of the water that reaches this nation is very imperfect, both in time and space. It varies from season to season and year to year, from drought to flood in the same area, and from the lush and "evergreen" Pacific Northwest to the parched and often barren Southwest.

Imperfect Utilization

Man in the past generally has been either unable or unwilling to capture, hold, reuse, purify, or transport the generous quantities of water he has received annually. There have been specific instances in which he has utilized all of these conservation measures on a limited scale; but for the most part, he has preferred to locate where abundant fresh water was readily available. Such choice of location may not be practical in the future as people and industries are forced into less desirable areas. Water still cannot be transported economically over thousands of miles as is true with oil or natural gas.[3]

Rapidly Increasing Needs

Increases in population, of course, lie at the bottom of water problems for many areas, including the United States. But even more important is the constantly rising U.S. standard of living, with its increasing demands for sanitation, recreation, industrial products and services, and agricultural products. An average of 30 tons of water is required to grow one bushel of wheat and 100 gallons of water to make one pound of rayon. Some rayon plants use more than 800 million gallons of water in a single eight-hour shift, and the steel industry uses some 5 billion gallons a day.

---

[3] This may change as the unit value of water increases and-or the economics of transporting it declines in the future.

Variations in water availability from area to area have influenced settlement and development of the country, and greater concentrations of population and industry are found in areas affording an abundant water supply. The "nonwater" areas have been avoided thus far, but individual families, as well as industry and agriculture, are finding it necessary to expand into more arid regions as the population rises. And technology is slowly coming to the rescue. Industry, for example, has various ways of circumventing its needs for fresh water, with air cooling and the use of saline or brackish water among the most widely used substitutes. Petroleum refineries and chemical plants have long used water as a coolant, with 80 percent of their water loss in the past occurring through evaporation during the cooling process; many refineries have changed over to air cooling in order to free themselves from heavy dependence on abundant water supplies. One cannot estimate yet how many other industries will follow this example, but there is no question that they must. Technological developments that reduce evaporation in agriculture also are coming into use; since expensive irrigation is heavily concentrated in the arid and semi-arid areas of the United States (about 80 percent of the water withdrawn for irrigation is used in the West), reduction of evaporation is a major concern in agriculture.

Water Resource Squandering

Americans have seriously abused and wasted their water resources in many parts of the country. They have "mined" underground supplies and they have dumped all kinds of wastes in their surface lakes, but more recently the worst offenders have been industrial effluent and metropolitan sewage. A typical example is Galveston Bay, along the Texas Gulf Coast, where fishermen catch and eat fish from the waters that have served as the dumping grounds for raw sewage from various coastal cities and towns. Occasionally efforts at correcting one water problem will create new ones; Louisiana Congressman Allen Ellender complained in the Congress as early as 1966 that flood control projects already built in his area had cut off fresh water, thereby permitting salt water to seep in to take its place. He said that thousands of acres of fresh-water marshes had become vast lakes of salt water, making it impossible to grow livestock feed and also causing wildlife to disappear. In another case, the Environmental Protection Agency analyzed the drinking water of 80 U.S. cities in 1975 for suspected carcinogens, substances that cause cancer. The concern was that chlorination of a city water supply could chemically alter organic pollutants in the water, changing them to dangerous carcinogens.

PROBLEM NOT NEW

Water resources and their development have been a source of concern in the United States for many decades; only the character and scope have changed in our time. In fact, water and its availability was a major problem to the great western civilizations of centuries ago. Sanskrit writings that date back 20 centuries before the Christian era describe various methods for making foul water pure, including boiling and filtering through sand and gravel. In Julius Caesar's day the city of Alexandria used aqueducts to transport water from the Nile to cisterns, where a simple sedimentation process purified it for drinking. Earlier aqueducts existed in remote times in Babylonia, Assyria, and Egypt. Rome was served by nine aqueducts in the early days of the Christian era.

In the United States public issues concerning water have erupted

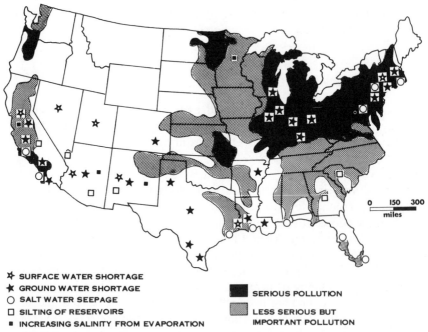

✻ SURFACE WATER SHORTAGE
★ GROUND WATER SHORTAGE
○ SALT WATER SEEPAGE
☐ SILTING OF RESERVOIRS
■ INCREASING SALINITY FROM EVAPORATION

■ SERIOUS POLLUTION

▨ LESS SERIOUS BUT
   IMPORTANT POLLUTION

0   150   300
          miles

No area of the United States can ignore its water problems; the widespread and serious nature of some problems are indicated partially on this map.

FIGURE 8. Water problems in the United States. Adapted from American Geographical Society.

sporadically at the local, state, and national levels for more than 150 years. It has been of such concern that a whole body of "water laws" has evolved. Today, however, the necessity for wise water allocation is more pressing than ever before, and the problem of scarcity—created by rising population, industrial growth, and increasing pollution—is further complicated by conflicting claims of navigation, hydro power, flood control, wildlife conservation, recreation, and sanitation.

ENGINEERING, GEOGRAPHY, AND ECONOMICS ARE INVOLVED

The proper allocation of water resources is the concern of everyone, but water planning and development projects should specifically involve three main professional groups: engineers, geographers, and economists. Any one of the groups may work independently on some feature of a water project, but all three must be inseparably interwoven and coordinated if maximum utility is to be attained.

All three disciplines are needed because each approaches the undertaking differently. The engineer is project-oriented. He exploits or develops the water resources and builds the dam, reservoir, or purification plant. He is concerned with how the dam should be erected, while the geographer and economist are more concerned with whether the dam should be built at a particular location—or whether it should be built at all. The geographer wants to know how the project will change the region; his emphasis is on man and his physical environment. The resource economist is system-oriented and is more interested in the aggregate economy and its members; he also wants to include abstract alternatives in his consideration of the project. His aggregate approach involves, among other considerations, entire watersheds and their management.

UNLIMITED V. LIMITED SUPPLIES

Water resources are unlimited only if, after use, they can be reused again and again. Almost all water in the world has been obtained from the recurring annual flow received from the hydrologic cycle, or from accumulated geologic storage or stocks from past ages. The latter sources include underground accumulations, lakes, swamps, rivers, and ice.

All of these sources, however, are affected by many troublesome variations. Among these are: (1) fluctuations in amounts, (2) periodic depletion of stocks, (3) variations in geography or the location of available supplies, (4) differences in quality and-or temperature, and (5) varying levels of reuse and reusability of the available water.

FIGURE 9. To win battles against ever-changing types and sources of pollution, it often is not "how much" information is gathered that counts, but how rapidly it can be garnered, evaluated, and utilized. Thus, sophisticated, fast monitoring equipment is employed to "patrol" the health of many watersheds—especially those such as the Ohio, which holds myriads of industrial users of the valley's water. Environmental monitoring units such as the one shown have been developed. These units contain a wide range of sensoring and analytical equipment to produce year-to-date information, as well as operational data displays. Courtesy Westinghouse Electric Corporation, 1973.

But not all water needs to be of the same quality, and not all water captured by man is consumed, which leads to a misunderstanding.

WATER USE V. CONSUMPTION

Many of those who predict water shortages in the future fail to distinguish between water use and water consumption.

Industry is a large *user* of water, but is a *minuscule* consumer of it. Most industrial water intake is used for cooling; then it is discharged in almost undiminished volume. A good example of this is the steam-electric power industry, which vaporizes (consumes) only $7/10$ of 1 percent of the water it uses. On the other hand, agriculture is both a user and a consumer; 60 percent of the water it takes for irrigation is lost into the atmosphere by evapo-transpiration. (Transpiration is the loss of fluid through an animal membrane in the form of a vapor or the emission of watery vapor from the surface of plant parts.) So the problems are quite different for industry and agriculture.

Industry, already a small consumer of water, can reduce its consumption still further by diminishing evaporation of its coolant (possibly even changing to air cooling processes). If industry can greatly accelerate development of technology for reusing water and for successfully preventing contamination of the water that is discharged, it will not aggravate local water problems. About the only additional water that it will require will be for industrial growth and expansion.

The water problem for agriculture is far different. Agriculture must develop more efficient allocation of its water, with less waste in its consumption and less evaporation when it is used. For agriculture, of course, the bulk of the research into technological change must be borne by government or by some industry that has a product to sell to farmers, because agriculture, which comes close to being a purely competitive market structure, cannot profitably undertake its own research. For example, the petroleum industry has done much to help agriculture reduce water losses caused by evaporation and seepage. Thin chemical films on the surfaces of lakes and irrigation ditches can decrease evaporation; plastic liners for farm tanks can reduce seepage; and soil covers can reduce irrigation by slowing evaporation (one company developed polyethylene strips that can be unrolled over planted seed rows, and another produced an "agricultural mulch," which is an extremely thin asphalt-like coating that can be sprayed on rows during the planting process).

METROPOLITAN WATER USE

It has been estimated that, on the average, U.S. cities *use* about seven-eighths and *consume* about one-eighth of their gross water withdrawals. The water is used for such facilities as sanitation and sewage; it is consumed for such purposes as watering yards (evapo-transpiration) and washing cars (evaporation). Most city waste-treatment processes are archaic, and the present practice of "flushing" wastes requires vast amounts of water; perhaps the day will come when a new, more efficient method will replace the current water-wasting practice of sewage disposal by dilution. Scientists have solved this problem for space ships.

The widespread use of detergents has created further water problems in the world. Up to, and including, World War II, animal fat and vegetable oil were used in the manufacture of soap. But soaps made from these basic oils and fats had two disadvantages; when used with hard water, the soap gave poor cleaning results, and war-time needs for explosives and gun powder caused shortages of the basic ingredients. So technology produced a synthetic oil to replace animal fat and vegetable oil.

In the 1930s a process developed by Universal Oil Products produced a synthetic detergent by alkylating benzene with chlorinated kerosene fractions, but the results left much to be desired.[4] In the late 1940s soap manufacturers' interest in synthetic detergents heightened, and a better process was developed under the leadership of Standard Oil Company of California, by sulfonating the alkylate of benzene and propylene tetramer. This new method became so well accepted that by 1968 more than 75 percent of the U.S. detergent and soap market was represented by synthetic detergents. However, products from this type of alkylate were not digested by the bacteria in sewage disposal plants, and the plants could not remove the chemically strong detergents from the water. Sewage plants became mountains of suds, the foam flowed into waterways and created navigation hazards, and most of the detergent remained in the water, much to the displeasure of downstream users. Then technology came to the rescue again, and soap manufacturers, at the prompting of the federal government, turned to the use of biodegradable detergents synthesized from straight-chain alkylbenzenes, which can be broken down by bacteria in sewage treatment plants, streams, and rivers. The change was completed by 1965; then a new problem arose. Manufacturers added phosphorus to the detergents to "soften" water; but the phosphorus served as a nutrient for algae and the algae-bloom turned water bodies to murky-green, slimy, foul-smelling wastes with diminished oxygen and reduced fish population. A public outcry in the 1970s caused detergent manufacturers to reduce the phosphorus content, but another ingredient—enzymes—has remained an "unknown" ecological factor. The long-term effects of enzymes on man and nature remain to be seen, and many researchers predict an eventual return to basic vegetable oils and-or animal fats.

The detergent problem is one that may well be on its way to solution, but it is only one of many problems still existing in the world of water.

COMPETITION FOR EXISTING WATER SUPPLIES

Nature gave us water but no directions for its use, and competition for this vital resource takes many forms.

---

[4] Esso Research and Engineering Company, "Petroleum—Nature's Storehouse for Chemicals" (Linden, New Jersey: Esso Research and Engineering Company, 1961), p. 16.

FIGURE 10. WATER WITHDRAWALS AND CONSUMPTIVE USES

(Billion gallons daily)

Purpose	1954 Gross withdrawals	%	Consumptive uses	%	1980 Gross withdrawals	Consumptive uses	2000 Gross withdrawals	Consumptive uses
Irrigation	176.1	58.6	103.9	94.9	167.0	104.5	184.5	126.3
Municipal	16.7	5.6	2.1	1.9	28.6	3.7	42.2	5.5
Manufacturing	31.9	10.6	2.8	2.5	101.6	8.7	229.2	20.8
Mining	1.5	0.5	0.3	0.3	2.7	0.6	3.4	0.7
Steam-electric power	74.1	24.7	0.4	0.4	258.9	1.7	429.4	2.9
Total	300.3	100.0	109.5	100.0	558.9	119.3	888.4	156.3

Source: Report of the Senate Select Committee on National Water Resources, 1961.

One question that arises is, who has the legal title to water when the supply is limited? Does the initial right belong to municipalities, industries, navigation interests, those who must irrigate, power producers, wildlife enthusiasts, recreation interests, or those who want to put it into storage? Even when there is ample supply, other competitive claims arise. For example, the construction of a large dam can make available a vast quantity of water, the use of which may kindle heated disputes. Navigation interests want the dam operated to maintain a constant water level; irrigation interests insist that the water be stored for off-peak, dry seasons; flood-control interests demand a dry pool behind the dam; and power people need a high head of water.

Another form of competition is interregional in nature. Should people who live or work upstream have prior claim to the water? Everyone obviously cannot be located upstream, and the rights of those downstream must also be protected.

Finally there is the question of whether water should be used indiscriminately to meet today's needs, or be saved and protected for future generations. In the past classical economists favored the principle of "current individual rights"; today's resource economists are more concerned with society's needs tomorrow, and the day thereafter.[5]

WATER ALLOCATION

Current water allocation techniques are bogged down in rather archaic terms: fair share, beneficial users, needs, moral rights, legal rights, precedent, historical rights, English law, and dry-country law. Not only are new ways and means of measuring efficient water allocation needed, but there is an obligation to go beyond that and determine the most beneficial resource mix that will create the best environment in which man can live and work. This will necessitate a far broader scope—not a "one dam, one plan," but a "one river, one plan" or even a "one watershed, one plan" approach, and it will require programs such as water distribution, flood control, irrigation, navigation, soil conservation, water storage, hydropower, reforestation, aquifer recharging, wildlife protection, and spreading.

Toward this end, watershed planning and control are reaching new heights in the 1970s through applications of automatically operated instru-

---

[5] Some students have questioned the right of anyone to speak for "society" and they wonder how anyone knows what "society" really wants. In a democracy, this must be determined at the election polls, with recognition given to the fact that such decisions often are made by minority factions or pressure groups; in other forms of government, the rulers decide what "society" wants, and—to paraphrase *Alice in Wonderland*—a "word" means what they choose it to mean, nothing more and nothing less.

mentation and data recording and reporting devices. Today, entire watersheds can be monitored and policed by strategically placed instrumentation units. These units include chromatographs (to separate the ingredients in a stream), spectrometers (to identify the various components separated), recorders and cybernated red-flag wavers (to announce when a change or pollutant has been identified). Thus, by carefully locating these units, authorities can diligently watch entire watersheds, and pollutants and polluters can be identified early enough so that corrective measures can be taken *before* vast harm occurs.

The technology and know-how are available, and only the implementation remains to be accomplished. Given the current state of public "alarm" and the success of pilot operations, it should be expected that the entire nation will be provided with watershed monitoring within two or three decades. Laws and enabling legislation must catch up with current technical capabilities.

In the United States national thinking on the subject of water control may be changing from a policy of "let local people do it" to one of extensive federal intervention. A Presidential Advisory Committee on Water Resources Policy reported to President Eisenhower back in 1955: "There is no 'national' water problem. . . . Instead, there are nation-wide problems relating to the use and development of water resources which vary widely between different sections of the country, and frequently between local areas." Businessmen have argued in the past that local controls are best because this method avoids the unnecessary expense involved when a federal bureaucracy tries to equate all areas of the nation. They have contended that national standards which cover all situations make it impossible to do an effective job anywhere, and local control-people usually can be counted on to recognize the problems of their particular locale and take a more "reasonable" point of view.

On the other hand, advocates of national minimums and national standards maintain that water is fugacious—it knows no state lines or city limits —and that local groups are too susceptible to pressure organizations and too willing to procrastinate. It is a dismal fact that almost without exception all surface fresh water in the United States has been contaminated to some degree, and many fresh-water aquifers are badly polluted or depleted. Streams are filled with sediment, industrial wastes, and raw sewage, and most state laws have been ineffective in controlling water pollution.

President Johnson, early in his administration, sought federal power to control entire watersheds, and if the watershed concept becomes a national reality, it will virtually blanket the country with federal control. In another approach, the Congress adopted in 1965 a Water Quality Act, which gave the states two years to develop their own standards for waters within their boundaries, or face federal governmental action. When the deadline approached, a chief of the federal Water Pollution Control Agency found that one-third of the states had failed to act,[6] but the deadline was extended and eventually all states acted.[7]

President Nixon continued to support by words and deeds the national insistence on good water quality throughout the United States. For example, the Nixon Administration called for strict enforcement by the Corps of Engineers of an old 1899 law that was "uncovered" recently. The Federal Refuse Act of 1899, possibly the most powerful tool yet passed by the Congress for cleaning national waterways, applies to some 40,000 river polluters, who must obtain (and few had) dumping permits to discharge factory materials into any navigable stream. Failure to obtain a license is punishable by a daily fine of $500 to $2500, and a strong feature of the law awards one-half of the fine assessed to any citizen who obtains evidence to help the Corps of Engineers get a conviction.[8] President Ford also continued to support good water quality enforcement.

Still another area in which the federal government plans to exercise an increasing influence is that of water research.

RESEARCH POSSIBILITIES

The cost of this nation's pollution control efforts in years ahead may well exceed the amount spent on the United States' "race to the moon," but pollution control is only part of the problem. Research possibilities into proper water availability and utilization are numerous, and include some of the following:

Better Utilization of Surface Water

Currently, only about 6 percent of the nation's average annual rainfall is used by inhabitants of the United States. This water falls relatively fresh and unpolluted; not only is research needed into ways of preventing its subsequent pollution, but a search also should be made for better retention methods, whether by use of dams, surface reservoirs, underground aquifers, or by some storage technique not now practiced.

Ground Water Supplies

Extensive research is needed in the area of ground water sources. This includes research into means of discovery, movement of water through

---

[6] *Chemical Week,* December 3, 1966, p. 25.

[7] *Business Week,* April 27, 1968, p. 35.

[8] *The Reader's Digest,* XCVIII, No. 589 (May, 1971), pp. 31–38.

the ground, capacities of aquifers, recharge areas and their capacities, measurements of underground waters, and chemical analysis. Since much of the nation's water comes from subsurface sources, additional knowledge is essential concerning this means of supply.

Saline Water Conversion

The United States became serious about obtaining fresh water from sea and brackish water sources in the 1950s, when the Congress approved the Saline Water Act of 1952 and the Secretary of the Interior established an Office of Saline Water. The initial act provided $2 million, only a "drop in the bucket," but it was a start. By 1967, the Congress had appropriated $112 million for research and development programs, and it authorized the appropriation of up to $185 million more during the five-year period ending in 1972. Also, the Atomic Energy Commission authorized the expenditure of $200 million between 1965 and 1975 on nuclear work related to desalting.

Five saline water conversion demonstration plants (three for converting sea water and two for purifying brackish water) were constructed, with

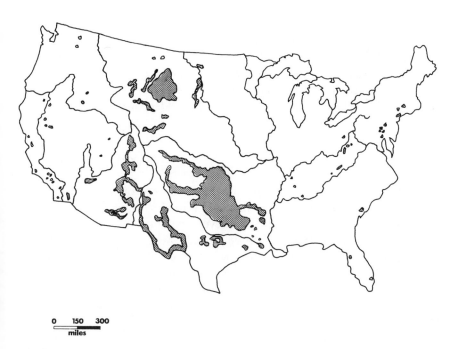

0   150   300
miles

FIGURE 11. Brackish water areas in the United States. Adapted from Office of Saline Water, U.S. Department of the Interior.

the main objective the reduction of conversion costs. It cost $4.00 to desalt 1000 gallons of seawater in 1952; by the 1970s, the cost had been reduced to about 22 cents, and large plants were being either constructed or completed at locations ranging from Florida to Southern California to the northeastern states. Meanwhile, water costs from conventional supplies of natural water increased through the years so that saline conversion is now economically feasible.

Other nations of the world also have been constructing plants, and Australia announced in 1975 that it had completed a new plant at Melbourne that uses an entirely new process, a synthetic resin filtration process.

Conversion of Brackish Waters

Some areas with a fresh-water shortage are amply supplied with brackish water, which offers a hope for solution in the not-too-distant future. The cost of demineralizing brackish water is not as great as the expense of ocean-water desalination and the former holds more promise— especially for agriculture and industry, whose requirements, as far as purity is concerned, are not as demanding as human requirements.

Waste-Treatment Processes

As pointed out earlier, the present archaic practice of "flushing" wastes requires vast amounts of water and large storage facilities. A more efficient system than dilution is needed, and a breakthrough on this may be possible if the sanitation engineer obtains more fundamental research from the biologists, chemists and physicists who understand the behavior of organic and inorganic pollutants.

Weather Modification

Some people still have hopes for the discovery of better techniques for inducing rainfall by artificial methods (cloud seeding with dry ice or silver iodide was used initially); however, experiments so far have not proved promising (a recent effort in Florida brought heavy rain in the wrong place—and hail), and more than research alone is required in this area. Extensive laws and favorable court decisions will be needed if man is to succeed in changing the "acts of God." For example, where does the legal responsibility lie when man-induced rain reduces attendance at a sports event, prevents a contractor from completing his job on time, or ruins a farmer's crop?

A Senate Select Committee on National Water Resources has reported that agriculture accounts for 95 percent of the nation's water consumption,[9] and much of the agricultural water is wasted through evaporation. Water lost to the atmosphere in 17 western states is estimated to be twice that withdrawn for public use in the entire United States. Through research, various substances that reduce evaporation of large water bodies have been developed, and various techniques of lining reservoirs to prevent seepage have been tested and used. The spreading of chemical films on water bodies reduces evaporation effectively if there is neither wind nor wave action; either of these conditions reduces the efficiency of this technique. Much work still needs to be done to reduce water losses in transit (as the irrigation water moves from its source to the plants) and additional research is needed to ensure that no more than the proper quantity of water is applied, and at the proper time, to various crops that are heavily irrigated.

Transpiration is another problem in agricultural consumption of water. This evaporation of moisture from plant surfaces such as leaves can be reduced by less dependence on water-loving plants and more development of water-efficient crops (which use less water) or even the development of salt-tolerant crops. In western areas of water shortages, for example, conventional lawns and shrubbery around homes could be replaced by desert grasses and shrubs, and nonbeneficial vegetation along canals could be eliminated. Manipulation and proper management of forest vegetation in less arid regions is another area for more research.

The widespread use of weirs (small dams, embankments, or levees) to raise the level of water in streams so that the water spreads over land in distributaries, or is drained into "recharge wells," promises to become more and more common. Tilling on farms will lead to low, accumulation areas where the water thus collected will be allowed to "seep" into the ground or to enter recharge wells, rather than its being "flushed" through tile pipes or drainage ditches immediately into the nearest stream for rapid drainage to the sea. There also will have to be improvements in farmers' comprehension of the problems entailed in better water utilization.

Similarly, along coastlines such as Long Island and sections of the Southern California coast, batteries of fresh-water recharge wells will parallel the sealine. The fresh water thus injected into the ground will form

---

[9] The reader is reminded that water that is consumed is not available for reuse until it has gone through the hydrologic cycle again. About 65 percent of the nation's gross annual withdrawal of water is *used* and available for reuse; but, of the remaining 35 percent that is *consumed,* virtually all of it goes into irrigation—mostly in the arid and semiarid West—and this is where evaporation assumes the role of an expensive thief.

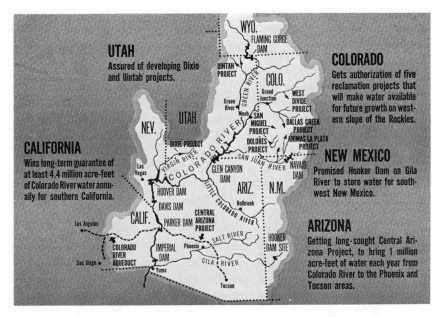

FIGURE 12. New plan for the Colorado River—big benefits for five states. Reprinted from U.S. News & World Report. Copyright 1968 U.S. News & World Report, Inc.

barriers or dams of fresh water to prevent (or even repel) incursions of salt water.[10] These and other techniques can be expected through time to ameliorate at least some water problems. All is not hopeless, and there are many measures that man can take to solve his water problems.

Watershed and Service-Area Development

Finally extensive research is needed on overall, integrated watersheds and their service areas. As discussed earlier, this will require the combined efforts of engineers, ecologists, geographers, meteorologists, and economists —in fact, most categories of scientists and social scientists. And, already noted, the research must consider not just the one project in isolation, but also its relation to others in the watershed and service area.

FUTURE OF FRESH WATER RESOURCES MANAGEMENT

The management of this nation's water resources today fails to reach either social or economic optimums in supply and use. There are at least

---

[10] In this connection, it is important to note that where fresh water and salt water meet, there tends to be a line of discontinuity and that fresh water repulses salt water.

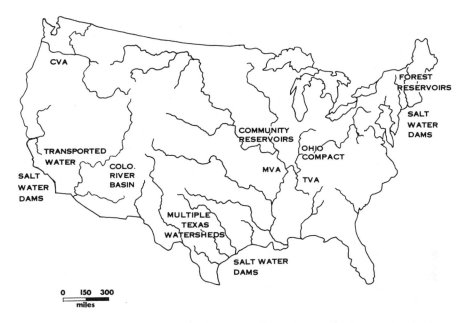

FIGURE 13. Different types of watershed management in the United States. Compiled by the authors.

three reasons for this: (1) wrong jurisdictional allocations; (2) difficulty of our establishing priorities under existing customs, laws, mores, and controls; and, (3) difficulty of our establishing economic allocations for varying classes of water use.

Because of existing problems and because of a real or imagined crisis in local water supplies, society (chiefly through its government and government-supported research) is seeking a "massive" solution to the nation's fresh water woes. The consequence has been for the nation to look to technology or "le grande" water projects, rather than the maximization of local aspects of fresh water use and reuse management. For example, the Fort Peck Dam, or schemes to bring north Canadian or Alaskan waters to Texas, or efforts to produce unlimited fresh water from the oceans, all capture man's imagination and raise hopes of reaching goals not easily attained within even a few generations. To a significant degree, this results in false, uneconomical survey research and feasibility programs.

Instead, during the balance of this millennium, more meaningful water resources development programs are likely to include:

1. Improved allocations of existing sources of fresh water to induce considerations of absolute supply, law and policies

121

2. Establishment of standards, to include measurements, with geographic levels or bench marks for individuals and industries, general welfare (health and economics), and considerations of human goals, wants, and needs

3. Establishment of monitoring systems, using chromotography, spectography, recorders, and analyzers in establishing point (2) above

4. Programs to manage wildlife, especially fish management or marine balance

5. Programs to manage land utilization so as to optimize watershed development, including rural zoning or use of slopes and flood plain areas

6. Ground water and aquifer surveys and research in an effort to manage better underground flows, to protect the flows from excess pollution, and to maintain water tables; also to determine which ground water supplies are stores and which are flows

7. Continued emphasis on desalination of sea water, with special attention given to brackish coastal backwaters or ground waters

8. Development of interstate or regional—and even international—compacts to aid in the management of water resources on a broader basis

9. Continued and expanded interest in interbasin water movements (e.g., movement of Mississippi River water to the Great Lakes or to the Gulf Coast of Texas)

10. Continued developments of inland navigation

11. Further research in efforts to understand weather sufficiently so that, at some future date, weather modification and control might become a reality

12. Programs that, in effect, chain or festoon population centers and industries from inland points to sea-level locations for use and reuse of waters as they travel enroute to the ocean

In the meantime, the seeking of priorities and funding for these programs promise to consume much legislative time and effort, and to drain off research talents, engineering skills, and construction capabilities from other sectors of total economic effort. The struggle to maximize water resources promises to be long-lasting—perhaps even everlasting, so long as man exists.

INLAND WATERWAYS

Inland waterways have served as a resource to man almost since the very beginning of civilization. Man was using nearby rivers and streams (for drinking, washing, catching of food—and later for traveling) even before he first gained enough courage to venture onto the seas.

This brief discussion of waterways cannot possibly treat them in a manner that is commensurate with their vital role in economic activity, both past and present.[11] They unquestionably are a resource, since they serve numerous important functions for man; but their current value (and their diversity as a resource today) is not as great as the potential afforded by seas and oceans, the subject of the next section.

By the time that the United States had begun to use the canoe and dugout or pirogue, European waterways had long been contributing to their various regions' economic progress. In America the canoe gave way to the flatboat and keelboat; but upstream navigation was severely limited by the means of propulsion—poles, oars, and sails. Commercial steam-boating did not make its appearance until shortly after 1800; but then the volume of traffic on inland waterways began to increase sharply, until a rapid growth of roads and railroads led to the abandonment of many U.S. canals and the decline of river transportation (except for the Great Lakes). Recent decades, mostly since World War II, have witnessed a resurgence of inland waterway transportation in the United States, especially since its waterway development has been following the pattern of western Europe, where rivers and canals are developed jointly with drainage, flood control, navigation, irrigation, and electric power generation projects.

The U.S. federal government has connected bays with short canals to form an intercoastal waterway along both the Atlantic and Gulf of Mexico coastlines from New York down to Brownsville, Texas; and the Missouri, Illinois, Ohio, Cumberland, Tennessee, Arkansas, and Mississippi, and the Columbia in the West, are all important inland waterways today. The St. Lawrence Seaway, plied by small ocean vessels that can reach all major Great Lakes ports, and the Hudson are the most important water-ways in the Northeast. But unlike all the major rivers of Europe, some of the longer U.S. waterways still are little used for transportation.

The Rhine, in Europe, is the world's most intensively used river. Other important European rivers are the Danube, Elbe, Oder, Seine, Vistula, and Rhône, but canals are especially significant in Europe. Russia has the Volga, with its major navigable tributaries, and the Don River; while China has its Yangtze (with the Grand Canal), and the Mekong, Ganges, and Irrawaddy. Africa has the Nile, which has gained importance since the 1969 completion of the Aswan Dam, and the Congo, which is navigable in some sections.

Brazil's Amazon is well-suited to navigation because it runs through a large land mass and has a very low gradient; but the area that it serves

---

[11] For additional discussions of the transportation aspects of inland waterways, see one of the economic geography textbooks, such as William Van Royen and Nels A. Bengtson, *Fundamentals of Economic Geography* (Englewood Cliffs, N.J.: Prentice-Hall, Inc., 1964), or Richard M. Highsmith, Jr., and Ray M. Northam, *World Economic Activities: A Geographic Analysis* (New York: Harcourt, Brace & World, Inc., 1968).

has very little economic activity. Both the Amazon and China's Yangtze permit small oceangoing vessels to penetrate considerable distances inland. In southern South America, the Paraná-Paraguay system serves parts of Argentina, Brazil, and Paraguay. Most South American rivers have an extremely high gradient with waterfalls, which makes extensive use for transportation impossible, but which will offer many sites for hydroelectric power generation once the need for it arises.

Inland waterways have been discussed mostly from the viewpoint of transportation; but their value as sources of water (for industry, municipalities, recreation, irrigation, and energy production) is equally as important— if not more so, inasmuch as most of the transportation could be accomplished (usually at greater cost) by other means of travel.

As a source of fresh water for municipalities and industrial users, inland waterways are of incalculable value. Virtually every major U.S. city is located on a navigable waterway (with a few exceptions like Denver and Dallas–Fort Worth). Figure 10 indicates that municipalities are expected to withdraw some 28 billion gallons of water daily by 1980, and most of it will come from the major waterways. Industry is an even larger user of water, with its needs estimated at 101 billion gallons daily by 1980; but steam-electric power needs, estimated to reach 258 billion gallons of water daily by 1980, constitute the largest usage by far. Most of this water will come from inland waterways.

Without rivers as a source of fresh water, the agriculturally rich Imperial Valley would not have been possible, for it was part of the Colorado Desert before waters from the Colorado River were brought in for irrigation. And the highly productive Rio Grande Valley of Texas would not have been possible without waters from the river that divides the United States from Mexico. There are endless examples, especially if one considers the subject on a world basis.

OCEAN RESOURCES

The earth, with more than 70 percent of its surface covered by water, occasionally has been called the Blue Planet; when viewed from space, the earth appears as a world of blue with only patches of green. Even in an era characterized by an emphasis on space exploration, man increasingly is turning to the seas around him with renewed interest.

The seas have been a resource almost since the dawn of mankind,[12]

---

[12] Undoubtedly the water bodies' initial importance on earth was their influence on weather and climate; however, if one upholds the functional approach to resource development, explained in earlier chapters of this book, he would have to say that the water bodies were not a resource until man, using his culture on nature, made a concentrated effort to utilize the sea—probably for food and transportation in that order.

but until recently man has used the vast water bodies rather indifferently, without much scientific curiosity or goals of full utilization. He has employed the sea as a nomad uses the grasslands or a primitive hunter uses the forests. Now, however, oceans are becoming one of the world's most promising economic frontiers, as the earth's expanding population endeavors to mobilize the resources that it will need to survive, and as the more advanced nations strive to disburse available funds in an optimum allocation to hydrospace v. aerospace—inner space v. outer space.[13]

Any encyclopedia or atlas can give the important statistics about the sea: among other things readers will discover that, of the surface of the earth (roughly 197 million square miles) some 70.8 percent is occupied by seas that average a depth of 12,450 feet, or 2.38 miles, and almost 10 percent of the remaining "landed" area is covered by inland rivers, streams, lakes, lagoons, swamps, etc. Earth may have been misnamed, for its surface includes much more water than dry land. The seas contain 98 percent of the hydrogen and oxygen on earth, and they are the sources of all fresh water, with 80,000 cubic miles of seawater evaporated each year and returned to the surface as some form of precipitation. The total volume of the sea is 328 million cubic miles of water. Another interesting, and one of the most amazing, facts about this important resource is that an estimated four-fifths of the living organisms on earth are in the sea.

Technically, oceanographers designate only three bodies of water as oceans: the Atlantic, Pacific, and Indian; all others are called either seas, bays, or gulfs in their terminology. Such distinctions are not relevant to this discussion, and the remainder of this chapter will use the terms oceans and seas as synonymous to designate various large bodies of salt water.

Vast quantities of material were written about the seas during the 1960s, as man expanded his knowledge in a desire to mobilize these vast areas and increase his resource base. The decade of the 1970s is reflecting even more interest. But existing "maps" of the deep ocean floors are about

---

[13] One notable illustration of this duel for funds came in 1966, when the Congress voted to favor outer space over inner space and eliminated support for the National Science Foundation's Project Mohole—so named because scientists planned to penetrate the Mohorovicic Discontinuity, which lies between the earth's crust and its mantle. The 82-day test drilling program was to take place about 115 miles northeast of Maui in the Hawaiian group, where the Pacific Ocean is 14,000 feet deep and the mantle is only about 31,000 feet below sea level (J. E. Kastrop, "Project Mohole," *Petroleum Engineer,* March, 1965). Scientists had hoped that the project would shed light on such age-old questions as: How old is the earth? How was the earth formed? What is the origin of ocean waters? Is there evidence to support the theory of continental drift? What is the origin of the moon? Is the earth cooling or heating and how is heat distributed with depth? What causes earthquakes and can they be predicted? How did life on earth begin? (J. E. Kastrop, "New Drilling Technology Certain from Project Mohole," *Petroleum Engineer,* July, 1964). Lack of funds caused abandonment of the project.

as accurate as were maps of the land masses in the 1700s, and the water masses historically have remained the *mare incognitum* (unknown oceans) of the past. There can be no doubt that the sea is one of man's most basic resources. This chapter is intended as a study of how the sea has served as a resource in the past and how it can be mobilized for additional utilization in the future.

Through the years the seas have served man in numerous ways. They have been a source of his food and water, and at the same time a depository and a collector of his garbage; they have provided recreation and transportation for peoples of different countries, while forming national boundaries; they have contributed inanimate energy, chemicals, and minerals; and they exert an important influence on weather and climate throughout the globe.

The following discussion cannot be taken as showing an order of significance, for the priorities of importance vary with the needs of each nation in the world.

OCEANS AFFECT WEATHER AND CLIMATE

Large water bodies have immeasurable impact upon onshore climatic conditions. Anyone who has experienced the violence of a hurricane, typhoon, or other vicious storm is aware of the tremendous forces that nature can generate in the warm tropical seas; but as Chapter Seven points out, the effect of large water bodies is even more important in influencing daily conditions on the landed areas of various continents. If land is touched by cold offshore currents and the prevailing wind blows from water to shore, the onshore area will be a vast arid wasteland; on the other hand, warm offshore water with winds blowing toward the shore will result in lush vegetation. This is because the air above the water is either warmed or cooled by it, and warmer air holds more moisture, while cooler air carries less.

Oceans also tend to stabilize temperatures on nearby land, both daily and seasonally, inasmuch as water neither attains the same temperature as adjacent land areas nor cools at the same rate.[14] It has been noted that the ocean, as the globe's great regulator and stabilizer of temperatures, is like a savings bank for solar energy, taking deposits during periods of excessive insolation and paying them back during periods of want.[15] Such a stabiliz-

---

[14] This is because water, with a higher specific heat, takes five times as much energy to warm one degree as does a similar volume of dry earth, and because water reflects some of the sun's rays, transmits heat over a greater area, permits insolation to penetrate deeper, and has the ability to overturn or mix so that warm water rises and cold water falls in the winter.

[15] Rachel L. Carson, *The Sea Around Us* (New York: Oxford University Press, 1951), p. 172.

ing influence has an important effect on economic activity along the shore-lines. Favorable climatic conditions support fruit and vegetable crops, create popular places to live and work, and even encourage an array of resort areas. The North Atlantic Drift has been called the "current of civilization" because, where it flows into the higher middle latitudes, it makes land-cropping possible and this in turn supports the populous economic beehive of Europe. The same latitudes on other continents, which do not benefit from the warm waters of the North Atlantic Drift, are extremely cold and sparsely populated—Siberia, Greenland, and eastern Canada.

"Everybody talks about the weather, but nobody does anything about it" was a classic observation made, not by Mark Twain as commonly attributed, but by an editorial writer named Charles D. Warner back in 1897 in *The Hartford Courant*. Today's technological man is working to change that statement. The ocean and the atmosphere comprise a gigantic energy-exchanging "machine" that alters both atmospheric and ocean weather conditions. But until recently meteorological scientists were hampered in weather forecasting by a lack of information, with only about 5 percent of the world's surface, mostly land, surveyed by weather instruments. Introduction in the late 1960s of such weather satellites as Tiros and Nimbus, and the adaptation of high-speed electronic computers, have removed some of the forecaster's reliance on guesswork and intuition, and are a step in the direction of doing something about the weather. The vast ocean expanses are now under the watchful eye of man's orbiting reporters; oceanographers also are benefiting from photographs and other data collected from space vehicles.

Man is seriously considering altering ocean resource potentials by blocking or diverting ocean currents. For example, if a floating dam were to be constructed across the 30-mile-wide Bering Strait (between Alaska and Siberia), the cold waters of the Arctic would be blocked and would thereby permit the warm waters of the Japan (Kuroshio) Current to warm Kamchatka and other east coast areas of Siberia. However, if this *is* done, the danger is real that the cold Labrador Current would be intensified, further chilling the east coast of North America. So again, the need to consider (in balance) all projects aimed at altering the "resource balance of nature" is evident.

SOURCE OF FRESH WATER

Large water bodies of the world are currently serving man as a source of fresh water in two ways: first, nature's hydrologic cycle distills fresh water from the ocean brine and distributes it over land; and second, today's technological man is developing the direct technique of desalting ocean water.

Water passes through an interesting cycle, as discussed previously in this chapter. It enters the atmosphere as moisture evaporates from the land and its water bodies, from plants and animals (through transpiration and perspiration), and, more important, from the vast oceans. Then winds transport the vapor over land, where it falls as precipitation. Since the oceans contain 97 percent of the earth's moisture, they are the main source of fresh water, and nature, itself, does most of the work by purifying salt-water through evaporation, by transporting the moisture with windpower, and by releasing the precipitation through orographic, convectional, or cyclonic weather patterns.

There was a time when nature was relatively quite bountiful in providing pure water in sufficient areas for man's needs. But as people and their industries expanded into newer and more arid regions, and their water requirements increased,[16] nature appeared more niggardly, until now man is having to turn to his own technological devices to supply his water needs.[17]

By the mid-1960s, fresh water already was flowing from spigots supplied by more than 200 desalting plants in the world,[18] and the United States, in an effort to find a cheap, efficient technique, has tested five different methods with pilot plants in various parts of the country.[19] Cost is still the major consideration, but much progress has been made in finding cheaper sources of energy, in spreading costs by multiple operations (such

---

[16] Although every aspect of the U. S. economy is increasing in size, problems arise in the disparity of the increases. For example, the rise in household water needs is considerably greater than that which would be anticipated because of the increase in population, and the rise in industrial water requirements exceeds the increase in manufacturing. Two things—a rising American standard of living and greater utilization by industry of higher water usage devices and water consuming machines—have brought about such unequal increases.

[17] At the turn of the century, Americans used about 40 billion gallons of water per day; the figure doubled by 1920, doubled again by 1944, and doubled once more by 1965. A 1967 mimeographed publication by the Office of Saline Water, *More Fresh Water at Lower Costs,* estimated current use of water in the United States at 375 billion gallons per day and reported that water use was increasing at the rate of 25,000 gallons per minute.

[18] About one-half of these plants were using the distillation processes, with the largest a submerged tube plant in Aruba with a rated capacity of 3.4 million gallons per day; most of the 200 plants of all types desalinating water were small, turning out a total of only 50 million gallons daily (see Justine Farr Rodriguez, Economic Research Division, The Chase Manhattan Bank, *Water Supply,* mimeographed, February, 1967).

[19] U. S. Department of the Interior, Office of Saline Water, *Saline Water Conversion* (Washington, D.C.: Government Printing Office, n.d.), lists the pilot plants as: Freeport, Tex., long-tube vertical multiple-effect distillation; San Diego, Calif., multistage flash distillation; Webster, S.D., electrodialysis (membrane process); Roswell, N.M., forced-circulation vapor-compression; and Wrightsville Beach, N.C., freezing.

as electric generation), and in diluting more expensive pure water from desalination plants with cheaper, less-pure water from other sources. A 2,620,000-gallon-per-day "flash" process desalination plant began operations in Key West, Florida, in 1967, and Los Angeles is converting sea water from a nuclear-powered 150 million-gallon-a-day plant; the United States and Mexico are considering a billion-gallon-a-day plant on the Gulf of California in the 1980s.

Another area for future development is thought to be the large freshwater springs that lie on the continental shelves, pouring unseen and unused into the sea. Some authorities believe that, once the required techniques and apparatus are developed, it might be cheaper, gallon for gallon, to tap some of these springs than to desalinate sea water.[20] But to date, man has found it most feasible (economically and technically) to process the brackish waters of coastal areas (especially such areas as the U.S. Gulf Coast) and extract fresh water.

SOURCE OF ENERGY

Falling water has been used for many generations to run water wheels for grinding wheat and other grains, and more recently to generate electricity. Tides of the oceans may be used in much the same way, for the ocean water not only falls on a regular basis, but also alternately rises, and this periodic vertical movement of the tides represents an enormous store of potential power that is not dissimilar in effect to that found in waterfalls or rapidly moving rivers and streams.

Many parts of the world have tides that potentially are great enough to run turbines, and these in turn could generate electricity—this represents an inexhaustible source of energy that could continue as long as the moon and sun exert their gravitational pull on large bodies of water. It might be briefly noted here that moving water has tremendous power; a one-acre-inch of water weighs more than 113 tons (at 8.4 pounds per gallon), and moving water has the ability to move objects with a force equal to the sixth power of the moving water's velocity.

Two tides a day of large and almost equal amplitude, which is the difference between the water levels at high and low tides, offer excellent conditions for tidal energy exploration. Sites where tidal energy is economically recoverable with today's technology are rather rare; but four areas have received the most study in recent years by France, England, Russia, and Canada. Interest waned in the 1960s, but a quadrupling of oil prices in

---

[20] "Ocean Engineering Takes the Plunge," *Fortune,* LXXIII (June, 1966), p. 216.

1974 stimulated interest again. The world's first large-scale tidal power plant (generating 544 million kilowatt-hours of electricity a year) was completed in 1967 by France on the Rance River estuary between Dinard and Saint-Malo. The French also are looking to the possibility of a larger plant off the cost of Brittany. The Russians built a tiny, experimental plant in Kislaya Guba (600 miles north of Murmansk) and then started work on a much larger plant in an inlet of the White Sea. Britain has studied the possibility of a plant on the Severn River near Bristol, and Canada has seriously considered the construction of a tidal plant in the Bay of Fundy, between Nova Scotia and New Brunswick.[21]

Use of the sea as a source of inanimate energy in the future has a number of advantages, including relatively low-cost, pollution-free, long-life plant operation and the ability to store energy for brief periods of time; but there also are a number of disadvantages, one of which is adverse location. While use of the oceans as a source of energy is not significant today, the potentials are tremendous, and research and technological developments undoubtedly will make this a valuable resource in the future.

NATIONAL BOUNDARIES

The ocean can be both a barrier and a frontier, and either way it serves as a resource under the functional concept of resources.

Until recent times an ocean separated nations; now it connects them. There was a time when the ocean was as restrictive to trade as a large desert (and to some extent, that is still true); however, such restrictions have been greatly reduced by modern ocean transportation, discoveries of rich fishing areas, attractions of local minerals over the world, and increased desire for foreign trade. The Pacific Ocean was a far greater obstacle to trade than the Atlantic. The size and shape of the Pacific Ocean have made it a formidable barrier between America and Asia, for it measures more than 12,000 miles wide near the equator, and measures only slightly less than that from Alaska to the Antartica. On the other hand, the Atlantic Ocean roughly is only one-half the size of the Pacific and is much narrower, with a form something like a misshapen hourglass. It measures just 1800 miles from Brazil to Africa, and only 2000 miles

---

[21] Palmer Cosslett Putnam, *Energy in the Future* (New York: Van Nostrand, 1953), pp. 196–97; *The Wall Street Journal,* September 23, 1974, p. 4; *Business Week,* November 9, 1974, p. 115. Another possible source of energy is ocean thermal conversion, but only limited interest has been expressed in this source in recent years (see *The National Observer,* January 11, 1975, p. 10). The first experiments in this method date back to 1930 in Cuba, but scientists estimate that it will be the late 1980s before a plant can be operational because of many legal and technical problems.

from Newfoundland to Ireland. It is understandable that the United States developed extensive trade with countries across the Atlantic long before such trade was developed with countries to the west. However, especially following World War II, trade and commerce, both surface and air, have developed and now "tie together" the far-flung resources around the ocean, including Australia, Oceania, Japan, Southeast Asia, Alaska, Canada, and the United States.

Oceans also serve man in that they furnish many nations with national borders that are rarely contested (and are seldom invaded). Shorelines have been far less susceptible to attack by neighboring countries than land borders, which periodically trigger boundary disputes over the world. In the case of ocean boundaries, the disputes usually concern offshore waters and the extent of various countries' claims to sovereignty over such waters. Today, fishing rights seemingly touch off most wrangles, followed closely by offshore oil claims, but the day is rapidly approaching when "battles" for other minerals may multiply the number and severity of such disputes manyfold.

The U.S. Department of State has noted that "growing nationalism in a world fraught with tensions . . . causes many nations to look seaward, whether apprehensive as to securing their domain or to extending it." The State Department further noted that offshore claims over the world are "always increasing, never decreasing." [22] There are three basic motivating factors behind the establishment of national claims to offshore waters: resource utilization, enforcement of national laws, and defense. A serious difficulty concerning offshore claims has been the lack of uniformity existing among countries of the world. Some claim three nautical miles as the distance from the coast of their territorial sea, others claim six miles, while still others protect 12 miles; as extreme cases, Guinea claims 130 nautical miles as the breadth of its territorial sea, while certain west coast countries of Latin America (Chile, Costa Rica, Ecuador, El Salvador, Honduras, and Peru) have offshore claims extending 200 miles seaward,[23] mostly because fishing is so important to them.

GIGANTIC SETTLING PONDS

Oceans are important depositories for various forms of refuse from the continental masses. In the past they have been a resource because they

---

[22] U.S. Department of State, *Sovereignty of the Sea,* Geographic Bulletin No. 3 (Washington, D.C.: Government Printing Office, 1965), p. 1.

[23] *Ibid.,* pp. 26–27. One nautical mile equals 1.15 statute miles. Significantly, at one point, Ecuador was holding more than 75 fishing vessels of United States registry for having invaded the 200-mile sanctuary claimed by that country (*Daily Oklahoman,* January 19–20–31, 1971, p. 1).

served as giant "cesspools" for man's wastes; he has dumped enormous amounts of junk and debris—from beer cans to automobile bodies—in the water offshore. More recently, oceans have been increasingly used as depositories for raw city sewage, and even for the radioactive wastes of man's atomic energy programs.[24]

However, the oceans serve as settling ponds in an even more important way. They are the depository for millions of tons of refuse discarded from the continents daily by nature. The Misssissippi River alone discharges annually into the Gulf of Mexico 785 billion cubic yards of material.[25] This includes valuable minerals which move to sea in solution or by suspension and saltation. About one-half of the known elements have been identified in seawater and undoubtedly many others will be discovered in the future; probably most of the elements found on land also occur in the oceans in solution. This has caused one writer to comment that taking minerals from the land is like living on one's savings; but mining the ocean is living on income.[26]

Included among materials known to be dissolved in the sea are the chlorides that give saltwater its familiar salinity, all of the gases found in earth's atmosphere, and a large number of less-abundant materials—gypsum, potassium sulfate, and calcium carbonate in fair quantities, and such rare elements as uranium, gold, and silver. It was estimated that, at 1960 prices, there was $20,000 worth of gold in each cubic mile of seawater; unfortunately, it probably would cost 2½ times as much to extract the gold as it would be worth, and there is no interest in such an operation right now.[27] Some of the minerals dissolved from land and collected in oceans, such as iron, silicon, and calcium, are used by sea plants and animals in their life processes and in effect are removed from the water; consequently, the quantity of these elements in solution is less than one would expect to find if he estimated it from the accumulation recently supplied by rivers and streams feeding into the oceans. However, the "salt" ions are extremely soluble and not utilized by plants and animals, and therefore

---

[24] One disadvantage of man's using fissionable sources of energy is that radioactive wastes must be disposed of (this will not be a problem once fusionable materials are in use); to date many of these wastes have been sealed in containers and discarded in the ocean. This practice must have its limitations somewhere in the future; it has been estimated that to supply the current U. S. power needs with fission, the nation would have to dispose of radioactive wastes equal to many thousands of atomic bombs.

[25] Lester E. Klimm et al., *Introductory Economic Geography* (3rd ed.) (New York: Harcourt, Brace and Company, 1956), p. 30.

[26] Robert C. Cowen, *Frontiers of the Sea* (Garden City, N.Y.: Doubleday and Co., Inc., 1960), p. 259.

[27] Robert B. Abel, "Resources of the Ocean," *Navy, The Magazine of Sea Power,* VII, No. 12 (December, 1964), p. 35. Recent increases in gold prices may change this position in time.

represent a relatively higher percentage of the ocean's content than one would estimate from their relatively low rate of flow in the rivers.[28]

Current utilization of valuable ocean minerals and their future potentials are discussed later in this chapter.

RECREATION

The value of oceans as sources of recreation may not be fully recognized by most people; but man is increasingly emphasizing his need for leisure time, especially in the industrialized nations, and economic activity associated with that leisure is becoming more and more significant. Certainly this is an area where man is mobilizing the seas as a resource. Water recreation includes such diverse activities as fishing, boating, and scuba diving; sunbathing, surfing, and swimming; using seaside hotels, parks, and public beaches. Annual sales of skindiving and underwater fishing apparatus, photography, and other equipment alone total some $50 million in the United States and more than $40 million in the remainder of the world.[29] The day will come when underwater aquatic parks, tours, and motel-resort facilities further increase the value of the sea as a resource.

OCEAN TRANSPORTATION

Oceans also are a resource for man because they offer a relatively low-cost means of transportation. Until rail lines and paved roads were developed in comparatively recent times, inland and oceanic water transportation was the only feasible means of moving bulky goods. Thus, most of the world's large cities, colonial developments, and early industrial cities were located on or near the world's water routes. In early America lower cost water transportation favored the building of expensive canals instead of roads whenever possible.

The thousands of vessels that traverse the oceans today have a combined capacity which would be sufficient to carry about one-half of the world's total production of wheat or corn or rice. Practically all of the earth's freight that is transported more than 3,000 miles goes by ship, and water vessels still account for much of the shorter hauls, too. Although today's transoceanic airlines are moving increasing numbers of passengers, long-distance transit of cargo by air, while growing rapidly, is still rela-

---

[28] L. Don Leet and Sheldon Judson, *Physical Geology* (Englewood Cliffs, N.J.: Prentice-Hall, Inc., 1965), p. 223.

[29] *Battelle Technical Review,* December, 1965, p. 10.

tively small; the sea lanes continue to furnish the longest binding links among the world's economies.

In the days of sailing ships, ocean currents and wind directions were critical, for they determined the trade routes and thus much of the economic activities. Though today's modern steamships have a choice of routes, their navigators still often follow the currents and winds in order to gain speed, avoid icebergs, save fuel and time, carry greater payloads, and traverse the oceans with greater safety in storms (it is safer to move with the current in a storm than against it).

Ocean transport, although requiring great capital initially, is lower-cost relative to other means of transportation in the long haul for a number of reasons:

1. Oceans are free highways. There are no taxes, no construction costs, no roadbeds or right-of-ways, and no maintenance. Of course there are the important costs of dredging harbors, providing navigation aids and rescue potential, and building port facilities—and these can be very expensive; but they are not significantly greater than corresponding costs of building airfields, railyards, or other loading and unloading dock facilities.

2. Transshipments are often unnecessary. Unbroken worldwide ocean voyages usually can be undertaken without the transfer of goods from one carrier to another, as ships make various ports of call, and container services now are widely available and growing rapidly.

3. Routes can change. As commercial conditions shift over the world in time, the direction of various shipping routes can easily be changed for ocean-going traffic; ships need only to alter their ports of call, and there is no need to build new highways or special rail lines to accommodate newly developing commercial areas.

4. Part of the propelling force is free. To the extent that ships can utilize them, nature's winds and ocean currents give a free propelling force that saves fuel and time, permits greater payloads, and reduces shipping costs.

5. Vehicle is relatively low-cost to build. It costs much less to build a ship capable of carrying 50,000 tons of cargo, for example, than to build overland transportation capable of carrying an equivalent tonnage by truck or rail.

6. Smaller operating costs. A ship requires a smaller crew and much less fuel (there is less friction in water) than is needed to move an equivalent cargo tonnage overland. Similarly, maintenance crews are relatively smaller per ton hauled.

7. Bulkier goods are possible. Generally, the bulkier the goods, the higher the total transport costs, and if the commodity is very large and low in value per unit, overland transportation costs can become quite high in proportion to that value (e.g., coal or building stone). So there is a tendency to move the bulkiest goods by water if at all possible.

8. Free government services. Various governmental bodies not only help finance port and harbor projects, just as they helped the railroads in an earlier era

with free right-of-ways, or the airlines today with airports, but they also furnish many free operating services along the shipping lanes. These include free radio-beacon operators, lighthouses, and emergency assistance, which are basically needed for the merchant marine fleets but also are available without costs for shippers.

There are still a limited number of major shipping lanes today, as almost any economic atlas will show.[30] World shipping has a tendency to converge on Western Europe as incoming vessels carry foodstuffs and raw materials toward Europe and manufactured goods move on the outbound voyages. Almost 40 percent of all ocean voyages either originate or terminate in the coastal waters between the southern point of Norway and the northwestern edge of Spain. Many of the ocean-going raw materials entering European ports are bulky items—crude oil, rubber and wool, or meat and grains like wheat and corn—which Europe either produces in insufficient quantities or not at all. Europe, once an important exporter of coal, now is even a net importer of this bulky cargo.

There are two major trunk lines and four other very important ocean shipping routes in the world, and most of them converge on Western Europe.

SOURCE OF FOOD

For centuries the sea has provided man with food. Fish still are the most important resource of the sea, and fishing remains one of the most important economic activities. Probably the first sailors learned to navigate the sea by piloting fishing vessels; and unquestionably the rise of world naval powers has occurred among fishing people—in Carthage, Greece, England, The Netherlands, and Norway. Civilian and naval shipping crews usually have come from men trained originally in fishing fleets.

Fish

The total fish catch in the world amounts to more than 70 million short tons annually,[31] and the commercial catch has been increasing at a

---

[30] For example, see *Goode's World Atlas* (Chicago: Rand McNally & Company, 1964), p. 44; or discussions of shipping routes in William Van Royen and Nels A. Bengtson, *Fundamentals of Economic Geography* (4th ed.) (Englewood Cliffs, N.J.: Prentice-Hall, Inc., 1964), pp. 562–69; John W. Alexander, *Economic Geography* (Englewood Cliffs, N.J.: Prentice-Hall, Inc., 1963), pp. 508–10; Richard S. Thoman, *The Geography of Economic Activity* (New York: McGraw-Hill Book Company, Inc., 1962), pp. 168–69.

[31] It was 76.4 million short tons in 1970; U.S. Bureau of the Census, *Statistical Abstract of the United States: 1972* (93rd edition). Washington, D.C., 1972, p. 825. Later editions report similar figures.

rate of 6 percent a year. Peru, Japan, China, the United States, India, Spain, Canada, and Denmark report the largest annual catches.

Fish food from the sea is becoming more important in the world because of recent population explosions and because of the great amount of hunger found over the earth; but man has hardly tapped the seafood supply around him. Large, fertile areas can be found in every ocean, except possibly the Indian and Arctic Oceans.

Fishing is still at the "hunting and collecting" stage of organization—though technology has produced the factory ships and catchers—and presently accounts for only 1 or 2 percent of man's food supply. The sea is estimated to be potentially more productive per square mile than land; but man has done very little thus far to utilize it properly. One note of caution should be sounded, however. Many popular magazine articles have described the oceans as limitless reservoirs of food, and thus such bodies of water are considered an ultimate solution to food demand problems created by explosive population trends. This may or may not be true.

The sea is not an *inexhaustible* resource insofar as fishing is concerned; but if properly managed and worked, it can serve indefinitely as a *renewable* resource. Some estimates place the possible fish catch at nearly five times the current rate, without depletion, but such estimates are much easier to make than to substantiate. Man must learn much more about the sea before he attempts a rate of extraction indicated by such a projected catch, for there are a number of bothersome factors to be considered; unlimited exploitation without proper research could prove dangerous.[32] First, it is quite possible to upset the balance of nature in the sea; if a certain species of fish is exhausted, other fish that feed upon that species may be destroyed. And if man destroys a certain species, he may cause a very great increase in other species upon which the first type feeds and may disrupt the ecological food pyramid. This is another case of a flow resource that will serve man indefinitely as long as he properly mobilizes it without upsetting the ecology of nature and so destroying his resource through ignorance or indifference.

Ichthyologists already have identified more than 25,000 species of fish, but only about 6 percent are ever used by man, and not more than 2 percent are used to a significant degree.[33] Some 12 species make up about 75 percent of today's commercial catch in the world; about one-third are in the herring family (including sardines, menhaden, and anchovies), about one-fourth are in the cod family (cod, hake, haddock, and pollack), less than

---

[32] For many people food from the world fisheries is a major factor in individual survival; but with nations such as Iceland, Newfoundland, and Norway, where fisheries are the dominant economic activity, it is more a question of national survival.

[33] Lionel A. Walford, *Living Resources of the Sea* (New York: The Ronald Press Company, 1958), pp. 228–29.

one-tenth are mackerel (or such relatives as bonitos and tunas), and a small portion are flounders, rockfishes, basses, snappers, weakfishes, or other miscellaneous groups.

How well a species of fish can contribute to a nation's economy depends upon a number of factors: abundance in numbers; concentration in an area; regularity of habits so that fishermen can find them in certain places and at certain times; accessibility in areas not too deep or otherwise unworkable; palatable, nutritious, and esthetically pleasing; firm-fleshed enough not to spoil during transportation back to port; and capable of being preserved in some form.[34]

About 85 percent of all fish caught are taken in the middle latitudes for various economic and geological reasons. The economic explanations of middle-latitude concentrations may be summarized briefly as follows: [35]

1. Dense populations in middle latitudes. Of the four main commercial fishing regions, three (northeast United States, northwest Europe, and Asia) have dense populations, while only one (northwest United States) does not.
2. Limited arable land. Many areas of high fish consumption (e.g., Norway, Iceland, United Kingdom, Japan) have a low ratio of arable acres of land per person.[36]
3. Dietary patterns. Because of religious, cultural, or market limitations, much of the middle-latitude population is forced to eat fish instead of meat (the relatively higher price of meat is one market limitation, for example).
4. Nonfood uses. An increasing use of fish to produce agricultural fertilizers, animal feeds, and oils has developed in the middle latitudes; included for nonfood use are menhaden from U.S. offshores and anchovettas from waters off Peru.

The geomorphological attractiveness of the middle latitudes includes:

1. Continental drainage. Dissolved minerals and organic matter run from the continents into the ocean, where they support the biotic pyramid—forming food and nutrients for microscopic animal and plant life (plankton), which is eaten by some large fish (herring, menhaden, and mackerel) or by small fish that in turn become food for larger carnivorous fish. This continental drainage is especially significant in the middle latitudes of the Northern Hemisphere.
2. Shallow continental shelf waters. About two-thirds of all known seafishes

---

[34] Ibid., p. 227.

[35] These points are not significant enough to this discussion of the sea as a resource to warrant detailed analysis here; but an excellent elaboration can be found in Alexander, op. cit., pp. 75–80.

[36] Arability is defined for this purpose as "capable of being cultivated with today's level of technology and cultural development."

live on continental shelves in depths of less than 100 fathoms, and since the shelves are relatively narrow, most species live within 20 miles of land to spawn or because of the availability of food.[37] Most of the shallow offshore waters are in the middle latitudes, chiefly in the North.

3. Mixing ocean waters. As nutrients resulting from the continental runoff move into the ocean, they have a tendency to sink or settle to the bottom—beyond reach of animal and plant life which stays nearer the surface to obtain sunlight. However, certain conditions prevailing in the middle latitudes help bring these nutrients near the surface again: the water is churned or mixed by convection (the falling of cold water and rising of warm water); by colliding currents, as cold water from the poles and warm water from the tropics conflict; or by upwelling, as surface water swings away from the land and is replaced by deeper water that brings nutrients with it.

4. Onshore forests. Nature was kind to man when it placed large, well-developed softwood forests near the shorelines in the middle latitudes. The wood from these forests is utilized for small fishing boats, for smoking fish, and for making marketing containers such as boxes, crates, and barrels. This marketing aspect is especially important in middle latitudes, in which Canada, the United States, and Western Europe are located.

5. Irregular shorelines. For some geomorphological reason, the middle latitudes tend to have a greater irregularity in their shorelines, and such indented areas furnish better natural harbor facilities where fishermen operate more easily. This abundance of natural harbors has stimulated the development of port facilities needed for commercial fishing.

6. Cool waters and cool climates. As if the above-mentioned reasons were not enough, the middle latitudes furnish a happy combination of cool waters and atmospheric temperatures which are particularly conducive to commercial fishing. Warm tropical waters tend to produce fish with a higher oil content, while colder waters seem to make the fish more palatable. Cooler waters also have less bacterial action, which in warm waters of low latitudes tends to destroy nutrients (fish food) at a faster rate. Also, for some undetermined reason, cold-water fish tend to run in schools more so than in low latitudes, and this makes it easier for commercial fishermen to gather a boatload of one particular type of fish. Furthermore, the cooler middle and higher latitude climates require less icing-down of fish (the subsistence economies of the tropics generally cannot afford such a luxury as ice), and middle latitude fishermen can travel greater distances from shore without having the fish spoil before they return to port.

What about future food possibilities from the oceans? As was noted earlier, the seas are not an inexhaustible source of fish food; but they are a renewable source if properly managed in the future. Some day man must

---

[37] Walford, op. cit., p. 230. Most plant life cannot live deeper than 200 feet of water because reduced sunlight does not permit photosynthesis.

abandon his current dependence on "searching out and capturing" the fish, and turn instead to raising and harvesting them in an age of aquaculture, if he is ever to realize full mobilization of the oceans' food sources.[38] Purely mathematically derived trendlines of potential world population sizes are frightening, and, while it is unlikely that such astronomical figures will ever be realized, even the current world food situation offers staggering problems. A majority of the world population today lives in hunger, an estimated two-thirds of the people suffer from lack of protein and more than 100 million are stricken with kwashiorkor.[39]

Fish Concentrate

One possibility for alleviating world hunger is the production of a powdered fish concentrate developed in the United States; it is 80 percent protein, compared with only about 20 percent protein found in meat. The concentrate is obtained by grinding and powdering the fish so that a tasteless flour is produced. It is not practical to consider this fish concentrate as a food substitute, but rather as a supplement that can be added to the daily diet—especially in areas where that diet consists primarily of grains low in protein. Not only is the fish concentrate tasteless, but it also has the advantage of being produced just as well from "trash" fish as from the best tuna or cod, and production of sufficient protein to supply the entire world's needs could be obtained at a cost of less than one cent per day per person.[40] When initially manufactured, the flour was made from the entire fish— heads, fins, and intestines included—but objections from the U.S. Pure Food and Drug Administration brought modifications in the process so that now only the "edible" portion of the fish is used. While there is little religious objection to the eating of fish flour, since it is not animal meat, there remain some social and cultural taboos.[41]

---

[38] Aquaculture is at least 500 years old in Asia, but, for the remainder of the world, it still has not "come of age."

[39] A disease caused by lack of protein requirements; it is the familiar "pot-belly" appearance seen among people, especially babies and children, who subsist almost entirely on certain grains. See George A. W. Boehm, "Aquaculture," *Britannica Book of the Year,* 1965, p. 116; and Andrew Hamilton, "The Skipper at Scripps," *Think,* XXIX (November-December, 1963), p. 13.

[40] "Fish Flour for the Hungry Millions," *Sea Secrets,* X (May, 1966), p. 5; marketing efforts by a Swedish firm are described in *Business Week,* November 14, 1970, p. 112.

[41] There might be less objection to eating a protein concentrate produced like yeast from petroleum or natural gas; this possibility is not covered at this time because the present emphasis is on the sea (though oil and natural gas may come from offshore).

Much of the literature about ocean food sources deals with plankton and the vital role it may play in future years. Plankton is a collective term used for that segment of marine life that drifts under the influence of ocean currents, and includes phytoplankton (microscopic plants) and zooplankton (microscopic animals).[42] When supplies of nutrient salts are sufficient, and the light and temperature are conducive, the unicellular plants can double their numbers daily.

Copepods, the most abundant zooplankton, contain 70 to 77 percent protein, 5 to 19 percent fat, and up to 4 percent carbohydrates,[43] while phytoplankton contain less food value, but are rich in certain vitamins. From a standpoint of efficiency alone, man could best use the sea as food by eating plankton directly.[44] However, on a large scale, there are numerous formidable obstacles: the quantity in any given body of water varies greatly yearly, seasonally, and even daily; plankton are difficult to collect in quantity by man; some species are poisonous and could ruin a whole catch; and plankton, as food, tastes like finely ground gravel spiked with cod liver oil.

For these reasons, plankton has been discussed more than it has been eaten. Authorities seem to agree that talk of feeding the world's growing billions on plankton soup is just that—and it appears that plankton harvesting must be left to the sea creatures best fitted to do so, such as whales and herring, unless fantastic technological and cultural breakthroughs occur.

Seaweed

Considerable exploration has been undertaken in recent years on the use of seaweed as a food. Algae and kelp (a form of alga that reaches lengths of up to hundreds of feet) and seaweeds that seem to be plentiful along the coastlines, especially in temperate and cool seas. Total tonnage in all waters of the world is impressive, and the seaweed crop could be harvested two or three times a year by boats equipped with underwater cut-

---

[42] By definition, however, something as large as the jellyfish must be classed as plankton too, for it drifts with the currents (the word "plankton" was derived from a Greek word meaning "drifting").

[43] Walford, op. cit., p. 123, taken originally from Johannes von Krey, "Eine neue Methode zur quantitativen Bestimmung des Planktons," *Kieler Meeresforschungen,* VII (1950), pp. 58–75.

[44] Since most of what a living creature eats goes into growth, energy, and sustenance of life, the next best thing would be to eat fish that live on plankton (like herring) than fish that eat other fish (like cod).

ters.[45] There are various forms of marine algae—green, blue, blue-green, red, and brown, depending upon their principal pigmentation. The red and brown have proved to have the most significant commercial value so far, and make up about 95 percent of the known deposits of seaweed.

The red algae, which range from single cells of microscopic size through broad-fronded plants three to five feet long, are most widely used as a source of food. The brown algae, which grow up to 20 feet long, are of negligible importance as human food, especially in the Western World, for the brown type extracts more minerals from seawaters and the carbohydrates are less digestible for man. A few blue-green and green algae, among them sea lettuce, are eaten in various places, particularly the Orient and Oceania, as vegetables and garnishes, or for flavoring.[46]

A small brown alga is used in Japan for preserving mushrooms, and another genus of it is eaten as food by the Japanese; but the world over, the brown version is used much more extensively for animal feed, fertilizers, and as a source of such industrial products as iodine, soda, potash, acids, textiles, and paper. Seaweeds are not a satisfactory food when used exclusively for sheep, cows, horses, pigs, and poultry; but they are excellent as supplementary feed when used in a proportion of about 15 percent of the normal ration.[47]

There are more than a dozen factories that manufacture meal from brown seaweeds, including some located in the United States, Nova Scotia, France, Denmark, Eire, the Netherlands, Scotland, Norway, and South Africa. The brown version makes a better fertilizer than the average barnyard manure, for it not only has at least two-thirds as much nitrogen, one-third or more as much phosphoric acid, and about twice as much potash, but it also makes a good soil conditioner.[48] Seaweeds also have been an excellent source of antibiotics, and as a war-time source of acetone, acetone oils, potassium chloride, ethyl esters, and organic acids. Algin factories currently located in the United States, United Kingdom, Spain, France, and Japan make a product widely used by the food industries as stabilizers for ice cream (to prevent whey separation), icing, malted milk, canned meats and cheese, as an emulsifying agent in mayonnaise and other salad dressings, and as an ingredient in jellies. For nonfood applications seaweed products are used in pharmaceutical emulsions, pills, tablets, ointments, hand

---

[45] Aylesa Forsee, *Beneath Land and Sea* (Philadelphia: Macrae Smith Company, 1962), p. 46. One problem is that the annual tonnage of seaweed grown in a given area varies greatly from year to year.

[46] Walford, op. cit., pp. 276–77.

[47] Ibid., p. 280.

[48] Uses listed in this paragraph are based upon Walford, op. cit., pp. 181–85.

lotions, toothpastes, shaving creams, and sizing materials for the textile, paper, latex, and leather finishing industries.

Red alga, which is quite high in vitamin content, has been used for more than 300 years in the manufacture of gel-forming chemicals. It is currently used as a gelling agent in jelly candies and similar sweets, is pressed into rolls for chewing like gum, and is used as a stabilizer in sherbet, pies, meringues, and salad dressings. The Japanese make a dish from red alga that they call *nori,* and other algae can be boiled, eaten raw with vinegar, or cooked into a seaweed candy.

A new type of white algae has been raised that has a naturally pleasant flavor; when dried, it resembles flour and can be baked into cake and bread.[49]

The potential of seaweed as an important resource from the sea is sizable and certainly warrants man's full mobilization efforts; however, its utilization will depend not only on technological change, but also on cultural adaptation.

Invertebrates and Sea Mammals

Some saltwater invertebrates and mammals have been very significant as sources of food in the past. While their import will continue to be felt in some areas of the world, the degree of their economic impact probably will vary inversely with man's need for food generally.

Invertebrates compose almost 90 percent of the mass of nonplant life in the sea, but very few of the enormous number of species meet the requirements necessary to be considered a source of human food; those generally considered as food are oysters, clams, scallops, lobsters, shrimps, and squid.[50]

Marine mammals, including whales, dolphins, seals, walruses, sirenians, and sea otters, have a higher proportion of species that are useful than any other group of sea animals, but the populations are relatively small and the rate of production is rather low.[51]

Much has been written about the threat of overpopulation. For the world as a whole, it is a problem of the future; but for many parts of the globe, it is a problem of immediate and fearful concern, and it has been

---

[49] William J. Cromie, *Exploring the Secrets of the Sea* (Englewood Cliffs, N.J.: Prentice-Hall, Inc., 1962), p. 262.

[50] Also mussels and cockles in Europe and the Orient, marine snails in the Orient, abalones in North America and the Orient, octopi in southern Europe and the Orient, crabs in the United States and Japan, and even barnacles in Chile and the Mediterranean.

[51] Walford, op. cit., p. 256.

for a long time. If the carrying capacity of a certain region cannot support even a meager number of people, that area is overpopulated. Obviously, the upper limit of earth's population does not depend on the provision of "elbow room" for people, but on the amount of food that can be produced. On an acre-for-acre basis, the sea is more productive of organic food than land, and because the ocean bodies, which currently furnish only about 1 percent of the world's food, cover more than 70 percent of the globe, the potential is obvious.

SOURCE OF MINERALS

The possibilities offered by the sea as a source of food is evident from the preceding discussion, but scientists studying the earth's water bodies during the International Geophysical Year (1958) concluded that the difference between present and future use of the sea will be every bit as great for minerals as for food. More recent years have been confirming this conclusion.

Man currently utilizes a number of techniques to obtain a limited supply of minerals from the ocean. From seawater, itself, he extracts magnesium, manganese, phosphorus, bromine, boron, and potassium salts. From beneath the sea, he obtains petroleum, natural gas, and sulfur primarily, although the Japanese have a 13-million-ton-a-year coal mine that drifts 60 feet below the ocean floor from an entrance on land, and an oil company found gold with deep dredges in Nome Sands off Norton Sound in Alaska.[52] Tin ore is being mined at 90-foot depths off Thailand and is being smelted at a plant completed in the fall of 1965, and coal is mined from an underwater tunnel off Nova Scotia and New Brunswick; aragonite is taken off the Bahamas.[53]

However, another important possibility is the mineral content lying on the ocean floor, itself. For some years the Japanese have dredged up iron ore from the magnetite-rich sands in Tokyo Bay, recovering 7 million tons of iron during a four-year period.[54] Iron ore also is mined off Newfoundland, and tin is dredged in waters of varying depths off Indonesia,

---

52 Robert Reniero, "Mining the Ocean Floor," *Business Week,* June 30, 1962, p. 143; and Robert F. Crossley, "Our newest frontier is underwater!" *Popular Mechanics,* CXXV (May, 1966), p. 97. Rich veins on Nome's beaches yielded more than $100 million worth of gold from mines, and it was assumed that the veins extended out under the ocean.

53 "Is there a gold mine in the ocean?" *Business Week,* April 9, 1966, p. 94.

54 Robert Revelle, "The Research Frontier," *The Saturday Review,* XLVII (October 3, 1964), p. 60; and Clark M. Eichelberger, "The Promise of the Seas' Bounty," *The Saturday Review,* XLIX (June 18, 1966), p. 21.

Thailand, and Malaysia.[55] American interests have obtained diamonds from the ocean floor off southwest Africa's coastline by the use of a vacuum process aboard barges.[56] These are only a few examples that are periodically reported; but one other less colorful illustration should be cited: a few forward-looking construction firms are profiting elsewhere in the world from recovery of sea-floor sand and gravel—an unglamorous business, but one that may prove the most profitable of all in the future, as burgeoning world populations gradually require ever-increasing amounts of building materials and at the same time cover more and more land deposits of these materials.

Titanium-bearing sands are believed to exist off the coasts of Florida, India, Japan, and Australia,[57] and the United States now needs increasing quantities of this unusual metal which is used in aerospace, supersonic transports, rocket motor cases, pressure vessels containing super-cold liquid nitrogen and hydrogen, desalination plants and chemical processing. In fact, titanium is among eight minerals (antimony, bismuth, gold, mercury, platinum, tantalum, tin, and rutile—a source of titanium) for which the U.S. Geological Survey's Office of Minerals Exploration announced that it will pay up to 75 percent of private investors' exploration costs.[58]

Without a doubt, petroleum, natural gas, and sulfur constitute the greatest mineral recovery from the oceans to date, as evidenced by hundreds of odd-looking towers that dot the Gulf of Mexico, offshore in Southern California, in the North Sea, in Alaskan waters, and elsewhere. This was the first major recovery of mineral resources from the ocean (except for salt) and still is the most remunerative. A Dow Chemical Company plant at Freeport, Texas, where the highest average temperature of water adjacent to U.S. coasts is found, extracts chemically all the magnesium produced in the United States, and three-fourths of the U.S. bromine supply, from seawater, and is doing it profitably; but this is a special situation where the mineral is rather highly concentrated in the water and costs of recovering the product from land by conventional methods are quite high. Innumerable uses of magnesium include airplane manufacturing, insulating materials, printing inks, toothpastes, medicines, and war implements like incendiary bombs, star shells, and tracer ammunition; magnesium com-

---

[55] Crossley, op. cit., p. 97; Abel, op. cit., p. 35; Revelle, op. cit., p. 61.

[56] Lloyd Mallan, *Secrets of the Sea* (Greenwich, Conn.: Fawcett Publications, Inc., 1965), pp. 33–34; and Eichelberger, op. cit., p. 21. Reports indicated that the yield was some 1,000 carats of good diamonds daily, with the diamond-bearing gravels producing some five carats per ton—five times the average inland diamond field. No one knows for sure whether the diamonds originated on the ocean bottom or were washed there from the land over geological time.

[57] Eichelberger, op. cit., p. 21.

[58] *U.S. News & World Report*, October 2, 1967. Historically titanium production has been a "boom or bust" industry, but now it is "booming" and prospects are bright.

pounds also are used as refractory materials in lining smelting furnaces, and in pharmaceuticals, fertilizers, rayon, and paper. Bromine is important in producing high-test gasoline, sedatives, fire extinguishers, photographic chemicals, dyestuffs, and chemical warfare materials.[59]

A great deal of effort has been devoted to devising methods for extracting gold from seawater, but no economically successful method has yet been found. It is estimated that the oceans of the world contain more than 6 million tons of gold—enough to make a pile weighing almost as much as the Great Pyramid of Egypt and worth about 18 times as much as the current world gold supply—but a ton of seawater contains only 2 to 60 milligrams of gold and no one as yet is rushing to mine the sea for gold, as was noted earlier. Robert B. Abel, executive secretary of the Interagency Committee on Oceanography, estimated in 1964 that there was $20,000 worth of gold in each cubic mile of seawater, but it probably would cost $50,000 to extract it.[60]

Globigerina ooze, a type of sediment, covers about 50 percent of the ocean floor and contains as much as 95 percent calcium carbonate. Extensive deposits lie within a few hundred miles of most countries with sea coasts, and the ooze may someday serve as a source of cement for those nations with no domestic deposits of cement-grade limestone.[61]

The mineral content of ocean water is estimated to be only about 35 parts per 1,000 parts of water (and 27 of those 35 parts are salt), but when one considers that the oceans cover some 137 million square miles, averaging 12,500 feet deep, he is awed by the potential of the seawater. The elements, in order of their abundance, are:[62]

Chlorine	Fluorine	Copper	Lanthanum
Sodium	Nitrogen	Zinc	Yttrium
Magnesium	Aluminum	Lead	Nickel
Sulfur	Rudibium	Selenium	Scandium
Calcium	Lithium	Cesium	Mercury
Potassium	Phosphorus	Uranium	Gold
Bromine	Barium	Molybdenum	Radium
Carbon	Iodine	Thorium	Cadmium
Strontium	Arsenic	Cerium	Chromium
Boron	Iron	Silver	Cobalt
Silicon	Manganese	Vanadium	Tin

---

[59] Excellent discussions of the extraction processes and utilization techniques of the minerals can be found in John L. Mero, *The Mineral Resources of the Sea* (New York: Elsevier Publishing Co., 1964).

[60] Abel, op. cit., p. 35. These figures predate the rapid price fluctuations of the 1970s.

[61] *Scientific American*, CCIII (December, 1960), p. 70.

[62] H. U. Sverdrup, Martin W. Johnson, and Richard H. Fleming, *The Oceans* (Englewood Cliffs, N.J.: Prentice-Hall, Inc., 1959). Exact amounts of each are not given because they vary from place to place in the oceans.

Scientists from 18 countries released a report early in 1971 saying that there is evidence that the oceans contain sufficient minerals to meet the world's needs for at least a century.[63] The scientists said, among many other things, that the earth's oceans contain astronomical amounts of dissolved solids, that more than $7 billion worth of minerals were produced from the sea annually as the world entered the 1970s, and that oil and gas deposits under the seabed may exceed those available on land.

However, economic costs and limitations of man's technological know-how remain the primary obstacles.[64] The payoff may well be the recovery of an almost inexhaustible supply of important materials, but the investment will have to be tremendous. But with costs of obtaining raw materials from the earth rising each year (as such materials become increasingly dear) and with costs of obtaining similar materials from the ocean bottom decreasing as technology advances, there should be a time in the future when the two cost curves cross for any particular mineral and it will become commercially feasible to extract that material from seawater for industrial uses. For some minerals these cost curves may cross in the near future; but for others that time may still be far in the future.

In an interesting series of experiments conducted under the sponsorship of the United States Office of Saline Water in conjunction with private industry, chemical "by-products" are being extracted from salt water before the salt-water desalination process takes place; the object is to reduce thereby the cost of obtaining fresh water from the sea. Through a series of highly technical processes, the following minerals and chemicals already were being salvaged back in the early 1960s: magnesium ammonium phosphate, magnesia, potash, caustic soda solution, halogens, boron, zinc, copper, uranium, molybdenum, bromine, and sodium hydroxide.[65]

Manganese is the mineral to which oceanographers and mining engineers look for the next breakthrough in ocean recovery. This would be a major development, for the United States now imports almost all manga-

---

[63] Associated Press stories carried in publications of May 31, 1971, quoted a "Report on the Application of Science and Technology to Development," a report made to the United Nations Economic and Social Council.

[64] Another obstacle that must be solved some day is the fact that legal considerations affecting ocean mining are nebulous and encouraging to claim jumpers. Traditionally, open waters have been free, and thus a nation that is attempting to mine the ocean far from its shores might have to "fight off" invading nations; but for the American free-enterpriser, the problems go even beyond that, for individuals have no rights on the open seas—only sovereign nations have rights—and thus a private mining project at sea would be subject not only to the whims of foreign governments, but to those of its own government, as well. The problem may surface soon, as the U.S. government made plans in early 1974 to encourage oil exploration in the Atlantic's deep-water Continental Slope, beyond the Continental Shelf.

[65] "CPI's Treasure Hunt," *Chemical Week*, XCV (September 26, 1964), pp. 81–82.

nese and the U.S.S.R. currently has about two-thirds of the world's known reserves of this vital ferroalloy metal which has so many uses and advantages, including that of adding tensile strength and abrasion resistance to steel. It has been established that manganese exists in nodules of varying sizes over most of the Pacific floor.[66] They also are found in the Atlantic and Indian Oceans, but the Pacific seems most promising as a source. These nodules apparently consist of about 50 percent manganese, 27 percent iron, 2 percent copper and other metals (e.g., nickel, cobalt).

Nodules are natural concentrations of minerals and range in size from microscopic bits to those that weigh almost a ton. The black potato-shaped objects tend to get larger and much more plentiful in deeper water. They are formed whenever metal particles are washed down from mountains and soils on the continents. Such metal particles attach to other particles and tend to form solid masses as they move out to sea (the process is very similar to that of making rock candy). As nodules reach deep water, they begin to sink and pick up other elements such as copper, lead, and zinc.[67] Once they reach the ocean bottom, they begin to grow at a rate of about one millimeter per 1,000 years. At present, there are approximately 1.5 trillion tons of these nodules on the ocean floor.[68] Dr. John Mero of the Newport News Shipbuilding and Drydock Company has calculated the growth of manganese nodules in all of the Pacific Ocean to be 10 billion tons per year, far surpassing any conceivable consumption by man.

Nonmetallic nodules found in the shallow waters of Southern California are thought to contain about 60 million tons of phosphatic materials.[69] The major uses of phosphorus are in the match and fertilizer industries. A mineral with the greatest potential economic importance to the United States may be potash (potassium), another basic nutrient used by farmers to stimulate crop production; potash is one of the three primary components, with nitrates and phosphorus, in fertilizers. World consumption of

---

[66] Abel, op. cit., p. 35.

[67] The search operations for nodules is a well-kept secret, but it has been estimated that as many as 30 companies and several governments had spent as much as $300 million by 1974 in development of technology to mine the deep, and another $300 million to $500 million is poised to pump into the business by the end of 1976. Those competing in the race to mine the oceans contend that technology is fairly well in hand already, and at least three commercial mines could be operating before 1980—and maybe sooner. See *The Wall Street Journal,* September 21, 1973, p. 1.

[68] "Scraping the Bottom," *Newsweek,* April 15, 1963, p. 66. Figures concerning the growth rates and the estimated quantities vary with different scientists; *The Wall Street Journal,* September 21, 1973, p. 1, lists nodular growth rates as 16 million tons a year.

[69] "Is there a gold mine in the ocean?" *Business Week,* April 9, 1966, p. 94. Also see "CPI's Treasure Hunt," op. cit., and Reniero, op. cit., pp. 143–44.

potash is enormous and attempts to mine potash from the ocean bottom have taken place off the southern coast of California.[70]

CONCLUSION

The oceans, which constitute seven-tenths of the earth's surface, have served as a resource almost since the dawn of mankind, but through the ages their value remained rather constant until recent years. Today man is beginning to view the ocean in a new perspective, and its vital role in his survival is becoming better appreciated.

The vast water bodies are unquestionably important for their influence on world weather and climate, as means of less-expensive transportation, as collecting basins for continental matter, as national boundaries, and as connecting links among nations. But they will become even more valuable in the future as renewable sources of food and minerals, and as inexhaustible sources of fresh water and energy.

Oceanography has been characterized as a science of five parts—physics, chemistry, geology, meteorology, and biology—but certainly the roles that geographers and economists, and probably other related disciplines, can contribute should not be ignored. There are virtually no limits to the benefits that man can derive from the oceans if he properly mobilizes his efforts toward their full utilization. The severest limitation is man's adherence to tradition. No attempt has been made here to describe developing technology in the area of ocean exploration and utilization, for this segment of oceanography is changing so rapidly that any discussion of "latest" developments undoubtedly soon will become obsolete.[71] The 1960s saw man's mobilization of the sea gain real momentum and "get into full swing." By the mid-1960s more than 300 of the United States' largest manufacturers were sharing in the military undersea budget for research and development,[72] and the programs have continued to expand since then. If anyone wonders why the Americans are pouring billions of dollars (a still very inadequate sum) into ocean mobilization efforts, he can take a clue from the words spoken by G. V. Petrovich, a scientist in the Soviet Union (whose oceanographic research fleet is some eight times larger than that

---

[70] Abel, op. cit., p. 36.

[71] For example, one program has started development of a small, manned submersible capable of operating eventually at depths down to 6,000 meters (only 2 percent of the oceans are deeper); and scientists are experimenting with silicone-rubber "gills" that already enable hamsters, mice, and rabbits to breathe oxygen directly from seawater—so it is only a matter of time and technology before man can equip himself with such gills.

[72] *Dun's Review and Modern Industry*, June, 1966, p. 32.

of the United States'): "The nation that first learns to understand the seas will control them. And the nation that controls the seas . . . will control the world." [73] Many American scientists seem to agree.

SELECTED BIBLIOGRAPHY

BARDACH, JOHN E., *Harvest of the Sea*. New York: Harper & Row Publishers, 1968.

BAZELL, ROBERT J., "Arid Land Agriculture: Shaikh Up in Arizona Research," *Science*, March 12, 1971, pp. 989–90.

CHORLEY, RICHARD (ed.), *Water, Earth and Man: A Synthesis of Hydrology, Geomorphology and Socio-Economic Geography*. London: Methuen & Co., Ltd., 1969.

COOTNER, PAUL H., and GEORGE O. G. LÖF, *Water Demand for Steam Electric Generation: An Economic Projection Model* (Resources for the Future, Inc.). Baltimore: The Johns Hopkins Press, 1965.

FORMAN, JONATHAN, and OLLIE E. FINK (eds.), *Water and Man: A Study in Ecology*. Columbus, Ohio: Friends of the Land, 1950.

FOSTER ASSOCIATES, *The Role of Petroleum and Natural Gas from the Outer Continental Shelf in the National Supply of Petroleum and Natural Gas*. Washington, D.C.: U.S. Bureau of Land Management, Government Printing Office, 1970.

GULLION, EDMUND A. (ed.), *Uses of the Seas*. Englewood Cliffs, N.J.: Prentice-Hall, Inc., 1968.

HURST, CHARLES K., *Water in International Affairs*. Toronto: Canadian Institute of International Affairs, 1956.

JAMES L. DOUGLAS, and ROBERT R. LEE, *Economics of Water Resources Planning*. New York: McGraw-Hill Book Company, Inc., 1971.

KNEESE, ALLEN V., and STEPHEN C. SMITH (eds.), *Water Research: Economic Analysis, Water Management, Evaluation Problems, Water Reallocation, Political and Administrative Problems, Hydrology and Engineering, Research and Needs* (Resources for the Future, Inc.). Baltimore: The Johns Hopkins Press, 1966.

LEEDS, HILL, and JEWITT, INC., *Economic and Institutional Analysis of Wastewater Reclamation and Reuse Projects* (Prepared for Office of Water Resources Research). Washington, D.C.: Government Printing Office, 1971.

LOFTAS, TONY, *The Last Resource: Man's Exploitation of the Oceans* (rev. ed.). Chicago: Henry Regnery Company, 1970.

---

[73] Ibid., p. 80. It is not a new idea, of course; Sir Walter Raleigh once said, "Whoever commands the seas, commands the trade, whoever commands the trade . . . , commands the riches of the world. . . ."

MERO, JOHN L., *The Mineral Resources of the Sea.* New York: Elsevier Publishing Company, 1965.

MILLER, DAVID WILLIAM, JAMES J. GERAGHTY, and ROBERT S. COLLINS, *Water Atlas of the United States: Basic Facts About the Nation's Water Resources.* Port Washington, N.Y.: Water Information Center, 1962.

MILNE, LORUS JOHNSON, and MARGERY MILNE, *Water and Life.* New York: Atheneum, 1967.

MOSS, FRANK E.. *The Water Crisis.* New York: Frederick A. Praeger, Publishers, 1967.

NACE, RAYMOND L., *Water and Man: A World View (The International Hydrological Decade).* Paris: UNESCO, 1969.

NATIONAL RESEARCH COUNCIL, COMMITTEE ON OCEANOGRAPHY, *Economic Benefits from Oceanographic Research, A Special Report.* Washington, D.C.: National Academy of Sciences, 1964.

NATIONAL RESEARCH COUNCIL, COMMITTEE ON WATER, *Water and Choice in the Colorado Basin: An Example of Alternatives in Water Management.* Washington, D.C.: National Academy of Sciences, 1968.

NIKOLAIEFF, GEORGE A. (ed.), *The Water Crisis.* New York: The H. W. Wilson Company, 1967.

"No Lull in the Battle Over Offshore Limits," *Business Week,* January 15, 1972, p. 40.

NORTH, WHEELER J., "Giant Kelp: Sequoias of the Sea," *National Geographic,* August, 1972, pp. 250–69.

SAUNDERS, ROBERT J., *Forecasting Water Demand: An Inter- and Intra-Community Study.* Morgantown, W.V.: Bureau of Business Research, West Virginia University, 1969.

UNITED NATIONS, DEPARTMENT OF ECONOMIC AND SOCIAL AFFAIRS, RESOURCES AND TRANSPORT DIVISION, *Water Desalination in Developing Countries.* New York: United Nations, 1964.

WOLLMAN, NATHANIEL, and GILBERT W. BONEM, *The Outlook for Water: Quality, Quantity, and National Growth* (Resources for the Future, Inc.). Baltimore: The Johns Hopkins Press, 1971.

SIX

LAND:
THE RENEWABLE RESOURCE

Land means *many and different things* to *many and different people.*
To some, land means the soil and its ability to produce crops. To most
economists, land is one of the "property" resources and includes "all natural
[physical] resources—all 'free gifts of nature' which are usable in the productive process." [1] To others, land implies space, site, location, or spatial
relations. To still others, land implies ownership, status, affluence, influence,
and even power.

For purposes of this discussion, land implies all of these things and
more. Land implies *man,* as man relates to his place of habitation, work,
travel, worship, and recreation. Land is his *home* and how this home relates to other things. It is his *place of work* and how the particular shop,
store, center, factory, plant, or production complex relates to other things.
In all these examples of land, man is implicit, and his culture is essential.
Land values and man's goals, wants, and needs are directly and, at the

---

[1] Campbell R. McConnell, *Economics: Principles, Problems, and Policies,* 2nd
ed. (New York: McGraw-Hill Book Company, Inc., 1966), pp. 24–25. McConnell
further states that such resources as arable land, forests, mineral and oil deposits,
and water resources come under this general classification. This "free gifts of nature"
idea is not fully compatible with the *resource* economist's view that man, through his
culture, *creates* the resource out of the neutral material furnished by nature.

151

same time, indirectly related; yet the term *land* transcends economic implications to encompass pride, security, confidence, landscape, scenery, beauty, and even religious commitment. Land is a mixture of nature and man along with man's institutions (his culture).

To discuss land *in toto* may be impossible, but that the attempt must be made in any consideration of resources is almost axiomatic. Therefore, despite the danger of treating only subunits of the whole, this chapter—"Land: the Renewable Resource"—is presented for the purpose of laying some foundation.

Furthermore, in this chapter *land* will not include discussions of seas and oceans—although water must be considered in terms of the spatial relations of land in juxtaposition with aquifers, rivers, lakes, or seas. Land, for the purposes of this chapter, is described in terms of area, quality of soil, physical features, moisture, drainage, slope, and spatial relations. Predictably, there is an acute concern with the kinds and quality of economic activity that a given area can support, both now and in the future.

What land use is current? What is possible? What is best? Should a given area be in field crops, forests, grasses, or simply left in a natural state? Should a river valley be dammed and flooded? Should an area be used for farming, forestry, ranching, recreation, wildlife preservation, or water storage? These are some of the resource-oriented questions of land. How can land be used to aid man best in attainment of his and society's goals, wants, and needs? In this regard, we should note that although land, on this closed planetary system, is finite in character, it can be altered in many ways and degrees. For example, land can be altered by the addition of fertilizer and water; conversely, the "washing out" of such minerals as salt will, at a cost, allow crops to be harvested on formerly barren ground. The addition of greenhouses and the application of light and heat will permit land to be cropped, even above the Arctic Circle. Similarly, as we shall see in Chapter Eight, mineral deposits become economically attractive to man only when there is sufficient demand and technological feasibility. In this way, "ore" bodies are created, just as reclamation projects can *make* "land" for agricultural purposes.

These land and land-related topics are organized under the subheading of: (1) Primary Uses of Land—Croplands, Grazing Resources, Forests, (2) Urban Land, (3) Recreation, (4) Space and Spatial Relations, (5) Location and Spatial Relations, and (6) Land Perception.

PRIMARY USES OF LAND

The greatest users of land are the primary producing activities of man—agriculture, grazing, forestry, fishing, hunting, and mining (treated in Chapter Eight). Significantly, even though the primary occupations are the big users of land, in the more developed countries where manufacturing and service occupations lead in total employment, recreation land is in demand, and land areas set aside for this purpose take on sizable proportions. In general, most primary producing land areas result in low productivity per individual, as measured in goods or money. In contrast, mining, manufacturing, and service activities produce relatively more intensive uses of land per worker productivity. Thus, historically, this latter group has been given priority by societies. To date, commercial, residential, industrial, and governmental uses of land development have been favored, being given a higher position in the existing scheme of man's culture than have more bucolic purposes—and this is especially so in the more developed countries. It is only within the past 100 years that man, mostly through his governments, has seen fit to set aside parks, preserves, recreation areas, and research areas.

Croplands

By and large, even with the world's burgeoning population, only a small share of land is used for crops. Europe, with its burden of inhabitants, uses only one-third of its land for crops. The United States uses approximately one-fourth for crops, and the Union of Soviet Socialist Republics uses less than 10 percent. In other parts of the world, less than 5 percent is cultivated for crops.

Despite tremendous strides in the application of technologies to agriculture, the potential for farming—although not yet maximized—is definitely limited by nature and varies greatly from one part of the world to another. What agriculture is possible depends chiefly on six factors: (1) climates, (2) soils, (3) landforms, (4) markets, (5) governmental influences, and (6) social values and goals.

Climates. Plant yields are maximum under certain combinations of light, wind, temperature, and moisture. Any one of these may be the critical factor. For example, tung trees do well only within 30 miles of the 30th parallel; cotton requires at least 200 consecutive frost-free days; and rubber trees require a minimum of 90 inches of rain, yet are retarded if their roots are flooded. Such factors as winds (direction, as well as velocity) and modifications due to water, air drainage, exposure, and other climatic vagaries also play important roles in determining whether a given climate has the potential to become a positive resource. Precipitation rates may be offset by evaporation rates.

Soils. As with the climate potential, soils also vary greatly from area to area; and, to a great extent, their variations correspond to the climate prevailing in a given area. Soil variations include such factors as develop-

FIGURE 14. Agriculture technologies might well be epitomized by the cotton picker. The inset emphasizes the complexities of this type of machinery, while the view of the air-conditoned cab, equipped with tape deck and AM-FM radio, depicts the sophistication of its operator. Thus, the machine becomes the tie between the enabling land and climate on the one hand and the sophisticated, technologically oriented farmer on the other. Courtesy Deere and Company.

mental age (whether there are identifiable strata or horizons), structure, fertilizer requirements, drainage, capacity to hold moisture, minerals, and color. The existence of essential plant nutrients, their depth, and the looseness of soil particles (root crops do best in loose, friable, well-drained, still-moist soils) are also important. By and large, the world's best agricultural lands are the so-called chernozems, or black/brown earths, of the Ukraine and of Iowa and its peripheral states. Some of the poorest soils, due primarily to leaching and oxidation, are the soils of the tropical rainforests or the excessively cold and arid soils of tundra areas. Thus, most of the world's estimated 3.2 billion acres of land that are in crops are in the middle latitudes. Of the estimated 20 percent under crops in the low latitudes, probably only one-half are producing in any given year; the balance, because of heavy leaching of minerals, is idle or fallow.

Landforms. Slopes, because of drainage and associated erosional problems, are decisive factors in agricultural activities. Flat lands are preferred for most crops, but air drainage and adiabatic heating, as well as

154

water drainage, provide attractive conditions for some crops such as fruit trees, grapes, and hay.

Markets. Finances, tastes, preservatives, customs, and physical distribution systems also are determinants of what is grown on any given agricultural resource potential. These factors set limits on how much machinery (as against hard labor) is available, whether fertilizers can be used, or even what crops may be grown.

Governmental Influences. Governments play an increasing role in agricultural development throughout the world. Soil conservation programs, water-storage systems, reclamation projects, price supports for selected crops, crop quotas, and even secondary factors such as rural electrification, rural postal services, credit, research programs, herbicides, pesticides, equipment technology, and farmstead construction aids are deciding factors in the evolving agricultural patterns—given the requisite favorable environmental conditions. Almost all governments are interested in the promotion of food production for their people.

Social Values and Goals. The basic values and goals of a people and their culture, including the technology that they have evolved under their value systems to attain these goals, determine which crops are preferred. Even food likes and dislikes, the ratio of population to area, and whether machinery and other technologies and learnings can be applied—all are important factors in determining agricultural land uses.

Agricultural Patterns Based on Resource Potentials. In total, the impact of the various resource bases on agriculture has resulted in the evolution of nine rather distinct types of agricultural production patterns:

1. Livestock and crops—mixed cropping with livestock as the major role; usually found in middle latitudes.
2. Specialized higher-middle latitude cropping—includes most of the world's wheat lands.
3. Commercial mixed grains—chiefly corn (maize), wheat, oats, or rye with some livestock feeding on middle latitude farms; however, most grains are sold for cash.
4. Dairying—nearly always in middle latitudes with feed crops and pastures dominant.
5. Southern Europe and Coastal Mediterranean—intensive cropping on relatively small land units (usually under 25 acres) and including grains, fruits, nuts, and (with irrigation) off-season fruits and vegetables.
6. Reclamation cropping—middle and low latitude desert areas with aid of irrigation; includes cotton, alfalfa, and off-season fruits and vegetables.

7. Plantation/commercial tropical cropping—relatively large tracts of land in low latitudes producing essentially one crop (e.g., rubber, bananas, etc.).

8. Family or communal tropical cropping—usually nonintensive agriculture with small land units, variety of crops prevalent, and de-emphasis of livestock.

9. Oriental cropping—perhaps the most intensive form of cropping; small land units, often in separate land parcels (except certain Chinese communes); produces wide variety of food crops; multiple cropping of rice is most common, followed by a wide choice of vegetables; only livestock are chickens and pigs, although interest in beef cattle is strong in more affluent areas of Japan.

Although the chief agricultural commodities are legend and myriad in form and practice, there are certain significant generalizations that can be drawn about the more important/valuable crops:

1. There are more acres in wheat than any other crop.
2. More people subsist on rice than any other crop.
3. Corn gives the greatest yield by value per acre.
4. Potatoes give the greatest yield by weight per acre.
5. Beans and peas are grown by nearly all peoples.
6. Sugar cane, coconuts, and bananas are the staples of the tropics and (after transportation) are important sources of foods and industrial products throughout the world.

In contrast to Malthusian theory, the world has not yet developed any appreciable shortage of arable land; rather, local shortages result chiefly from marketing and from educational and economic difficulties, along with problems related to the application of scientific knowledge and developing technologies. While nature (temperature, moisture, topography, and soil characteristics) may set the outer limits on arability of land, culture is still the major determinant of whether the land is cultivated.

Grazing Resources

Immense areas of the United States, and of the world, are used primarily for the grazing of livestock. In terms of people employed, grazing is relatively minor; but in terms of extent, it is major. For the most part, grazing lands are those areas marginal or submarginal to croplands. Land capable of more intensive uses are—except where listed under a government-sponsored program to reduce production—used for growing crops. In fact, the dust bowls of interior United States or the drier margins of the Ukraine are results of pressures to crop marginal lands. Even so, grazing generally represents a more intensive use of the lands than do forests. Thus, grazing is usually residual to cropping, and forests are usually residual to both.

Historically, grazing lands have been the domain of nomad or pioneer settlers. Where land had not been legally appropriated, herds and flocks were grazed. Eventually, most grazing lands came under some form of legal control (recently, in the 1940s and 1950s, this took place even in the Kirghiz and Kazakh areas of the U.S.S.R.). The tendency has been for grazing areas to be held in ever larger consolidations. For example, the King Ranch in Texas has over 1 million acres; some of the new Sovkotzki, or State farms, in the U.S.S.R. exceed several millions of acres; and the Outback areas of Australia have evolved under huge land holdings. Early overgrazing seemingly "mined" the soil of these areas.

Today, however, given the residual nature of their relatively poor soils, marginal climates, and rough terrain, there is considerable evidence that range operators have mastered techniques for measuring livestock capacities of their lands, and most of these lands are being managed with at least some view toward the future. Still, pressures are being applied constantly to increase production—especially in the more industrialized nations—and, consequently, damage can be (and in many cases is) severe. This is particularly true on leased lands if they are not adequately controlled. Even so, this damage is slight when compared with the inroads that cropping has made on what probably should be land devoted to grazing. The seeds of a return to dustbowl days exist in such states as Oklahoma and Kansas, where vast areas are used for growing wheat rather than "native" grasses.

The same situation is indicated for the lands of the Emba Basin and other steppe areas recently put under the plow in the U.S.S.R. The red spring rains in Romania and the Ukrainian dust storms in August suggest that the recently opened State farms located throughout vast areas where annual rainfall totals nine inches may be hazardous and of doubtful wisdom in the long run. Recurring dry cycles in the African Sudan, in certain sections of Brazil, and in other similar marginal areas suggest that the problem is worldwide in scope and, with the destruction of productive lands and widespread dust storms, of universal interest and concern.

In addition to possible dust-related problems, grazing lands are of concern in watershed management. As major contributors of stream sediment and sudden runoff waters, grazing lands influence entire drainage systems even out of proportion to area and amount of precipitation received.

In summary, these are the resource-development problems of grazing lands. For the most part, no really overriding policy issues exist in the cases mentioned under cropland uses and, as we shall see, under forest, urban recreation, and reclamation land uses. There is widespread general concern that productivity be maintained and the land not abused, but there are no very significant or pressing issues. The lack of concern about grazing lands, as compared with forestry, for example, is evident in the contrast between the relatively small tracts of so-called virgin prairies that have been set aside for preservation and study, and the vast public and private areas set aside in forests.

Forests

Mostly residual to the cropping and grazing resources discussed earlier in this chapter, forest resource mobilization is the arena in which *timber empires* and *industrial empires* meet. It is also the arena in which man has fought out some of the evolving principles of land use within the body politic; and it is where the forces of conservation and preservation have made their stand. Thus, forests are treated here in detail otherwise seemingly out of proportion to their empirical importance.

Domestically, the outgrowth of this meeting of empires in the United States is the forest-products industry, the fourth most important industry in the nation's economy. The significance of basic forest resources in the United States may be understood better when translated into terms of employment. More than 3 million workers in many parts of the United States depend on forest resources as the main basis upon which manufacturing values are added. Timber processing, manufacture of wood products, construction, and transportation and marketing of wood products in recent years have accounted for more than $25 billion, or approximately 5 percent annually of the nation's gross national product.[2]

Present patterns of forest resource mobilization in the United States have, for the most part, evolved since World War II. Following the war, a new approach to forest products manufacturing began to take form through vertical and horizontal integration, mergers, and cooperative agreements among lumbering firms, lumber mills, and wood processors. There is today a still-expanding pattern of manufacturing that includes the harvesting of timber, the acquiring of prime timberlands upon which these raw materials grow, and the processing of the harvested wood into pulp, paper, chemicals (with production established to make use of wood waste), plywoods, hardboards, and flake-board—all to the nearly total use of each tree harvested.

Prior to the emergence of the present-day gigantic firms that are

---

[2] U.S. Department of Agriculture, *Forest Service,* Forest Resource Report No. 17, February, 1965, p. iii.

mobilizing the nation's forest resources, the U.S. Forest Service was the primary preservation and conservation organization in the nation. Indeed, the struggle between preservation and conservation is still timely and, in many aspects, is centered on the nation's timbered lands.

Forest Conservation v. Preservation. Following an early period when the tradition of the land was based upon an abundant forest resource, the pendulum of public attitudes concerning forests swung, among much of the nation's population, from exploitation and abuse toward preservation,[3] rather than toward conservation (or what proponents of conservation consider wise use).[4]

To understand this shift in the pendulum's swing, one only has to picture the great early-day surge of peoples across the prairies and grasslands, the settlement of great cities along the rivers, the construction of connecting transportation lines (primarily rail) based largely upon the cutting of pine forests in the Great Lakes region, and, indeed, the entire settlement of a nation based upon timber. With the passing of the frontier period, however, attitudes toward the forest resource shifted. It soon became clear that the timberlands were not without limit and in fact were being rapidly reduced by policies of "cut out and get out."

The destruction left behind by such policies, in turn, set off new forces. Initially, the reaction produced movements toward the designation of national parks and (more recently) wilderness areas on the one hand and national forests on the other. A comparison of national parks (and wilderness areas) with national forests depicts the difference between preservation and conservation. National parks and wilderness areas are usually based on natural or historical sites and, wherever possible, are *preserved* in their original state. Some 7 million acres of forest lands presently in national parks are not logged, nor is hunting allowed, and other uses are strictly regulated. Additional acreages are similarly controlled in the nation's wilderness areas.

In contrast, the national forests are kept in perpetual crops of timber,

---

[3] Preservation, in the context of this chapter, is defined as "to keep intact."

[4] In this chapter the terms *conservation* and *wise use* are synonymous. The point made in Chapter Two, that resources *are not*—they *become,* and that there is no such thing as a *natural* resource is illustrated again in regard to the timberlands of North America. For the early European explorers and to settlers of the Atlantic coast, the overpowering, awesome, unbroken canopy of virgin forests shaped the course of United States history. And, enigmatically, as awesome and mysterious a barrier as forests were to the early settlers, still they found that they could habitate only forest areas. Indeed, the early settlers could destroy the forest and clear land for agriculture more easily than they could break up the heavy sod of virgin grasslands or irrigate the desert. Also, the early settlers used timber for fuel, fortifications, housing, transportation, weapons, and tools. They found in the forests such potential food sources as maple syrup, nuts, edible roots, dyes, and tanning materials.

and specified grazing and mining also are allowed. Particularly in the western states, the latter two uses of timberlands are important adjuncts of the national forest, or *conservation,* concept. Sportsmen such as hunters, fishermen, campers, and hikers are welcome not only in the national forests, but also in the forests of most "conservation-minded" timber firms and individuals.

In national forests, logging usually is done by private companies under the supervision of government foresters; techniques of producing perpetual crops of timber are followed. But national forests are not the only areas in which perpetual forestry techniques are practiced. For example, as early as 1900, one of the nation's leading timber companies made a basic decision that, wherever possible, it would retain its land base after the harvest of timber. This, in itself, was a departure from earlier company policies of "cut out and get out." [5]

To understand further the conflicting reasoning behind the views of preservationists, as opposed to the beliefs of conservationists, one might do well to remember that those who destroyed the forests in the early days of this country were cheered on and even recognized as progressives—the settlers of this rugged wilderness. And, as Stewart L. Udall points out in his book *The Quiet Crisis,* it was not until after 1800 that cities clamored for lumber in wholesale lots and enterprisers learned to organize men and machines to produce it. Then came the circular saw and the steam mill. Shortly afterward, the wood-pulp process for making paper was invented, and there began a frantic wood rush that stripped most U.S. forests and helped puncture the myth of superabundance. [6] Thus, there was originally widespread and general support for those who cut timber and prepared the land for others who would later come and try to farm it.

In this era of construction, lumbering activities made the forest industry the nation's largest producer. The basic forest resources were readily available, immigrant labor was low in cost, and little capital was needed to outfit a mill and begin production. Timber cutting began on the East Coast and swept across the nation, literally cutting off and removing the white pine climax vegetation of such states as Wisconsin, Michigan, and much of Minnesota. Forests were considered unlimited; there was enough wood for thousands of years; so, it was thought, why not cut and—as a sort of by-product—make room for others to come and farm the land after you got out? Not only were the timbermen responsible for devastation of forests, but the farmers who followed added to the damage. To clear the

---

[5] Harry E. Morgan, Jr., "The High Yield Forest" (Address delivered at the Shareholders' Annual Meeting of the Weyerhaeuser Timber Co., Tacoma, Wash., April 13, 1967), p. 8.

[6] Stewart L. Udall, *The Quiet Crisis* (New York: Holt, Rinehart and Winston, 1963), p. 55.

land further, they set huge fires, which, in turn, swept away and destroyed (along with the soil resource) additional thousands and thousands of acres of excellent virgin timberland.

It was an era of either free or extremely cheap land—land that could be had almost for the asking. But even if it had to be purchased, the cost was a small consideration for the return that could be realized in selling the necessary wood and timber to build the nation's cities and railroads. Furthermore, in this era of poor survey knowledge, often when private lands were cut, the surrounding lands—both private and public—also were swept up and stripped of their forests. Still, the myth prevailed that the forest resource was inexhaustible.

It was against the background of this widespread destruction that the preservationist-conservationist (the difference between the two terms had not been clearly spelled out or widely accepted), such as John Muir,[7] Frederick Law Olmsted,[8] and others, began to heed and to advocate adoption of certain suggestions of still earlier naturalists such as Emerson [9] and Thoreau,[10] who by this time had become widely read and recognized. Although these earlier naturalists had not advocated public action regarding forests, they at least temporarily prevented the destruction of small remnants of the nation's natural timbered landscape.

An early sign that conservation or preservation measures would some day become a way of life in the United States was the bill signed by President Lincoln in 1864 establishing the Yosemite area as a reserve; later

---

[7] John Muir, A.M., LL.O. (1838–1914), born in Scotland, became internationally famous as an explorer and naturalist, became especially well-known for his knowledge of, and visionary plans for, continental United States. His numerous publications and editorial responsibilities dealt chiefly with background studies for national park proposals. He was one of the outstanding early conservationists, with the period of his greatest influence extending from the later decades of the nineteenth century through the early years of the twentieth; his heritage, however, has lasted beyond his death.

[8] Frederick Law Olmsted (1822–1903) was a powerful motivating force in the emergence of an organized conservation movement during President Theodore Roosevelt's administration. Olmsted was a landscape architect, and owing to his influential position as Superintendent of New York's Central Park as well as to his planning of park systems in Chicago, Buffalo, Boston, and the grounds of the National Capitol at Washington, he was instrumental in securing the Yosemite Valley as a national reservation. Later Yosemite was to become a national park.

[9] Ralph Waldo Emerson (1803–1882) assisted, through his essays and poetry, in the establishment of new, broadened values for physical resources. Although he died in 1882, his contributions, which led to a conservationist movement, were made prior to 1865.

[10] Henry David Thoreau (1817–1862), a contemporary of Emerson, became a leader in the transcendentalist movement of the middle 1800s and devoted much of his time and talent to writing an appreciation of nature. His literary impact did much to develop attitudes that regarded bucolic settings as a resource worthy of being "set aside" for the sheer benefit and enjoyment of the areas themselves.

it was ceded to California as the projected first national park of the country, although the first national park to be established as such by Congress was Yellowstone National Park, now in the state of Wyoming.

Thus, by the turn of the century, with some 40 years' experience behind it, the conservationist-preservationist movement had established itself as a force to be reckoned with on the American scene. Through the understanding leadership of President Theodore Roosevelt and such naturalists as Muir and preservationist-conservationist Governor Gifford Pinchot of Pennsylvania, the movement was well established.[11] Also, by this time some of the true costs of forest destruction were being comprehended. Not only was there an immediate impact due to an inadequate supply of lumber, but there was also an awareness of the less direct—although perhaps even more serious—long-range impacts upon soil and water storage. Thus, the prospect of continued forest destruction was especially ominous in the eyes of those who foresaw the intensity of these two dangers. And, to this date, the struggle over whether to preserve and/or conserve domestic forest resources has not yet been resolved.

Today the commercial forestry-lumbering industries are practicing what they define as conservation, which is the wise use of the forest lands; but there are still those who advocate the setting aside of preservation lands, as typified by various wilderness area proposals placed before Congress.[12] The problem today is a race to preserve what little wilderness remains against the insatiable appetite of a burgeoning population that demands more space—space for living and space for basic resources with which to satisfy human wants and needs. Indeed, Stewart Udall has pointed out that the nation has less than three decades in which to establish wilderness areas.[13]

Thus, it is against this background of urgency that U.S. commercial forest interests must currently garner the necessary timberlands to meet demands for their services and products, and, at the same time endeavor to harness the forest resource to the satisfaction of the citizenry. Striving toward this dual goal, modern-day, forest-related industries are sharing their stewardship of the land by allowing their forest acres to be used for recreation, by cooperating in watershed development and water runoff control, and by developing and practicing perpetual forestry techniques. However, in light of long-range commitments being made on the one hand

---

[11] U.S. Department of Agriculture, *Forest Service,* Forest Resource Report No. 17, February, 1965, p. 118.

[12] The Wilderness Act (Senate Bill 4, First Session 90th Congress, January 14, 1963—Interior and Insular Affairs) established a national policy for preserving the remains of wilderness resources. The Act established the National Wilderness Preservation System made up of areas of primeval America that are still wilderness and capable of being kept that way without interference with other purposes now being served by such lands.

[13] Udall, op. cit., p. 181.

by Congress and state legislatures, and on the other by the private forest empire, there is no prospect that the contest between preservationists and conservationists will end in the near future. Indeed, in a country as rich as the United States, perhaps the struggle should go on and there should always be maintained both preservation tracts and conservation forests.

Today's Potential Forest Timber Resources. Forest resources of the United States still occupy some 760 million acres, or nearly one-third of the 2.3 billion acres of land in the 50 states of the Union. In turn, two-thirds of the forested area (some 500 million acres) is defined as commercial forest land, which means that it is suitable and available for the growing of continuous crops of saw logs or other industrial timber products. The remaining one-third is noncommercial. This latter area is so classed either because of low productivity or inaccessibility or because it has been set aside for public use, such as reservations for recreation.

Of some 900 species of trees in the United States, fewer than 100 are used to produce commercial timber. In turn, probably more than 90 percent of all United States timber comes from some 30 species found in the nation's six major forest areas as classified by the U.S. Forest Service. In terms of their extent, these six areas are (1) central hardwood forests, (2) southern forests, (3) Rocky Mountain forests, (4) northern forests, (5) Pacific coast forests, and (6) tropical forests.

Forest Areas Continue to Increase. As we have already seen, since the early settlement of this country there has been an almost continuous encroachment of farms, cities, highways, and other cultural features upon the forest lands. However, since the middle 1930s there has been an abandonment of crop land—particularly in the South and in certain areas of the central hardwood forests—resulting in a reversion to timber growing that has more than offset losses of forest lands in other areas.[14] Only in the eastern Gulf states have forest areas declined in a relative sense, mostly as a result of the conversion of forest areas to pasture. For example, in areas throughout much of Alabama, Mississippi, and Tennessee, commercial forest lands increased as much as 8 percent in the 10-year period from 1953 to 1963, reflecting sweeping changes in the agricultural economy of those areas.[15] For the most part, these lands are former croplands—in many cases worn out or else placed in forests under the soil-bank program [16]—that

---

[14] Forest Resource Report, op. cit., p. 77.

[15] Ibid., p. 77.

[16] The Soil Conservation and Domestic Allotment Act of 1935 (as amended) provides that the Secretary of Agriculture shall expand, utilize, and develop a soil-building program; and the Soil Bank Act of 1956 directs the Secretary of Agriculture to formulate and carry out an acreage reserve program to compensate would-be producers of certain crops (wheat, cotton, corn, and rice) for reducing their acreages of these commodities below their farm acreage allotments as set under the Agricultural Adjustment Act of 1938.

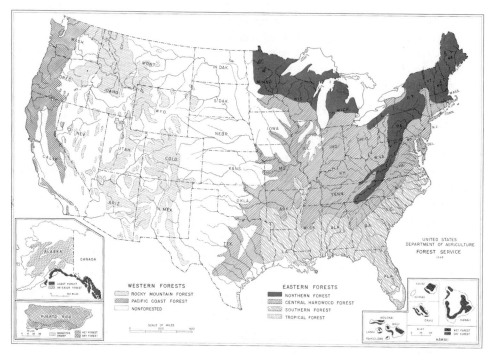

FIGURE 15. Western and Eastern forests. Courtesy U. S. Department of Agriculture, Forest Service, 1948.

must be restocked artificially, or slowly by nature, before timber crops can be mobilized at some future date.

In contrast, most of the timberlands lost have been of relatively high growing capabilities, and quite often the timber formerly standing on such land was not utilized when cut. Most of these areas have been taken over for highways, industrial plants, urbanization, recreation centers, and other land uses that deny opportunities for tree growth.

Thus, since 1900 the interrelations between forestry science and technology have immensely altered man's exploitation patterns of the forests. As noted, the acceleration of wasteful practices regarding U.S. forests has been more than offset by progress in the restoration and upgrading of commercial forest areas, including farm lot forests.[17] A reliable picture of the net effects of these changes is just now becoming available. The changes have done much to strengthen the conservationist's hand—at least to prevent indiscriminate inroads by preservation areas into his present holdings. That these signs of "progress" are timely is emphasized by the recognition

---

[17] Forest Resource Report, op. cit., p. 2.

that machine-powered techniques of mobilizing forest resources have underscored the interdependence of the wood-product supplier and the consumer.

Mobilization of Forest Resources. The United States, with about 7 percent of the world's forest resources, is both the greatest producer and the largest consumer of wood and wood products. This country produces more than 30 percent and uses nearly 40 percent of the world's total industrial forest resource output. Two hundred years after the Revolutionary War, forests still occupy one-third of the nation's land. And, as noted earlier, two-thirds of this forest area, or 509 million acres, is defined as commercial forest land; that is, it is suitable and available for producing continuous crops of saw logs or other timber products for industrial uses.[18]

Work continues toward the development of new, faster-growing trees in almost all sections of the country. This includes the development of seed orchards. One firm has developed Douglas fir seedlings through a seed orchard program selected from mature scions grafted on the young trees. The result is the production of young trees with more than twice the vigor of the average fir seedling, and cross-pollination effects of these "super trees" have been explored.[19] Genetic experimentation also is underway on the "big three" southern pines—short-leaf, long-leaf, and loblolly. Here, too, as with almost all of the nation's forest types, scion banks are being established and seed orchards developed.

In addition to today's forest technology, which calls for the selection of seeds from scions obtained from grafts to healthy root stock and for controlled genetic fertilization, seeds are camouflaged from their natural predators, and seedlings are protected. Standing forests, young and old, are now fertilized from the air—cutting as much as 10 to 15 years from the time needed for trees to reach marketable size—and the use of helicopters, aircraft, insecticides, and fire protection also enables forests today to produce more board feet than are cut on an annual basis. Moreover, forest lumbering equipment—essentially machinery—has been developed to make timber cutting more efficient. Heavy machinery means that larger-sized boles can be handled with less damage than formerly was possible, hydraulically operated saws can reach greater heights and make more efficient cuts, and other powerful machine units permit more roots to be grubbed from the soil so that, ordinarily, more of the entire tree is used than ever before.

Even the computer has been employed in this effort to utilize more efficiently the resources of the forests. For example, the computer now assists in allocating logs to the most profitable end-products, and this effort is being extended even to the product, itself, so that computer programs

---

[18] Ibid., pp. 75–77.
[19] The Georgia-Pacific Corporation, *Growth,* VIII, No. 1 (March, 1967), p. 5.

trim paper more economically and evaluate paper machine scheduling alternatives. The result is a significant cost saving through a reduction in the amount of trim and through the choice of an optimum size paper for cuts. Computers also are aiding management in its assigning of both the sizing of logs and the daily orders for specific operations.

Not only are computers used to program the processing equipment, orders, and inventories, but they also are employed to record the forest resource, itself, and to simulate forest growth and other natural activities. The advanced firms are recording forest activities as they occur and are analyzing them in on-line decision-making processes. They are developing rapid feedback on how forecasts work out, and this enables management to make value judgments based on updated facts far more rapidly than ever before. Forecasts, decades in advance, are more accurate, and this allows forest mobilization firms to synchronize their reforestation and forest purchase plans with the markets and to project these plans for decades into the future —a requirement that is essential in industries where the time-lag (for raw material production) may well be 30 to 40 years.

Although today's forest area in the 50 states has been reduced to some 30 to 35 percent of the nation's total area—primarily due to land clearing for farming, highway use, urban development, and other miscellaneous purposes—the new annual growth of timber actually exceeds the amount being cut. This is a development attained only since the mid-1960s. Prior to that time, the amount cut exceeded the amount added by growth.[20]

The reduction in forest area has not been uniform throughout the nation; it has taken place primarily in the eastern half of the country, where the present forest area approximates only one-half of the original amount. In the West, and particularly in Alaska, most originally forested areas still exist as sources of timber, although much of the area has been reduced in productivity. However, the area standing in forests is only one means of measuring scope and perhaps is not as important as the standing-board-footage measurement. The board footage has been reduced through the years by perhaps three-fourths. Here again there is a difference between areas; the eastern forests probably contain less than 15 percent of their original stands, while the West and Alaska still have perhaps as much as two-thirds to three-fourths of the original board footage.

With still other factors to be considered pertaining to timberlands, it might be timely at this point to emphasize that the only significance of such perusal lies in an effort to determine in what direction the nation is moving in the mobilization of its forest resources.

---

[20] Jim Breetveld, *Treasure of the Timberlands* (New York: Scholastic Book Services, 1967), p. 5. The National Wildlife Federation reported in 1971, again, that the timber growth rate was continuing to increase over the amount cut.

In this regard, a key factor is the general increase of hardwoods in board footage at a rate faster than they are being cut; but, in contrast, softwoods are being cut faster than growth is taking place.[21] In some areas—particularly in Great Lakes and eastern areas—almost all of the original softwoods have been removed. This is not entirely unfavorable, however, because younger trees in these areas have a much more rapid rate of growth than do some of the older stands that contain larger, more mature trees. The main drawback is the absence of large-sized timbers, so that forest resources for such items as poles or cut-lumber are definitely not as readily available as they were 60 or 70 years ago.[22] Nevertheless, total volume of wood is now greater at the end of each year and, for some forest product uses, the prospect of supply is definitely bright.

Much of the optimism regarding future total forest resources stems from the success of research efforts by larger forest-product firms. Indeed, a decline in the relative importance of public forests is of special interest today. Until the late 1950s, publicly owned forests, especially federal forests, accounted for more than 40 percent of the total board footage available. Now, however, the larger forest-product companies are adding to their lands and improving the existing stands at rates greater than those taking place in the public sector. Similarly, improvements are occurring in regard to higher-valued timbers and especially on the aforementioned heavily cut-over softwoods lands. Nevertheless, public forests remain a significant source of forest resources within the United States.

Especially important at this time are improved management techniques applied to the forests, both public and private. For many years the public sector performed much of the research and was far better financed than were the private sectors. In contrast, today there is no prior claim to the knowledge that makes intensively cultivated perpetual forests possible. Even smaller private forests often replant and gain rates of growth comparable to those which, in the past, have been attained only by the better-managed lands of large forest-product corporations and by the public forests.

Another factor that affects current forestry practices of both large and small enterprises is the fact that standing forests, on the average, are not profitable unless the operation is vast. In general, forests show growth rates of less than 3 percent annually; especially when compared with other

---

[21] Ibid., p. 17. Some regions are exceptions to this national pattern. George E. Kelly, vice president for the Southern Forest Institute, noted that the pulp and paper, lumber, and plywood industries planted 493 million seedlings during the 1970–71 planting season; almost all were softwoods, and the South's forests now have more trees growing than at any time in the past 30 to 35 years (*Northwest Arkansas Times,* November 24, 1971, p. 12).

[22] Ibid., p. 5.

investment opportunities, a standing tree, once it attains a merchantable size, represents a relatively low rate of growth for its owner. Consequently, there is a temptation to cut such trees and invest capital in more profitable undertakings. Thus, small-forest owners often succumb to inducements to sell their timberlands to large corporations or public forests. Further augmenting the reasons for disposing of their forest holdings are the many years that it takes before a profitable second cutting is possible. Such long intervals may exceed generations, and this, with the low return per year of investment, favors the development of forests by large corporations or by the public sector.

Forest Resource Based on Production. The forest, as it stands, is actually more than a single raw material. It is a group of closely related materials possessing many varied properties that are extremely versatile in their utility. Although trees are one of the most familiar of all raw materials, they seem to be less widely understood by the layman than are other basic resources. In general, the qualities that make wood attractive to man are many: wood is easily worked, is strong for its weight and an excellent insulator; it stores well, wears well, absorbs shock and vibration, and can be readily changed into different physical forms or chemical components. Thus, it is adaptable by man to meet a great variety of needs.

Although varying widely from species to species, wood is generally composed of carbon, hydrogen, and oxygen in specific proportions. It is approximately 50 percent cellulose, some 25 percent lignin, 20 percent hemicellulose, 5 to 10 percent water-soluble extractives, and a trace of ash. Many chemical applications of wood have resulted from industry's ability to separate the lignin and cellulose and transfer these materials into usable products. As a result of man's ability to utilize the derivatives of wood or portions of wood, the commercial forest mobilization industries are able to produce a wide variety of products.

Forest Resource Mobilization Outlook. The U.S. Forest Service, in a recent appraisal of trends in the nation's timber industry, studied and projected the outlook for timber supplies and demands to the year 2000. The information presented was designed to provide a basis for judgment as to whether timber resources in the United States would be adequate to support the demands of the anticipated national population levels in the decades ahead.

The principal highlights and conclusions of the study are paraphrased and summarized below; they are most significant in this consideration of forest resource mobilization.[23]

---

[23] Forest Resource Report, op. cit., p. 1.

1. Demands for timber products are projected to increase by 80 percent by the year 2000. To meet these projected demands for roundwood, the cut of saw timber in U.S. forests—after allowances for imports—is estimated to rise from 48.4 billion board feet in 1962 to 81 billion board feet in 2000. Projections for individual products show wide variations in prospective rates of growth and consumption. For example, the estimated demands for pulpwood and for plywood and veneer by the end of the century are 2.7 times the 1962 level of consumption, while the demands for lumber are projected to rise only about 43 percent during the same period. The use of fuel wood by 2000 is assumed to decline by a further 55 percent, even with the present emphasis on charcoal as a home commodity.

2. Continued major expansion of population and economic growth is anticipated. Population in these projections is assumed to rise from 187 million people in 1962 to 325 million people by 2000, a 74 percent increase. Gross National Product is assumed to increase 3.5 times in this period, per capita income nearly 100 percent, and total use of raw materials roughly 100 percent. (The study was made before the impact of present-day birth control techniques and with the announcement by the U.S. Bureau of Census that the actual population birth rate in the United States, in percentage, was at an all-time low in 1967 and continued low in subsequent years. What these will mean to this projection is conjectural at this point.) [24]

3. Continued technological improvements in production and marketing in the forest industries will be essential to achieve projected demands for timber. Since 1930, industrial timber products have represented a fairly constant 22.5 percent of all industrial raw materials consumed in the United States. Some wood products, notably lumber, have failed to hold their own in the mix of raw material used. But such displacement has been roughly offset by increased use of other industrial wood products such as container board, plywoods, flakeboard and hardwoods. The projected demands for wood products represent about 21 percent of the estimated total industrial raw materials that will be consumed by the year 2000. To keep pace with this production level, the timber mobilizing industries will be expected to continue to improve their technology and increase their efficiency of timbers harvested.

4. Imports of timber products will likely increase somewhat, but most timber required to supply future U.S. markets is expected to come from domestic forests. Imports of lumber, newsprint, and other forest products represent about 13 percent of the total roundwood consumed currently in U.S. markets for timber products. Imports make up about 11 percent of the total lumber, 19 percent of the pulp and paper products, and about half of the hardwood veneer and plywood used. (Here again, it should be pointed out that in the late 1960s, many large U.S. timber mobilizing firms turned more and more to forests overseas for specialized woods and for low-cost labor.

---

[24] See, for example, the St. Regis Paper Company, *Annual Report,* 1966, p. 20.

FIGURE 16. COMMERCIAL FORESTS IN THE UNITED STATES, BY TYPE OWNERSHIP AND SECTION, 1963

Type of Ownership	Total U.S. Area	Total U.S. Proportion	North	South	Rocky Mountains	Pacific Coast
	Thousand acres	Percent	Thousand acres	Thousand acres	Thousand acres	Thousand acres
PUBLIC						
Federal:						
National forest	96,804	19	10,265	10,476	43,398	32,665
Bureau of Land Management	5426	1	81	27	2076	3242
Bureau of Indian Affairs	6461	1	1198	251	2816	2196
Other Federal	4485	1	964	3308	31	182
Total Federal	113,176	22	12,508	14,062	48,321	38,285
State	20,844	4	12,751	2164	2340	3589
County and municipal	7848	2	6748	656	83	361
PRIVATE						
Forest industry						
Pulp and paper	35,022	7	10,797	21,614		2611
Lumber	26,113	5	2996	12,551	2535	8031
Other	5493	1	523	3257		1713
Total industry	66,628	13	14,316	37,422	2535	12,355
Farm	151,017	30	55,503	78,897	8769	7848
Miscellaneous private	149,332	29	69,963	67,868	3575	7926
All ownerships	**508,845**	**100**	**171,789**	**201,069**	**65,623**	**70,364**

Source: U.S., Department of Agriculture, *Timber Trends in the United States*, Forest Resource Report No. 17, February, 1965, **p. 102.**

FIGURE 17. PROPORTIONS OF COMMERCIAL FOREST AREA, INVENTORIES, GROWTH, AND CUT IN THE UNITED STATES, BY OWNERSHIP, IN PERCENTAGES

Ownership	Commercial forest area	Growing Stock			Sawtimber		
		Inventory	Growth	Cut	Inventory	Growth	Cut
National forest	19	37	14	18	46	16	22
Other public	9	10	8	7	10	8	8
Forest industry	13	15	20	26	16	22	30
Farm and miscellaneous	59	38	58	49	28	54	40
Total	100	100	100	100	100	100	100

Source: U.S., Department of Agriculture, *Timber Trends in the United States,* Forest Resource Report No. 17, February, 1965, p. 107.

171

Thus, it would not be surprising to find that the United States, by the year 2000, will be importing, in percentage, considerably more timber than this study was able to project when it was written.) [25]

5. Timber supply-demand relations in the United States have generally improved since World War II. Growth of both softwood and hardwood timber has steadily increased in that period as a result of increasingly effective forestry programs. Fire protection, in particular, has paved the way for extensive natural restocking of land, and there is currently a wave of young timber now reaching sufficient size to be counted in timber inventories. Planting, thinning, and other cultural work have contributed in smaller ways to the continuing buildup of forest stocks in nearly all of the designated U.S. commercial forest lands. In contrast to these favorable trends in timber volume, however, the quality of available timber supplies has continued to diminish. Cutting of industrial timber products in U.S. forests also has increased in recent years—but more slowly than growth. The total cut, including fuel wood, has declined slightly. As a result of these divergent trends, growth of saw timber in the East in 1962 exceeded the cut by a substantial margin—by 90 percent for softwoods and 60 percent for hardwoods. In the West, where most timber is still in old growth stands, supplies available for harvest continue to exceed the actual cut.

6. Prospective U.S. timber growth and inventories, with recent levels of forest management, appear sufficient to meet projected demands of the next two or three decades, if not in the latter years of this century. These total "supplies of growing stock" are expected to rise from about 17 billion cubic feet in 1962 to a peak of approximately 19 billion cubic feet around 1980. In terms of saw timber projected, supplies rise from about 67 billion board feet in 1962 to, roughly, 74 billion board feet in 1980. Significantly, in the beginning of the 1980s projected timber supplies are expected to decline in the light of recent levels of forest management, in contrast to a continuing rise in the projected cut. By 1990, projected supplies of saw timber approximately equal the projected cut. By 2000, projected supplies fall short of the projected cut by about 16 percent, or 13 billion board feet. (Here, again, the study was made before some of the fertilization and other reforestry techniques now available were fully worked out. Some of the new techniques, particularly the fertilization of forests from the air, may well reverse or postpone the date when expected timbers will no longer provide for the nation's markets.)

7. Declining timber quality represents a major problem for wood-using industries. The availability of different tree species, sizes, and grades is also a significant factor in appraising the nation's timber situation. Here, again, as we have noted, new types of products from smaller trees, such as flakeboard and hardboard, may also help to postpone the date when reduced quality means the end of domestic timber supplies. Nevertheless, further declines in tree size (and quality) can be expected if timber cut and growth

25 Ibid.

follow the projections of the Forest Service study of 1962. This is especially true in western stands, where similar marked declines in the proportion of cut from larger and more valuable trees are in prospect.

8. The timber supply outlook is relatively favorable for the pulp and paper sector, but not as encouraging for the lumber and plywood groups. For industries dependent primarily upon wood fiber, including, particularly, the pulp and paper sector, the outlook for timber supplies appears relatively favorable, even though further adjustments to smaller timber and greater use of hardwoods appear necessary. In recent years, this category has achieved an impressive increase in the use of hardwoods from 14 percent of the total pulpwood used in 1950 to 20 percent in 1962. Use of chips from sawmill and plywood plant residues has increased even more sharply, rising from 6 percent of the total pulpwood used in 1950 to 21 percent in 1962. Further adaptations of available timber supplies appear technically feasible in this sector. Similarly, the development of flakeboard and hardboard, by such firms as the Georgia-Pacific Corporation, augur well for postponement of the day when lumber and plywood companies will not be able to meet their market demands. It is particularly significant that within the lumber and plywood sectors, trends in timber size and quality point to rising costs of production and increased marketing problems, unless marked improvements in technology are achieved. The development of the above-mentioned types of board indicates that technology may well be able to breach the gap in forest resources for the lumber and plywood sectors; and it is particularly significant that, especially regarding the adequacy of raw materials, they do not depend upon the total inventory of fiber, but rather on the operable supply of wood of desirable quality and sufficient size and volume to permit low-cost processing and production of saleable products.

9. Projected timber demands to the year 2000 could be met with more intensive forest management and utilization. It is generally recognized that the nation's commercial forest lands can produce the needed timber resources for this country if the knowledge of forest management already realized can be applied. The number of technical forestry measures that could be applied today include timber stand improvement, planting or seeding of productive sites, selection of seed and scions, planting of desirable species, increasing fire protection, development of techniques for fighting insects and plant diseases, more complete utilization of timber in wood and manufacturing plants, acceleration of road construction programs for fire protection and for rendering forest areas more readily accessible for the application of management techniques, and research and development efforts to provide knowledge for a more efficient management of forest resources and mobilization in the decades ahead.

10. Forest industries depend on farm and miscellaneous ownership for more than one-half of their raw material requirements. Production of timber on lands owned by farmers and miscellaneous private owners is a key to the expansion of forest resources in the next 50 years. These ownerships, which include about 60 percent of the commercial forest land in the United States,

contain 40 percent of the current inventory of growing stock, and it will be necessary to establish forest management techniques before it is possible for these areas to contain their proper percentage of inventory as well as area.

11. The long-range outlook and the uncertainties of projections must be considered in formulating forest programs. Indications are that supplies of timber over the next two or three decades can support a substantial expansion of markets for products, although trends in timber quality represent an increasingly serious problem. Also, the climate and soil resources cover a sufficient area so that, if adequate forestry programs and management techniques are applied, the U.S. timber supply will continue to meet the needs and wants of the population.

Just what impact kenaf and comparable developments will have on future timber requirements remains to be seen. Paper can be manufactured from inexpensive kenaf, a fast-growing plant that looks like marijuana and that can be harvested annually instead of every 15 years, as is required for pine. Currently, only two factors obstruct development of kenaf in southern Florida (where climate is almost entirely frost-free): one is a shortage of seeds; the other is the fact that the kenaf plant is a host for the pink bollworm, which is a threat to cotton. Once these two problems can be solved, there seems little doubt that kenaf will be raised in quantities sufficient to alleviate paper shortages.

Urban Land

Much world population is already, or else fast becoming, urbanized. Probably 60 percent of the world's population already lives in cities, and there are virtually waves of people exchanging rural settings for urban patterns, whether by actual migration or simply by being overtaken by urbanization. The trend is worldwide. (Tokyo has about 10 percent of Japan's population; Europe is even more urbanized than is the United States; indeed, even in Latin America most of the population is concentrated in such major megapolises as Mexico City, Rio de Janeiro, and Buenos Aires.)

Urban land uses include a host of land-based activities, ranging from residential through commercial, industrial, and transportation—land to live on, land for streets and alleys, stores, parking, parks and government buildings, schools and churches, to name but a few. Some land is held in idleness by speculators, who are awaiting a propitious time and purpose before proceeding with its development. Many more cities, especially in the United States, annex vast territories so as to shape, chiefly through zoning restrictions, the patterns of urban settlement for decades ahead. Or they may annex land simply to protect a watershed, aquifer, or recreation area. In any event, it is clear that land will continue to be available for urban development for a long time because less than 1 percent of the total land area of the United States (Hawaii and Alaska included) is now occupied by cities. In a micro sense, it is becoming increasingly apparent that the present urbanized areas are in trouble because of the very high tactical, strategic, and intrinsic value of the land in relation to the general land mass. In fact, over 90 percent of the people of the United States live and work along, or at the focal points of, some 12 transportation routeways (see Figure 18). The critical nature of land along the routeways is well illustrated by the fact that industrial/commercial holdings occupy and stretch for literally hundreds of miles. For example, riparian land along the navigable rivers and streams—even hundreds of miles upstream and downstream from major terminal cities—already is held either for predetermined purposes or by land speculators who are waiting for values and pressure of land needs to match their expectations.

Indeed, along some stretches of routeways, riparian land is no longer available, e.g., between Baton Rouge and New Orleans, along the Rhine, Upper Ohio, etc. In addition, the land needs of a city depend on its history of development, its purpose, and its size. Some cities crowd upwards of 90,000 people per square mile, as is the case with some sections of New

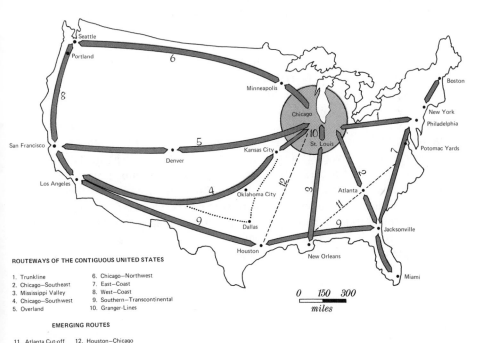

ROUTEWAYS OF THE CONTIGUOUS UNITED STATES

1. Trunkline
2. Chicago—Southeast
3. Mississippi Valley
4. Chicago—Southwest
5. Overland
6. Chicago—Northwest
7. East—Coast
8. West—Coast
9. Southern—Transcontinental
10. Granger-Lines

EMERGING ROUTES

11. Atlanta Cut-off   12. Houston—Chicago

•••••Dallas Distortion

0   150   300
miles

FIGURE 18. Routeways of the contiguous United States.

York City and Chicago; other cities, such as Houston, will average fewer than 1500 people per square mile. New York and Chicago developed before the automobile; Houston's growth has been entirely automobile-oriented. Also, the first two are older cities; Houston's growth is more recent; historically, as cities grow, the more intensive use develops near the core. Similarly, rectangular or circular patterns tend to produce heavier densities than do strip or radiating urban conglomerations.

In terms of size, most older cities of a million or more population will have densities ranging from 9000 to 14,000 persons per square mile. The density of smaller cities will range downward to averages of fewer than 4000—with some automobile-oriented cities such as Oklahoma City and Wichita having fewer than 1500 persons per square mile. The Chicago Transit Authority feels that no market for mass transit exists where densities of fewer than 9000 people per square mile exist.[26] It would seem, then, that far more intensive use can be made of such cities as Houston [27] and even New York.[28] This factor, when combined with a temporary decline in population growth, suggests that the pressures on urban land use are more related to individual and social values than to the amount and quality of land per se. In turn, the significance of this observation is the implication that, if urban problems are anticipated with understanding, their solution is not a function of lack of space but of the priorities and expectations that man has placed on a particular piece of real estate.

Admittedly, many unknown factors in the trends of U.S. population growth need to be revealed before definitive answers on land/space needs can be determined. What of family size? After the current surge of child-bearing ages passes, what of population trends? Will there be fewer households tomorrow because of changing social patterns? Will people in new lifestyles and patterns prefer the urban core or the fringe? Will a zero population growth level be attained—or even approximated? Even so, unless immigration is severely curtailed, young population increments will be continually added to the urban areas, swelling the numbers in succeeding generations; and, as immigrants take up residence in cities and their numbers continue to be augmented, there seems little chance that urban population growth rates will ever stand still or decline. Even though ample land/space is indicated for continued urban developments, it is a fact that approximately one-third of all urban development "covers over" productive

---

[26] *Chicago Area Transportation Study,* III, Chicago, State of Illinois, 1959–63, p. 14.

[27] Charles G. Burck, "The Good Life in a New Corporate Capital," *Fortune,* February, 1971, p. 92.

[28] Eleanore Carruth, "New York Hangs Out the For Rent Sign," *Fortune,* February, 1971, p. 86.

soils or destroys some of the more beautiful sites. For these considerations, perhaps planners and developers need to substitute mobility for place. That is, they might put urban developments in poorer agricultural areas or in less scenic locations, and then landscape. Or, by using mass transit, they might connect noncontiguous urban areas; in this manner, ravines, poor soil areas, and other less promising productive areas can be used for urban purposes, thereby enhancing a nation's total land/space potential. Clearly, a need to substitute mobility for place will become more acute as certain established areas become either "polluted," "taxed," or "extracted" out of production; then it might well become necessary to substitute transportation for space to provide time and place utility.

Changes in Urban Land Use. Not only does the amount of land required for an urban center vary with the history or stage of development, but more land and perhaps continuing land requirements are also indicated. There promises to be more cities in the future with more and more people living in ever-larger urban conglomerations. To date, the more acute problems have been centered in the core city, or related to it, and the suburbs— made possible by, and at the same time a product of, automobile affluence and mobility—have provided succor and release. In the suburbs, more land has been available for residential, industrial, and commercial uses. Shopping centers with what seemed at the time adequate parking space were developed. Even so, many of the ills and problems of the core city are now emerging in the suburbs. Even with the use of more land per capita, the increased dependence on the automobile—which in turn has produced a need of more land for broader streets, parking spaces, two- and three-car garages and driveways—has in effect produced crowded neighborhoods and a high degree of personal infringement. On many streets, service stations have been located on corner lots, and intervening large residential units have been converted into multiple apartment units, offices, or service centers so that so-called commercial strips have resulted. With time, economic pressures build, and the properties on either side of existing commercial strips gradually change in intensity.

Other suburban problem areas relate to shifts in transportation patterns. For example, in the suburbs of Chicago, the electric commuter trains and the Chicago, Aurora and Elgin, North Shore, and South Shore electric interurban systems—all important factors in shaping the pattern of suburban development—no longer exist, and this has effectively isolated suburbs so that their citizens seldom relate to the central city for either employment or recreation. Even the major transportation focal point, O'Hare Airfield, has moved to the suburbs. The long-range effect has been to produce suburb core center problems with both commercial and residential decay. Thus, the problems of the core city are only repeated many times throughout the older suburbs.[29]

Politics of Urban Blight. Further compounding the land-use problems of urban areas are the political patterns that have evolved. Fragmented and/or overlapping political units which duplicate jobs, functions, and controls—often with varying standards and goals—only confuse matters and stymie or neutralize progress. Vested interests and differing capacities to raise funds combine to produce great differences in juxtaposition. In turn, these heighten misunderstandings and ineffectiveness in man's dealing with land problems. For, as is the case with core urban land, individual values, goals, and wants that depend on land uses can be attained only through some form of public or quasi-public action. This implies a body politic that has been excessively fractured and weighted down with layers of governing bodies, each with varying constituencies or purposes. Significantly, the total image suggests that land-use progress depends upon, or must await, progress in government effectiveness.

Recreation Land

Recreation land is plentiful, yet scarce. The meaning of the term *recreation land* varies from person to person. For some, it means scenery, undisturbed nature, wildlife preserves, picnicking, hiking, camping, or hunting. For others, it means golf, sports contests, gunnery ranges, tennis courts, swimming pools, art work and art shows, libraries, or historical sites. Whatever the form, land is required. Without this space to "get off the daily merry-go-round," human physical and mental health must suffer. Opportunities for physical conditioning—a chance to relax, to escape claustrophobia, to change pace, to alter perspective, or to gain succor from other sources of stress—are vital to individual health and social well-being. Although the matter is here too briefly stated, for all of these reasons land for recreation is critical now, and it promises to become even more critical and, therefore, more highly valued in the future.

Recreation lands may be either private or public. Also, they may be classed according to types of use: (1) activity bases (parks, ball fields, golf courses, swimming pools), (2) topography/biological (grade, picturesque or unique physical features such as gorge, mountain, lake, dunes, beach area, vegetation, or fauna), (3) combined use (state parks with

---

[29] In the Chicago area, Maywood, Evanston, and Waukegan illustrate the point. In Los Angeles, too, early suburbs were aligned with Southern Pacific and other tracks—long abandoned, but nevertheless contributing to the many urban cores of that metropolitan complex.

scenery, golf courses, airfields, man-made lakes for fishing, boating, water skiing). In addition, recreation areas may be classed according to distance from populated centers, whether measured in miles, time, or cost. Today, in the public sector, the greatest need is for more combined-use facilities close to metropolitan areas. If located within a one- or two-hour drive, supposedly such recreation facilities could be reached by more people and could serve better in terms of frequency of use—provided that traffic congestion does not prevent widely based participation.

Subject to cyclical, peak-period use, often the roads, parking areas, services, and other attendant infrastructures are overbuilt in terms of average needs. Thus, they are both space-using and costly, compounding land demands. Yet, it is this very mobility, combined with more leisure time, higher income, and the press of population, that has created the need/demand for such recreational areas.

As a result of the foregoing, one of the prime needs, attainable in the United States chiefly through political action, is at least statewide zoning (if not interstate zoning) so that suitable areas may be designated for future recreational development—at such time as sufficient demand exists or sufficient funds warrant development.

Similarly, on the *international* scale, private investors such as financially potent international airline and international hotel chains are laying claim to, and building major edifices on, attractive physical sites throughout the world. This activity, comparable to the lodges which U.S. railroads earlier constructed in or close to national parks or scenic areas,[30] has now been extended to even the most remote islands of Oceania.[31] In the long-range view, it is not too difficult nor too imaginative to see the desirability of man's setting aside, for public use, certain beach areas, vistas, or waterbodies. Clearly, man is not yet ready to tackle problems of international zoning, but the day is not too far away when he will attempt this complex task.

That millions of visitors annually crowd into even such remote national parks as Yellowstone or such man-made recreational areas as Lake Texoma is evidence of both the acceptance of, and the pressures for, additional recreation areas. How much land will be needed? To date, no adequate techniques or measurements have been devised to foretell how much recreational land will be needed. Thus, until meaningful correlations and inferences can be drawn from population, income, leisure time, educational levels, and time/distance cost factors, perhaps it is better to err

---

[30] For example, Yellowstone National Park; Banff and Lake Louise in Canada; and French Licks, Indiana, to name but a few.

[31] Both Continental and American Airlines have been active in building hotels on South Pacific islands as "destinations" for air travelers.

on the high side and zone, or designate, more land than can reasonably be developed—even at the cost of taking such land off tax rolls.

Even more difficult to resolve are such recreation-related problems as ultimate land-use. For example, should a river valley be maintained, or should the valley be dammed and the waters of the stream impounded to form a lake? [32] Or should pipelines, freeways, or fully protected rail lines be granted rights of eminent domain even if the "ecological balance" is broken as a result of their construction? [33] Currently, no satisfactory technical or political system has been devised to aid in rendering wise decisions on priorities. Toward this end, some hope that the emergence of a Department of Natural Resources at the federal level will provide the organization, research, and requisite allocation of funds with which to progress toward more satisfactory solutions to recreational land-use problems. At the same time, and at the opposite end of the classification, cities, towns, counties, and states must consider the wisdom of their creating recreational land-use projects as integral to better urban development and including public and quasi-public recreational projects as adjuncts to the development of mass transit systems. For example, parks, golf courses, trails, and other similar activity facilities could be made integral to a mass transit line, connecting recreationally oriented, traffic-generating points on the line.[34]

In the meantime, it is vividly clear that policies must be evolved that will ensure the eventual development of meaningful recreational land-use ratios to other land uses.

SITE OR LAND, SPACE, AND INFRASTRUCTURE

Land as space and the associated spatial relations of land—in contrast to land as a factor of production per se—are some of the key indicators of this resource. Facets of spatial or area resources are: (1) site, (2) location and spatial relations, (3) size, shape, and depth of land area, and (4) infrastructures.

The term *site* refers to a *specific* parcel of land occupied, or to be occupied, by a specific structure (or group of structures) ranging from a building or farm to an industrial complex, a military base, a farming region, or community/urban development. In turn, the use or suitability of

---

[32] Current debates concern the Snake River of Idaho, Oregon, and Washington; the Illinois and White River Valleys of Arkansas, etc.

[33] The proposed Prudhoe Bay–to–Anchorage pipeline, as contested by the Sierra Club, is an example approved by the Congress in 1973.

[34] Would-be users could conceivably rent electric carts or other sports equipment at certain stations located near golf courses, tennis courts, riding stables, and hiking trails.

a site includes the shape of an area, grade, base material, soil/groundwater, drainage, and such infrastructures as exist or are available to the site (including all utilities, lighting, roads, parking, and walkways).

A plant site may be rectangular, square, or irregular in pattern. In any case, the layout or arrangement of production lines, terminals, docks, storage, ingress, egress, and attendant office space will be governed or even limited accordingly. Similarly, some plants or crops (in farming) require level land that may or may not be available. Level land is generously available for industrial purposes on the Texas Gulf Coastal Plain but is definitely limited in the valley and ridge country of West Virginia. The kind, depth, structural strength, and physical and chemical properties of base materials and soils often will set the value of a site. Firm foundations might easily be reached in New York or Chicago, where rock or glacial gravels are encountered. In contrast, on the underlying soft clays of the Norfolk, Virginia, area, foundations are costly and—for large buildings or heavy machinery—are even impossible to develop. In the glacial gravels of Wisconsin, foundation beds are relatively easy to establish, in contrast to the occasional muck soils encountered in the same state, or to the faulting, fine clays of southeastern Arkansas.

Groundwater and drainage, too, are forces to be reckoned with in site development. Water purity, temperature, mineral content, dependability of sources, and drainage possibilities are all important considerations. Often the drainage features for an airport, plant, or highway interchange are the most difficult and costly aspects of development when a land resource is being developed.

Finally, the availability or projected costs of arranging for the necessary infrastructures may determine the real resource potential of a particular site—assuming that it otherwise has a suitable location or desired spatial relation to other features or factors.

LOCATION AND SPATIAL RELATIONS

Perhaps the most significant aspect of land resources is their relation to other areas and other things. Distance or proximity to and from mines, fields, forests, or markets is important, and distance from friend or foe geographically affects international trade, international politics, and international security. Nor are these distance factors static. Formerly isolated areas, as such, are no longer isolated with the advent of air travel; and even certain areas that were opened as stepping-stone airports [35] for the early

---

[35] Trinidad, Greenland, Nova Scotia, Iceland, and Dakar became important airfield sites during World War II; for the most part, the facilities developed then have now been either retired or placed on standby for emergency bases.

world air routes are now back in isolation with the advent of the longer-range and faster jets.

Similarly, England's position in the center of the so-called Land Hemisphere gave it an early advantage in terms of the sailing vessel. Later, faster and larger vessels reduced the relative advantage of location for that country.

On a different scale, transportation developments almost always produce counteradvantages and disadvantages. For example, an interstate highway separates and isolates as well as unites. An interstate highway cuts counties in two and, for those who do not own or control land at points of access to such highways, it means a relative disadvantage in terms of micro scales of mobility.

New major regional airports, such as the Dallas–Fort Worth Regional Airport, or O'Hare Airfield at Chicago, favor interests with nearby facilities. And—because of the use of seemingly ever-larger equipment—smaller air terminals will lose even existing services when people or freight move by highway to the supersonic airport of tomorrow. Another illustration of the dynamics of spatial relations is the idle facilities of many formerly busy railroad towns and river ports.

For many communities, and even for states, it has become a full-time job of citizens to organize, scheme, struggle, and even fight to maintain the relative advantage of their city's or state's spatial relations. In this regard, Dallas exemplifies what can be done with an out-of-the-way location. Dallas exists on man-made facilities and, at the same time, exists even in spite of them. Fort Worth is an older city and has more radiating rail and highway routes; yet Dallas's Love Field early attracted more flights and certified routeways. From this beginning, Dallas grew. The resultant disadvantage of this to surrounding areas is to be seen, for example, in Fort Worth's continuing struggle to "catch up" economically and in the fact that citizens of Houston—an even larger city—still must go to Dallas for airline connections. Also, Houston's mail still is routed through Dallas for handling, and many shipments that come through Houston's port go to Dallas to be opened—only to have many of these same shipments return later to Houston. In fact, Houston's vassal position was almost complete until the National Aeronautics and Space Administration (NASA) located its Manned Space Control Center at nearby Clear Lake. Subsequent to this development, and in response to it, the Civil Aeroneautics Board belatedly saw sufficient justification to grant east-west transcontinental air routes so that now Houston's air service more nearly approaches its needs. Still, today, many connecting flights to numerous major locations can be made only through Dallas.

The size, shape, and depth of land areas, whether controlled by an individual, corporation, or political body(s)—including nations and coalitions of nations—are important resource considerations. On the one hand, the greater the extent of a controlled land, the better the chances that it will contain useable minerals, productive soils, and favorable climates. On the other hand, and as an offsetting disadvantage, distances may be costly, and intervening obstacles may hinder—or even prevent—resource development.

Similarly, shape of a controlled area is important. An area intended for an industrial plant may offer better layout potential if it is square rather than rectangular. Thus, an industrial site on the undulating glacial gravel surface of northern Illinois might offer a better opportunity for an efficient plant arrangement than, for example, the same amount of land area strung along a river valley in West Virginia. Shape is also important in terms of transportation and mobility patterns. By way of illustration, a single, central rail line suffices to serve most of Chile or Norway, but a radiating pattern is needed to serve France, and a grid system is required for nations shaped like the United States.

Of importance from a military point of view, size, shape, and depth offer certain advantages or disadvantages. Compact nations may find political and economic unity not hard to achieve, but they lack the depth needed as a military buffer or for dispersion or maneuvering of troops. In contrast, nations having adequate space may find the costs of overcoming distance self-defeating, or they may find it impossible to attain the degree of economic and political cohesiveness requisite for effectiveness. Quite often water or topographic barriers are compensating factors, enhancing unity despite large areas such as are found in Australia (due to surrounding reefs and water barriers) or differing languages, as in Switzerland, where blocking mountain barriers provide protection from outside forces.

Although treated only briefly, the size, shape, and depth of land areas are powerful factors shaping, restricting, or permitting full utilization of total resource potential attendant upon "land."

LAND PERCEPTION

Almost by way of summary and review of this chapter on land, it is appropriate to consider how land is perceived. The chapter began with the statement that land means *many and different things* to *many and different individuals*. How one perceives land is a highly subjective matter. For example, few citizens of the United States believed that Hitler's Germany actually needed *Lebensraum* (living space) and thus felt that it was unjustified in resorting to military measures to obtain land. Landless urbanites look at residential lots of suburbia with envy and suburbanites look on farm holdings as too large. In turn, the farmer, faced with the problem of fully utilizing his costly machinery, sees his land unit as too small. Still others consider the responsibilities of caring for their land as onerous and they long for the carefree urban life.

As noted earlier, urban areas use less than 1 percent of the land. The U.S. farmland produces surpluses of foodstuffs (except when unusually adverse weather conditions occur), and there is no demonstrable world-wide shortage of land. Yet, China has moved into Tibet, while the U.S.S.R., North Vietnam, Nepal, India, and other neighbors look with apprehension at China's moves along their frontiers. Even the United States, thousands of miles away, perceives China's land concerns as ominous and has taken to arms to prevent certain land from falling under the control of the "foe." The United States and many other nations perceive land as "for their citizens" and have placed immigration quotas that they hope will prolong the day of ultimate overcrowding (for them). Japan, frustrated in its World War II attempts to gain more land by force, has turned to an alternative, economic means of gaining land by having "world corporations" accomplish national policies aimed at using land in absentia (e.g., in Alaska, Australia, etc.).

The world has long had land-starved or land-hungry people; this is not a new problem. In fact, most wars have been fought over land (or the minerals in it). Yet often land has not been perceived by the masses as worthy of sacrificing life; in such cases a battle for land sometimes would be translated into terms of a moral crusade or an "ism," and the war would thus be placed on a supposedly loftier plane. Still, the depth and feeling with which some peoples perceive land is expressed by such terms as "Fatherland," "Motherland," or simply "my land." And national mottos or other such forms of inculcation have helped prepare or condition people to accept death (for some) for the sake of their country. Groups have long considered it appropriate and honorable for the individual to lay down his life for the "national territory." In fact, Robert Ardrey, in his book *The Territorial Imperative,* attempts to develop the point that man has an inherent desire or drive to control land.[36] Land thus perceived is part and parcel of man; man and land are inseparable. At the very least, man cannot be studied or considered meaningfully without consideration of land.

SUMMARY

Thus, how land is perceived depends entirely on the background values, goals, and wants of the perceiver. That land-use is basically pri-

---

[36] Robert Ardrey, *The Territorial Imperative* (New York: Atheneum Publishers, 1966). He notes that this also is true of the "prouder animals."

mary (agricultural), urban (including secondary and tertiary endeavors), and recreationally or spatially oriented is a part of man's record. That it is a major part of history is incontestable. The evidence is empirical; it can be measured. However, despite all the dire predictions of intolerable pressing populations on the land, there is not now, nor is there imminent, any shortage of land. The problems of land are those of perception. How should it be used? Should land be managed privately, publicly, or by some combination of these? The forester sees trees; the cattleman, grass; the farmer, crops; the urbanite, large and more spacious cities; the concrete salesman, more land in paved highways; the manufacturer of transportation equipment, certain land economies in mass transit systems; the oilman and military planner, a need for a pipeline regardless of ecological damage; the Sierra Club member, scenery and undisturbed nature; and so on ad infinitum. Land *is;* but, more importantly, land is *how it is perceived.* Land is finite, and land-use is limited by money (or lack of it), technology, topography, soil, climate, ores, size, shape, depth, and physical and political controls. More importantly—historically and for the future—land-use is more likely to be a function of man's willingness to "work the land" intensively or extensively, and whether, or to what extent, he exercises his inherent territorial imperative. Will man continue to be willing to die for the "Fatherland" or the "Motherland," for "My Land" or "Our Land"?

SELECTED BIBLIOGRAPHY

BARNEY, DANIEL R., *The Last Stand.* New York: Grossman Publishers, 1974.

BARTHOLOMEW, HARLAND, assisted by Jack Wood, *Land Uses in American Cities.* Cambridge, Mass.: Harvard University Press, 1955.

BELLUSH, JEWEL, and MURRAY HAUSKNECHT (eds.), *Urban Renewal: People, Politics and Planning.* Garden City, N.Y.: Anchor Books, Doubleday & Company, Inc., 1967.

BERESFORD-PEIRSE, HENRY, *Forests, Food, and People.* Rome: Food and Agriculture Organization of the United Nations, 1968.

CHANG, JEN-HU, *Climate and Agriculture: An Ecological Survey.* Chicago: Aldine Publishing Company, 1968.

CLAWSON, MARION, with CHARLES L. STEWART, *Land Use Information: A Critical Survey of U.S. Statistics, Including Possibilities for Greater Uniformity* (Resources for the Future, Inc.). Baltimore: The Johns Hopkins Press, 1965.

Food and Agriculture Organization of the United Nations, Forestry Division, *Grazing and Forest Economy.* Rome: Food and Agriculture Organization of the United Nations, 1953.

Foss, PHILLIP O., *Politics and Grass: The Administration of Grazing on the Public Domain.* Seattle: University of Washington Press, 1960.

HARING, JOSEPH E. (ed.), *Urban and Regional Economics: Perspectives for Public Action.* Boston: Houghton Mifflin Company, 1971.

HOWITZ, ELEANOR C. J., *Clearcutting: A View from the Top.* Washington, D.C.: Acropolis Books, Ltd., 1974.

HOYT, HOMER, *Urban Land Use Requirements, 1968–2000; The Land Area Required for the Future of the Urban Population in the United States.* Washington, D.C.: Homer Hoyt Institute, The American University, 1968.

HYAMS, EDWARD S., *Soil Civilization.* New York: Thames and Hudson, 1952.

ISE, JOHN, *Our National Park Policy; A Critical History* (Resources for the Future, Inc.). Baltimore: The Johns Hopkins Press, 1961.

JOHNSON, D. GALE, and ROBERT L. GUSTAFSON, *Grain Yields and the American Food Supply; An Analysis of Yield Changes and Possibilities.* Chicago: University of Chicago Press, 1962.

MACHATSCHEK, FRITZ, *Geomorphology,* trans. D. J. Davis, ed. K. M. Clayton. New York: American Elsevier Publishing Company, Inc., 1969.

MILLER, E. WILLARD, *A Geography of Manufacturing.* Englewood Cliffs, N.J.: Prentice-Hall, Inc., 1962.

OLSON, SHERRY H., *The Depletion Myth; A History of Railroad Use of Timber.* Cambridge, Mass.: Harvard University Press, 1971.

RAKHMANOV, V. V., *Role of Forests in Water Conservation,* trans. A. Gourevitch and L. M. Hughes. Washington, D.C.: Published for U.S. Department of Agriculture and the National Science Foundation by the Israel Program for Scientific Translations, 1966.

SARTORIUS, PETER, and HANS HENLE, *Forestry and Economic Development.* New York: Frederick A. Praeger, Publishers, 1968.

SIEGAN, BERNARD H., *Land Use Without Zoning.* Lexington, Mass.: Lexington Books, D. C. Heath and Company, 1972.

STAMP, L. DUDLEY (ed.), *A History of Land Use in Arid Regions.* Paris: UNESCO, 1961.

STONE, CHRISTOPHER D., *Should Trees Have Standing?* Los Altos, Calif.: William Kaufmann, Inc., 1974.

STRONG, ANN LOUISE, *Planned Urban Environments: Sweden, Finland, Israel, The Netherlands, France.* Baltimore: The Johns Hopkins Press, 1971.

THOMSEN, FREDERICK LUNDY, *Agricultural Marketing.* New York: McGraw-Hill Book Company, Inc., 1951.

U.S. Congress, Senate Committee on Banking, Housing and Urban Affairs, Subcommittee on Housing and Urban Affairs, *Land-Use, Planning, and Management Programs,* Hearings, 92nd Congress, 1st Session. Washington, D.C.: Government Printing Office, 1971.

U.S. Department of Agriculture, *Crops in Peace and War—The Yearbook of Agriculture, 1950–51*. Washington, D.C.: Government Printing Office, 1951.

U.S. Department of Agriculture, Forest Service, *Timber Trends in the United States*. Washington, D.C.: Government Printing Office, 1965.

U.S. Department of Agriculture, U.S. Soil Conservation Service, *Soil Classification: A Comprehensive System*. Washington, D.C.: Government Printing Office, 1960.

VILENSKII, D. G., *Soil Science* (3rd Engl. ed.), trans. A. Berron and Z. S. Cole. Washington, D.C.: Published for the National Science Foundation and U.S. Department of Agriculture by the Israel Program for Scientific Translations, 1960.

WHYTE, R. O., *Crop Production and Environment*. London: Faber and Faber, 1960.

SEVEN

AIR:
THE UBIQUITOUS
BUT TROUBLED RESOURCE

The air that man breathes is yet another vital flow resource that can last indefinitely—unless it becomes badly abused and hindered in its ability to flow by man's ignorance or disregard for the functions of nature. Just as man can utilize his culture to improve upon nature in developing needed resources, so can he use his culture to hamper and destroy nature. It is only in recent years that technological man—especially in industrialized countries—has realized the necessity for conserving or protecting the air he breathes, one of the most basic resources that he has.

PUBLIC AWAKENING

Air pollution is a problem that plagues most industrialized nations in varying degrees. But, because the problem has descended upon nations gradually, they have tended to ignore it as a threat until the ill-usage of air takes on alarming proportions. Then, as more and more people become aware of the personal harm they face, the public, itself, becomes concerned and begins mobilizing its resources against the threat.

Of the world's industrialized areas, the United States has shown meaningful public concern for air purification, beginning with the early 1960s.

During the two preceding decades, Americans listening to radios and, later, watching television laughed with unconcern as comics joked about the Pittsburgh smoke and the Los Angeles smog; but no one laughs any more.

The problem of tainted air would not be of such immensity if the population were distributed evenly over the United States. However, more than one-half of the population resides on only 1 percent of the nation's land area, and two-thirds of the people cover only 9 percent of the space. Thus, the people crowd closely together, accompanied by their air-polluting automobiles and trucks, chimneys and incinerators. And the problem is compounded by the fact that many manufacturing and industrial operations, power plants, and public waste-burning and transportation facilities are located in the same thickly settled areas.

Adding to pollution conditions still further are two unusual climatic conditions over which man has little control—air traps and temperature inversions, where radiation of the earth's heat creates a cold air layer near the ground with a warmer air layer above it (see Figure 19). This traps the contaminated air near the ground, and the resulting smog becomes especially noticeable—and bothersome—in the mornings and evenings, when workers are moving to and from their jobs in heavy traffic. The major variables affecting the nature and seriousness of the air pollution problem at any one time and place are: types of pollutants, quantity of pollutants, wind speed and direction, topography, sunlight, precipitation, decrease or increase in air temperature with height, and susceptibility of the individual to particular pollutants or combinations of pollutants.[1]

Air pollution often is referred to as a problem created by today's modern way of life. In the United States, this view is supported by the fact that there are more than 100 million cars, trucks, and buses on the streets and highways spewing pollutants into the air breathed by an ever-increasing population; this air is used and further polluted by an industry of unprecedented expansion and diversification. By the time *pollution* had become a familiar household word in the 1960s, every community with 2500 or more people—which includes 90 percent of the nation's metropolitan population —was suffering from air pollution caused by more than 150 million tons of gases, dusts, and fumes being discharged into the air annually.[2]

But only the dimensions of the problem are new; man-made contam-

---

[1] U.S. Department of Health, Education and Welfare, Public Health Service, *Today and Tomorrow in Air Pollution*, No. 1555, (Washington, D.C.: Government Printing Office, 1968), p. 29.

[2] The National Center for Air Pollution Control, U.S. Department of Health, Education and Welfare, estimated that unless new controls were applied, the annual total of air pollutants would rise from 129 million tons in 1965 to 215 million tons in 1980, and to 404 million tons in the year 2000 (see *U.S. News & World Report,* August 19, 1968, p. 61).

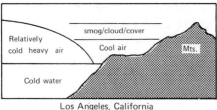

Los Angeles, California
(cross-section)

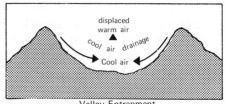

Valley Entrapment
Donora, Pennsylvania
Klagenfurt, Austria
Meuse Valley, Belgium, etc.
(cross-section)

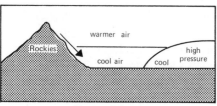

Denver, Colorado
(cross-section)

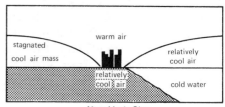

New York City
(cross-section)

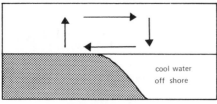

Boston, Massachusetts
Coastal Seabreeze
(cross-section)

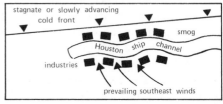

Houston, Texas
Prevailing Breeze
(bird's eye-view)

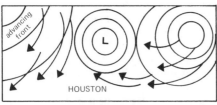

Houston, Texas
Backing Cyclonic Winds
(bird's eye-view)

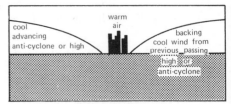

Houston, Texas
Backing Cyclonic Winds
(cross-section)

FIGURE 19. Examples of inversion or cool air entrapment.

inants (as distinguished from nature's own dusts and pollens, which also pollute) are as old as civilization. The first fires built by cavemen fouled the air to a limited extent. For thousands of years, a nighttime smoke haze has hung low over the villages and fields of the Middle East; and the haze exists today in almost every part of the world where farmers burn grass and brush to obtain fertilizing ash from them. European countries have been burning soft coal and peat as fuel for more than 1000 years, thereby feeding the air with ever-increasing amounts of gases and soot. In the year 1306, King Edward I of England issued a royal proclamation prohibiting the use of soft coal in London while Parliament was in session, upon penalty of "great fines and ransomes" because of the smoke and greasy soot that it created. Today, air in Ankara, Turkey, is severely polluted from the widespread use of lignite as fuel.

POLLUTION IS CUMULATIVE

There are two fundamental causes that underlie a progressive nation's air pollution problems. One is a growing population and its insatiable demands for industrial products and services, especially the internal combustion engine; the other is an ever-increasing standard of living. The harmful effect arising from the presence of these two conditions is cumulative, and the problems of air pollution will surely get worse before the situation gets better (what is being done and what can be accomplished are discussed later in this chapter).

NATIONAL GROWTH

Towns and industries of a century ago were relatively few, comparatively small, and well dispersed. The wastes that they discharged into the air caused little concern and generally went unnoticed unless an unusual climatic condition created a special problem. But as populated areas grew in scale and numbers and became more concentrated, their aerial wastes multiplied.

Recent statistics indicate a population growth in the United States of 1.3 percent a year, and the nation is becoming more urbanized. Larger metropolitan areas, which accounted for two-thirds of the population in the 1960s, will probably include 85 percent of the nation's residents by the 1980s.[3] This growth will require a great many more vehicles, additional electric generation (much of it from coal and fuel oil), plus a large

---

[3] U.S. Department of Health, Education and Welfare, op. cit., p. 7.

increase in space heating, refuse burning, the number of factories, and other primary air contaminators. The major polluters of the U.S. atmosphere were estimated in the "pre-control period" as follows:[4]

Polluter	Million Tons Annually	Percent of Total
Transportation	74.8	59.8
Manufacturing	23.4	18.7
Electric Power	15.7	12.6
Space Heating	7.8	6.2
Refuse Burning	3.3	2.6

There are hundreds of varieties of pollutants released by a wide array of sources over the nation—especially in metropolitan areas. The pollutant expelled in the greatest quantity is carbon monoxide (estimated to account for about 52 percent of the total annual discharge), the toxic gas coming from gasoline- and diesel-fired vehicles. Transportation also releases most of the hydrocarbons (some 12 percent of the total pollution), and—along with the electric power industry—most of the oxides of nitrogen (6 percent). Electric power also accounts for the oxides of sulfur (18 percent), which are released from the coal and fuel oil used as the source of energy, while industry—with electric power generation running a close second— emits most of the particulate matter (10 percent of the total annual discharge). The other pollutants (2 percent) are many and varied.

A NEW WAY OF LIFE

To a certain extent, pollution is the price the nation is paying for an ever-rising standard of living and a better way of life. The peasant villages of Europe or South America are mostly free of smog, but they are also lacking in bathtubs, refrigerators, two cars per family (or even one car), packaged frozen foods, and the wide array of other products and services found in so many American homes. "Convenience" foods, for example, come wrapped in paper, foil, and plastics that are easy to use but difficult to dispose of in a metropolitan area; they go into the incinerator instead of to the garbage dump, adding immeasurably to the tons of soot and ash poured into the air. A significant part of the nation's foul air pours out of household chimneys, office buildings, and municipal incinerators.

In the past, the layman generally assumed that there was so much

---

[4] Justine Farr Rodriguez and Joan Mahfouz, "Air Pollution" (New York: The Chase Manhattan Bank, Economic Research Division, 1967).

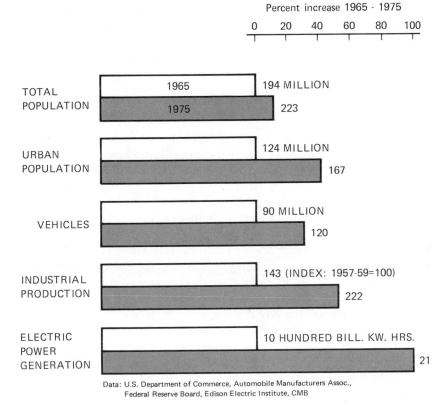

Percent increase 1965 - 1975

| | 0 | 20 | 40 | 60 | 80 | 100 |

TOTAL POPULATION — 1965 — 194 MILLION — 1975 — 223

URBAN POPULATION — 124 MILLION — 167

VEHICLES — 90 MILLION — 120

INDUSTRIAL PRODUCTION — 143 (INDEX: 1957-59=100) — 222

ELECTRIC POWER GENERATION — 10 HUNDRED BILL. KW. HRS. — 21

Data: U.S. Department of Commerce, Automobile Manufacturers Assoc.,
Federal Reserve Board, Edison Electric Institute, CMB

FIGURE 20. The sources of pollution are growing. Adapted from The Chase Manhattan Bank, "Business in Brief," No. 72 (February, 1967).

air surrounding the earth that even tons of solid and gaseous material poured into it would never be noticed. It is true that estimates show about 6×10^{15} tons of air on earth,[5] and thus the 150 million tons of pollutants spewed forth into that air each year amounts to only about one ton of pollutants for each 40 million tons of air. However, just as figures showing the amount of water on earth give little solace to inhabitants of areas that receive only four inches of rainfall a year, so figures showing the ability of the atmosphere to dilute pollution are of little consolation to areas where the pollutants tend to concentrate. Unfortunately, the very thin layer of atmosphere—rising little more than 100 feet above ground—

[5] Louis J. Battan, *The Unclean Sky* (New York: Doubleday & Co., 1966), p. 15, arrives at the figure by multiplying the pressure at sea level (14.7 pounds per square inch) times the earth's surface area (8×10^{17} pounds, or 6×10^{15} tons of air).

in which people spend their lives also contains, with few exceptions, the sources of most of our pollution.[6] Add to this the considerable concentrations in certain areas of the country of both population and pollution sources, and the problem multiplies in the seriousness of its consequences.

AIR POLLUTION DAMAGE

The damage inflicted by air pollution is enormous yet difficult to measure in dollars and cents. Some sources estimate that the yearly cost exceeds $12 billion in the United States alone; but a multiple of that figure would be difficult to dispute, especially if we consider values to which a price tag cannot be attached.[7]

The most obvious losses come from damage to building stone, metals, fabrics, leather, paper, paint, and rubber. Certain building stones, especially limestone, deteriorate when the air is unusually concentrated with carbon dioxide; mixed with a high humidity, it can produce carbonic acid, which discolors stone and scars its surface. A small quantity of hydrogen sulfide gas in the air can badly discolor painted surfaces if the paint contains lead. Another form of property damage is dirtied automobiles, homes, and clothing (annual cleaning bills can be extensive), and the extent of damage is far greater in the industrialized cities than in the more remote rural areas. There also are crop losses that are blamed on air pollution; the damage caused to precision parts in machinery is difficult to estimate; reduced visibility—resulting in larger lighting bills, accidents, and inconvenience to travelers—is also a cost; and the depreciated values of neighborhood property because of continuing pollution must be considered.

Damage to public health is still another cost that has not been accurately assayed. Medical care is expensive, days of unproductivity cannot be regained, and fatalities sometimes occur. Some authorities, reacting in the extreme, refer to the "deadly effect masked in every type of respiratory ailment from asthma to bronchitis to lung cancer," [8] while others point

---

[6] The atmosphere of the entire earth is becoming increasingly polluted. Because the winds and air masses transport the pollution, scientists have recorded an increase in certain contaminants (e.g., sulfur oxides) even in the North Polar region.

[7] The tall granite spire with which Thothmes III, ruler of Egypt, sought to glorify himself withstood the sun and sand of the Sahara for 35 centuries. The 2000-ton obelisk was finally transported to New York in 1880, where it is now being gradually dissolved by the air. Sulfurous gases—and New York has more of these toxic gases than any other American city—form a very weak sulfuric acid that coats everything in the city, eating away at limestone, etching marble, and attacking even granite. (From a New York Herald Tribune News Service story printed in *The Houston Post*, April 3, 1966, sec. 1, p. 2.)

[8] "The Filth We Breathe," *Science Digest*, May, 1963, pp. 4–11.

out that the serious effects of pollution on health are far from conclusive.

However, several serious incidents have occurred to leave little doubt that health problems can arise from contaminated air. In Donora, Pennsylvania, in October, 1948, a four-day temperature inversion clamped an impenetrable lid over the area and so concentrated the air pollutants that 20 residents died of respiratory failure. In London in December, 1952, another four-day killer smog resulted in more than 4000 excess deaths that were directly or indirectly the result of pollution. And in 1963, a deadly smog was blamed for the deaths of 400 New Yorkers. These cases were extreme and may not occur in those areas a second time—just as tornadoes do not usually sweep the same path clean on two separate occasions—but less dramatic situations do recur in some locales time and again.[9] And in all probability, killer smogs will make headlines again in certain parts of the world.

POSSIBLE SOLUTIONS

By the 1970s, control of air (and water) pollution had become one of the fastest-rising sectors of capital spending by American industry. Under public and governmental pressure, almost every major industry began to report large annual expenditure increases in both research and equipment designed to abate air pollution. The annual outlay for research and development alone more than doubled between 1960 and 1970 and is expected to go as high as $80 billion by the year 2000.[10] The nation was beginning to mature in its approach to air pollution.

In earlier days, cities tried to meet the pollution problem by deliberately segregating industry into a particular area of town; every major city had its industrial area, where grime and dirt were expected and slums accepted. Later, improved transportation facilities encouraged industry to move away from such slumlike areas and relocate in the country, where pollution could be dispersed and would go unnoticed; but the increasing population and growth of cities gradually encircled the industries again,

---

[9] In 1968, 60 members of the UCLA medical faculty signed a statement advising everyone who could do so to move away from the smoggiest parts of Los Angeles, San Bernardino, and Riverside counties because air pollution was a major health hazard during much of the year (*Los Angeles Times,* August 11, 1968). The conditions had not improved by the mid-1970s.

[10] U.S. Department of Health, Education and Welfare, op. cit., p. 14. The Council on Environmental Quality estimated (see an Associated Press story carried in newspapers on September 18, 1973) that the United States must spend some $274 billion during the decade 1972–1981 on environmental cleanup; the total included an estimated $121.3 billion for water pollution, $41.8 billion for solid wastes, and $105.6 billion for air pollution control and prevention.

resulting in a recurrence of the problems. Also, many small, isolated communities, though at first welcoming the establishment of such plants, eventually discovered that they became in effect "vassals of the plant." For, as long as the polluting continued, few (all too often none) other industries would locate there. Thus, in effect they also became "captives" of the polluting plant.[11]

Now, in the latter half of the twentieth century, the realization has come that, instead of seeking stopgap solutions or fleeing from the situation, the communities must solve the pollution problem on the existing premises. The cost to industry of purifying the air will run into billions of dollars, with part of the expenditures not recoverable except through higher prices for products sold to consumers. In terms of capital costs, the cleanest cement-making plant may cost 10 percent more to build, the cleanest refinery 1 percent or more, the cleanest integrated steel mill 3 to 5 percent more, and the cleanest foundry smelt shop 15 to 20 percent more.[12] The industries that will be hardest hit are those producing electric power, chemicals, metals, petroleum, and pulp.

However, not all expenditures on pollution control equipment need be a net loss to industry; a portion of the cost can be offset by recovery of wasted by-products. For example, in Los Angeles petroleum refiners found that in eliminating sulfur from refinery exhausts, they could recover 600 tons a day of waste gases and convert much in these sulfuric gases into useful by-products. Some pollution control authorities are beginning to define pollution as something that has no recoverable value, while the useful materials exhausted into the air are considered to be wasted valuable by-products.

It should be remembered, however, that pollution by industry is only a part of the nation's problem. A more culpable contributor to foul air in the 1960s was the various modes of transportation. Suggested solutions to this problem ranged initially from expensive modifications on vehicles to complete abandonment of fossil fuels as a source of energy and the eventual substitution of electric vehicles. Extensive research financed by government, suppliers of fossil fuels, and vehicle manufacturers probably will make the extreme measures unnecessary.

---

[11] For example, Blackwell, an isolated community in northcentral Oklahoma, had an offending zinc smelter with automation and a depressed market. Many employees were laid off, but "The Chimney" continued to spew out an all-pervading white dust, and the town, with a surplus labor force, had no opportunity for new plants. Fortunately for the town, Blackwell Zinc announced that it would close by 1974, and within 17 months after the announcement four new industries—with a combined payroll equal to Blackwell Zinc's original employment—had located there (*Tulsa Daily World,* October 2, 1973, p. B-1).

[12] Rodriguez and Mahfouz, op. cit.

FIGURE 21. *Before* and *after* scenes of the Hayden copper smelter in El Paso, Texas. *Top* shows particulate matter—visible portion of stack plume—and sulfur dioxide being dispersed into the atmosphere. *Bottom* shows new process "on stream." Planning for this plant, begun in 1966, was part of a $50-million program to improve air quality in the vicinty of the copper smelters. Courtesy ASARCO (American Smelting and Refining Company).

Any discussion on ways and means of solving polluted air problems would have to include government action.[13] The first federal legislation on air pollution was passed in 1955, and activity accelerated considerably after passage of the 1963 Clean Air Act and its 1965 amendment. Such

---

[13] The cost of air pollution abatement must be borne by one or more of the following: consumers (in higher prices), labor (in lower wages), raw-material suppliers (in lower prices), stockholders (in lower dividends), and society (in subsidies of some form). There is a question whether those who try to keep the air clean should bear the cost; perhaps those in the industry who do not make the effort should be penalized with a graduated tax on pollutants emitted, with the revenue used to subsidize those who do abate.

legislation offered financial support to states, regions, and localities that originated or maintained air pollution control, contributed additional funds for research, and established standards for federal intervention in cases of interstate pollution (and, upon request, intrastate pollution). After the Clean Air Act was enacted, government expenditures on pollution problems began to increase annually at an average rate of about 15 percent.

There has not been, and there may never be, full agreement on two basic questions: Where should the incidence of pollution control costs fall? [14] Where should the authority to enforce such controls lie? The arguments are similar to those offered in water pollution abatement,[15] with much of the economy's industrial segment believing that air pollution should be realistically recognized as a local or regional problem that interferes with individual or community well-being in varying degrees, while much of the nation's nonindustrial segment views it as a broader problem requiring national mobilization to protect one of the country's most basic resources—clean air.

Furthermore, opinions differ widely concerning what approach pollution controls should take. Some theoreticians see current efforts toward depolluting air and water as only intermediate measures; in fact, they envision the day when each economic entity (e.g., a city) is a closed loop, similar to a space capsule in which astronauts reconstitute everything—even their own waste.

This idea has merit.[16] It is an important fact that the American consumer actually *consumes* nothing; he only *uses* things and then tries to burn, bury, grind, dump, or flush his wastes. Natural laws decree that nothing is ever really consumed, except when, as Albert Einstein theorized, it is turned into energy (and then, once expended, it shows up again in some physical form). Economists, with relatively few exceptions, hypothesize about various techniques for producing and distributing goods for consumption—without paying much heed to what happens after the "consumer" buys the goods. At least the old tin can used to rust away in time; but the "immortal" aluminum can may last forever, and many of today's glass bottles and jars—and hardy plastic containers—may last almost as long. The U.S. per capita output of solid wastes has been estimated at running more than 1600 pounds a year, and the figure is rising some 4 percent

---

[14] Costs run high. U.S. Steel estimates that pollution control equipment accounted for 10 percent of its $100 million cost for a new plant at Baytown, Texas (*Time*, May 17, 1971, p. 46), and Phillips Petroleum Company says that 12 percent of the cost of its carbon black plant at Orange, Texas, went for pollution control devices ("Conserve and Protect," a pamphlet by Phillips Petroleum Company, 1971).

[15] See the discussion on water pollution control in Chapter Five.

[16] Two good articles on this subject can be found in The Chase Manhattan Bank, "Business in Brief," No. 72 (February, 1967), and "The Age of Effluence," *Time*, May 10, 1968, pp. 52–53.

annually; New York City alone dumps 200 million gallons of raw sewage into the Hudson River, and each square mile of Manhattan produces some 375,000 pounds of solid waste a day—with most of it being incinerated, and much of that drifting into the air as fly ash.[17]

For a while yet, man's residual matter can still be "thrown away"— burned, buried, or dumped into the streams, rivers, lakes, and bays. However, as the National Academy of Sciences has noted, the day will come when there is no longer an "away," as the earth becomes more crowded and one person's trash basket is another's living space. Then man cannot even be content with merely depolluting what he is presently befouling— although that is an important first step that man must take before he can rush headlong into the future. Some authorities have come to call pollution "resources out of place" [18] and see a trend toward the recycling of an ever-increasing amount of the materials used by man. Currently, scrap or reprocessed material constitutes the "raw material" for 50 percent of the U.S. steel production, 56 percent of the copper, 12 percent of the rubber, and 21 percent of the paper produced.[19] There are indications that this is only the beginning of man's efforts to make new goods from reprocessed materials. Pollution is really a problem of proper utilization of resources, and recycling is a major part of the answer.

The greatest public concern over air and water pollution has been shown in the United States in recent years, but other industrialized nations are experiencing a growing pollution problem (e.g., Japan and Germany's Ruhr Valley). And some day the currently less-developed nations will look to the United States for guidance and solutions as they, too, follow a similar path of national growth. Meanwhile, other nations are being affected by U.S. efforts at pollution control.[20]

Progress in some areas appears eminent and promising. At least three of these are worth mentioning: (1) the external combusion engine, (2) cleaner fuels for existing equipment, and (3) fusion power.

THE EXTERNAL COMBUSTION ENGINE

Automobile mobility is the basis of most of modern man's living, working, and social patterns. The automobile's *infernal* combustion engine has already been cited as one of man's greatest causes of air pollution. A

---

[17] *Time,* loc. cit.

[18] The Chase Manhattan Bank, op. cit.

[19] Ibid. By 1975, unfortunately, paper recycling had declined temporarily because of the cost factor.

[20] International trade is affected, for example. Auto manufacturers in other countries must meet U.S. antipollution standards if they want to export cars to America.

less polluting power plant would go far in preserving much of man's investment in lifestyles, patterns, goals, and values—recognizing, of course, that there would be massive job and investment dislocations attendant upon any widespread abandonment of the "internal" combustion engine. Such dislocations likely would spread out to encompass the iron and steel machining industries, petroleum refining and distribution systems, and service industries. Offsetting such catastrophic disadvantages would be a lower-cost power unit—lower in initial manufacturing costs, servicing and replacement costs, and fuel costs.

One such "external" engine has reached the production stage.[21] The only volume emissions produced are water and carbon dioxide; other emissions are very small in volume and present no toxic threat. This engine burns at atmospheric pressure, resulting in less pollution. Burners are used to raise the temperature of freon (gas), which would turn the gears of a turbine engine; the engine would not be in contact with flame, and metal wear and fatigue would be much less than in the now conventional internal combustion engine. That such an engine is revolutionary in scope and highly salutary in terms of long-range effects on air (and noise abatement) is an understatement. Such a power plant would completely change not only the concept of automobile manufacturing, but also the entire system of producing and marketing motor fuels, lubrication, and maintenance. The technology is here; how long will it be before economic and cultural factors will embrace its widespread application? And, as revolutionary as the Minto Engine might be, it is mere child's-play in terms of long-range environmental impact as compared with the prospects of "cleaner fuels" or, eventually, "fusion power."

Still other steps are being sought, and tests of feasibility are under way. One such measure being studied on a large scale is the use of propane as a clean-burning, noncorrosive liquid fuel with high heat content in motor vehicles. In comparable ways, other LPG (liquefied petroleum gas) products are being given serious consideration as substitutes for "less clean" fuels and/or feedstocks. Ethane is one such hydrocarbon that, if anticipated demands result in even a slight price increase, is available and could be used as a cleaner chemical feedstock than fuels currently in use.

Immediate prospects indicate that LPGs will be widely adopted as fuels and, when available at lower costs, as chemical feedstock. To this end, the federal government issued a proclamation that permits unlimited imporation of LPG and natural gas liquids from Canada and Venezuela.[22]

---

[21] The Minto Engine, costing $100, running on almost any combustible fuel, expected to last almost a lifetime, and causing almost no air pollution (*The Oklahoma Journal*, February 25, 1971, p. 14).

[22] "More LPG—Mainly for Burning," *Chemical Week*, January 6, 1971, p. 15.

In addition, because of broad-based demands for cleaner fuels, domestic firms are developing increased capacities.[23] Technology is thus helping to reduce air pollution.

Fusion power is beyond doubt man's great hope to abate, and then avoid, future air pollution. The prospects of fusion power are within the foreseeable reach of man.[24]

Fusion power requires no burning of the world's oxygen or hydrocarbons, and no unwanted combustion by-products are released, which, in turn, must be dumped into the atmosphere. Neither are radioactive wastes produced as a part of the fuel cycle. With fusion power, the fuel cycle enters a closed system, long a goal of man, rather than a linear system, as is currently necessary. Any reaction products are neutrons or nonradioactive helium and hydrogen and radioactive tritium nuclei. However, in contrast to nuclear fission processes now in use, which produce radioactive materials in abundance, the radioactive tritium nuclei can be returned to the system and actually constitute a fuel (see Figure 22). Such a system depends on the development either of new materials that will contain or withstand the tremendously high temperatures released, or of some other means of holding heat away from materials—such as through a magnetic field or gravity control. In any event, a pilot plant probably will be feasible within two or three decades.

The significance of this development, when it arrives, might be likened to the impacts of the steam engine, diesel power, the internal combustion engine, the jet turbine, and the electric computer—all compressed into a very brief period. Miniaturization, or application of fusion power, might well mean production of a nonpolluting supersonic transport (SST) and most other conceivable power requirements of man. The impact and impingements of this potential technology on economic and cultural patterns are beyond comprehension, but that one of the environmental results to be anticipated is "clean air" gives man real hope and reestablishes faith and meaningful goals, ultimately, in "technology." In the meantime, man must live within the parameters of his present technology, economy (and cultures). Toward this end, the United States Congress enacted, and the executive branch of the Federal Government inaugurated, the 1970 Clean Air Act.

---

23 Ibid.

24 William C. Cough and Bernard J. Eastland, "The Prospects of Fusion Power," *Scientific American,* CCXXIV, No. 2 (February, 1971), pp. 50–64. In mid-1973, the Environmental Protection Agency cautioned the Atomic Energy Commission (see an Associated Press story carried in publications on September 17, 1973) not to commit itself to the controversial atomic "breeder reactor" until it had considered other methods of generating power—atomic fusion power, solar energy, wind or tidal power, geothermal steam, etc.

PRESENT LINEAR POWER SYSTEMS

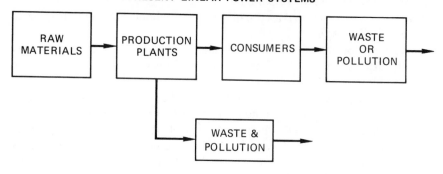

HOPED FOR FUSION (CLOSED) SYSTEM

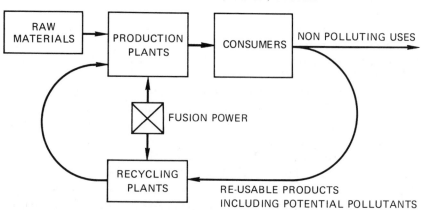

FIGURE 22. Present linear power systems. Diagrams based on Cough and Eastland.

This act, implemented by the Environmental Protection Agency, has as its undergirding provision the establishment of minimal (acceptable) air pollution standards. The very fact that man finds any justification in accepting some degree of air pollution testifies to the power of the forces that our economy and culture have set in motion. However, that man just a year later, in 1971, was seeking to attain even purer air was evident in new powers that the executive branch of the Federal Government sought for its Environmental Protection Agency. These proposed new powers, building on the 1970 Clean Air Act, asked for abatement of air pollution from both moving and stationary sources. The Federal Government subsequently banned leaded gasoline for 1975-model and later automobiles and limited the permissible sulfur content in bulk fuels (such as those used for electric power generation).

The unleaded gasoline reduced automobile pollution emissions, but became a highly controversial and expensive change. Proponents of lead additives maintained that combustion efficiencies more than offset damage from what lead compounds might be released in the burning processes; however, opponents pointed out the recognized dangers of lead and lead compounds to humans and property.

The limitation on sulfur in bulk fuels chiefly affected factories, large heating units, and electric power generating plants that use fossil fuels. The problem, in brief, is to tie the controls of air pollution to the marketplace in some meaningful way. Regulation per se is largely negative in approach and restrictive in nature, whereas society's atmospheric needs and goals would probably be better served if regulation were complemented by recovery rebates.

Thus, it now seems that the widespread revulsion to and revolt against the pollution of man's atmosphere, rather than bringing a *simpler life* and *simpler technology,* promises to produce (in time) an even more complex life (technologically and culturally). Man may have to live within the parameters of air limitations, owing to the finite nature of the atmosphere; but he *need not* sacrifice values of clean air if he uses the technologies available to him and, at the same time, works toward "closed systems" of fuel use or power generation, rather than the open, or "linear," systems currently employed.

The discussion in this chapter has concentrated mostly on *pollution* of air, the flow resource. Of course, air also serves as a resource in other ways—for example, as a source of energy (windmills and other forms of wind power), transportation (planes and other means of travel), raw materials (nitrogen, neon, and other products used by man). However, the detrimental effects of contaminated air are of the greatest concern to today's advanced worldwide society, and some nations have given a high priority to the solution of this problem—which is the major thrust of this chapter.

SELECTED BIBLIOGRAPHY

"Air Pollution and Forests: A Study Still in its Infancy," *Science News,* January 6, 1973, p. 7.

ASHTON, ROBERT, JR., "Black Sky Over the Southwest," *National Parks & Conservation Magazine,* October, 1971, pp. 25–28.

CHANLETT, EMIL T., *Environmental Protection.* New York: McGraw-Hill Book Company, 1973.

COUGHLIN, R. W., A. F. SAROFIM, and N. J. WEINSTEIN (eds.), *Air Pollution and Its Control.* New York: American Institute of Chemical Engineers, 1972.

DETWYLER, THOMAS R. (ed.), *Man's Impact on Environment* (Part III). New York: McGraw-Hill Book Company, 1971.

LILLIE, ROBERT J., *Air Pollutants Affecting the Performance of Domestic Animals: A Literature Review.* Washington, D.C.: U.S. Agricultural Research Service, Government Printing Office, 1970.

"Pollution Dilemma: How Clean Is Clean Air?," *Business Week,* July 15, 1972, p. 92.

SCORER, RICHARD S., *Air Pollution.* New York: Pergamon Press, Inc., 1968.

SCOTT, DAVID L., *Pollution in the Electric Power Industry.* Lexington, Mass.: D. C. Heath and Company, 1973.

"Smog City," *Newsweek,* June 12, 1972, pp. 14–15.

STRAUSS, WERNER (ed.), *Air Pollution Control.* New York: Wiley-Interscience, 1971.

ROSSANO, A. T., JR. (ed.), *Air Pollution Control; Guide Book for Management.* Stamford, Conn.: Environmental Science Service Division, E.R.A., Inc., 1969.

U.S. Department of Health, Education and Welfare, *Today and Tomorrow in Air Pollution* (Public Health Service Publication No. 1555). Washington, D.C.: Government Printing Office, 1968.

WOLFF, ANTHONY, "The Price of Power," *Harper,* May, 1972, pp. 36–38.

EIGHT

MINERALS AS BASIC STEPPING STONES TO CIVILIZATIONS AND SOCIAL ACHIEVEMENT

A cursory consideration of minerals may yield an initial opinion that they are not as important in the United States economy as they once were. The minerals industries, like their physical resource counterparts—lumbering and farming—represent a steadily declining share of the total economy. Still, all other aspects of the economy—manufacturing, transportation, marketing, defense, exploration, research and development, education, fine arts, and government—depend on minerals, those substances obtained *from* the earth's crust (except for water) rather than *on* that crust (such as plants or livestock).

So basic are minerals to man's scheme of things that his very affluence hinges on his access to minerals in usable quality and volume. Indeed, "the doctrine of affluence is based upon the assumption that this earth's supplies (or substitutes for them) are adequate for universal affluence." [1] Whether the earth may one day, through technology breakthroughs (such as fusion power), provide all of the minerals desired by man remains to be seen. What is clear is that a shortage of many minerals exists now and for the near future, and unless man learns better utilization techniques, he

---

[1] Charles L. Park, Jr., *Affluence in Jeopardy: Minerals and the Political Economy* (San Francisco: Freeman and Company, 1970), p. 3.

may even have to "give up" the *advantages* of some minerals that are accessible (e.g., lead, mercury, etc.).

Minerals, in common with other forms of physical resources, have been the focal point of *use* struggles, especially during the past 25 years. World War II caused such *use* inroads on known reserves of iron ore, copper, and other minerals that widespread concern led to fears that the nation's industrial, economic, and military might would be limited by shortages. Some interests called for nationally sponsored stockpiling on a grand scale in order to "save" minerals for the future. Other interests deemed that stockpiling per se would seriously retard industrial and economic growth, thus restricting the ability of a nation to provide necessary work opportunities and even to defend herself. These groups advocated a dynamic policy of resource development, including exploration and technical beneficiation of those minerals that nature had to offer.

A nearly worldwide adoption of policies leading to rapid economic growth and technological advancement in mining and ore beneficiation has sustained high output levels and has increased knowledge of reserves. Since World War II, unprecedented economic and technological progress not only has occurred but also has been accompanied by—even made possible by—new and still-evolving political actions and alignments. For example, the oil exporting nations of the world have wielded tremendous political and economic strength through their International Union. All of Western Europe and Japan are now, to an unprecedented degree, dependent upon this organization's political and economic policies. Thus, the world has entered a new era in mineral development. Nevertheless, there are certain key mineral characteristics that conceptually, and in terms of their effects on man, differ only in degree, as compared with 25, 50, 100, or even 1000 years ago.

From these few observations, it is clear that minerals are "fund resources" with unique characteristics.

MINERAL CHARACTERISTICS

Most *minerals* are used for one of three purposes: to produce, to control, or to conserve some form of energy or heat. This concept in turn, then, provides a convenient and logical division of minerals into fuels, metals, and nonmetals. The fuel minerals are sources of energy or heat; metals serve to control energy or heat; and the nonmetals are most often used in static structures to conserve heat (such as in homes, offices, and plants) or conserve energy by providing smooth rights-of-way (such as roads, railroads, airfields, and port and terminal facilities). All three categories have at least seven common characteristics that are critical for a society to understand and appreciate if that society is to maximize its use of minerals: (1) minerals are found in localized deposits, (2) exploration for minerals and their development usually are costly, time consuming, and politically and/or economically hazardous, (3) most mineral deposits are relatively short-lived, (4) demand for minerals is increasing at an increasing rate, (5) some stockpiling or scheduling of reserve mineral supplies is needed, (6) most primary metals industries are oriented toward a single resource, and (7) mineral exploitation leaves an indelible mark on the environment.

Minerals Are Found in Localized Deposits

In contrast to soils, climates, and most other categories of physical resources, most minerals are found in limited areas. This leads to dominance—or even control—by a few individuals, corporations, political subdivisions, even states and nations. The immediate impact is to raise questions of who has the "rights to control"; and the long-range effect is to produce governmental administrative procedures or controls on minerals (including pricing). Also, the long-range impact has included the emergence of relatively rich individual or national super-economies, corporations, or political entities. At the same time, the long-range impact has been to make individuals, peoples, and nations interdependent. For example, Japan is dependent on U.S., Australian, Canadian, and South African coal; the U.S.S.R. is dependent on Hungary for aluminum; the United States depends on many nations for iron ore, on Malaysia for tin, and on South Korea for tungsten.

Exploration for Minerals and Their Development Usually Are Costly, Time Consuming, and Politically and/or Economically Hazardous

With few exceptions, the most readily discovered, the most accessible, and the richest mineral deposits are developed and mined first. Subsequent findings and mining operations are, by and large, more costly, difficult, and often hazardous. Often, in the absence of assured markets and/or highly stable political situations, other incentives are substituted by governments to ensure minerals for their industries and, in turn, for the benefit of individuals, public welfare, and/or defense. In light of a logarithmic growth in interdependence and competition, the exploration and development of foreign deposits are currently receiving strong attention. However, reliance on foreign deposits is costlier and riskier than reliance on domestic deposits because, in addition to the hazards of operating and marketing a mineral over great distances, there are the added risks of expropriation.[2] Thus, during World War II, the United States offered a $10,000 reward for the discovery of a sizeable domestic uranium deposit. Similarly, the U.S.S.R. has used competition between exploration teams to further its knowledge of domestic minerals; *still, to date, no nation has discovered or developed self-sufficiency in minerals.*

Some of the major problems inherent in modern-day mineral exploration and development are capital requirements. To open a new nickel mine somewhere or to explore for oil on the North Slope of Alaska requires billions (not millions) of dollars, and the prospects are for ever-higher costs in this category. It is little wonder that many mining firms are avoiding increased exploration expenditures, and more and more are devoting available funds to the development of whatever technology is required to bring *known deposits* into production.[3]

Most Mineral Deposits Are Relatively Short-Lived

Most minerals are fund, rather than flow, resources.[4] Even such once-vast deposits as the hematite ore bodies of Minnesota, Wisconsin, and Michigan have been exhausted. This characteristic of minerals brings into play the constant need for further exploration and development, as mentioned earlier, and makes mandatory adequate reserves as a hedge against depletion. Indeed, it is the exhaustible nature of mineral resources in use that, in the long run, makes future operations possible only on an increasing cost basis; it also often means mine abandonment with attendant social costs in jobs and loss of tax bases, not to mention obvious esthetic and alternate-land-use problems.

Perhaps of even more significance is the fact that mine depletion—even potential, if not actual—causes industry and even entire nations to concern themselves with problems of reuse (e.g., scrap metal) and substitutes (e.g., nylon rope for steel cable) and the establishment of national reserves through licensing, law, import tariffs, subsidies, and continuous exploration and development programs.

---

[2] For example, Chile has expropriated nearly all formerly foreign-owned and developed mines. See "Anaconda Earnings Drop On Lower Income From Chilean Mines," *Skillings Mining Review,* LX, No. 32 (August 7, 1971), p. 16. Overthrow of the Marxist government in late 1973 may reverse the trend in this country.

[3] Union Oil Company allocated a larger and larger share of its total budget to the problems of extracting oil from Colorado shales, rather than to further oil well drilling; and U.S. iron ore processors continue to extract and pelletize Minnesota taconites, rather than rely on further exploration for promising hematite and other ore bodies of less costly use.

[4] There are some exceptions to this statement. For example, iron *ore* is formed in some of Sweden's lakes rapidly enough to enable this country to "farm and harvest" iron ore.

FIGURE 23. Scale model of proposed Coppertown, USA, recently unveiled in Calumet, Michigan. An attempt to turn an abandoned mining wasteland into an economic entity is planned. Courtesy Universial Oil Products Company.

Demand for Minerals Is Increasing at an Increasing Rate

Industrial/cultural/technological demands are far more significant in the growth of mineral consumption than are population increases per se. This principle was set forth clearly in the President's Materials Policy Commission (the so-called Paley Commission) in 1952.[5] That it is still a valid principle in mineral forecasting is made evident in the Bureau of Mines publication *Mineral Facts and Problems,* where, for purposes of predicting mineral consumption, an annual population growth factor of 1.6 percent was combined with a projected industrial growth factor of 4.2 percent to produce a mineral consumption forecast of annual growth rates in the range of 3.4 percent to 5.5 percent.[6] Cultural and technological influences on the mineral industries have had an even greater overall impact on the pattern of consumption—especially under a technology that proliferates new material forms. Indeed, the demands for many minerals are out-

[5] No better statement exists than in "Resources for Freedom," President's Materials Policy Commission, II (Washington, D.C.: Government Printing Office, 1952), p. 111.

[6] U.S., Department of the Interior, Bureau of Mines, *Mineral Facts and Problems,* Bulletin No. 650 (Washington, D.C.: Government Printing Office, 1970).

stripping the ability of mining industries to produce; and in certain cases (such as with the nonferrous metals), total real costs have been rising at a faster rate than costs in the economy as a whole. The implication is becoming ever clearer that the ultimate brake on just how affluent the American society *can* become may well be critical mineral shortages. In the meantime, man is proceeding blithely forward, "making progress." Evidently most people believe that "technology will find a way" before it is too late, and so far these people may have been correct. Nevertheless, relatively recent public comprehension of just how tight and limited the "closed planetary system" is, combined with the daily sight, smell, taste, and feel of pollution, suggests to even the casual observer that the earth is, indeed, limited and that some point where man no longer will be willing to "pay the cost" may be approaching. Certainly, the *counter* affluence of the *counter* culture, seemingly at large in most industrialized nations of the world, supports this contention.

Some Stockpiling or Scheduling of Reserve Mineral Supplies Is Needed

The element of uncertainty in the adequacy of most mineral supplies makes mandatory both a knowledge of reserves and a response (usually stockpiling) to that knowledge. In the United States, as with most industrial nations, governmental bodies consider this problem of sufficient moment that the U. S. Bureau of Mines, Department of the Interior (perhaps soon to be incorporated into a Department of Natural Resources) and state geological survey units are publicly supported to develop knowledge of resources and to forecast future needs. Further supporting their efforts is additional information on minerals gathered and produced by the State and Defense departments and other intelligence sources, such as the Central Intelligence Agency and Office of Emergency Preparedness,[7] as well as by industry.

In addition to national stockpiling policies, industries, too, find it expedient to stockpile. Indeed, most power generating plants, ore reduction firms, metal furnaces, and other users provide aboveground or in-plant storage space and equipment to maintain reserves. For example, it is estimated that the Commonwealth Edison Company of the Greater Chicago area alone maintains 12 million to 15 million tons of coal stockpiled at its electric generator plants; and the new Europort Iron Ore Terminal, commissioned in 1970 at Rotterdam, was stockpiling some 15

---

[7] Office of the Federal Archives and Records Service, General Services Administration, *United States Government Organization Manual, 1970–71* (Washington, D.C.: Government Printing Office, 1970). For greater expansion, see Appendix 8A.

million metric tons of iron ore by 1973.[8] Admittedly, many stockpiling operations are combined with blending operations; but this process, too, is only part of the problem of man's bringing widely scattered reserves together to mix and blend to a standard, so as to take advantage of existing, known reserves and to "trade off" the advantages of each in terms of minimizing costs, assuring standards, and meeting delivery schedules. Thus, one of the key characteristics of minerals is that, in order to develop minerals in volume, reserves and stockpiling are usually necessary.

Most Primary Metals Industries Are Oriented Toward a Single Resource

Most of the world's producers of primary metals focus on a single mineral; and it is usually the exception when even coproducts or by-products form significant facets of a mineral producer's market mix. There are some noteworthy exceptions to this generalization, such as: sulfur is reclaimed from sulfur oxides; other compounds are captured in the smelting process; and secondary minerals are obtained in processing the complex nickel ores mined in the Sudbury, Ontario, area. In the case of nickel, the rock or ore also contains sulfur, copper, iron, silver, gold, and other trace minerals—all by-products or coproducts. A concentration on one chief product by most mining companies makes it difficult for raw material suppliers to predict and interpret market changes.[9] To mitigate the problem, most of the world's mining companies cooperate collectively through associations (as in the United States) or as national monopolies and/or international cartels.

Operations through monopolies or cartels alleviate the impact of market losses and serve to hedge against high mine opening and development costs. Benefits to the public are important, too, because collective action in mineral production not only protects capital outlays, but also may aid in the establishment and administration of stable prices. Furthermore, such actions protect employees from cutthroat competition. Even so, price fluctuations are tremendous and can be devastating in their effects.[10] Copper, in contrast, dropped in price from 50 cents a pound to

---

[8] David N. Skillings, Jr., "Europort Iron Ore Terminal," *Skillings Mining Review*, LX, No. 21 (May 22, 1971).

[9] U.S. Bureau of Mines, op. cit., p. 3.

[10] The first antimony price move in 55 months was announced by National Lead Company on March 13, 1969. A 4½-cent increase to 48½ cents per pound was the beginning of a year-long series of advances. By March, 1970, domestic antimony reached $1.76 per pound f.o.b., Laredo, Texas, and the European imports soared to $4.00 a pound at New York. Source: Robert A. Putney, Marketing Manager, Metal Division, National Lead Company: personal communication, 1970.

less than 30 cents within a year. In one case, the purchasers' production plans were upset; in the other, mining operations dropped to unprofitable levels.

Mineral Exploitation Leaves an Indelible Mark on the Environment

Hardly any sizeable areas of the world remain untouched by the hand of either the prospector or the miner. Tunnels carved high in the Rockies, valleys filled with gangue in Arizona, entire counties literally turned upside down in Illinois and Indiana, farmland honeycombed with hundreds of miles of mine railroad tunnels in Missouri, chat piles dotting eastern Oklahoma, subsiding lands lost along the Pacific and Gulf coasts—

FIGURE 24. This vertical photograph from some 70,000 feet shows many of the 73,000 oil and gas wells in Ector County, Texas. The city shown is Odessa, and all the black spots are well sites. Service roads and pipelines are also evident. It is little wonder that residents in these areas are resentful of the concern for Alaskan caribou, and are not too sympathetic with fuel-short East Coast citizens who refuse to allow offshore drilling or new petrochemical and refinery construction. Courtesy U.S. Department of Agriculture.

all stand as testimony to man's all-pervasive search for minerals. Acid lakes and streams, huge quarry pits from gravel, stone, coal, iron, copper, and molybdenum mines, leveled mountains, ugly mine tipples—many of which have been abandoned along with access rails, loading docks, and scattered equipment—and numerous ghost towns are additional, seemingly ubiquitous evidence that mining leaves nearly indelible marks.

Even more severe are some of the environmental effects of man's mineral use. Mercurial poisons have turned formerly sky-blue, sparkling lakes into gray, dull, lifeless bodies worse than useless to man. Sulfur and lead fumes pollute earth's atmosphere, and ash and acids from minerals rain from the skies. Man has learned that a mineral-based civilization extracts a cost in terms of health and esthetics. What ultimate limit can man tolerate? What *will* he tolerate? Answers to these questions are being argued today as citizens, through their governments, set pollution standards and begin to monitor air, water, and food and animal chains for dangerous violations. Indeed, man's use of some minerals, such as mercury, may already be coming to an end, and the use of still other minerals, such as lead, may be seriously curtailed.

The image of mining as the despoiler persists—even after restorative measures, which have been demonstrated as both feasible and successful, are guaranteed by the posting of bonds or the setting aside of funds to make restoration. As a result, some mining firms find their plans stymied.[11] Even in the face of high unemployment pressures, environmental arguments are voiced against the opening of new mines. And, whether environmental considerations may be used to hide nationalism or some other aspiration, the passions aroused when environmental aspects are publicized indicate that future mining may well become more costly, requiring much more time and public education before actual operations can begin. In turn, these cost and time factors may widen the geographic search for minerals and result in buyers purchasing from several alternative sources.

ENERGY SYSTEMS

Perhaps the energy source of greatest imaginable potential to help man attain his wants and goals is fusion. However, until fusion becomes practical, the constantly expanding demands for energy will necessarily be answered by the conventional fossil fuels (petroleum, coal, and natural gas), other fossil fuels (uranium and thorium), and hydropower. Probably fossil-fuel electric generating plants will still be the major source of utility

---

[11] George P. Lutjen, "The Curious Case of the Puerto Rican Copper Mines," *Engineering and Mining Journal*, CLXXII, No. 2, February, 1971, p. 75.

electricity in the year 2000,[12] and energy resources are expected to dominate the total mineral requirement through this millennium.[13]

Until man develops the capability of controlling fusion, which ultimately will dominate all aspects of *energy* development, a major development will be the systematization of all aspects of energy production. Toward this end, firms currently dealing with energy resources—oil, coal, natural gas, uranium, thorium (and hydropower)—are horizontally extending their operations to include all sources of power and are billing themselves as *energy companies*. These firms produce a range of both primary and secondary products. Perhaps the most important aspect of this movement has been the lateral movement of major oil firms [14] to include coal, uranium and/or thorium production (many of these same oil firms also are extending their operations vertically, including chemicals, pharmaceuticals, rubber, etc.). The chief motivating force is to make such firms more responsive to changes in the market place. And that markets *are* changing is apparent in light of shifts in the fuels being used; for example, there have been shifts away from low grade coals (because of high sulfur and ash content) to oil and natural gas. Indeed, there now are significant warnings that the demand for natural gas as fuel for utilities and home heating is about to outrun available supplies [15]—at least until pricing structures change to abet new exploration and development or to facilitate operations to convert coal to natural gas.

It must be expected that the mix of energy fuels will remain in a constant state of change until there are breakthroughs in technology that result in the general use of fusion. In fact, the industrialized nations of the non-Communist world—including the United States—are *fast* running out of *low-cost* fuel minerals. Furthermore, as we have already observed, the oil-rich nations have organized for the purposes of "getting more" for their petroleum, including an industrial capability in most cases. Thus, the eventual effect will be to strain the ability of the industrial nations of Western Europe, as well as Japan and the United States, to pay the ever-higher prices that are being demanded for oil from Venezuela, Algeria, the Near East, and other oil exporting areas. One important development stemming from this action has been a return to coal—only to find that vast North American coal reserves are limited in usefulness

---

[12] U.S. Bureau of Mines, op. cit., p. 6.

[13] Ibid.

[14] Typical of such firms calling themselves *energy companies* and ranking high among the world's largest corporations are Royal Dutch Shell, Gulf Oil Corp., Ashland Oil Corp., Kerr-McGee Corp., and Exxon (the world's largest in 1975).

[15] ArkLa Gas and Power Company cancelled industrial contracts for gas (*Arkansas Gazette,* August 14, 1971, p. 1). This was the first of many such announcements.

because of the sulfur and ash content that creates adverse environmental effects. Similarly, natural gas is in low supply, and technologies to get oil and gas from shale and coal, although known, are costly and limited because of environmental effects.

Further compounding today's energy pattern is the use of nuclear fuels such as uranium and thorium, which also are extremely difficult to handle. To date, no satisfactory long-range solutions are available; without such solutions, there is an ultimate limit on how much energy man can expect from these fuels. England has already felt the limitations of energy parameters; and no doubt, without fusion, even the United States will learn that its ability to produce energy will be stifled. Oil, particularly, is basic to future industrial operations and growth, and, by 1980, the United States—until recent efforts at self-sufficiency—was expected to be importing more than 50 percent of its annual consumption.[16] Currently, vast domestic shortages of oil and gas are real. The cost to the United States for oil imports in 1974 was approximately $15 billion and, against this backdrop, U.S. natural gas reserves were expected to continue to decline. Simply put, the situation *must* change.

Combined, these pressures are being felt politically and economically. Just as was the case with NASA's goal-oriented approach,[17] when the need for fusion becomes a politically expedient goal (because of more general recognition of the critical importance of fusion power to the ultimate success of any pollution-free energy system), then adequate financing will become available and that goal—fusion—likely will be attained. Fusion is currently in an even more advanced stage than fission was at the time that Einstein wrote his letter to President Franklin Delano Roosevelt (early in World War II).[18] Discussions in the field have shifted from questions of pure scientific feasibility to considerations of related technological, economic, and social matters.[19] *Indeed, the awesome, vast, all-encompassing impact that fusion holds for man has had at least short-term adverse effects on nuclear power stations and other power plants.* In view of the prospect that fusion energy may become a reality within the pay-out period of present power plant construction, what should the policies of electric utility companies be regarding such new, perhaps short-lived, construction? Russian sources have stated that it will be possible

---

[16] "Raw Materials—You Get What You Pay For," *Forbes,* August 1, 1971, p. 20.

[17] NASA (National Aeronautics and Space Administration) had for its goal "doing the impossible"—reaching the moon.

[18] Ultimately, the Manhattan Project was the organized effort to attain controlled fission; a similar project and effort might well hasten the day when fusion (already here) becomes practical for everyday use.

[19] William C. Gough and Bernard J. Eastland, "The Prospects of Fusion Power," *Scientific American,* CCXXIV, No. 2 (February, 1971), pp. 50–64.

for the U.S.S.R. to begin industrial production of fusion reactors by 1990–1995. Some U.S. predictions set 1980 as a possible date, assuming that adequate financing for engineering studies and technological progress is available.[20] And today's experiments with laser beams reinforce the hope for solutions to the "fusion key." In any event, if man is to arrive at the point in resource development and materials use at which total recycling and the changing and control of matter become a reality, fusion holds the key; as such, it deserves to become a national—even international—goal of the highest order.

Coal

  Until the advent of fusion, coal appears to be entering a period of interim growth and emphasis. Coal at present is competitive with oil and gas in all areas except in the production of gasolines and similar petroleum products. Even here, it is reassuring to know that coal *is* an alternative resource from which can be obtained synthetic gas and liquid fuel, although it was less economically feasible prior to the mid-1970s.

  Although the mining of coal in the U.S. declined after a 1947 peak of 631 million short tons (to a low in 1961 of 403 million short tons),[21] coal mining climbed again to 600 million tons by 1971.[22] Coal continues to be intensively competitive with oil and gas for all energy areas but home heating and gasolines. Currently, much coal is going overseas, mostly to Western Europe and Japan—and increased volumes are being used for electric generating.[23] Although it has not yet materialized in significant volume, the decline of anthracite mining also seems to have been reversed because of that fuel's high carbon, low sulfur, and low ash content. Especially in gas-deficient areas, anthracite *does* offer less pollution than is the case with bituminous and lignite coals. Also, with a growing practice of beneficiating ores through cintering and a growing demand for high-

---

[20] D. R. de Halas, "Psychofusion," *Nuclear News*, March, 1971, p. 16.

[21] Bureau of Mines, op. cit., p. 35. Prior to entry by major energy companies into the coal industry in the 1960s, coal was a dying and desperate industry with inadequate net revenue, rapidly rising costs (which were 50 percent labor at the mine), virtually no research (except some done by government), markets disappearing to other energy forms, and risk capital refusing to enter the industry. Also, prospects of atomic power (which did not materialize) frightened many marginal mines to close down.

[22] James R. McCartney, "Coal Industry to Have Greatest Year in 1971," *Skillings Mining Review*, LX, No. 9 (February 27, 1971), p. 13.

[23] The high point in exports was 1970 (with 72 million tons exported), and then the amounts began to decline somewhat. See U.S. Bureau of the Census, *Statistical Abstract of the United States: 1974* (95th edition) (Washington, D.C.: Government Printing Office, 1974), p. 516.

grade foundry coke, anthracite production should increase; however, as it is costly to mine and transport (compared with other energy sources), anthracite will continue in relatively modest demand.

Currently, the bituminous coal industry is under attack for environmental damage—especially for its surface mining techniques. However, more than 40 percent of U.S. coal is mined this way, and such production is essential to meet the demand. Restorative methods and attendant supportive financing are constantly making progress, and, in some extreme cases, tax bases even show gains following post-mining improvements.[24] Moreover, not all aspects of strip-mining of coal are necessarily destructive.

Where coal is deep and in sufficiently thick seams to warrant shaft or drift mining, there seems little doubt that underground mining offers certain environmental advantages. However, even in underground mining there are gangue disposal and surface subsidence problems, plus the relatively high cost of mining per se and attendant health and safety factors. In contrast, there are important resource development and use trade-offs regarding surface techniques of strip or auger mining that literally overturn the surface and seemingly destroy the value of the "land." For example, surface mining is not as dangerous to the health and safety of miners. Also, seams of coal too thin to be obtained in any other way can be utilized. Not only does surface mining add to available coal resources, but the cost of mining operations per se is also far less, and the savings are real—especially when one considers the limited value of much of the land so mined in its original state. To date, *most* land used in surface mining has been marginal to submarginal in terms of its income-producing capability, as compared with such post-mining uses as recreation, wildlife, managed forests, farming, homesites, air fields, water supply source, or other specialized uses. Indeed, in level land, the ridges and valleys left over from strip mining can constitute welcome relief, whereas leveled land resulting from mining in hill country may become valuable for farming, plant sites, or recreation areas.

Thus, while open pit or strip mining *can* be very damaging in the absence of controls—and there are uncounted examples of abuse (two Kentucky counties outlawed strip mining, and other areas, such as West Virginia, considered action)—the basic process itself should not be condemned completely. Any form of mining is hostile to the *natural* environment; but one cannot assume that the natural environment is always perfect.

Worldwide, bituminous coal—especially coking bituminous—holds the key to the economic and industrial strength of nations. Evidently the U.S.S.R. (in Siberia) holds the world's largest share of proven reserves, although the United States is self-sufficient, with adequate supplies for the

---

[24] "Strip Coal Mining . . . The Total Benefit Industry," *Coal Age,* April, 1966, p. 13.

foreseeable future and even beyond. The U.S.S.R. is especially well endowed—handicapped only in terms of the distance of known deposits
from established industrial districts. Even China has large reserves of coal,
requiring only developmental funds or investments. Thus, the long-range
prospects are good that coal can help fill the void in man's energy picture
until fusion comes into use. This capability will hold even if present projections of U.S. production in excess of one billion tons per year are
realized.

There is currently a worldwide shortage of available aboveground
coal; it is simply not available, even at prices that increased at unbelievable
rates within one year.[25] In many northern hemisphere industrial districts,
winter cutbacks in production have been necessary.

To protect investments most coal mining firms require large-volume,
long-term coal purchase contracts. This practice favors large users and
larger operations. Eventually the practice will result in *smaller* firms that
will operate *smaller* mines in order to serve *smaller* customers. Such mines
are likely to be less capable of environmental restoration or of mining
better quality coals in terms of their pollution effects.

Current shortages are likely to continue until the rates for fossil fuel
are clarified to a degree that will enable coal producing firms to make long-
range financial commitments. The policies of such administrative agencies
as the Federal Power Commission must allow increases in natural gas
rates, which in effect have acted as a ceiling on all fuel rates, thus preventing adequate returns on coal mining investments. Then, too, the prodigious
coal requirements of rapidly industrializing countries (such as West Germany and Japan) have placed added strains on present coal production.
For example, throughout most of 1969 and 1970 Japanese firms had a
standing offer throughout the United States of $1 more per ton for any
available coal, with the result that many U.S. producers skimmed coal
from deliveries to their long-term domestic customers. This, in turn, reduced aboveground stockpiles to such low levels that the U.S. power generating industry became exceedingly vulnerable to strikes or even threats of
strikes—again escalating the cost of coal.

The total effect of these many related forces—some obvious, others
infinitely more subtle—will be to increase worldwide coal production.
Toward this end, numerous economic webs are being spun to include such
widespread coal mining developments as the U.S. government-subsidized
training of miners to open a captive coal mine (Howe Coal Co.) in
Oklahoma to produce for Japanese markets.[26] Similar developments have

---

[25] "Coal Shortages Chill Chemical Profits Hopes," *Chemical Week*, CX, No. 9,
October 21, 1970, p. 21. By 1974, some coal was selling at approximately $20 a ton.

[26] U.S., Department of the Interior, Bureau of Mines, *Mineral Industry Surveys*, BOMR-223, Bartlesville, Oklahoma, December 12, 1968.

taken place between Japan and captive Australian coal mines. Ancillary developments in the U.S. include an entire new port complex at Port Arthur, Texas, and the implementation of unit train operations between mine and port.

In summary, it is significant that (until the advent of fusion) coal remains *the key mineral* undergirding industry. Historically, coal as a fuel and as a source of iron-smelting coke and chemical by-products has remained the basis of modern industry. The world's industrial leaders—the United States, the Union of Soviet Socialist Republics, and West and East Germany—are the leading producers of coal. The early rise and dominance of England as an industrial power was based upon easily obtained coal supplies. England's relative and absolute decline is similarly due to the depletion of readily accessible coal supplies.

Japan, too, early had a domestic source; but, as that island empire's industrial growth outstripped its supplies, it seized additional supplies in Korea and Manchuria by force of arms. When stripped of these sources by the subsequent events of World War II, Japan extended special efforts to purchase coal by arranging to finance the opening of overseas mines in the United States, Australia, South Africa, and Canada so as to create a diversified source pattern and thereby ensure the necessary coal with which to "stoke" Japanese industry.

Coal's importance is further highlighted by the fact that it is one of the basic foundations of the European Common Market.[27] In terms of its versatility in being used as fuel, coke, or chemical base, coal is without peer; it is the premier of all mineral resources.

Petroleum

Whereas coal can be considered the most basic fuel of the 1970s, petroleum will be sought as the most valuable. Ease of obtaining petroleum and the relative ease of processing and transporting products derived from oil account for petroleum's popularity over coal. It has been so effortless for man to enter oil into commerce that probably more than 90 percent of the total fuel used in transporting man and his goods depends on petroleum for energy. Similarly, probably 30 percent or more of all space heating depends on oil, and the lion's share of all products derived from organic chemicals stems from petroleum. Petroleum is especially important to man's transportation schemes, and modern transportation based on jet, diesel, and gasoline engines would be infinitely more costly, if not economically impossible, without petroleum.

---

[27] The European Coal and Steel Community—France, Belgium, Luxembourg, Italy, the Netherlands, and West Germany—agreed to the so-called Schuman Plan as early as 1952.

Most of the world's known oil resides in a relatively few producing fields. Three-fourths of the petroleum produced outside of the U.S.S.R. and China comes from 71 fields.[28] These are listed in Figure 25. The techniques used in petroleum exploration, drilling, and extraction, even though well established, are constantly undergoing modification in light of new geophysical knowledge.[29] Even so, the techniques are known and the necessary capital is available or can be obtained; the real problems are political—even military—considerations.

Members of the Organization of Petroleum Exporting Countries (OPEC) are demanding more and more shares in the assets, profits, and management of oil companies drilling in their territories. More embargoes are threatened unless member nations [30] receive higher taxes and royalties (and even majority ownership) from the producing companies—previous commitments notwithstanding. In 1970 major oil companies granted OPEC members, which produce more than 90 percent of the world's petroleum exports, higher taxes and profits.[31] Now these nations want more than profits from their petroleum fields; they want a full partnership in the world's technology. How far to go in this direction now provides the background for the world's "oil politics." In fact, the world's "shortage" of petroleum is more political than geological.

One effect, with both short- and long-range implications, is to prompt the international oil firms to press and expand their search for new reserves. Speed will be required if a rampant inflation of petroleum prices is to be halted or reversed.[32]

Inherent in the worldwide problem is the fact that probably two-thirds of the earth's petroleum reserves are in the Near East—Saudi Arabia, Iran, Iraq, Kuwait, etc. Thus, the "power of oil" is concentrated, and the international petroleum operators must find alternative sources. Elsewhere, as in Algeria, assets of foreign petroleum companies have been

---

[28] Robert J. Burke and Frank J. Gardner, "The World's Monster Oil Fields, and How They Rank," *The Oil and Gas Journal*, LXVII, No. 2 (January 13, 1969), pp. 43–49.

[29] Books and other publications detailing petroleum exploration, drilling, extraction, and transportation are myriad. One needs to find the very latest publication, however, because change is occurring rapidly.

[30] OPEC included 13 members in 1975—Algeria, Ecuador, Gabon, Indonesia, Iran, Iraq, Kuwait, Libya, Nigeria, Qatar, Saudi Arabia, the United Arab Emirates, and Venezuela.

[31] By late 1973, the OPEC nations had agreed on a new record world price for their petroleum, established a built-in annual percentage increase (to offset world inflation), and voted to support Libya's take-over of 51 percent ownership of Libyan production by foreign oil companies.

[32] Foreign crude oil, priced at about $2.30 a barrel in early 1973, climbed in some cases to an unbelievable $17 a barrel by the end of that year (see an Associated Press story in newspapers of December 24, 1973), and the end of OPEC's monopoly pricing was not in sight. At the time, U.S. oil sold around $7 per barrel.

FIGURE 25. RANKING OF THE WORLD'S LARGEST OIL FIELDS BY ULTIMATE RECOVERABLE OIL

Area	Number of fields
Middle East	38
North America	11
South America	7
Africa	11
Asia Pacific	4

Rank	Field, Country	Discovered	Ultimate recoverable oil (billion bbls)
SUPER GIANTS—MORE THAN 10 BILLION BBL			
1	Greater Burgan, Kuwait	1938	62.0
2	Ghawar, Saudi Arabia	1948	45.0
3	Bolivar Coastal Field, Venezuela	1922	30.0
4	Safaniya-Khafji, Saudi Arabia-Neutral Zone	1951	25.0
5	Kirkuk, Iraq	1927	15.0
6	Rumaila, Iraq	1953	13.6
5 TO 10 BILLION BBL			
7	Agha Jari, Iran	1938	9.5
8	Abqaiq, Saudi Arabia	1941	9.0
9	Gach Saran, Iran	1928	8.0
10	Sarir, Libya	1961	8.0
11	Raudhatain, Kuwait	1955	7.7
12	Minas, Sumatra	1944	7.0
13	Manifa, Saudi Arabia	1957	6.0
14	Marun, Iran	1964	6.0
15	Ahwaz, Iran	1959	6.0
16	East Texas, U.S.A.	1930	6.0
2 TO 5 BILLION BBL			
17	Bibi Hakimeh, Iran	1962	4.5
18	Sabriya, Kuwait	1958	4.0
19	Murban Bu Hasa, Abu Dhabi	1962	3.0
20	Faris, Iran	1964	3.0
21	Qatif, Saudi Arabia	1945	3.0
22	Lama, Venezuela	1957	2.7
23	Hassi Messaoud, Algeria	1956	2.7
24	Wilmington, California, U.S.A.	1935	2.6
25	Khursaniya, Saudi Arabia	1956	2.5

FIGURE 25. (cont.)

Rank	Field, Country	Discovered	Ultimate recoverable oil (billion bbls)
26	Wafra, Neutral Zone	1953	2.5
27	Abu Sa'fah, Saudi Arabia	1963	2.5
28	Dukhan, Qatar	1940	2.4
29	Zelten, Libya	1959	2.2
30	Poza Rica, Mexico	1930	2.0
31	Minagish, Kuwait	1959	2.0
32	Gialo, Libya	1961	2.0
33	Duri, Indonesia	1941	2.0
34	Murban Bab, Abu Dhabi	1954	2.0
35	Umm Shaif, Abu Dhabi	1958	2.0

1 TO 2 BILLION BBL

Rank	Field, Country	Discovered	Ultimate recoverable oil (billion bbls)
36	Haft Kel, Iran	1928	1.9
37	Masjid-i-Sulaiman, Iran	1908	1.9
38	Zubair, Iraq	1948	1.9
39	Idd el-Shargi, Qatar	1960	1.8
40	Pembina, Canada	1953	1.8
41	Amal, Libya	1959	1.7
42	Sassan, Iran	1967	1.5
43	Khurais, Saudi Arabia	1957	1.5
44	Idris A, Libya	1967	1.4
45	Elk Hills, California, U.S.A.	1920	1.4
46	Berri, Saudi Arabia	1964	1.4
47	Lamar, Venezuela	1957	1.3
48	Karanj, Iran	1963	1.3
49	Swan Hills, Canada	1957	1.3
50	Midway Sunset, California, U.S.A.	1901	1.3
51	B field, Cabinda	1966	1.2
52	Yates, Texas, U.S.A.	1926	1.2
53	Idris D, Libya	1967	1.2
54	Kelly-Snyder, Texas, U.S.A.	1948	1.2
55	Huntington Beach, California, U.S.A.	1920	1.2
56	Bai Hassan, Iraq	1953	1.2
57	Oficina, Venezuela	1937	1.1
58	Maydan Mahzam, Qatar	1963	1.1
59	Ebano Panuco, Mexico	1901	1.0
60	Seria, Brunei	1929	1.0
61	Boscan, Venezuela	1946	1.0
62	El Morgan, Egypt	1965	1.0
63	La Paz, Venezuela	1925	1.0

FIGURE 25. (cont.)

Rank	Field, Country	Discovered	Ultimate recoverable oil (billion bbls)
64	Quiriquire, Venezuela	1928	1.0
65	Dammam, Saudi Arabia	1938	1.0
66	Kingfish, Australia.	1967	1.0
67	Zaraitaine, Algeria	1958	1.0
68	Darius, Iran	1961	1.0
69	Fahud, Oman	1964	1.0
70	Samah, Libya	1962	1.0
71	Rostam, Iran	1967	1.0

Source: *The Oil and Gas Journal,* January 13, 1969, pp. 44–45.

nationalized, thus further weakening the producing and marketing capabilities of the established traders. Still other nations, such as Libya, have seized all petroleum assets in their borders and obtained 51 percent ownership.

Increased erosion of traditional and potential markets is further affecting the competitive position of international oil operators. In addition to the formation of OPEC, there is the success that many countries have had in developing their own domestic supplies—whether they came from offshore, such as the North Sea in the case of Norway, or inland, as in the case of China, which is self-sufficient in oil and gas.[33]

Even domestic politics, especially in the United States, is serving to deepen the problems of international oil companies. Environmentalists temporarily halted the construction of a pipeline from the Alaskan Prudhoe Bay field; when it is built, the extra costs and delay necessitated to overcome political opposition will make transport of Prudhoe Bay oil very expensive. And when the uniquely high costs of the Alaskan pipeline are added to the high costs of exploring and drilling in this remote, bleak, and climatically forbidding area, it may deter the actual full operation of this field for many more years. Only the high cost of monies already invested are causing oil companies to send more funds into this area at this time.

Thus, the search goes on and with limited success. The North Sea is producing some oil; and in Africa, Canada, the South China Sea, and

[33] "Red China Nears Self-Sufficiency in Oil," *The Oil and Gas Journal,* LXVIII, No. 40 (October 5, 1970), pp. 78–79. The huge Taching oil field in northwest China accounts for more than one-half of its production, which is now great enough that China tripled its 1974 oil commitment to Japan from 1 million tons to 3 million a year. There are 7.1 barrels or 298.2 gallons of oil in one metric ton.

FIGURE 26. Costs of drilling on the North Slope are illustrated in this photograph of operations in central Alaska, not far from Fairbanks. North Slope operations are significantly more remote, in barren permafrost lands, where all-new technology is required. Courtesy Exxon Company, Houston, Texas, U.S.A.

the Upper Amazon, the search continues. Even though a consensus of geological writings suggests that there are no more oil reserves comparable to those of the Near East, the combined impact of the current worldwide search will offset the leverage of any one particular region or organization in time. The vast reserves of the U.S.S.R., the U.S.A., and even China are such that, when combined with coal, shale, nuclear, and other energy sources, any braking effect on man's technological "progress" will be both temporary and relatively slight.

U.S. Domestic Shortages of Fuel Oil

The 1970s found the United States facing a prolonged fuel oil and natural gas shortage. Even preventive measures, taken by the federal government, only mitigated the problem slightly; the oil and gas industry characteristically has approximately a five-year lag between the time when changes in demand and/or supply are officially recognized and the time

FIGURE 27. The search goes on. Seismographic teams, such as the one shown in this photograph operating in far West Texas, conduct an ever-widening search, while new drilling rigs attempt to bore ever deeper. Costs necessarily increase. Courtesy Exxon Company, Houston Texas, U.S.A.

when effective action can be forthcoming. For purposes of analysis, three questions are pertinent:

1. Why did the shortages occur?
2. How can the problem be temporarily alleviated?
3. How can the problem be prevented in the future?

The hypothesis is that there is not an actual shortage of fuel oil, but rather a shortage of *cheap* fuel oil and difficulties in the refining and distribution of petroleum and fuel oil. These problems must be weighed in view of the U.S. oil industry, consumers, and oil policies—federal and state—and the world oil market.

Elimination of quotas and prorationing, along with the relaxing of pollution laws, can alleviate the problem on a temporary basis; but long-range plans must include (1) a revised petroleum policy, (2) an increase in mineral efficiency, and (3) a switch to other types of fuels.

The principle area of deficiency is the Atlantic Coastal Region, since

FIGURE 28. AREAS OF POWER SHORTAGES

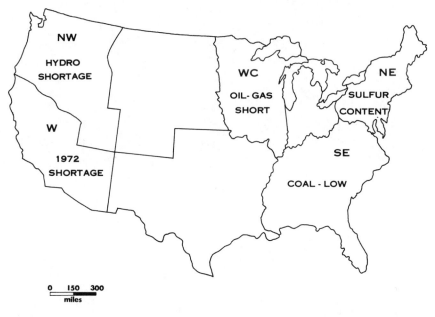

Source: Business Week, October 3, 1970.

it relies heavily on imports. Most of the United States is facing a shortage as demands increase and supplies dwindle. (See Figure 28.)

Among the reasons for this shortage are:

1. Temporary shortage of tankers—owing to Suez Canal closing (now open), decreased production in Libya, and blockage of a major pipeline. This was alleviated later.
2. Higher priced products—the domestic refiners prefer to produce higher-priced petroleum products instead of the cheaper ones.
3. Sulfur content—because of the various pollution regulations, oil with a high sulfur content cannot be used.
4. Nuclear plants—nuclear plants have failed to expand as predicted, thus placing more emphasis on conventional sources of power.
5. Mid-East oil supply—Libya reduced production and Syria blocked the major Trans-Arabian oil pipeline to the Mediterranean; then the Arabs instigated an embargo and continued to play world politics with their oil.
6. Shortages of coal—coal shortages have occurred due to exports to Japan, environmental problems, and the U.S. Mine Safety Act, which forced some marginally profitable mines to shut down. This shortage has manifested

226

itself in the demand for more fuel oil and natural gas (which were in short supply).

7. Power demand—the United States has been increasing its power demand by 8 percent a year (with consumption doubling each decade), and demand forecasts in the late 1960s and 1970s were far too low, relative to what developed.[34]

8. Equipment failures—brownouts and blackouts have become more common as generators fail and/or break down, partly because of overloads and in-insufficient capacity.

9. Environment consciousness—companies are forced to use better grades and less available fuel as regulations are tightened on the use of pollutant products.

10. Natural gas shortage—demand for natural gas is at its highest level, but producers are unable to meet it because production and distribution channels are limited.

11. Imports—the East Coast imports over 80 percent of its supply and, owing to Middle East troubles and increased world consumption, U.S. East Coast supplies stay dangerously low.

12. Change in societal attitudes—an American attitude against bigness and its profitability resulted in a drastic decline in U.S. exploratory wildcat oil and gas wells, which can lead to new fields; this obstruction included the Kennedy administration's area pricing of natural gas production (growing out of a 1954 Supreme Court decision in the Phillips Case), and later congressional reductions in the oil and gas industry's percentage depletion allowances.

Serious shortage can be averted *if* (1) winters are not severe; (2) there are no labor troubles in the coal fields or railroad lines; and (3) the Middle East does not flare up.

There are many estimates as to the severity of the shortage, ranging from deficiencies of 250,000 barrels per day (usually abbreviated as bbl/day or just B/D) upward in the eastern United States alone. Forecasts are very difficult because of such variables as price, Mid-East politics, domestic environmental requirements, and the like. The major suppliers of oil for the United States have been domestic producers, but foreign sources are becoming increasingly important—especially to the East Coast Region (see Figure 29). The major source regions for imports have been

---

[34] For a discussion of power-consumption trends, see David L. Scott and L. D. Belzung, "Analysis of Growth in the Electric Power Industry," *Atlantic Economic Review,* July-August, 1973, pp. 48–51. For a detailed discussion of background to the energy crisis, see L. D. Belzung, "The Energy Crunch. Its Past and Future," *Arkansas Business and Economic Review,* Winter, 1973, pp. 23–27.

FIGURE 29. INTERNATIONAL OIL TRADE
(thousand bbl/day)

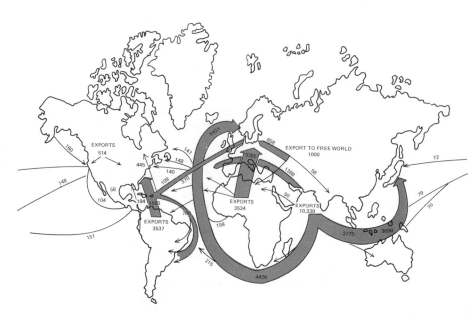

Source: Office of Oil and Gas, Department of the Interior, July, 1968.

Canada and Latin America (but Canada is becoming self-serving with its production, and Venezuela advanced to 1975 its 1985 deadline for taking over majority ownership of foreign holdings in the nation). Other countries will export more oil to the United States if its trade barriers are lowered and if it handles its foreign policy "right."

Figures 30 and 31 give a graphic example of how the U.S. oil picture can change rapidly during a period of shortages. Figure 30 shows a 1970 view, with about one-fourth of the U.S. supply expected to come from the Middle East in 1980 only if crude oil prices remained at $2.00 a barrel or less. Figure 31 shows the 1973 projections—still approximately one-fourth—even though Mid-East prices rose from $2.30 to $11.00 (and, in one case, to $17.00) a barrel for oil, with Arab embargoes, during the single year and wiped out price differentials between U.S. and foreign production. By 1975, Canada and Venezuela had reduced oil shipments to the United States, and Americans were no longer getting more than half of their imported oil from the Western Hemisphere. By the time the reader sees this book, undoubtedly the U.S. oil picture will have turned in a new direction. But the United States is a nation of crises; its citizens did not get

FIGURE 30. THE 1970 OIL PICTURE
(United States Oil Market [million bbl/day])

	1968		1975			1980	
		3.30	Wellhead Price	2.00	3.30	Wellhead Price	2.00
Arab	.4	.1		.5	.1		1.3
Non-Arab *	.1	.2		1.5	.4		4.0
Latin Amer.	1.5	2.1		2.0	2.7		3.7
Canada	.5	1.9		1.8	2.6		1.5
Domestic	10.6	12.4		11.2	13.5		9.5
Total	13.1	16.7		17.0	19.3		20.0

* Exclude Western Hemisphere and Soviet Bloc.
Source: The Economist of London, February 28, 1970, pp. 62–63.

PRICE BREAKDOWN (price/bbl in $)

Louisiana Crude		Mid-East Crude
3.30	Wellhead Price	1.40
.46	Freight to East Coast	
.14	Transport to Port	.74
—	Tariff	.105
$3.90	Total	$2.24

Source: The Economist of London, February 28, 1970, p. 63.

FIGURE 31. MIDEAST OIL—SEE HOW IT SPREADS
(Mid-East Exports)

	1972 Oil Consumption (millions tons)	Percentage from Middle East * in 1972	Projected percentage from Middle East * by 1980
United States	854	4%	25%
Western Europe	775	72%	50%
Japan	261	78%	88%

* Including Libya.

Source: Newsweek, September 17, 1973, p. 35.

the atomic bomb until an all-out effort was needed in World War II to beat the Germans to it; they did not look to outer space until the Russians were there; they did not worry collectively about the environment until they could hardly see or breathe; they did not become concerned about crime and drugs until virtual epidemics developed; and they did not think about a fuel shortage until the service stations ran dry and homes became cold.

In the past the low price of foreign crude oil and U.S. quotas influenced the amount of foreign oil that could enter this country. The permanent lowering of trade barriers has been, and will continue to be, essentially a problem of "security" versus "efficiency." As foreign oil prices first met, and then pushed up, domestic prices during the early 1970s, the consumer felt the pinch, but the long-run effect was unquestionably beneficial since it stimulated development of domestic activities in coal conversion, shale-oil development, tar-sands utilization, and deeper (and much more expensive) petroleum exploration. It also focused attention on the need for alternative energy sources—solar, geothermal, fission, fusion, etc.

Conflicting Values

Conflicting values between pollution controls versus free use, the home industry versus foreign imports, and refinery conversion versus higher-priced products have combined to produce an overall power shortage. The problem of supplying the East Coast with fuel oil is intertwined with these variables plus the international intangibles. The federal government's initiation of controls over fuel distribution, begun in the winter of 1973, was a recognition that voluntary mechanisms do not always work in the short run under a free-enterprise system, and it can not work when prices are restrained.

Temporary Solution to the Fuel Oil Crisis

The fuel oil crisis in the United States was a long time coming, and it was obvious early to those people who would analyze it. It was temporarily alleviated through the use of increased (or removed) quotas, decreases in state prorationing, voluntary increases in domestic production, some restrictions on consumption, and government intervention. But the price mechanism still remains as a major part of the solution. Historically, the United States has been accustomed to *cheap* energy; unfortunately for the consumer, *that luxury is gone forever*. The complexity of the situation and the variables that enter into the problem-solving area are presented later in this chapter.

The quota system of the early 1970s limited the amount of petroleum imported to about 20 percent of the total domestic production (see Appendix 8B). Advocates of the system pointed out that it was increasing supply, lowering costs, and promoting greater efficiency of the oil industry. Opponents contended that the percentage, without a large increase, was crippling the home industry, reducing incentives for exploration, and forcing small producers out of the business.

The policy appeared feasible since it allowed more imports, even though the potential savings were not passed on to consumers. The steps taken by the federal government to ease import barriers during the U.S. energy crisis helped; but they did not solve the problem.

One potential problem of any increase in imports is that, with a tanker shortage (and the country has no means of handling supertankers at all), the United States still has difficulty in obtaining overseas oil. This is aside from the problems of OPEC monopolistic price moves, Mid-East politics, and a mounting balance-of-payments deficit.

Prorationing

Another available measure was increases in prorationing. Prorationing is a state limitation of the quantity of oil produced by each operator to some fractional part of total productive capacity (maximum efficiency rate) of a well. Historically, it is a technique imposed by the major oil producing states to attempt to limit production to forecast demand, so as to make the best use of resources by preventing physical and economic waste.[35] A second economic effect was that prorationing stabilized the price structure of the industry.

By mid-1972, all U.S. oil producing states had raised production allowables to the MER limits (except where fields might be damaged). It is unreasonable to expect that prorationing will be terminated permanently, since it not only stabilizes the industry but also maintains a stable income for the states (which receive tax revenue from oil production).

Increase in Domestic Refining

A third possible solution to the fuel oil problem in the United States is for domestic manufacturing (refining) to increase its output of fuel oil

---

[35] An example of physical waste is reduced oil recovery from a reservoir because of too-rapid recovery; economic waste would be the drilling of more wells than are needed.

and residuals; but the long-range trend is to decrease the yields of low-value products as technology improves.[36] Some of the major oil companies began increasing their output of fuel oils as early as 1970; but such measures were admittedly stopgap attempts and not economically feasible on a long-term basis unless the market price of fuel oil and residuals can move much closer to the going price of the crude oil from which they are obtained.

Extensive alteration of the refinery mix in the United States would have required considerable additions to existing facilities; and, while the oil industry could see the shortages coming, a relatively depressed market in the early 1970s prevented investment capital from moving into refinery construction.[37] Only after the price structure rose considerably, as the nation approached the mid-1970s, was the capital forthcoming. But, there was still the problem of the lengthy time-lag that is characteristic of the oil industry and the American expectation that fuel oil and residuals must be priced far below the going price of the crude oil from which they are refined. Widespread elaborate plans for U.S. refinery expansion were announced immediately after the 1973–74 Arab embargo, but virtually all plans were cancelled by 1975, when the oil companies had a chance to analyze the economic picture more thoroughly.

Other Methods

Additional ways of averting short-range crises might include:

1. Slowing down the economy
2. Lowering the standard of living
3. Increasing use of other fuels
4. Imposing rationing

Any one of these means constitutes a crisis, in and of itself, and can be used only in a "true" emergency, or as a public gesture by private firms, or under governmental compulsions.

---

[36] U.S. Department of the Interior, Office of Oil and Gas, *United States Petroleum Through 1980* (Washington, D.C.: Government Printing Office, 1968), p. 66.

[37] The domestic oil industry "topped out" in 1972, when new refinery construction came to a standstill (just at a time when it was needed most), and for the very sound capitalistic reason that it just was not too good an investment to build additional immensely expensive facilities. The percentage depletion allowance had been cut; there was uncertainty over low-lead versus no-lead gasoline for the future; there were demands for increased imports instead of domestic exploration; environmentalists had halted production from offshore waters and Alaska; price increases were artificially restrained; and reformers complained about oil and gas industry profit margins and advertising expenditures.

FIGURE 32. Clearly, before even a large corporation is willing to invest the requisite millions of dollars in a complex refinery, such as this one located in Baton Rouge, assured markets and raw materials are essential. While the market is assured in the United States, dependable raw material supplies have long been in question. Compounding the problem have been legal restrictions and public resistance to the construction of such refineries where they are needed—chiefly on the East Coast. Courtesy Exxon Company, Houston, Texas, U.S.A.

Solutions

Long-range solutions involve an increase in domestic production, the continuation of some imports, and greater efficiencies—as well as conversion to other fuels. Future shortages can be circumvented only by the implementation of new and practical mineral policies that take into consideration *both* the domestic and foreign political and economic situations.

Future U.S. Sources of Petroleum

Although there is no question the United States experienced a temporary, real shortage of oil, the foreseeable probability is slim that a severe, *lasting* shortage will develop. Local refinery capacities, costs, government controls, or inadequate planning could cause additional temporary or local deficits, but there are vast *known* deposits of oil and large areas of *probable* oil deposits, as well as the enormous reserves of oil shale and tar sands. Given the existing capital, transportation means, and technology, there will not be an "actual" shortage of oil in the near future. As the United States looks overseas, however, the problem of national security forces the government either to reevaluate its position or to look toward new sources of power. Domestic availability and environmental considerations become cost factors.

Outlook for Domestic Shortages

Throughout the 1970s domestic demand for fuel is expected to continue to increase at a rate calculated to outstrip any reserves developed, thus directing domestic users more and more toward foreign sources. The most affected areas will be the East and West coasts because they now face fuel shortages, are still undergoing rapid economic development, and have all *but* supertanker facilities to handle imports. As indicated in Figures 33 and 34, there are several areas of future production. But, in

FIGURE 33. EVALUATION OF FUTURE AREAS OF PETROLEUM PRODUCTION

Area	Amount	Capital	Trans-porta-tion	Tech-nology	Govern-mental Atti-tudes	Overall Feasi-bility	Depend-ability
Alaska	A	A	C	B	B	B	A
Indonesia	B	A	B	A	A	A	A
Southeast Asia	A	A	B	B	A	A	B
North Sea	A	A	B	B	B	B	A
Ecuador	A	B	B	A	B	B	B
Siberia	A?	A	C	B	C	C	C
Nigeria	B	B	A	A	B	B	C
Middle East	A	A	A	A	B	B	C
Algeria	B	A	A	A	B	B	B
S. & N. Africa	A	A	A	A	B	B	C

Criteria: A = favorable for development
B = intermediate position
C = unfavorable

Note: The decisions are based upon the judgment of the writers (including study of the subject and their general understanding of the areas). The list is not all-inclusive, but does include different parts of the world where recent oil discoveries have been made. The magnitude and feasibility of these sites is still a matter of conjecture; therefore, this chart is a guide to, rather than a complete study of, the oil picture. Criteria are based upon the U.S. viewpoint in areas where applicable.

addition to these sources and the above-mentioned techniques, the United States will continue to turn to current supply areas (Figure 34).

Technological advances in the areas of exploration, drilling, production, and transportation (pipelines, supertankers, etc.) are a key to avoiding future crises. The list of new opportunities is very broad, and the likelihood of more efficient techniques for oil utilization also is very strong.

However, technology itself is not the sole answer to the problem—government policies can be equally important in arriving at solutions to the recurring domestic oil crises. For one thing, future government policies toward imports can be expected to soften, out of necessity and because of demand for lower-priced oil. Admittedly, changes will be slow, because the government will be challenged by the small domestic companies and by leaders in oil producing states. Governmentally administered controls are likely to be the key to future oil policies and prices in the United States (see Appendix 8C).

FIGURE 34a. WORLDWIDE OIL PICTURE, 1970

Country	Reserves (1000 bbl)	Production (1000 bbl/d)	Refining– Crude (1000 bbl/d)	Feasibility
Australia	2,500,000	41.3	320.0	B—14
Indonesia	9,000,000	724.6	282.2	B—15
West Germany	700,000	155.6	2358.6	C—16
Middle East	317,522,000	12,263.2	2437.9	
Iran	55,000,000	3314.4	644.8	B—14
Iraq	27,500,000	1529.0	103.5	B—14
Kuwait	68,000,000	2518.0	489.0	A—12
Muscat-Oman	5,000,000	317.6	———	C—16
Neutral Zone	13,000,000	454.8	———	B—15
Saudi Arabia	140,000,000	2914.6	377.0	A—13
Africa	54,679,000	4998.9	784.9	
Algeria	8,000,000	936.6	48.3	B—15
Egypt	5,000,000	236.4	175.0	C—18
Libya	35,000,000	3066.7	9.5	C—16
Nigeria	5,000,000	537.3	46.0	C—18
Argentina	4,000,000	339.0	457.2	A—13
Mexico	6,000,000	405.1	494.5	A—12
Venezuela	14,750,000	3580.0	1313.4	A— 9
Canada	8,782,000	1200.0	1400.0	A—10
United States	38,700,000	9177.6	12,600.0	
West Hemisphere	76,661,750	15,406.5	19,112.5	
Total Free World	463,780,400	34,147.5	41,842.6	
Communist World	60,000,000	7118.6	———	
Total World	523,780,000	41,266.1	———	

FIGURE 34b. CRITERIA AFFECTING FEASIBILITY

PROXIMITY

1 = Western Hemisphere
2 = On water body
3 = Inland

HOME DEMAND

1 = Low
2 = Moderate
3 = High

RESERVES

1 = Over 30 billion barrels
2 = Over 10 billion barrels
3 = Under 10 billion barrels

STABILITY

1 = High
2 = Moderate
3 = Extremely variable

PRODUCTION

1 = Over 1000 bbl/day
2 = Under 1000 bbl/day

ATTITUDE TOWARD U.S.

1 = Friendly
2 = Neutral
3 = Virtually hostile

INFRASTRUCTURE

1 = Advanced
2 = Semideveloped
3 = Poorly developed

GRADE STRUCTURE (totals from above)
7—13—A = good
14—15—B = fair
16—20—C = poor

Natural Gas

Historically, natural gas production was a "by-product" of petroleum production. Most gas in the early development of oil fields was flared, allowed to escape, or occasionally used in developing the field where the gas happened to be coming to the surface. On rare occasions, a large oil company (Exxon in the Katy Field near Houston) could afford to reinject natural gas into the reservoir and hold it for several decades until markets were available.

Worldwide natural gas development and utilization still lag far behind petroleum because of transportation problems. The continuing development of pipelines, even across the Mediterranean,[38] the development of super-cold pressurized tankers to move liquid natural gas in volume across oceans, plus the relatively fast growth of energy markets depending on natural gas—

---

[38] Williams Brothers Pipeline Company of Tulsa, Oklahoma, announced intentions of surveying and engineering a pipeline from North Africa across the Straits of Gibraltar to Western Europe.

236

all are changing past patterns, and gas fields are being sought now for their natural gas content alone. This is especially true within the United States and the U.S.S.R., and today nearly all industrial nations are looking for sources of energy.

In the United States in 1970, approximately one-third of all energy consumed was natural gas. Natural gas consumption has been increasing at a rate of nearly 6 percent per year (whereas petroleum growth has experienced an average annual rate of increase of less than 4 percent). However, because of economic manipulation in response to political pressure, it is now clear that the United States and other highly industrialized nations are facing acute shortages. And, for the most part, these shortages have been effected by economic regulation rather than by geological shortages of gas per se.

In the United States, the natural gas industry has been regulated by the Federal Power Commission, which, since the mid-1950s, has kept well-head prices of most gas at such unrealistically low levels as to discourage exploration, drilling, and development of attendant pipeline systems to keep new supplies flowing. In the Phillips decision of 1954, the Supreme Court, in effect, applied common carrier pricing techniques—because of an earlier Interstate Pipeline Act—to natural gas prices at the well-head if the gas were intended for interstate commerce. Other explanations for the low gas prices and growing domestic shortage are:

1. Early accumulation of discovered gas reserves in and around developed oil fields (at a time when there was little market for gas)
2. Rapid development of pipeline technology, and pipeline expansion based on this technology
3. Effects of price inflation on coal and oil energy forms (but, because of regulation, these effects were not passed on to natural gas)
4. Clean characteristics of gas for home heating, making it more desirable
5. Rapid development of industrial markets based on low-cost, so-called interruptible rates on off-peak-season gas supplies
6. Current emphasis on environmental considerations
7. The effects of long-term contracts, which have acted as a lid on price increases

In the long run, prospects for supplies of natural gas depend on what regulation (or deregulation) discourages or encourages production. Unless price increases are allowed that will encourage adequate levels of exploration and discovery, natural gas shortages result.

Congressional action about the turn of this decade also reduced considerably the oil and gas percentage depletion allowance (cutting the amount of tax-exempt income received by oil or gas producers), and this discouraged wildcat activity.

Further clouding the issue are long-established and continuing arguments among preservationists, conservationists, and energy producers themselves. Some people argue that shortages should be encouraged to the point that rationing becomes necessary. Producers of competing fuels (like coal) and those who transport the fuels understandably support this position. They argue on the side of the preservationists and conservationists that natural gas should be allocated first—or even reserved exclusively—for home heating and cooking. Industrial needs, they say, ought to be met with coal, nuclear, and other nonhydrocarbon energy sources. At this time, no clear-cut course of action has been set; the oil and gas industry has repeatedly convinced enough congressmen to vote against this so-called National Fuels Policy.[39]

In the United States, even with all of the exploration that has occurred, there is still no accurate estimate of potential natural gas reserves. Elsewhere in the world, with the possible exception of the U.S.S.R. and North Africa, gas reserves are still being found only coincidental to petroleum fields.

The importance of natural gas to the Soviet economy is highlighted by the Soviet Union's pronouncement that it has located the world's largest gas reserves. Based on finds in and around the Arctic Circle in western Siberia, the Soviet Union claims in excess of 10 trillion cubic meters of natural gas.[40] Based on such estimates, the U.S.S.R. is planning a 1250 mile pipeline from field to industrial markets in the Moscow-Leningrad area. In addition, because of the presence of these natural gas resources, that country is planning to develop the region as an economic whole, including cities in excess of 100,000 people working in developing and supplying the fields, a gamut of petrochemical plants, power plants, lumber mills, and service facilities. In all, over 32 separate natural gas fields have been defined, and, when finished, a pipeline system of more than 12,500 miles will serve the fields. This U.S.S.R. potential development well illustrates the basic building-block characteristics of mineral resources in changing cultures and in social achievement.

Nuclear Fuels

Man's "on again–off again" interest in nuclear fuels is currently "on again." Nuclear fuel applications are currently looking favorable to society

---

[39] There are many valid arguments both for and against such a national policy enacted into law, and the conclusions one draws depend mostly upon the assumptions with which one starts. At any rate, the issue is not likely to arise again soon, because the coal industry (the main advocate of such a policy) is currently healthier than it was in the early 1960s, and many large oil companies have now entered the coal business.

[40] "Soviet Biggest in Gas?" *Chemical Week,* June 28, 1969, p. 18.

after the experience of an initial period of rapid growth during 1965–1968. A wave of concern over adverse environmental problems attendant with radioactive waste disposal—from the mining and milling of uranium ores through refining, fabrication, and use as a fuel—developed strong political support that served to act as a brake on "progress." [41] A lag in market development also acted to restrain or prevent a rapid buildup of nuclear applications.

Now, however, rising costs of fossil fuels and, with volume production, a lowering of costs for nuclear fuel materials are exerting inexorable pressures for nuclear power plant construction. The higher capital outlays required for nuclear power plants can now be recovered because nuclear fuels are less costly than fossil fuels. In fact, as this nation entered the 1970s, it appeared that fossil fuels were simply not available for certain areas.[42] As a result, plans for nuclear-based power plants, rather than fossil-fueled plants, are being implemented,[43] and the Atomic Energy Commission (AEC) estimated that U.S. nuclear capacity will increase from less than 1 percent of its total output to more than 50 percent by the year 2000. Perhaps the largest boom in adopting nuclear fuel applications will take place with the advent of commercialized fast-breeder reactors, expected in the 1980s in the United States. The French already have tested the fast-breeder reactor with a 250,000 kilowatt pilot plant.

In recognition of these expected developments, many oil and gas companies, international as well as domestic, have expanded into uranium production operations; [44] and mining, electronic, and aviation industries,[45] too, are moving to join the race to see who will be providing nuclear fuels in the coming decades. Toward this end, the federally sponsored AEC was gradually withdrawing from operational activities in favor of supervisory controls. The AEC ceased to exist after January 19, 1975, and its licensing and regulatory functions were taken over by the newly created Nuclear Regulatory Commission (NRC). Further promising to bring lower costs to the nuclear fuels facet of the economy is foreign competition.[46]

In support of this expected growth and further possible advances in

---

[41] For a detailed development of nuclear fuels, their historical development, industry technology, geology, market, and hazards, see: Joseph A. DeCarlo and Charles E. Short, "Uranium," *Mineral Facts and Problems,* U.S. Department of the Interior, Bureau of Mines (Washington, D.C.: Government Printing Office, 1970), p. 219.

[42] "Nuclear Power Is Looking Better All The Time," *Chemical Week,* September 16, 1970, p. 22.

[43] Ibid.

[44] Continental Oil Co., Texaco Co., Kerr-McGee, Gulf Oil Co., Getty Oil Co., Skelly Oil Co., Atlantic Richfield, Combustion Engineering, etc., ibid.

[45] Amarillo Minerals, General Electric, North American–Rockwell, etc., ibid.

[46] Yellow cake (a form of U_3O_8) from Britain's AEC and Australia's Mary Kathleen Limited plants, ibid.

technology, U.S. domestic uranium requirements will move from a 1968 level of 2700 short tons to an estimated 65,000 by the year 2000.[47] Even though an import quota is expected to be implemented before long, this volume of uranium will provide for one-half of the nation's anticipated needs. France is planning to go ahead with commercial liquid metal fast-breeder reactors, which can use the waste products from nuclear reactors.[48] Significantly, worldwide developments, although lagging behind the U.S. rate of increasing nuclear fuel dependence, will be sufficient to create competition for the more readily available uranium. As a result, by the 1990s the cost of nuclear fuels can be expected to rise to a level where competing fuels might once again receive attention. Attendant upon these advances in nuclear fuel applications, miscellaneous or ancillary applications are expected to be met from already-produced supplies of depleted uranium stocks.

Solutions to problems concerning endangered health and environment are needed and can be expected with time, added capital, and technological breakthroughs. However, such developments will no doubt add to the cost of power produced, so that uranium and thorium nuclear fuels are not—and will not be—the clear-cut panacea leading to abundant, low-cost power that is so often predicted.

Other Energy Systems

Until fusion power becomes a practical reality, the United States and the world, in addition to intensifying their exploration and development of natural gas and uranium, will extend their searchings into other forms of energy. There was a wide array of proposals—to turn garbage and animal wastes into oil or natural gas, to propel automobiles with hydrogen (the fuel used in spaceships) or hydrides, etc.—but the best near-term candidates for energy appear to be oil shales and tar sands, although shortages of water required by current technologies may limit potential growth of these sources. Also, the possibility that prices of competing energy sources may decline again—making shale and tar sand production uneconomical —has dampened enthusiasm for them.

Oil Shales and Tar Sands

Although marginally commercially competitive with coal, petroleum, or natural gas as sources of energy, oil shales and tar sands offer potential oil reserves; the technology exists, at a cost, to turn these materials into

---

[47] Joseph A. DeCarlo and Charles E. Short, op. cit., p. 240.
[48] David Brand, *The Wall Street Journal,* January 28, 1975, p. 26.

FIGURE 35. An indirect dry cooling tower system for a 200-million-watt steam turbine generator. Indirect dry-type cooling systems lend themselves to far higher ratings (1000-million watts or more), which make them attractive for use with nuclear power plants. Courtesy GKN Birwelco Ltd., Birmingham, England.

energy resources. Especially well endowed with oil shale and tar sand deposits are the United States, Canada,[49] the Union of Soviet Socialist Republics, Mainland China, Sweden, and Australia; and extrapolations from various estimates indicate that these energy sources alone would last for some 300 to 350 years at 1970 rates of consumption.

A degree of urgency in regard to developing competitive technology levels for oil shales and tar sands is evident in the announced energy policies of the United States.[50] The U.S. Bureau of Mines operates, under federal

---

[49] The first tar sands mining and processing complex was opened in 1967 by Great Canadian Oil Sands, Ltd., a subsidiary of Sun Oil, at Fort McMurray, Alberta, along the Athabasca River. Union Oil Co. expects to complete the first private commercial U.S. oil-shale conversion plant in 1979 in western Colorado.

[50] "Proposal to Reopen Shale Research Facility Studied," *Tulsa Daily World,* August 24, 1971, p. B–11.

sponsorship,[51] the Anvil Point oil shale research facility on U.S. Navy oil shale reserve land near Rifle, Colorado. Even here, environmental considerations promise to add to costs and to slow developmental work.[52] The Bureau of Mines plans to operate under contract to private firms housing machine shops, laboratories, crushers, refineries, mines, mining equipment, and water and sewage systems. Other countries, such as Sweden and the U.S.S.R., operate similar facilities.

Even so, cost considerations indicate slow progress and the need for further relative increases in the price of energy from more "conventional" sources.

Hydroenergy

Limited by locations—where running water in regular regimes and in large volumes is found and where optimum climate and nonsoluble rock formations exist—hydropower (chiefly hydroelectric power) resources are definitely limited and relatively well developed. Significantly, because of attendant dependence on a reliable watershed and, in turn, on land uses within a watershed, most hydroelectric plants are government sponsored, developed, and operated.[53] Private operations are, for the most part, conducted as a "utility" and are operated in conjunction with—or supplementally to—an electric power system grid. Only a few corporations and private firms, usually historical remnants, operate hydroelectric power units for their own consumption.

For the world as a whole, about one-fifth of the produced electricity depends on hydroelectric sources. Yet, in some countries such as Canada and Norway, as much as 90 percent of the electricity is derived from flowing water; in the U.S.S.R. and Japan, about 50 percent; and in many countries of Western Europe, approximately 40 percent. And, with a continuous, growing world demand, hydropower development will be intensified.

Exotic Power Sources

Geothermal, wind, tidal, solar, and other exotic power sources, although currently insignificant in man's search for energy, stand in the wings.

---

[51] Adequate water supplies also continue to be a problem in oil shale operations.

[52] National Environmental Policy Act of 1969.

[53] For example, in the United States, even though long-term operations may be turned over to an authority (Tennessee Valley Authority, Missouri Valley Authority, etc.), during periods of development involving flood control, navigation, power production, and recreation, the Corps of Engineers or Department of Defense is responsible. However, if irrigation and land reclamation are paramount and hydropower is a secondary consideration, then the Bureau of Reclamation of the Department of the Interior is made responsible.

Geothermal power, although developed in Italy and elsewhere, has shown only the feasibility of known technologies. Vast geothermal areas in Alaska, Antarctica, the U.S.S.R., and elsewhere are available when the economics involved so indicate. Similarly, technologies for using planetary winds and solar radiation, or the tides and thermal differences of the sea, as power sources are known with only limitations of the cost and space factors holding back further developments until there are relative cost increases in more traditional fuel sources.

Outlook

For the world and in the face of limited proven and theoretical reserves, the consumption of natural gas, petroleum, and coal (in that order) is growing rapidly. For the short term, this trend will continue. In the long term, coal, oil shales, and tar sands—which hold the preponderance of the earth's fossil fuels—will come into play. Along with these trends will be layered, almost independently, the development of fission power plants, and, at least by the year 2000, it is hoped, fusion power sources.

MINERALS AS THE MEANS OF CONTROLLING OR CONSERVING ENERGY

The mineral economies of the United States and the world are undergoing constant change. As far-reaching and revolutionary as technological breakthroughs or change may be, there are few areas where the impact of science is more noticeable than in those minerals used to harness or conserve energy. The chief categories within these minerals are the: (1) ferrous category, (2) nonferrous category, and (3) nonmetallic category.

For the most part, these minerals are so-called *fund* resources (as compared with *flow* resources—see earlier discussions, Chapter Two). As such, their principal characteristics are significant factors in the various decision-making processes that determine whether any particular mineral will be used in quantity or with care and only after diligent searches for better or less costly substitutes. These resources can be "exhausted"—or, at least, the "ore bodies" favorable to man's exploitation at a given point in history (economically, politically, technologically, culturally, or militarily) may be exhausted. Whether any given mineral is literally used up is open to debate.[54] However, evidence that ore bodies can be depleted for use as a "resource" can be found in the abandoned iron mines of Pennsylvania and Minnesota, the desolate lead mines of Missouri, and the stark, quiet silver mines of Colorado. Perhaps for these reasons, the opening and exploitation of mines should be based on far greater deliberations than has

---

[54] U.S. Bureau of Mines, *Mineral Facts and Problems,* op. cit., pp. 7–9.

been the case historically. Man, in his hurry for progress, has all too often "mined out" and "gotten out," leaving economic and social ruin in his wake.

In fact, as most minerals are mined, milled, smelted, and refined for use within complicated resource systems and chains of systems, man has

FIGURE 36. View within a ball mill illustrating one facet of a resource chain requiring great capital and know-how to implement. Ball mills are used to pulverize coarse materials. Courtesy Stearns-Roger Corporation. Photo by Ray Manley.

introduced environmental pollutants that are now so severe as to preclude past use patterns for certain minerals. The list is long but of sufficient importance to warrant some illustration; therefore, mercury, sulfur, lead, and asbestos are discussed toward the end of this chapter as examples of environmental parameters to mineral development, or the "breaking" of resource chains.

Ferrous Minerals

One of the most basic of economic indicators is the demand for ferrous metals, which for purposes of convenience include the so-called ferrous alloys [55] that serve chiefly as additive elements in making steel

---

[55] The chief alloys added to iron ore to produce various grades and kinds of steel include: manganese, silicon, chromium, nickel, cobalt, columbium, tungsten, tantalum, molybdenum, and vanadium.

(and/or steel alloys). Historically, the locational bases of iron and steel mills have been: (1) the ready availability of good coking coal deposits, (2) ready access to iron ore deposits, (3) break-in-transit on transportation modes, (4) iron and steel markets, and (5) labor. Where favorable combinations of these factors are to be found, iron and steel milling, rolling, and processing are found. The flowlines of iron and steel making, the critical points, and the location of activities are especially well developed and discussed in depth and breadth by Erich Zimmermann.[56] However, the great developments in regard to iron and steel manufacturing since the advent of Zimmermann's classical treatment will be discussed here under four headings: (1) worldwide dependence on international iron ore traffic, (2) beneficiation, pretreatment, and direct reduction of iron ores, and accompanying technological prospects, (3) growing recognition of, and attempts to cope with, environmental problems, and (4) need for new mining laws and policies.

Worldwide Dependence on International Iron Ore Traffic. It traditionally has been basic to the world's leading iron and steel producers that they have in-house deposits of iron ore. The United States had its Mesabi Range, France had its Lorraine deposits, and Britain originally had its local supplies. Germany, too, had its own supplies but early turned to its neighbors Luxembourg, France, Austria, Sweden, and Czechoslovakia for supplies. Between World Wars I and II, France, Germany, and Britain turned to sea movements of iron ore from Spain and North Africa. Since World War II, development of the world's more favorable iron ore deposits has been widespread and has reached points on every continent.

The big change to overseas deposits came during the 1960–1965 period. For example, within that five-year span, the transoceanic share of iron ore imports to Western Europe increased rapidly. In 1960, 64 percent of the imports came from other neighboring European countries. By 1965, non-European producers were supplying more than 51 percent.[57] Venezuela, which in 1960 was the biggest transoceanic supplier of ore to Western Europe, had been surpassed by Liberia, Brazil, and Mauritania. By 1965, Sweden was no longer Western Europe's largest nondomestic supplier of high quality iron ore.

The Australian Example. During this same five years, and during the remainder of the 1960s, Japanese and United States capital, markets, and know-how developed an Australian-Japanese-United States trade tri-

---

[56] Erich Zimmermann, *World Resources and Industries* (New York: Harper & Brothers, Publishers, 1951), pp. 648–54.

[57] Svenska Handelsbanken Index, *Economic Review,* Index No. 4, Stockholm, Sweden, 1967.

FIGURE 37. These outsized ore carriers, with bulk-handling equipment, work at Seven Islands ore terminals on the St. Lawrence estuary. Each unit is capable of handling 7620 tons of ore per hour, or two tons per second. A 100,000-ton deadweight bulk ore carrier can be loaded in 6½ hours. Courtesy M.A.N., Maschinenfabrik Augsburg-Nürnberg AG, West Germany.

angle based chiefly on Australia's iron ore (but also on such alloys as copper and nickel).[58]

The matter of Australia's iron ore reserves has had some contradictions. In 1888, a government geologist wrote that Australia had sufficient reserves to supply the world, but, since iron ore had no value in the Pacific region, there was no sense in bothering with iron minerals. By 1938, the Australian government placed a ban on the exportation of iron ore because estimates placed reserves at 368 million tons, a 50-year supply. In 1961, the Commonwealth lifted the embargo, and suddenly Australia had massive known reserves.

The man credited with discovery of large reserves in the Hammersly Range of Western Australia in 1952 is Langly George Hancock. Realizing the immensity of the project, he interviewed 30 large companies over the next eight years. He entered into an agreement with Kaiser Steel of Cali-

---

[58] Marshall E. Perry, "Australian Iron Ore Development and Japanese, American Participation," mimeographed (Norman, Okla.: University of Oklahoma, 1970), p. 8.

fornia in 1960, and a company was formed. The embargo was lifted the following year, and Hancock moved in teams, which he directed from the air, and claimed Mount Tom Price. This claim has over one-half billion tons of iron ore reserves.[59]

After negotiations with Japanese steel companies in 1965, the first step was soon taken to exploit the deposit, and Port Dampier facilities were started, with 182 miles of track laid, town sites built, and mine facilities constructed. By mid-1966, the first contract ore was loaded into the *Houn Maru,* bound for Japan, and three years later an average of 13 million tons of ore was being shipped—75 percent of it destined for Japan.[60] Contracts for an additional five million tons of ore per year were signed in 1969 with Japanese steel mills, which initiated the opening of a new mine and port facilities.

Although the Mount Tom Price group was the first on the scene, shortly before the sailing of the *Houn Maru,* the first ore from the Goldsworthy Mining Company left for Japan.[61] This company had prospected the area and found large reserves of ore (at 59 percent iron minimum) in excess of one billion tons.

The latest major project in Western Australia, the Mt. Newman Mining Company, is destined to become one of the largest in the world. It began shipping ore mined at Mt. Newman through Port Hedland in 1969. Capacity was projected to reach 20 million tons by 1975, and the ore was to go to Japanese, Australian, and Romanian steel mills. Japan was taking 12 million tons per year by 1975, or about 7 percent of its estimated requirements.[62]

In Tasmania, the Savage River Mines—a smaller, $80-million operation—began shipments in 1968 of iron ore pellets to Japan. This mining operation is owned 50 percent by Japanese interests and the remainder by a mixture of American and Australian companies. The operation is notable for a 53-mile slurry pipeline, the first successful long-distance heavy mineral line in existence; it feeds the 2.25-million-ton-per-year pellet plant.[63]

The preceding four examples of mining endeavors are sufficient to indicate the Australian trend, which obviously has a strong bias toward Japan. The Australian Bureau of Mineral Resources data show a total

---

[59] Ibid., p. 9.

[60] *Skillings Mining Review,* LIX, No. 1, January 3, 1970.

[61] Approximately the same facilities were constructed as the Hammersly group had built, except that the rail line was 71 miles long and port facilities were erected on an island at Port Hedland. Here, the operating company is owned by Consolidated Gold Fields Australia, Ltd., Cyprdu Mines Corp., and Utah Construction and Mining Company. *Skillings Mining Review,* LVIII, No. 39, September 27, 1969.

[62] It is another example of Japan's having obtained in peacetime what it could not get by force in World War II.

[63] *Skillings Mining Review,* LVIII, No. 49, December 6, 1969.

mineral export pattern changing from 33.3 percent to Japan in 1965 to 48.6 percent by 1968—all at the expense of Europe, percentage-wise, in mineral trade. In 1968 Japan took 85 percent of all iron ore exported, and projections show Japan to be consuming well over 90 percent of the iron ore exports in the 1970s. Japan also is taking considerable percentages of coal, alumina, nickel, and copper, and it has projected even larger purchases in the future.[64]

This Australian development has been partly at the expense of other— even established—producers such as Chile, Peru, Canada, and the United States.[65] Since 1965, equally large mines have been opened in Canada, Angola (West Africa), and the Soviet Union. Russia, the world's largest iron ore producer, has indicated plans to extend its exports to nations outside the Eastern bloc.[66]

Steel, too, has joined iron ore in the international character of its traffic patterns. For some steel-producing nations (such as the United States), the imports present both subtle and obvious problems. Low-cost, foreign-produced steel is seriously eroding domestic markets. From 1955 to 1965, imports almost doubled every three years.[67] Fears existed among domestic U.S. producers that, if trends continued, it would become unprofitable for them to stay in business.[68] Over the world, steel imports have almost tripled, with nearly 70 nations now producing. World capacity now exceeds world demand, and most nations—with output exceeding domestic demands—are keeping the United States market in mind. Lower labor costs and newer plants and technology combine to enable these recent comers among the world's steel producers to outproduce, in terms of cost, the older, established producing countries.[69]

The effects that imports have on domestic production in terms of employment, balance of payments, and other economic factors are combining to bring restraints on international trade. To illustrate, in 1967 the United States considered legislation that would restrict imports to 10 percent of domestic steel production.[70] Thus, steel quotas could become a core around which further trade barriers will develop.

The effect on U.S. production can be summarized best as follows:

---

[64] Australia Bureau of Mineral Resources, Geology and Geophysics, *Australian Mineral Industry, 1968 Review* (Canberra: Australian Government, 1968), pp. 14–22.

[65] Ibid.

[66] Index, op. cit., p. 2.

[67] "Dangerous Bargains," *Steelways,* March/April, 1968, p. 7.

[68] Ibid., p. 7. Imports began to rise at a slower rate after 1965; U.S. Bureau of the Census, *Statistical Abstract of the United States: 1974* (95th edition) (Washington, D.C.: Government Printing Office, 1974), p. 800.

[69] Ibid., p. 8.

[70] Ibid., p. 7.

FIGURE 38. STEEL IMPORTS INTO THE UNITED STATES

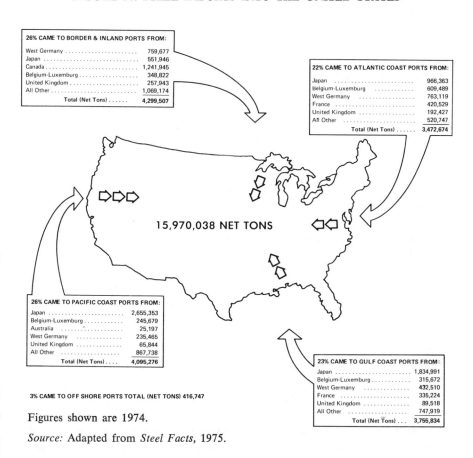

26% CAME TO BORDER & INLAND PORTS FROM:	
West Germany	759,677
Japan	551,946
Canada	1,241,945
Belgium-Luxemburg	348,822
United Kingdom	257,943
All Other	1,069,174
Total (Net Tons)	**4,299,507**

22% CAME TO ATLANTIC COAST PORTS FROM:	
Japan	966,363
Belgium-Luxemburg	609,489
West Germany	763,119
France	420,529
United Kingdom	192,427
All Other	520,747
Total (Net Tons)	**3,472,674**

15,970,038 NET TONS

26% CAME TO PACIFIC COAST PORTS FROM:	
Japan	2,655,353
Belgium-Luxemburg	245,679
Australia	25,197
West Germany	235,465
United Kingdom	65,844
All Other	867,738
Total (Net Tons)	**4,095,276**

3% CAME TO OFF SHORE PORTS TOTAL (NET TONS) 416,747

Figures shown are 1974.

Source: Adapted from *Steel Facts,* 1975.

23% CAME TO GULF COAST PORTS FROM:	
Japan	1,834,991
Belgium-Luxemburg	315,672
West Germany	432,510
France	335,224
United Kingdom	89,518
All Other	747,919
Total (Net Tons)	**3,755,834**

in 1949, domestic iron ore production amounted to 38 percent of the world's total. In 1959, this had dropped to 14 percent. In 1969, it was down to 12 percent. Net ore imports during this period increased from five million tons in 1969 to an estimated 52 million tons in 1973.

Further developments serving to firm up present iron and steel trade relations are investments in large facilities for the pretreatment and direct reduction of iron ores, and improvements in the transportation of bulky ores.

Beneficiation, Pretreatment, and Direct Reduction of Iron Ores and Accompanying Technological Prospects. Three-fourths of all iron ore mined throughout the world is sintered and/or pelletized. The iron content of ore prepared for transoceanic shipments is controlled, and this enhances the ease of transportation and lowers attendant costs. In fact today's mill speci-

249

fications demand that nearly all ore be beneficiated. Beneficiation crushes ores, sinters them, and then reconcentrates the particles into agglomerations of predetermined sizes. The exact processes used depend on the nature of the ores and their intended purpose.[71] The next step in the expected technological chain points to prereduction. In turn, there is the spreading adoption of "mini-steel plants" on coastal, deep-water sites, using fine ore loaded and unloaded as slurry through pipelines. The dried reduction technique used by the Hysla steel group of Mexico (plus similar techniques) is pointing the way [72] to still other presmelting steps in iron ore processing.

By way of summary, in 1960 one-half of the world's ore production was shipped to the furnace as run-of-the-mine product; by 1980, untreated ore will account for no more than 20 percent.[73] In the long run, grinding operations—although initially requiring more capital—are producing controlled smelter ores more cheaply; the result is lower-cost iron and steel.[74] Prereduction also complements scrap iron in the smelting techniques.

Changes in transportation technologies include ore slurry pipelines and 120,000-ton deep-sea iron ore carriers and ore-transfer systems that unload at rates approaching 10,000 tons per hour. The development of vast storage and ore-maintenance areas must be accompanying cost factors.

Trends emerging from the foregoing discussion are important. In some nations (notably the United States), there will be a decrease in technical assistance to overseas areas. In regard to iron and steel, postwar efforts to "build up" American allies and former foes alike have succeeded too well. Consequently, this country's domestic iron and steel economy is depressed; for example, Great Lakes ore shipments in the early 1970s were at their lowest point since 1936.[75] Japanese and West European steel of equal quality can be imported cheaper than it can be produced anywhere in the United States. What logically follows is the ability of those same foreign areas to produce iron- or steel-manufactured items such as automobiles, generators, and machine tools. Will earth-moving machinery and agricultural machinery be next? If it were not for national-defense arguments, economists would be tempted to note that the principle of comparative advantage should dictate abandonment by the United States of the iron- and steel-making business. Other nations seem to do it cheaper—and, thus, better!

Owing to the very basic building-block nature of iron and steel, these

---

[71] For a detailed discussion of the various techniques, see U.S. Bureau of Mines, *Mineral Facts and Problems,* op. cit., pp. 294–95.

[72] M. M. Fine, "Production and Utilization of Metallized Ore," *Skillings Mining Review,* LXI, No. 9, February 27, 1972, p. 1.

[73] Ibid., p. 14.

[74] Togues Astier, "Impact of Prereduction on Steel Making in Latin America," *Skillings Mining Review,* LXI, No. 11, March 11, 1972, p. 1.

[75] *Skillings Mining Review,* LXI, No. 5, January 29, 1972, p. 22.

eventualities seem to be causing many nations to turn to nationalism. Also, the currently rich nations are getting richer and the currently poor nations are becoming poorer.[76] Behind all of this is the fact that iron movements are no longer limited to a few "have" nations, for, as has been pointed out, iron ore and iron and steel movements are global in nature. These developments, plus the unknown aspects of environmental concern, have resulted in an unsettled situation throughout the industry—a situation that promises to last for at least a decade.

Growing Recognition of, and Attempts to Cope with, Environmental Problems. Environmental considerations evident in current iron and steel production include problems related to: (1) mining and ore beneficiation, (2) smelting and milling, and (3) iron and steel markets. In total, the impact of environmental protective movements in terms of cost, new equipment, and effect on employment in the iron and steel industry is most difficult to gauge. These costs will have an important impact, but they will be borne because of the very basic nature of the industry. The only alternative is to depend more and more on foreign iron and steel—which only moves the pollution problems of mining, smelting, and milling overseas and makes environmental problems of the iron and steel marketplace even more difficult to control.

Increased reliance on sintered and pelletized ore has had a corresponding effect on the construction and use of larger and improved beneficiation plants near the mines. Gangue disposal has become a problem, with its pollution of streams and lakes and even coastal sections of Lake Superior. As a general rule, it requires about three million tons of ore to produce two million tons of pelletized or sized ore; the difference constitutes costly disposal problems. And, where domestic ore must compete with foreign ore, the additional cost often prohibits profitable operations. Thus, hydraulic removal into a flowing stream or the waters of a nearby lake is only a short-run, temporary *economic* solution. In the long run, total *social* cost considerations suggest that these polluting measures are not acceptable. This raises the trade-off question: are Americans, as a nation, willing to forego the lower cost of imported ores and, in turn, support the higher costs of domestic ore development and use? Obviously, higher prices for domestic ores will be needed if adequate controls of mining spoils and gangue are to be realized.

Another point to consider is the fact that much of the legislation proposed from time to time would further reduce domestic mining activities—including iron ore production—and would force added dependence on

---

[76] This idea is not new, of course; it is touched upon in Gunnar Myrdal, *Economic Theory and Underdeveloped Regions* (London: Gerald Duckworth, 1957), and in Zimmermann's discussion of resource hierarchies, op. cit., pp. 140–41.

foreign sources.[77] For example, 427 legislative restrictions to mine development were put before the Congress in 1972 alone,[78] not to mention other measures that were introduced at the state and local levels.

Environmental considerations of iron and steel smelting and milling are tempered by the fact that U. S. producers are facing intensified competition at home and from abroad. Yet research and development efforts have resulted in new and improved techniques. Complete instrumentation has taken some of the guesswork out of these processes, produced cleaner stacks, given more uniform products, improved methods of mining and washing coal, and enhanced the preparation of coke.

Similarly, the use of oxygen in the open-hearth furnace not only speeds steel making, but produces less pollution. Although not yet feasible economically, the possibility of man's making steel directly from iron ore—without the long-used method of blast furnace processing—is now technically feasible.

Perhaps some of the most significant environmental considerations in iron and steel manufacturing technology have been in the area of water use. Beginning more than a decade ago, when Bethlehem Steel agreed to purchase sewage effluent from the city of Baltimore for purification and recycling use throughout the massive Sparrows Point, Maryland, iron and steel producing complex, in conjunction with individual plant efforts to abate both water [79] and air pollution, the industry has been making progress in learning to live within man's geographic/environmental parameters. Many changes have brought about improved water use: sources of pollution have been controlled more efficiently; filtering systems have been installed; "settling basins" that remove soil and dust have been built; chemicals and oils that remove fine particles and neutralize acids [80] have been utilized; and even the amount of water needed in iron and steel production has been reduced. Problems still exist; but it is significant that the attendant problems still limiting progress are economic in nature. These are related to the market.

Need for New Mining Laws and Policies. Major changes both in the marketplace and in the mining laws and policies will be necessary if iron and steel's chief environmental problems are to be solved. For example,

---

[77] S. Norman Kesten, "Legislation Will Reduce Mining Activity," *Skillings Mining Review,* LXI, No. 4, January 22, 1972, p. 5.

[78] Ibid.

[79] It takes approximately 45,000 to 55,000 gallons of water to produce a ton of steel. As early as 1967, Armco was spending millions of dollars annually in a water abatement program described in great detail in a corporate publication, *Armco Today* (Middletown, Ohio: Armco Steel Company, 1967), pp. 2–7.

[80] For example, in some steel plants, hydrochloric acid is used in pickling solutions rather than the customary sulfuric acid. The former is costlier to neutralize.

the scrap-processing industry's capacity to recycle metallics is not being used anywhere near its fullest potential because existing laws and regulations—or the lack of new enabling legislation—prevent better uses of scrap metals. An illustration of this is rail rates on iron ore and scrap, both regulated by the Interstate Commerce Commission. Current regulations fail to recognize that scrap iron and steel must compete with iron ore, and the ore enjoys far lower rail rates than does scrap. Consequently, movement of scrap from accumulation points to processing points is inhibited. To increase scrap utilization, legislation is needed relative to the pricing of metallic products so that the user is rewarded if he returns them to the scrap assembly point, or he is penalized if he does not. Also, just as mine owners receive depletion allowances that enable them to regain their capital investments when the mines or wells become exhausted, the scrap industry should have similar incentives in terms of their equipment needs. This relief would be especially timely in encouraging scrap firms to purchase and operate the latest available equipment to cut and size metal from junk automobiles and similar sources of metallic environmental pollution.

Against this background of rising costs for environmental controls and consumer resistance to mining activities and subsequent "spoiling the

FIGURE 39. Scrap, de-tinned cans, and shredded iron provide iron to precipitate copper in solution. The copper lodges on the pieces of metal and the iron goes into solution as iron sulfate. Scene is at the Copper Beach plant at Sahuarita, Arizona. Such uses of scrap metals require more favorable transportation rates for scrap (as against those for ores). Courtesy American Smelting and Refining Company.

countryside," the hard-pressed metal industries are becoming less able to meet the nation's mineral needs. What seems required are new laws that will permit mutually acceptable exploration and mining on federal lands, as well as continued freedom to enter into private and state land compacts to produce mine products. The current overreaction to environmental problems that result from mining activities, if not sensibly controlled, will only lead to greater mineral shortages and inflationary costs over the long run.

Nonferrous Minerals

The minerals in the nonferrous category are too numerous and diverse to describe in detail. Thus, it suffices to point out that aluminum, magnesium, titanium, and copper are the critical elements because they are the growth elements.

An insatiable demand in the United States and the world for electrical power is placing exceptional demands on copper and aluminum, while the jet age has stimulated growth and concentrated attention on such nonferrous metals as titanium and boron.

Some nonferrous metals, such as mercury, sulfur, and lead, are under heavy attack because of their adverse environmental effects. All producers of metals seem to be experiencing difficulties in controlling pollution problems attendant upon mining, processing, and scrap recycling.

In almost all cases—but especially in the case of tin, lead, and zinc—substitutes and replacements loom as threats to these industries.

Copper. The United States is the world's leading copper producer and consumer,[81] but worldwide demand for the metal is strong and increasing. Electrical equipment and supplies constitute approximately one-half of the demand. On the supply side, mining and metallurgical research related to more economic extraction and beneficiation of low-grade copper ores has increased the economic availability of immense tonnages of ore. Some of the more effective conservation practices of recent years include the reclamation of a major component of the U.S. copper supply from scrap, the recovery of copper by leaching from material too low in grade or unsuitable for beneficiation, and the obtaining of additional native copper by reworking old tailings with regrinding, flotation, and leaching.

In the United States, air pollution from copper smelting and refining operations has resulted in considerable state and local legislative action—laws either proposed or adopted—to control sulfur oxides and particulates. Thus, there has been considerable research recently into better methods of controlling sulfur oxide emissions, as well as research into ways of ensur-

---

[81] U.S. Bureau of Mines, *Mineral Facts and Problems,* op. cit., p. 541.

ing that the industry shall have adequate long-term water supplies with a minimum of water pollution.

Aluminum. Aluminum production is now a worldwide industry. There seems to be no shortage of bauxite and—with improved transportation to remote tropical areas rich in bauxite, plus development of techniques to utilize deep deposits or even clays—there appears to be no problem of supply of the source materials. Rather, the future seems to be more clouded by considerations of electricity costs to reduce alumina to aluminum; of the cost of cleaning stack gases of dust, carbon, and fluorides; of the restoration of mined-out bauxite areas; and of the disposal of fine red mud residue from the bauxite-to-alumina process. There is no question that demand will continue to increase as there are applications in almost all sectors of the economy.

Magnesium. An abundance of magnesium in seawater brines, magnesite, and dolomite might well provide a solution to some of the problems

FIGURE 40. Machine known as a "universal jumbo" operating in an underground mine. These jumbos are designed for one-man operation and provide improved efficiency and production. The need and use of such sophisticated equipment illustrates the principle that resources and their development depend on man's technologies and culture. Courtesy Gardner-Denver Company, Quincy, Illinois.

encountered with aluminum production simply through the substitution of magnesium for aluminum in many uses. Currently, the chief deterrent to this is the high cost of producing magnesium. This situation could well change rapidly—especially if one considers the residue pollution problems of alumina processing. There are no major pollution hazards in the production of magnesium, although there may be some indirect problems relating to use of limestone (or oysters) and energy—the other principal ingredients of the process.

Titanium. Titanium uses are chiefly for pigment, welding rods, and aircraft structural metals. It is produced from ilmenite and rutile, and the former is plentiful in the United States and is a major source of pigments (especially as an opacifier in paints, paper, and plastics); rutile is in short supply, not only in the United States but also worldwide. Recent research has been concentrated on finding feasible methods of producing structural metals from the relatively plentiful ilmenite. Environmental problems for titanium are similar to those encountered in the production of aluminum.

Mercury. Mercury—also known as quicksilver—has been used by man for more than 20 centuries (Aristotle mentioned it in the fourth century B.C.). Because it makes a good case study—substitutes exist for very few of its uses, and it is an example of a break in the resource chain—mercury will be examined in detail at this point.

Mercury is known in 25 minerals but is recovered almost entirely from the red sulfide known as cinnabar. During the past 500 years, mercury has gained importance by its use in pharmaceuticals, in industrial chemical processing, and as a poison. Although its poisonous qualities have been known for some time,[82] its effects were popularized by Lewis Carroll in *Alice in Wonderland,* where the author so characterizes the "Mad Hatter." [83]

Modern technology has expanded the use of mercury into the production of plastics, urethane and vinyl chloride, chemical acetaldehyde, batteries, silent switches, high-intensity street lights, fungicides, magnets, mildew inhibitors, caustic soda, chlor-alkali, and pulp and paper, as well as in sewage treatment and gold reclamation.[84]

The World Health Organization (WHO) established .05 parts per million (ppm) as the safe limit on mercury concentrations. Canada, how-

---

[82] *The Shorter Oxford Economic Atlas of the World,* 3rd ed. (Oxford: Oxford University Press, 1965), p. 94.

[83] Mercury was used in that day in the processing of fur into felt to make hats; after lengthy employment in the hat industry, the debilitating effects of mercury poisoning took its toll as brain damage.

[84] Carol E. Knapp, "Mercury in the Environment," *Environmental Science and Technology,* November, 1970, p. 890; for the chlor-alkali process, see "A Grim Pursuit of Quicksilver," *Business Week,* July 18, 1970, pp. 42, 44.

ever, set .5 ppm as the safe limit; for years, the United States accepted Canada's limit, but some scientists admit that no one is sure what is "really safe."

Because mercury exists in a natural state, there is a *natural* amount of its concentration. When this factor is combined with man's use of the metal, one finds mercury concentrations in soil, air, and water.[85]

As a fungicide treatment for grain seed, mercury protects the seed from fungi that hinder germination processes. Developed in Germany in about 1914, mercury fungicides came into common usage during the 1920s.[86] The danger to humans results from their eating wild game fowl that have eaten the grain. Other cases have resulted from misuse of the grain in feeding farm animals or in grinding meal for human consumption. A University of Toronto study of 300 foods showed that many grains were contaminated with mercury—especially wheat and rice.[87]

Scientists, knowing that mercury vapor was poisonous, have for years made it a practice to handle and store mercury in water to prevent vaporization. Since mercury is costly, the average laboratory technician or layman seldom considered it feasible to dispose of mercury, much less release it as effluent into rivers and lakes; yet, industry *has* flushed it in large quantities into water systems. The annual disposal rate in the United States may be as high as 1,200,000 pounds, and the dumping in Canada may amount to 250,000 pounds a year.[88] It has been estimated that 23,917,200 pounds of mercury was expelled into the U.S. environment between 1945 and 1970.[89] Mercury, lying on river and lake bottoms, will take centuries to deteriorate (if some way is not devised to remove it).

Fish can accumulate concentrations of mercury 3000 times the amount in surrounding water,[90] and the lethal nature of mercury poisoning for humans is such that one's eating three meals of contaminated fish within a

---

[85] Tests show that soils in the northeastern United States register mercury concentrations of .04 to .02 ppm, the air in the San Francisco Bay area has 2 nanograms of mercury during smoggy conditions, "clean water" in the northeastern U.S. has tested at .06 parts mercury per million, Santa Barbara Channel oil at 21 ppm; coal tests at about .5 ppm.

[86] Berton Rouèche, "Annals of Medicine," *New Yorker,* August 22, 1970, p. 64.

[87] *Business Week,* op. cit., p. 43. David W. Ehrenfield, *Biological Conservation* (New York: Holt, Rinehart and Winston, 1970), p. 48, notes that if the grain is eaten by chickens, the mercury collects in egg whites, which, if eaten by man, makes mercury accumulate in his brain, kidney and other tissues; this is organic mercury. For an explanation of how inorganic mercury in water bodies is ingested by fish and converted to organic mercury, see "Mercury and Mud," *Scientific American,* September, 1970, p. 86.

[88] *New York Times,* September 11, 1970, p. 1.

[89] "Legal Antidote for Mercury Pollution," *Business Week,* April 25, 1970, p. 31.

[90] *New York Times,* July 25, 1970, p. 22.

seven-day period can be fatal.[91] The half-life of mercury in fish tissue is 17 to 20 weeks.[92]

The worldwide human death toll has run high from consumption of mercury-contaminated fish, animals, birds, and seed grain.[93] When death does not occur, many individuals have been left as "living vegetables."

In an industrialized nation like the United States, prevention of mercury contamination is a complex problem that resists easy solutions. The Army Corps of Engineers has been charged since 1889 with monitoring all discharge into navigable waterways, and companies dumping effluent were supposed to itemize any substances that they felt "might have environmental effects"; but no one ever thought to look for mercury as an offender.[94] Also, there were some 60,000 registered pesticides used in the United States, and most contained some form of mercury; it was not until 1970 that the Pesticide Regulation Division of the Department of Agriculture banned the sale of all "mercury-laden" products, but subsequent court actions reversed the order on some such products.[95]

Of course, bans that halt the dumping of pollutants and the production of pollutants or contaminated food are only as good as their enforcement. Solutions are likely to be both expensive and lengthy in their implementation—and certainly resisted by those persons affected by such regulatory action.

First estimates of mercury poisoning in the United States considered it confined to the Great Lakes area; but later figures show that 33 states have some dangerous contamination of their waters.[96] By 1970, four states had closed some lakes and rivers to fishing—with Alabama placing a ban on 51,000 acres of water, including the Tennessee River. Of course, the economic impact to commercial fishermen and those businesses catering to sports fishermen, tourists, and recreation runs into uncounted millions of dollars—and many businesses are ruined forever.

---

[91] Jerome J. Knapp, "Mercury Poisoning (or) The Fish You Catch Can Kill You," *Field and Stream*, July, 1970, p. 44.

[92] Rouèche, op. cit., p. 64. This source also describes the symptoms of mercury poisoning.

[93] For a discussion of some of the cases, see Rouèche, ibid; Knapp, op. cit., p. 44; Harold Martin, "The Mad Hatter Visits Alice's Restaurant," *Today's Health*, October, 1970, p. 34; *Business Week*, op. cit., p. 44; Daniel Zwerdling, "And Now, Mercury," *The New Republic*, August 1, 1970, p. 17. The worst epidemic of mercury poisoning occurred in Iraq in 1972, when 6500 persons were admitted to hospitals and 459 deaths were recorded; rural families received methylmercury-fungicide-treated wheat seed grain from Mexico and, instead of planting the grain, used it to make home-made bread (*Wall Street Journal*, July 19, 1973, p. 12).

[94] Robert Sherrill, "Pesticide Irresponsibility: The Real Villains," *The Nation*, September 14, 1970, p. 210.

[95] "Deadly Mercury," *Sports Illustrated*, July 20, 1970, p. 9. The National Agriculture Chemical Association claims that there are "no substitutes for mercury fungicides" (*Business Week*, op. cit., p. 44).

[96] *New York Times*, September 11, 1970, p. 1.

While mercury pollution is, by the very nature of the metal's pattern of use, primarily a problem of economically advanced nations that have the technology and capital to support sophisticated industries, it is not limited to those countries. Secondary sources of pollution—resulting from pesticides, fungicides, and treated seed grains—also affect less-developed nations as well. It will take dedicated governments, an enlightened and determined populace, and a socially aware business community to correct man's resource-use pattern of mercury.

This discussion of mercury as a case study of man's break in the resource chain is rather lengthy; but it reflects only the beginning of investigations into the detrimental effects that other metals have on man and his environment. *Among others that have serious effects in varying degrees are lead, cadmium, zinc, arsenic, chromium, copper, barium, and selenium.*

Sulfur. As has been the case with mercury, sulfur dioxide issuing from smelters, generating plants, and chemical plants has become a major environmental concern. An estimated 37 million tons engulf the United States annually, and, if unchecked, the total could reach 61 million tons by 1980.[97] That this is not likely to happen is evident by legislation, either pending or approved, at both the state and federal levels.

One result of existing and pending legislation against sulfur dioxide is that producers and users of sour crude oil and sour natural gas [98] are now going into the production of sulfur for the market. Accelerating this trend are government-decreed, five-year amortizations of the equipment used in recovering the sulfur dioxide at the well, the stack, or the point of processing. Demonstration-grant monies will further hasten the abilities of such producers to recover sulfur rather than let it escape into atmosphere.

The Ducktown, Tennessee, precedent has shown the way for freight-rate reductions to move reclaimed sulfur competitively to market. The terrain around Ducktown previously resembled the barren moon's surface because SO_2 from a copper smelter smokestack would "wash" out of the atmosphere to form sulfuric acid on the ground. In the Ducktown court case, a decision required operators of the smelter to recover the sulfur waste being vented up the stack and, in turn, required the railroads serving the area to institute rates sufficiently low to make the sulfur price competitive in the marketplace.

The total impact, over time, will be to force the closing of many Frasch-process sulfur productions and to rely increasingly on the recovery

---

[97] Gordon Young and James P. Blair, "Pollution, Threat to Man's Only Home," *National Geographic,* December, 1970, p. 772.

[98] Sour crude oil and sour natural gas are high in sulfur content, as opposed to the "sweet" hydrocarbons, which contain little sulfur. Much of this impurity, if it is a high percentage, often is removed at the point of production (meaning near the well).

of otherwise waste sulfur. Much work remains to be done to perfect scrubbers and other technologies designed to eliminate stack sulfur.

Lead. Lead, too, has proved to have environmental parameters. Air over many North American cities has concentrations of lead 20 times greater than air over rural areas. The atmospheric lead content comes mostly from gasoline additives and the venting of burned lead alkyls. Man is now becoming fearful of the unnatural hazards in his being exposed to such high concentrations of lead.

For the immediate future, it appears that lead in urban dust and dirt is more likely to cause lead poisoning than is atmospheric lead. Certain workers, such as garage mechanics and traffic policemen, might be subject to hazardous levels more than other persons. However, for the most part lead poisoning has not reached the poisonous levels of mercury and sulfur, although there are parameters to be reckoned with, and technologies are being sought to bypass man's dependence on lead. Some lead poisonings—such as in paints—are no longer as much of a problem as they once were.

Asbestos. Asbestos is representative of numerous other products that are under careful scrutiny as being at least potentially dangerous to health. Asbestos occurrence in nature is limited to only three or four places in the world; Canada has the only economically feasible deposit. Such characteristics as its fire-resistance, electrical nonconductivity, and insulative nature to heat and cold have resulted in its being mined, even though its adverse effects on health are widely known and feared. In fact, its damaging effects on the lungs or other human membranes have quite literally forced development of substitute technologies. Thus, an example of man's mining of a deadly substance despite this knowledge and accompanying fears is destined to be terminated soon. Asbestos is now produced with great care and for only limited applications, and laws and building codes have been widely legislated either to prohibit its use or to specify detailed safety measures. Asbestos further illustrates the dynamic and constantly changing nature of resources.

In summary, man's use of vital minerals reflects—to a uniquely high degree—his needs and wants, his cultural values, and his willingness to accept substitutes for certain minerals when such substitutes can be used.

Man's Needs and Wants, Cultural Values, and Mineral Uses and Substitutions

It has been noted by some writers that it is a society's cultural values that determine what kinds of minerals that society will accept or demand.[99]

---

[99] Montrose Sommers and Jerome B. Kernan, *Columbia Journal of Business World,* II (March, 1967), pp. 89–97.

The question then arises: in the light of a need to find substitutes for minerals that are either characteristically hazardous or in short supply (particularly in view of unprecedented annual worldwide population increments and corresponding geometrically increasing demand for minerals), what is the future of mineral availability and consumption?

Humans seem to have an almost infinite ability to increase their numbers, while the resource base upon which they *currently* depend for support seems to be finite.[100] The question must be asked, then: how long can the demands of the population be met with existing resources? Technology has made great strides toward meeting these demands, and technology has the capacity to grow at astounding rates; but societal values and institutional patterns maintain a continuous "drag" on that potential growth. Cultures change and adapt at a much slower rate than technology would if it were

FIGURE 41. This sophisticated conveyor-belt system in rock salt mine at Borth, West Germany, shows literally the depth to which man applies his technology to meet his needs for key minerals. The lengths and capacities of horizontal haulage systems are increasing in size because of the availability of new materials and research models. The result permits not only deeper and more vast operations, in terms of distance, but it also opens doorways to uses of lower-grade ores. Courtesy GHH Sterkrade, a subsidiary of M.A.N., Maschinenfabrik Augsburg-Nürnberg AG, West Germany.

---

100 Actually, the resource base is finite only in the relatively short-run period; resource theory, as discussed in early chapters of this book, points out that *resources* is a dynamic concept that changes over time. What is a resource today may not be one tomorrow, and the reverse is also true.

permitted to progress unrestrained by culture. In today's world, the only lasting solution, within the parameters of this "dynamic-technology/cultural-lag" conflict, lies in some sort of worldwide policy of population stabilization. This would ensure that the population growth rate does not outrun the ability of inhibited technological change to meet resource demands. Certainly this thought is not new, and there is reason to believe that such population stabilization will take place; the only question really is, *when?*

Even if a stabilized world population can be achieved, greatly increased demands upon mineral resources will continue because of economic growth in all parts of the world. A nation could, of course, greatly limit or cut back on the use of its resource base in an attempt to conserve adequate supplies for future years (although this also would curtail growth). Or, the nation could blindly proceed to use its resources freely, with little real thought given to the concept of optimum use; this would leave the problems of ultimate exhaustion to future generations. The latter alternative might be intolerable to many readers, and the former will be only partially acceptable. A far more logical and sensible approach would be to work rapidly toward a concept of "most efficient use" of the nation's resource base, and—where applicable—develop *and force* the allocation of substitutes for minerals that are hazardous or in short supply. Undoubtedly, technology is capable of solving the myriad of problems associated with finding and developing suitable substitutes. The real problems of the future will come in the area of product acceptance—and that is a cultural problem rather than a technological obstacle.

Thus, detailed studies need to be undertaken to determine the number and diversity of products, existing or proposed, that could successfully serve (and be accepted) as effective substitutes. Such studies would include analyses of the cost factors involved in society's making the proposed substitution. If, for example, a particular metal used in household cookware could be put to better use for other purposes, serious consideration should be given to the use of substitute materials (glass or some other comparable material) for cookware. Of course, unless such a shift to substitutes were forced on society—and this would be contrary to the American tradition of consumer choice in a profit-oriented economy—business and government still would be faced with the uncertainty of consumer acceptance. It is here that the cultural traits that dominate a society will come into play.

The chief difficulty would be the fixed investment that manufacturers have in producing existing products. The capital outlay required to retool for the change in basic materials would be enormous; but there are ways that this could be handled by society. The transition could be made slowly, as in the replacement of antiquated equipment, with a minimal trauma; or, if the need for a change to substitutes is immediate enough for public concern, government subsidy (rapid tax write-offs, etc.) could be utilized. The important point is that a great deal of mineral savings could be accomplished without reducing product availability, and damaging environmental effects from the use of hazardous minerals could be alleviated.

SELECTED BIBLIOGRAPHY

BROOKS, DAVID B., *Supply and Competition in Minor Metals* (Resources for the Future, Inc.). Baltimore: The Johns Hopkins Press, 1965.

CLYDE, PAUL H., and BURTON F. BEERS, *The Far East*. Englewood Cliffs, N.J.: Prentice-Hall, Inc., 1966.

CHRISTENSON, C. L., *Economic Redevelopment in Bituminous Coal: The Special Case of Technological Advance in United States Coal Mines, 1930–1960*. Cambridge, Mass.: Harvard University Press, 1962.

DOHERTY, WILLIAM T., *Conservation in the United States, A Documentary History: Minerals*. New York: Chelsea House Publishers in Association with Van Nostrand Reinhold Co., 1971.

FRASCHÉ, DEAN F., *Mineral Resources: A Report Presented to the Committee on Natural Resources*. Washington, D.C.: National Academy of Sciences, National Research Council, 1962.

GRAYSON, C. JACKSON, JR., *Decisions Under Uncertainty: Drilling Operations by Oil and Gas Operators*. Boston: Harvard University, Division of Research, Graduate School of Business Administration, 1960.

GUILLAIN, ROBERT, *The Japanese Challenge*. Philadelphia: J. B. Lippincott Co., 1970.

LADOO, RAYMOND B., and W. M. MYERS, *Nonmetallic Minerals* (2nd ed.). New York: McGraw-Hill Book Company, Inc., 1951.

LAMEY, CARL A., *Metallic and Industrial Mineral Deposits*. New York: McGraw-Hill Book Company, 1966.

McDIVITT, JAMES F., *Minerals and Men; An Exploration of the World of Minerals and Its Effect on the World We Live In* (Resources for the Future, Inc.). Baltimore: The Johns Hopkins Press, 1965.

MANNERS, GERALD, *The Changing World Market for Iron Ore: An Economic Geography* (Resources for the Future, Inc.). Baltimore: The Johns Hopkins Press, 1971.

MANNERS, GERALD, *The Geography of Energy*. London: Hutchinson University Library, 1964.

McKNIGHT, THOMAS L., *Australia's Corner of the World: A Geographical Summation*. Englewood Cliffs, N.J.: Prentice-Hall, Inc., 1970.

NININGER, ROBERT D., *Minerals for Atomic Energy: A Guide to Exploration for Uranium, Thorium, Beryllium* (2nd ed.). Princeton, N.J.: D. Van Nostrand Company, Inc., 1956.

RUSSELL, WILLIAM L., *Principles of Petroleum Geology*. New York: McGraw-Hill Book Company, Inc., 1951.

SCHURR, SAM H., *Historical Statistics of Minerals in the United States* (Resources for the Future, Inc.). Washington, D.C.: Resources for the Future, Inc., 1966.

SMITH, WALTER S., and C. W. GRUBER, *Atmospheric Emissions from Coal Combustion; An Inventory Guide*. Cincinnati: U.S. Division of Air Pollution, 1966.

U.S. DEPARTMENT OF THE INTERIOR, BUREAU OF MINES, *Mineral Facts and Problems*. Washington, D.C.: Government Printing Office, 1970.

U.S. DEPARTMENT OF THE INTERIOR, Geological Survey, *Mercury in the Environment*, Geological Survey Professional Paper 713. Washington, D.C.: Government Printing Office, 1970.

U.S. DEPARTMENT OF THE INTERIOR, OFFICE OF OIL AND GAS, *Plain Facts About Oil*. Washington, D.C.: Government Printing Office, 1963.

VOSKUIL, WALTER H., *Minerals in Modern Industry*. Port Washington, N.Y.: Kennikat Press, 1970.

APPENDIX A

The Office of Civil and Defense Mobilization was changed by act of Congress to the Office of Emergency Planning on September 22, 1961. The name of this agency was changed again by Congress on October 21, 1968, to the Office of Emergency Preparedness.

The *U. S. Government Organization Manual of 1970/71* shows the following administrative organization for OEP:

Director

Deputy Director

Assistant Director

Director, National Resource Analysis Center
     Deputy Director, National Resource Analysis Center
     Chief, Materials Policy Division
     Chief, Systems Evaluation Division
     Chief, Resource Evaluation Division
     Chief, Economic Stabilization Division

Director, Government Preparedness Office
     Chief, Plans and Procedures Division

Chief, Guidance and Review Division
Chief, Special Facilities Division
Director, Field Operations Office
    Chief, Operational Analysis Division
    Chief, Disaster Assistance Division
    Chief, Field Services Division
Director of Planning Review
Director of Liaison
Director of Information
Director of Administration
General Counsel
Health Adviser

Purpose. To assist and advise the President in the coordination and determination of policy for all emergency preparedness activities.

Activities. To study and advise the President concerning use of resources such as manpower, materials, industrial capacity, transportation, communications, civil defense, stabilization of the civilian economy and rehabilitation after enemy attack.

The office also determines the kinds and quantities of strategic and critical materials to be acquired and stockpiled against a war emergency (this important activity was assigned to the OEP by the Strategic and Critical Materials Stock Piling Act of 1946).

The Trade Expansion Act of 1962 and the earlier Buy American Act of 1933 allow the OEP to investigate the impact of foreign imports and to consult with procuring agencies to determine buying policies of the United States "to determine if security is threatened."

One pertinent point about the OEP is: "It develops and maintains a complete capability for monitoring, evaluating, and projecting the status of the Nation's resources and economy to meet all types and degrees of national emergency; and analyzes present and future resource deficiencies and strengths. . . ."

Responsibilities. The OEP is responsible for developing and recommending emergency preparedness legislation for all levels of government; implementing and maintaining the readiness standby agencies and programs; and coordination of the National Defense Executive Reserve Program. It provides advice and assistance to Federal agencies regarding programs for the mobilization, allocation and utilization of national resources and coordinates emergency operating plans and action measures.

Source: U.S. Department of Commerce, *United States Government Organization Manual, 1970/71* (Washington, D.C.: Government Printing Office, 1970).

APPENDIX B

HOW HOUSEHOLDS WERE HEATED IN NORTHEASTERN UNITED STATES, 1965

Source	Percent
Gas	32.9
Petroleum	59.0
Coal	7.2
Electricity	.9

Source: *Competition and Growth in American Energy Markets* (Houston, Texas: Texas Eastern Transmission Corp., 1968), p. 27.

COMMERCIAL ENERGY
(percent)

	Gas	Petroleum	Coal	Electricity
1960	46.7	18.0	14.7	20.6
1965	50.1	17.7	6.0	26.7
1985	55.9	7.2	0.0	36.9

Source: *Competition and Growth in American Energy Markets* (Houston: Texas Eastern Transmission Corp., 1968), p. 34.

CONSUMPTION OF PETROLEUM
Quantities
(thousand bbl/day crude equivalent)

	Residential	Commercial	Industry	Transportation	Generated Power	Non-energy	Total
1947	772	126	1008	2768	134	353	5161
1965	1696	244	1725	6078	344	1163	11250
1985	1545	341	2876	12195	540	4998	22495

Source: *Competition and Growth in American Energy Markets* (Houston: Texas Eastern Transmission Corp., 1968), p. 57.

APPENDIX C

The Oil Import Administration, under the supervision of the Assistant Secretary–Mineral Resources, discharges the responsibilities imposed upon the Secretary of the Interior by Presidential Proclamation 3279 of March 10, 1959, as amended, "Adjusting Imports of Petroleum and Petroleum Products into the United States." This proclamation, in the interests of national security, imposes restrictions upon the importation of crude oil, unfinished petroleum oils, finished petroleum products, and residual fuel oil to be used as fuel. The Administration allocates imports of these commodities among qualified applicants and issues import licenses on the basis of such allocations.

OIL IMPORT APPEALS BOARD

The Oil Import Appeals Board was established by the Secretary of the Interior pursuant to authorization contained in Proclamation 3279 of March 10, 1959, as amended, "Adjusting Imports of Petroleum and Petroleum Products into the United States." The membership of the Board consists of one representative each from the Interior, Commerce and Justice Departments, designated by the respective Department heads.

The Board considers petitions from persons affected by the regulations issued by the Secretary of the Interior, implementing the Proclamation.

The Board is authorized, within specified limits, to modify an allocation granted by the Oil Import Administration on the grounds of exceptional hardship or error; to grant allocations for crude oil in special circumstances to persons with importing histories who are ineligible for allocations under the regulations; to grant allocations for finished products, on the ground of exceptional hardship, to persons who do not qualify under the regulations; and to review the revocation or suspension of any allocation or license. Decisions of the Board are final.

OFFICE OF OIL AND GAS

The Office of Oil and Gas was established May 6, 1946, by the Secretary of Interior in response to Presidential Letter of May 3, 1946.

It serves as a focal point for leadership and information on petroleum matters and is the principal channel of communications between the Federal Government, the petroleum industry and the oil producing states. It maintains the capability to respond to emergencies affecting the Nation's supply of oil and gas.

The Office of Oil and Gas maintains the Emergency Petroleum and Gas Administration to mobilize and direct the Nation's gas and petroleum industries in the event of a national emergency. It develops national petroleum readiness plans and assists the states and industry in their petroleum emergency plans. It coordinates the measures taken by the government and the petroleum industry regarding foreign oil supplies which threaten the national security. It conducts studies, domestic and worldwide, to maintain data on the adequacy of oil and gas to meet demands, to define deficient areas and to develop ways to alleviate actual or potential deficiencies. It provides leadership to the Federal Interagency Petroleum Statistics Program, provides advice and information on petroleum matters, and conducts an active interchange of information with the oil and gas industries through the National Petroleum Council and other advisory groups. It maintains liaison with the Interstate Oil Compact Commission and the conservation agencies of the oil producing states, and participates in a number of international groups having responsibilities for oil and gas.

Source: U.S. Department of Commerce, *United States Government Organization Manual, 1970/71* (Washington, D.C.: Government Printing Office, 1970).

NINE

THE CHEMICAL INDUSTRY: USER AND BUILDER OF RESOURCES

The chemical industry is both an extensive user and a prolific builder of resources. It is one of the fastest-growing industrial segments of the United States—indeed of the world—whether measured by employment, productive capacity, or variety of products.

Chemical processors are building their plants and marketing their wares in increasingly numerous and ever-widening circles (with only an occasional product circle disappearing) until, it would seem, they succeed in submerging the world's people under a sea of products and by-products (or pollutants and refuse). The chemical industry is awesome in terms of its gargantuan appetite for mineral resources, its interlocking, kaleidoscopic market and marketing channels (reinforced with bonds of reciprocity), its vast land requirements, and its impingements on the environment. Indeed, even the term *chemical industry* defies definition and causes the overly sensitive and socially aware individual to cry for a halt to any further "technological progress" in industrial chemistry.

The one thing in common among chemical industries is the characteristic that chemistry plays a basic role in the plant process. However, since nearly all manufacturing employs chemistry to some extent, the term *chemical industry* per se is most commonly applied to, and probably should be restricted to, those firms where a chemical reaction takes place under some attempts to control such a reaction, rather than in a plant which merely blends or mixes materials mechanically. In other words, chemical manufacturers are traditionally those that sell chemicals *as such* chiefly to other chemical manufacturers. Sometimes referred to as the *strictly chemical industries,* these firms produce heavy chemicals (such as sulfuric acid, caustic soda, and soda-ash), fine chemicals (drugs, dyes, etc.), and specialized chemicals (alcohols, plastics, gases, etc.).

By way of contrast, it is convenient to apply the term *allied chemical industry* to those firms that use chemicals in their plant processes for blending and/or mechanical mixing operations, and to use the term *chemical process industries* for those manufacturers that turn *natural* raw materials into a changed form that is more useful or acceptable to commerce (rayon, fuels, paper, ceramics, etc.). Significantly, there is no clear-cut boundary between these operations, and most companies are organized horizontally and vertically into conglomerates. The saying in vogue (both apropos and timely) that "the chemical industries are their own best customers" expresses a major concept that must be appreciated if one is to understand the industry. For example, this concept helps to explain why chemical plants are more often located in clusters. Exceptions to this phenomenon are unusual and are feasible only where a plant is located atop a volume of raw- or process-material sources, such as a salt dome, or alongside a stream (so as to have access to process, effluent, or coolant waters), or where a plant is producing a relatively high-value product for a national market (orlon, etc.), or in the event a plant produces a high-volume, low-value commodity for a local market (such as fertilizers). Other exceptions might be found (such as isolated plants in which air or water pollutants are prime economic factors in the production process), but these are rare and promise to become even more of an exception as more and more concern is given to the environment.

Still other factors currently affecting new chemical plant locations are the accordion effects of tight credit and marketing controls made possible and effective through electronic data processing and computer/ output decision making. Under conditions of tight credit, such as existed during the late 1960s and early 1970s, chemical industry locations are determined in the light of customer needs so that inventories can be held at a minimum, while plants depend on faster and more reliable transport timing. This, in effect, is causing some chemical producers to locate close to markets, rather than close to raw materials. Further effects of this development are often massive, even regional, in nature. For example, expected capital expenditures for new chemical plants in the South (where raw material, labor costs, and taxes are relatively low) are now in the process of being diverted to market-oriented sites in the North Central, New England, and Western states.[1]

---

[1] "New Headache for Site Seekers: Public Clamor over Pollution," *Chemical Week,* August 19, 1970, p. 52.

FIGURE 42

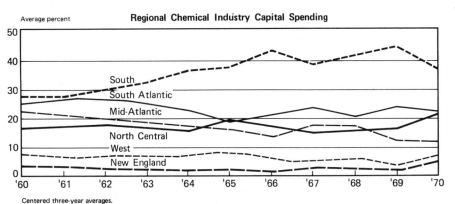

Centered three-year averages.
Regions: South: Tex., Okla., Ark., La., Ky., Tenn., Miss., Ala. South Atlantic: Del., Md., Va., W. Va., N.C., S.C., Fla., Ga., Wash. D.C. Mid-Atlantic: N.Y., N.J., Pa. North Central: O., Mich., Ind., Ill., Wis., Minn., Ia., Mo., N.D., S.D., Neb., Kan. West: Ariz., Calif., Colo., Ida., Mont., Nev., N.M., Ore., Utah, Wash., Wyo., Alaska, Hawaii. New England: Me., Vt., N.H., Conn., R.I., Mass.

Adapted from Manufacturing Chemicals Associates, Inc., *The Chemical Industries Facts Book* (Washington, D.C., 1969), pp. 21–24.

Further compounding the problems of new chemical plant locations is the fact that certain communities are actually denying sites because of ecological or esthetic considerations alone. In some cases local communities are joined by national conservation groups and certain agencies of the federal government to bar chemical plant developments,[2] thereby forcing them to select secondary or seemingly less "logical" locations.

The total impact of these various forces has been to produce an industry-wide state of flux and confusion as to what courses or principles to follow in making plant location decisions.

SUMMARY OF PRESENT PATTERNS
OF CHEMICAL MANUFACTURING

From World War II until the late 1960s, the pattern of chemical plant locations was away from relatively old concentrations in northern New Jersey and around Buffalo, New York. However, the early 1970s brought considerable renewed interest in modernizing and adding to the northern New Jersey chemical complex. The basis for this renewed interest lay in the above-mentioned trend to locate closer to markets and the expectation that imported feed stocks and even raw petroleum would soon become available on the East Coast.

The current national pattern of chemical locations shows six major concentrations: (1) Northern New Jersey, (2) Upper Ohio and Tribu-

---

[2] Ibid.

tary Valleys, (3) West End of Lake Erie, (4) Greater Chicago, (5) Texas-Louisiana Gulf Coast, and (6) Southern California. These are by far the largest concentrations of chemical plants within the United States. Secondary clusters of interdependent plants have been established where each plant either performs related steps in a given chemical process or depends on by-products [3] or wastes from nearby processors. Also, as has been noted, there is a scattering of individual plants that either process bulky, low-cost chemicals such as fertilizers for nearby local markets, or manufacture relatively high-cost chemical products such as synthetic fibers for regional or national markets. Recently, a few (mostly new) plants are being located so as to serve an especially demanding, specific customer.

SELECTED CHARACTERISTICS
OF CHEMICAL INDUSTRY

Characteristics common to most chemical plants include: (1) multi-faceted competition, (2) changing products, markets, and processes, (3) relatively high research and development budgets, (4) relatively high rates of obsolescence and depreciation, (5) multistage plant processes, (6) high capital investment per worker, who is relatively highly paid and technically prepared, (7) record of price stability, and (8) high degree of water-oriented plant location.

Multifaceted Competition

Competition within the chemical industry is especially keen. There is competition between raw materials—for example, petroleum versus animal fats for use in making detergents; there is competition between processes—for example, the derivation of nitrogen by at least 20 different processes; there is competition between products—for example, the many different kinds of permanent antifreeze; and there is strong and still growing competition from industries located overseas.[4] Such keen competition means that the selection of an optimum location for a chemical plant usually must be based on extremely sound industrial location advantages and

---

[3] Some manufacturers object to the term *by-product* because the layman often considers it a residual, unintentionally produced during the manufacture of another product, and thus costing the producer nothing. Actually, the by-product usually is produced intentionally in addition to the principal product and may be quite valuable.

[4] In the early 1970s the most extensive new-plant construction in the world was occurring in Western Europe—although Japan had the most new chemical plants for a single country; Japan's petrochemical growth was retarded later by the oil shortage. Albert H. Kislin, *CW Report I*, CXIV, No. 4 (January 23, 1974), pp. 32–37; *CW Report II*, CXIV, No. 5 (January 30, 1974), pp. 24–30.

that the transportation role is relatively important to the point of often being decisive in determining success. This importance of transportation, combined with the fact that other chemical manufacturers are the chemical industry's (own) best customers, has produced a clustering of chemical activity that implies that any change in products, markets, or processes is likely to have vast, sweeping, and accordianlike effects.

Changing Products, Markets, and Processes

Change is a constant companion—a "way of doing business"—in the operations of chemical manufacturers; few are the industries that surpass them in this respect. And, as if the increasing rate at which new products are being introduced were not enough, changes in these *products* and changes in the *processes* by which they are obtained [5] make the chemical industry extremely dynamic. A reliance on research and development programs using scientific exploration and experimentation and learning techniques, rather than on a sheer physical or mechanical exploitation of what nature affords, probably accounts in large measure for the constant state of change and flux inherent in chemical activities. Constant searching, discovering, and utilizing promise a continuation of past and present patterns of change—undoubtedly at an even accelerated rate.

Further compounding the increasing rate of change are the close and myriad interrelations among the plants and the users of their primary products and by-products. Often a major producer will find his market captured by a competitor that is selling the same substance, a substitute, or a comparable product (which might be obtained as a by-product from still another process). Thus, families of chemical manufacturers have evolved, with interfamily cooperation in amassing, processing, and developing systems to recall information from vast data banks that have been accumulated by the industry in order to "stay ahead of competition."

Relatively High Research and Development Budgets

If a chemical firm is to remain competitive, its cost outlay for processing and experimenting with such vast learnings is substantial. Most operating budgets of chemical firms reflect this need. Even so, unfavorable economic conditions, taxes levied without due consideration of the burden placed on chemical firms in the areas of research and develop-

---

[5] For example, teflon coatings for cooking utensils, introduced as a by-product of space exploration, proceeded through the introductory Teflon to Teflon I and then Teflon II, all in a span of less than a decade.

ment, or the premature "bleeding off of profits" by company leaders can stifle growth and progress. The required high qualifications of workers in the industry also increase the cost of research and development, and frequent product changes often necessitate significant and costly alterations in plant layout, equipment, and even location.

Relatively High Rates of Obsolescence and Depreciation

Provisions for nearly constant programs of research and development, pilot plant testing, modifications or reconstruction at existing plants, and new plant construction demand pricing, cash-flows, and cost accounting methods that provide for high obsolescence rates. And the nature of most chemical plants must include even rapid depreciation rates due to the corrosive nature of the materials and the extremely high temperatures and pressures required in most chemical processes. For example, the life expectancy of some pumps often can be measured in months and—in certain extreme situations—even in "one-time usage." Also, the disposal of highly toxic materials and equipment constitutes significant cost factors. That high costs of operation and depreciation are recognized as industry-wide problems is apparent from the fact that high-ranking congressmen advocate investment tax credits as a means of increasing cash flow within the industry so as to keep domestic production technologically current and abreast, if not ahead, of foreign production.[6]

Multistage Plant Processes

Unlike most other industries, the chemical industry tailors a plant for a specific commodity. Whereas production of a new or altered commodity hinges on merely the modification of existing equipment or lines for most other manufacturers, a new chemical commodity often requires new facilities. The impact has been to force new production facilities to come on line only after a series of developmental steps have been completed.

Step 1 or 2   Laboratory experimentation
Step 2 or 1   Recognition or awareness of a need or want
Step 3   Further experimentation with untried equipment or techniques
Step 4   Pilot plant
Step 5   Full-line production
Step 6   Full-market development

---

[6] Wilbur Mills, "Tax Credit On Again?," *Chemical Week,* July 28, 1971, p. 18.

Step 7   Modification(s) to maintain satisfactory market position

Step 8   Close down

A recognition of these steps (including number 8, close down) aids in one's understanding the attendant problems of obsolescence and depreciation mentioned above.

High Capital Investment per Worker, Who Is Relatively Highly Paid and Technically Prepared

The nearly constant growth in demand for technically competent workers has caused consistently higher average wage scales in the chemical industry than in most other industries. Indeed, competent chemical "know-how" has been so scarce that many chemical firms have hoarded brainpower. Employment rates rose steadily after the industry first got its start just before World War I. Only in 1970 and 1971 was this rise halted; owing partly to an excess of qualified people and partly to depressed economic conditions, layoffs of even technically qualified workers were recorded.[7] Even under the economic recession of the early 1970s, chemical workers fared better in contrast to the average for all industry, in terms both of salaries and wages paid and of job stability.[8] However, for the first time certain segments of the industry—such as the fiber producers—felt the pinch of declining markets, due to a slack economy and availability of imports, and undertook sizeable work force reductions. Even so, the heavy per-worker investment in plant and equipment, and the relatively few employees required, suggest that the chemical worker will generally continue in his favored role.

Record of Price Stability

Despite the high degree of competition existing in the chemical industry, prices were very stable until the threat of imports arose in the late 1960s and early 1970s. The size and economic strength of most large chemical firms, the high investment costs for research and development, the fact that the chemical industry is its own best customer, plus a large degree of market control by larger firms produced the stable price condition that existed over the years. Throughout the 1960s even the threat from foreign producers did not change this situation as U.S. chemical firms were sufficiently powerful to neutralize any encroachment from overseas. Today, however, the situation is altered. There are huge foreign chemical producers capable of outproducing and outmarketing even some of the largest

---

[7] "Chemical Workers Feel the Pinch," *Chemical Week,* February 17, 1971, p. 16.

[8] Ibid.

U.S. firms. The long-range economic, political, and military impacts of this development remain to be seen.[9]

High Degree of Water-Oriented Plant Location

More than 70 percent of all new petrochemical construction and approximately 65 percent of other post-World-War-II chemical construction in the United States have taken place along the nation's midwestern river and intracoastal canal routes. As we have already observed, following World War II the location pattern of new chemical plants was away from relatively older concentrations in northern New Jersey and near Buffalo. Shifts in new plant locations followed three chief courses. First, and most evident, are five major areas of plant construction and expansion: (1) Texas-Louisiana Gulf Coast, (2) Greater Chicago, (3) valleys of navigable tributaries of the Upper Ohio System, (4) west end of Lake Erie, and (5) Southern California, with the first area constituting by far the largest concentration. Second, clusters of new, interdependent plants developed, such as at Calvert City, Kentucky,[10] where each plant either performs related steps in a given chemical process or depends on by-products or wastes from neighboring processors. Third, and as previously mentioned, there has been a wide scattering of individual plants processing either bulky low-cost chemicals, such as fertilizers for local markets, or manufacturing relatively high-cost chemical products, such as synthetic fibers for regional or national markets. In any case, the greatest concentrations of United States chemical activity have been along the midwestern rivers and canals, and more than one-half million persons—an estimated 70 percent of all chemical manufacturing employees—are working in chemical plants along, or close to, these water routes.

More than 4000 different chemicals are produced along these routeways; indeed, one plant at Baton Rouge, Louisiana, alone produces more than 700 different commodities. Products vary greatly from section to section; some areas such as Chicago are highly diversified, others highly specialized.

Chemical activities on the East and West coasts are chiefly market oriented. In addition, there is a tendency in those areas to look to a future situation in which import quota restrictions will be relaxed and coastal chemical plants will then have wider access to relatively low-cost foreign feedstocks and other raw materials.

---

[9] To wit, President Nixon's proposal to add a 10 percent tariff and, at least temporarily, to halt gold sales for dollars (Address to the Nation, August 15, 1971).

[10] Based originally on a plant constructed by the Penn Salt Corporation.

FIGURE 43. CHIEF COMMODITY CLASSIFICATIONS BY SECTIONS OF ROUTEWAYS

Intracoastal Canal

Petrochemicals other than heavy chemicals; inorganic heavy chemicals; organic heavy chemicals; plastics, synthetic fibers and/or rubber; and extraction and/or shipping of basic raw materials—other than from agriculture.

Ohio Valley (including the Kanawha)

Inorganic heavy chemicals; silicones, plastics, synthetic fibers and/or rubber, coal and petrochemicals other than heavy chemicals; fertilizers, feed supplements, and insecticides; dyes, paints, enamels, varnishes, and lacquers; and soaps, detergents, bleaches, and allied products.

Illinois Waterway

Chemicals for processing and treatment of water, lumber, foods, metals, paper, leathers, adhesives, and abrasives; dyes, paints, enamels, varnishes, and lacquers; fertilizers, feed supplements, and insecticides; soaps, detergents, bleaches, and allied products; coal and petrochemicals other than heavy chemicals; and inorganic heavy chemicals.

Upper Mississippi (above Cairo)

Fertilizers, feed supplements, and insecticides; dyes, paints, enamels, varnishes, and lacquers; heavy inorganic chemicals; silicones, plastics, synthetic fibers and/or rubber; coal and petrochemicals other than heavy chemicals; and chemicals for processing and treatment of water, lumber, foods, metals, paper, leather, adhesives, and abrasives.

Lower Mississippi (below Cairo)

Fertilizers, feed supplements, and insecticides; inorganic heavy chemicals; petrochemicals other than heavy chemicals; organic heavy chemicals; and silicones, plastics, synthetic fibers and/or rubbers.

Cumberland-Tennessee Rivers

Fertilizers, feed supplements, and insecticides; silicones, plastics, synthetic fibers and/or rubber; inorganic heavy chemicals; extraction and/or shipping of basic raw materials—other than from agriculture and air reduction.*

Tombigbee-Warrior System

Inorganic heavy chemicals; fertilizers, feed supplements, and insecticides; coal and petrochemicals—other than heavy chemicals; chemical processing and treat-

FIGURE 43 (cont.)

ment of water, lumber, foods, metals, paper, leather, adhesives, and abrasives; and dyes, paints, enamels, varnishes, and lacquers.

Missouri River

Fertilizers, feed supplements, and insecticides; inorganic heavy chemicals; pharmaceuticals †; dyes, paints, enamels, varnishes, and lacquers; and chemical processing and treatment of water, lumber, foods, metals, paper, leathers, adhesives, and abrasives.

* Air reduction plants are found along each section of the waterways; they are especially numerous along the Ohio Valley and in the Houston and Chicago areas.

† Pharmaceuticals are concentrated chiefly along the Upper Mississippi (especially at St. Louis), the Illinois (especially Chicago), and the Ohio Valley (especially Louisville and Cincinnati).

The production of chemicals, by value added nationwide, is highlighted by the data presented in Figures 43 and 44. In turn, the data of Figure 44 serves to point up areas of present chemical activity, and Figure 45 suggests investment trends by regions.

WATERWAYS WELL ORIENTED TO RAW MATERIALS USED IN CHEMICAL PRODUCTION

The midwestern river and canal routes are favorably oriented with respect to raw materials used by the chemical industry (see Figure 46). In addition to those indicated on this map, there are other raw materials drawn in volume from agriculture, forests and seawater. Oil is found in volume along the existing waterway system; and, if ports are recognized as a "real source" of imported raw materials, then the relative orientation of these rivers and canals with respect to chemical development is even more favorable.

As a rule of thumb, chemical producers that rely on basic minerals are, for the most part, located close to deposits. Thus, the minerals most widely used in chemical manufacturing are shown by states in Figure 46. Similarly, inorganics are clustered near plants producing them (see Figure 48). Occasionally such plants are market oriented—usually near other chemical firms (see Figure 47). Likewise, chemical plants that use organics are located close to their points of production. Significantly, much of the nation's basic organic chemical production is located in three areas: (1) Texas-Louisiana, (2) California, and (3) Kentucky–West Virginia.

278

FIGURE 44. STATES SETTING THE PACE IN PRODUCTION OF CHEMICALS

The top 36 States *

		Value added, '67	Change from '63
1	New Jersey	$2,825.0	+ 34.3%
2	Texas	2,075.9	+ 26.2
3	New York	1,661.6	+ 21.0
4	Illinois	1,544.0	+ 26.6
5	Pennsylvania	1,370.6	+ 38.8
6	Ohio	1,341.8	+ 40.3
7	Tennessee	1,164.1	+ 40.8
8	California	1,118.5	+ 38.2
9	Michigan	1,039.7	+ 36.4
10	West Virginia	835.8	+ 6.7
11	Indiana	833.3	+ 39.5
12	Virginia	767.5	+ 26.0
13	Louisiana	676.8	+ 55.4
14	Missouri	545.6	+ 38.0
15	South Carolina	475.7	+ 38.8
16	Florida	448.9	+ 29.4
17	Maryland	422.3	+ 41.6
18	Alabama	412.7	+ 90.6
19	Connecticut	395.8	+ 48.9
20	Kentucky	391.3	+ 43.0
21	North Carolina	369.7	+ 35.3
22	Massachusetts	363.9	+ 33.8
23	Georgia	308.6	+ 40.0
24	Kansas	277.2	+ 52.9
25	Wisconsin	263.1	+ 61.3
26	Iowa	243.6	+ 60.1
27	Minnesota	217.1	+ 30.3
28	Delaware	(not disclosed)	
29	Washington	166.0	− 30.3
30	Mississippi	157.4	+ 51.9
31	Idaho	111.6	+ 48.4
32	Puerto Rico	99.3	+115.2
33	Arkansas	95.8	+ 34.4
34	Nebraska	91.9	+118.8
35	Colorado	55.3	+ 26.0
36	Rhode Island	55.1	+ 64.0

FIGURE 44 (cont.)

The top 36 urban areas

		Value added, '67	Change from '63
1	New York City-N.E. New Jersey	$3,292.5	+ 32.5%
2	Chicago-N.W. Indiana	1,309.2	+ 25.3
3	Philadelphia-Bristol-Camden	1,025.2	+ 32.0
4	Houston-Alvin-Freeport	836.4	+ 39.8
5	Los Angeles-Long Beach	617.8	+ 38.3
6	Cincinnati	529.5	+ 47.7
7	St. Louis-East St. Louis	487.8	+ 29.7
8	Detroit	322.0	− 0.8
9	Baltimore	321.0	+ 29.9
10	Louisville, Ky.	316.8	+ 39.7
11	Cleveland	299.5	+ 36.0
12	Indianapolis	285.2	+ 43.0
13	San Francisco	281.7	+ 32.7
14	Buffalo-Niagara Falls	227.7	+ 5.0
15	Kansas City	206.1	+ 36.6
16	Minneapolis-St. Paul	194.1	+ 35.1
17	Memphis	167.7	+ 30.7
18	Boston	145.8	+ 11.6
19	Dallas	126.5	+ 46.4
20	Pittsburgh	125.5	+ 18.6
21	Albany-Troy-Schenectady	118.0	+ 56.9
22	Springfield, Mass.	112.6	+ 54.7
23	Akron	86.4	+ 24.5
24	Grand Rapids, Mich.	84.3	+178.2
25	Tampa	79.9	—
26	Milwaukee	65.4	+ 18.7
27	Greensboro-Winston-Salem	64.9	—
28	Toledo	53.5	+ 48.6
29	Rochester, N.Y.	51.2	+ 30.6
30	New Orleans	48.5	+ 67.8
31	Denver	46.3	+ 19.3
32	Columbus, O.	46.0	− 4.2
33	Portland, Ore.	45.1	+ 27.0
34	Anaheim-Santa Ana, Calif.	44.6	+ 48.7
35	Allentown-Easton-Bethlehem, Pa.	36.5	− 3.2
36	San Jose, Calif.	34.2	+ 34.6

* Including Puerto Rico. Tables compiled by CW from U.S. Bureau of the Census data.

Source: Chemical Week, August 19, 1970.

FIGURE 45

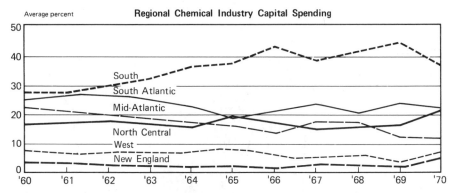

Average percent — Regional Chemical Industry Capital Spending

Centered three-year averages.
Regions: South: Tex., Okla., Ark., La., Ky., Tenn., Miss., Ala. South Atlantic: Del., Md., Va., W. Va., N.C., S.C., Fla., Ga., Wash. D.C. Mid-Atlantic: N.Y., N.J., Pa. North Central: O., Mich., Ind., Ill., Wis., Minn., Ia., Mo., N.D., S.D., Neb., Kan. West: Ariz., Calif., Colo., Ida., Mont., Nev., N.M., Ore., Utah, Wash., Wyo., Alaska, Hawaii. New England: Me., Vt., N.H., Conn., R.I., Mass.

Source: Adapted from Manufacturing Chemicals Association, Inc., *The Chemical Industry Facts Book* (Washington, D.C., 1969), pp. 21–24.

AVAILABILITY OF WATER AND ADEQUATE PLANT SITES

The specific location of most chemical plant sites within the general areas already discussed depends on: (1) adequate water supplies, (2) large, nearly level, tracts of land, (3) availability of low-cost electricity, and (4) an adequate supply of labor. Water requirements in chemical plants may run as high as 150,000 gallons per minute; plants using 50,000 gallons of water per minute are common. Even the 50,000-gallon figure equals the flow of streams usually considered rivers so that riparian sites on major waterways (or large lakes) are necessary.

Water requirements fall into three categories: (1) coolant, (2) plant processes, and (3) disposal medium for aqueous wastes. Although river water is used for all three, water used in most plant processes must be within a certain temperature range or degree of purity. Deep wells in alluvial bottom lands usually are used to meet such requirements. Although there are seemingly hundreds of miles of water-route land containing sites with adequate groundwater supplies awaiting future development, ground and surface water resources are still abundant only along the Upper Mississippi and Tennessee valleys and in the lake and bayou areas of Louisiana. Some Upper Mississippi River cities, such as Prairie du Chien, Wisconsin, have limited undeveloped supplies of pure water with an even temperature from sands and sandstones (e.g., Prairie du Chien's available water is esti-

FIGURE 46. ORIENTATION OF MIDWESTERN RIVER AND INTRACOASTAL CANAL ROUTES TO RAW MATERIALS CONSUMED IN CHEMICAL PRODUCTION

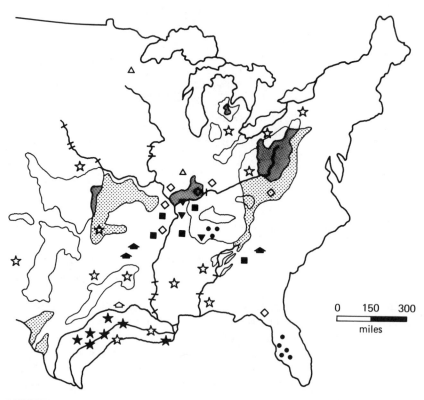

LEGEND

▨ COAL	
▢ PETROLEUM - NATURAL GAS	
▦ COAL & PETROLEUM- NATURAL GAS	
— NATURAL GAS PIPELINE RIVER CROSSING	
★ SULFUR	
☆ SALT	

■ BARITE
● PHOSPHATE
◇ LIMESTONE
▼ FLUORSPAR
△ ROCK PYRITE
♦ BAUXITE
⬡ SODIUM NITRATE

IMPORTED MATERIALS

PHOSPHATE FROM CURACAO
FLUORSPAR FROM MEXICO
BAUXITE FROM SURINAM
CHROME ORE FROM SOUTH AFRICA
MONAZITE FROM SOUTH AMERICA & AFRICA

Midwestern River and Canal Routes are favorably oriented in regard to basic raw materials used by the Chemical Industry.

282

FIGURE 47. CHEMICAL MARKETS *

Major chemical-using industries	Values of all chemicals consumed—1947 (millions of dollars)
Chemical industry	$2,655
Food and kindred products	1,451
Agriculture and fisheries	830
Textile mill products	800
Rubber products	604
Petroleum and coal products	213
Paper and allied products	183
Electrical machinery (except motors and generators)	178
Miscellaneous manufacturing	167
Apparel	142
Leather and leather products	126
Stone, clay and glass products	116
Motor vehicles	111
Iron and steel	99
Printing and publishing	97
Nonferrous metallurgy	85

* Although the data shown are old and no comparable data for a later date are available, the principle still holds that "the chemical industry is its own best customer"; see Jules Bakeman, "The Economics of the Chemical Industry" (Washington, D.C.: Manufacturing Chemists Association, 1970), pp. 4, 5, 8, 32, 58, 59, 61, and 66.

mated to be in excess of 7,500,000 gallons per 24-hour day); St. Paul and Minneapolis, both anxious to attract chemical industries, have some reserve supplies. Other rivers with available water are shown in Figure 49.

Chemical plants usually occupy large tracts of level land and, where clusters of interdependent plants are situated, areas of 5000 acres or larger may be needed. Here again, midwestern rivers and canals that traverse level glacial till plains, mature river bottoms, or recently emerged coastal plains provide hundreds of miles of nearly ideal riparian sites. Only along some sections of the Ohio and Tennessee rivers do steep valleys hinder the siting of chemical plants. Nearly everywhere along the waterways, drainage and/or flood control projects still afford dry sites.

CHEMICAL MARKETS

The chemical industry buys much of its own output—nearly one-half of the dollar value of all chemicals sold; this accounts to a large extent for the clustering of chemical plants. It also gives heightened importance to

283

FIGURE 48. "Resources are not; they become!" In no other facet of man's activities and his development of resources is the interrelation and interdependence of raw materials, technology, and culture more evident than in the chemical industry. This Odessa, Texas, chemical complex—the world's largest chemical concentration not on navigable water—includes several plastics plants, a rubber plant, and several pilot and experimental plants. Courtesy El Paso Products Company.

chemical plant affinities for riparian sites—especially the midwestern and southern river and canal routes, on the East Coast near New York, and in Southern California. The midwestern, southern, and Gulf Coast river and canal routes traverse the corn belt and the highly productive and complementary farmlands of the Middle South. The many food-processing centers associated with these rich agricultural areas constitute the bulk of the second largest category of chemical markets in the United States, and the fertilizer, insecticide, and livestock food supplement requirements of these areas constitute a great share of the third most important market category. Add to these the value of the chemical requirements of such iron and steel complexes as Pittsburgh, Youngstown, Cleveland, Greater Chicago, Gary, East St. Louis, and Houston; such petroleum refining centers as Baton Rouge, Houston, Wood River (Illinois), and Whiting (Indiana); the nation's largest soap and detergent plants; eight large pharmaceutical centers; hundreds of paint, varnish, enamel, and lacquer producers; large and growing synthetic fiber and rubber plants—and the sum constitutes the world's premier chemical market.

Significantly, certain auxiliary manufacturers, requisite to development of a large-scale chemical industry, are also important customers for the chemical industry. These include fabricators of metals, pipes, and valves;

284

instrumentation manufacturers; electroplating plants; machine shops, boiler and sheet works; foundries; research laboratories; producers of a wide range of containers; and refractory, heat, and air conditioning equipment plants, as well as heat and power generating stations. In combination, these plants tend to engender or enhance further chemical plant growth and development.

Foreign markets, growing at a particularly fast rate since the end of World War II, have changed drastically since even the 1950s, when European and Japanese chemical firms were still recovering and converting from the devastations of World War II. The growth of U.S. chemical imports has increased at rates in excess of 8 percent annually. Much of the increase has been in such chemical-using manufactured items as shoes, dyestuffs, synthetic fibers, and automobiles.[11] Also, U.S. chemical firms have lost overseas—and even domestic—markets to foreign producers.[12] The total impact of a loss in markets is to weaken, if not destroy, vast segments of the U.S. chemical industry. Currently, and in the years ahead, some of the major foreign policy goals of the United States must include efforts to preserve what has been developed; [13] and, if efforts to reason with the European Economic Community and Japan are not successful, then it should be anticipated that the structure of the United States chemical industry will undergo sweeping changes. Anticipated measures indicate that existing antitrust legislation will be eased, import quotas will be set, labor laws will be rethought and renegotiated, tax incentives will prevail, and the organization, location, and emphasis of the U.S. chemical industry will likely undergo vast changes, including mergers, reduction of duplicate production lines, further automation, higher per-worker plant investment, and work force reductions.

LABOR

Of the some 15,000 chemical establishments scattered throughout the country, the majority are relatively small, employing fewer than 500 workers. Indeed, most employ fewer than 25 people. However, the greater number of chemical workers are employed in large plants with 2500 or more workers.[14] Chemical plant labor is, for the most part, semiskilled. Although the workers are paid higher than the national average wage for this class of labor, employee costs constitute a relatively low charge against costs of

---

[11] *Chemical Week,* June 2, 1971, p. 21.

[12] Ibid.

[13] President Nixon's Address to the Nation, August 15, 1971.

[14] Jules Bakeman, "The Economics of the Chemical Industry" (Washington, D.C.: Manufacturing Chemists Association, 1970), pp. 191–93.

FIGURE 49. DROUGHT-RESISTANT RIVERS THAT CAN SUPPLY PROCESS AND COOLING WATER FOR PLANTS AND NAVIGATION TO MAJOR MARKETS

River	States	Discharge (cu. ft. per sec.) Max.	Min.	River	States	Discharge (cu. ft. per sec.) Max.	Min.
Alabama	Ala.	256,000	4450	Conecuh	Ala.	8120	497
Allegheny	Pa.	269,000	80	Connecticut	Conn, N.H.	282,000	112
Altamaha	Ga.	178,000	1430	Coosa	Ala., Ga.	73,200	940
Androscoggin	Me., N.H.	135,000	309	Coosawatee	Ga.	40,200	220
Apalachicola	Fla.	293,000	5300	Copper	Alaska	159,000	3830
Arkansas	Ark., Okla.	850,000	66	Coulitz	Wash.	139,000	998
Atchafalaya	La.	624,000	17,400	Cumberland	Ky., Tenn.	210,000	69
Bighorn	Mont., Wyo.	37,400	228	Current	Mo.	94,400	879
Black	Ark., Mo.	103,000	224	Delaware	Del., N.J., Pa.	329,000	412
Black	N.Y.	33,900	137	Deschutes	Ore.	43,600	3380
Black	Wis.	58,000	180	Duck	Tenn.	122,000	185
Blackfoot	Mont.	18,300	200	Edisto	S.C.	24,300	290
Bogue Chitto	La.	51,200	424	Escambia	Fla.	73,900	600
Brazos	Tex.	246,000	374	Etowah	Ga.	55,000	360
Broad	Ga., N.C., S.C.	119,000	108	Feather	Calif.	357,000	300
Cahaba	Ala.	85,200	188	Flathead	Mont.	82,800	198
Cape Fear	N.C.	*	170	Flint	Ga.	92,000	92
Carlson Creek	Alaska	4390	**	Fox	Wis.	24,000	138
Catawba	N.C., S.C.	177,000	90	French Broad	N.C., Tenn.	76,300	193
Cedar	Iowa	72,000	212	Gallatin	Mont.	7870	130
Chattahochie	Ala., Ga.	203,000	72	Gasconade	Mo.	96,400	271
Cheboygan	Mich.	1590	100	Grand	Mich.	54,000	381
Chehalis	Wash.	31,700	164	Grande Ronde	Ore.	30,000	436
Chena	Alaska	24,200	**	Green	Ky.	208,000	200
Chippewa	Wis.	102,000	1020	Green	Utah, Wyo.	68,100	196
Choctawatchee	Ala., Fla.	69,600	61	Gunnison	Colo.	35,700	106
Clark Fork	Ida., Mont.	153,000	115	Hatchie	Tenn.	59,000	217
Clearwater	Ida.	177,000	500	Hoh	Wash.	38,700	247
Clinch	Tenn.	51,100	108	Holston	Tenn.	59,600	470
Colorado	Ariz., Calif., Colo., Utah	220,000	286	Hudson	N.Y.	181,000	112
				Illinois	Ill.	123,000	2300
Columbia	Ore., Wash.	1,240,000	15,300	James	Va.	175,000	153

FIGURE 49. (cont.)

River	States	Discharge (cu. ft. per sec.) Max.	Min.
Juniata	Pa.	190,000	286
Kanawha	W.Va.	320,000	640
Kankakee	Ill., Ind.	75,900	154
Kansas	Kans.	510,000	160
Kasilof	Alaska	9090	**
Kenai	Alaska	20,600	190
Kennebec	Me.	58,800	110
Kickapoo	Wis.	10,300	161
Klamath	Calif.	425,000	1340
Klickitat	Wash.	25,500	466
Klutina	Alaska	9040	**
Kootena	Mont.	121,000	895
Kootena	Ida.	125,000	996
Kootenay	Mont.	98,000	994
Kuskokwim	Alaska	260,000	**
Leaf	Miss.	71,300	332
Lehigh	Pa.	92,000	160
Madison	Mont., Wyo.	7750	100
Mahoning	Pa.	23,000	125
Maksoutof	Alaska	2820	50
Manistee	Mich.	3570	540
Manistique	Mich.	13,600	288
Maquoketa	Iowa	48,000	105
Matanuska	Alaska	24,000	234
McKenzie	Ore.	88,200	1310
Menominee	Mich., Wis.	25,700	154
Meramec	Mo.	120,000	74
Merrimack	Mass., N.H.	173,000	147
Miami	O.	352,000	78
Mississippi	Ark., Iowa, Ky., La., Minn., Miss., Mo., Tenn., Wis.	2,080,000	65

River	States	Discharge (cu. ft. per sec.) Max.	Min.
Missouri	Iowa, Mo., Mont., Neb., N.D., S.D.	618,000	1320
Mohawk	N.Y.	130,000	213
Monongahela	Pa., W.Va.	140,000	204
Muskegon	Mich.	14,950	330
Muskingum	O.	126,000	218
Namekagon	Wis.	5200	113
Nenana	Alaska	28,500	**
Neuse	N.C.	25,900	124
New	Va., W.Va.	232,000	178
Newhalen	Alaska	29,600	**
Niagara	N.Y.	274,000	100,000
Nisqually	Wash.	20,800	176
Nooksack	Wash.	46,200	595
North Umpqua	Ore.	25,000	570
Obion	Tenn.	99,500	230
Ocmulgee	Ga.	83,500	128
Oconee	Ga.	96,700	59
Ogeechee	Ga.	26,300	131
Ohio	Ill., Ind., Ky., O., Pa., W.Va.	1,850,000	1800
Ontanagon	Mich.	42,000	260
Oostanaula	Ga.	47,000	408
Osage	Mo.	216,000	375
Oswegatchie	N.Y.	15,800	130
Oswego	N.Y.	37,500	353
Otter Creek	Vt.	11,000	100
Pascagoula	Miss.	154,000	696
Pearl	La., Miss.	60,000	289
Pecatonica	Ill., Wis.	15,200	132
Pee Dee	N.C., S.C.	270,000	50
Pend Oreille	Wash.	171,300	2200

FIGURE 49. (cont.)

River	States	Discharge (cu. ft. per sec.) Max.	Min.
Penobscot	Me.	126,000	1430
Pere Marquette	Mich.	2550	310
Pit	Calif.	37,100	570
Platte	Neb.	107,000	265
Potomac	D.C., Md., Va., W.Va.	484,000	216
Puyallup	Wash.	57,000	306
Rainy	Minn.	71,600	2200
Red	Ark., La., Okla., Tex.	400,000	130
Roanoke	N.C., Va.	261,000	55
Rock	Ill.	46,200	630
Root	Minn.	38,700	197
Roque	Ore.	135,000	444
Sabine	La., Tex.	121,000	270
Sacramento	Calif.	230,000	141
St. Croix	Me.	23,300	100
St. Croix	Wis.	54,900	75
St. John	Me.	121,000	510
St. Joseph	Mich.	20,200	420
St. Lawrence	N.Y.	315,000	139,000
St. Louis	Minn.	25,100	171
Salcha	Alaska	36,500	**
Salmon	Ida.	106,000	242
Salt	Wyo.	3520	216
San Joaquin	Calif.	79,000	184
Santiam	Ore.	161,000	260
Savannah	Ga., S.C.	350,000	492
Scioto	O.	177,000	244
Selway	Ida.	48,900	100
Seneca	N.Y.	16,700	373
Shenandoah	W.Va.	230,000	194
Skagit	Wash.	144,000	181
Skykomish	Wash.	88,700	315

River	States	Discharge (cu. ft. per sec.) Max.	Min.
Snake	Ida., Ore., Wash., Wyo.	369,000	50
South Fork	Tenn.	45,000	102
Spokane	Ida., Wash.	50,100	120
Sturgeon	Mich.	15,500	200
Susitna	Alaska	58,100	**
Susquehanna	Md., N.Y., Pa.	787,000	58
Tanana	Alaska	62,800	3800
Tazlina	Alaska	47,000	**
Tennessee	Ala., Tenn.	500,000	250
Tittabawassee	Mich.	34,000	111
Tombigbee	Ala., Miss.	217,000	50
Trinity	Calif.	190,000	162
Trinity	Tex.	184,000	102
Tuscarawas	O.	46,800	120
Tygart	W.Va.	22,500	129
Umpqua	Ore.	218,000	640
Wabash	Ill., Ind.	305,000	135
Wateree	S.C.	366,000	170
Wenatchee	Wash.	32,300	183
White	Ark., Mo.	324,000	90
White	Colo.	8160	53
White	Ind.	59,400	133
Willamette	Ore.	248,000	1990
Wisconsin	Wis.	80,800	90
Withlacoochee	Fla.	69,600	61
Wolf	Wis.	15,500	91
Yadkin	N.C.	80,200	177
Yazoo	Miss.	72,900	536
Yellow	Fla.	28,000	143
Yellowstone	Mont., Wyo.	138,000	389
Yukon	Alaska	282,000	**

* Maximum discharge figure not available.   ** Minimum discharge figure not available.   Source: *Chemical Week*, August 19, 1970.

production and, thus, have not been a major consideration in plant location. Increasingly, supervisory personnel and maintenance personnel are technically trained and qualified; they are paid relatively well to live where the raw material, market, and transportation demands of a plant may dictate.

TRANSPORTATION

Keen competition, both domestic and foreign, forces chemical processors to pay close attention to the economics of transportation. First, few chemical plants handling any appreciable volume can be successful without a rail siding; and since new trackage costs approximately $90,000 per mile, areas already served by good rail networks are preferred locations. Similarly, the value of good roads and road nets in an area can not be overemphasized. Pipelines, too, are essential to many chemical operations; indeed, promising chemical plant sites are possible where major petroleum or natural gas pipelines cross navigable streams or canals, or at points of bifurcation or distribution. The significance of this is evident in the huge petrochemical plants at Wood River, Illinois; Whiting, Indiana; Baton Rouge, Louisiana, etc. The point is further made by the fact that, at every point where trunk natural gas pipelines cross navigable inland river and canal routes, there are chemical plants (although most of these plants produce either anhydrous ammonia or carbon black).

Savings and enforced competition resulting from water transportation further enhance riparian sites and nearby locations.[15] Water carriers (and shippers) possess a wide range of equipment to move acids, phosphates, caustic soda, and other commodities on a scale to meet the demands of endless-belt and pipeline techniques. Some chemical firms operate whole fleets of tank cars, tank trucks, or ocean-going tankers (some of the newer barges have capacities exceeding 16,000 barrels, or the equivalent of nearly 70 railroad tank cars). There is special equipment (by water, rail, or truck) to move various chemicals. Tank equipment may be lined with glass, stainless steel, rubber, or other special materials to move the different kinds of acids. Hot caustic soda equipment may be insulated; there are pressurized units for the transportation of chlorine and propane or butane, stainless steel-lined equipment for industrial alcohols, insulated equipment for molten sulfur, and special units to transport styrene. Nor does this complete the list. Nearly all equipment designed to move chemicals in volume is self-unloading, and whether this includes pumps, endless belts, pneumatic

---

[15] Usually, chemical plants occupy large tracts of level land (a slope of 5 percent is about a maximum consistent with good engineering and earth-moving economies).

tubes, or huge shovels and buckets, nearly all represent significant fixed investments.

High-speed tows, flag trains, and "hot-shot" truck schedules all help to reduce the amount of capital tied up with in-transit materials. Also, equipment designed for use on the Gulf, rivers, canals, or the Great Lakes eliminates the necessity for many transshipment breaks. This last consideration is of special importance to shippers and movers of such items as Florida phosphate, which is marketed heavily in the Midwest, Great Lakes, and Middle South regions. Transportation patterns for chemicals are highlighted in Figure 50.

The combination of inflation-recession and foreign competition is currently placing more than usual emphasis on transportation; and the promise is that the same pressures will extend throughout most of the next decade. The early 1970s saw rail rates increase significantly—with further increases ahead—and truck rates rose even more, while additional ocean rate increases only compounded the problems attending transportation costs.

Transportation costs within the chemical industry to date have averaged between 25 and 30 percent. Current indications are that they will rise to 35 to 40 percent by 1980, unless methods can be found to alter the trends. Presently being tried are greater volume shipments by use of more water-borne movements, unit trains (or multiple-car rates), guaranteed shipments,[16] and other schemes. The chief impact, admittedly long range, promises to concentrate chemical production and marketing further. In addition, other riparian sites will be opened. The need and pressures for such new volume capacity routeways is highlighted by the fact that the Arkansas-Verdigris River project in Arkansas and Oklahoma, completed in 1971, has already attracted in excess of $300 million in chemical plant investments.[17] That change is underway is evident by the following excerpt:

What Moves Where: This year new data on the chemical industry's transportation patterns are available, for the first time since 1963, thanks to completion of the '67 Census of Transportation by the Dept. of Commerce.

The new figures show the Houston area as having originated 14.68 million tons of chemical products in '67, far eclipsing Chicago's 7.07 million tons. In '63, Chicago and Houston were virtually neck and neck at 9 mil-

---

16 A *shipper* guarantees a *carrier* that he will ship a minimum volume or percentage of his overall production requirements via that carrier's line.

17 Bureau of Business and Economic Research, mimeographed (Fayetteville, Ark: University of Arkansas, July 8, 1971). For a discussion of port development and rapid water-traffic growth along the Arkansas-Verdigris, see L. D. Belzung and M. H. Sonstegaard, *Regional Response Through Port Development: An Economic Case Study on the McClellan-Kerr Arkansas River Project,* IWR Contract 74–5 (Springfield, Va.: U.S. Department of Commerce, 1974).

lion tons. Boston, Pittsburgh, Philadelphia, San Francisco, and Los Angeles gained, while Buffalo and Cleveland declined.

Truck shipment continues to dominate chemical distribution, with more than half the tonnage originating in 18 of the 25 statistical regions surveyed. Houston was the most striking exception; trucks handled only 17.6% of the area's outbound tonnage. But that's up nearly six points from '65. Water (45.2%) has supplanted rail (36.8%) as the major transit mode in the Houston area. [See Figure 50.]

The census also details data on distance shipped and destinations. Shipments farther than 1000 miles are uncommon, except in the case of Houston, where the long hauls account for 29.6% of the tonnage shipped. Products originating in an area are, for the most part, shipped within that area or to adjacent ones. More than 45% of Houston's tonnage, for example, is shipped to points in the West South Central states.[18]

CHEMICALS AND ENVIRONMENT

A period of chemical industry history when manufacturers could dump, and did dump, unwanted materials or wastes into the skies, rivers, lakes, and seas seems to be drawing to a close. To date, the record of chemical producers and pollution has been extremely spotty. Some firms have long set high control standards on plant emissions; others have been flagrantly callous and unprincipled. Today, few if any chemical firms are unconcerned about the environmental impact of their operations. Some are even finding that their corporate plans are being stifled, blocked by public worry over environmental pollution—with that concern ranging the gamut from pure esthetics to the possible derangement of food chains resulting from the direct dumping of toxic poisons into the hydrologic cycle or planetary atmospheric system. Chemical firms, along with other industries, are feeling the restricting impact of tighter state and federal regulations.[19]

Added costs, construction delays, and increased site restrictions are being felt by the industry. Indeed, some firms have reached an impasse in new construction; [20] others have been able to proceed with new construc-

---

18 *Chemical Week,* August 19, 1970.

19 By the summer of 1972, President Nixon had fully operating an Environmental Protection Administration with a research, developmental, and enforcement staff of over 5000 persons. This executive unit of the federal government has now consolidated the responsibilities for air and water pollution control programs previously housed in the Departments of Interior and Health, Education and Welfare, as well as taken over pesticide programs formerly housed in the Department of Agriculture and the Pure Food and Drug Administration.

20 BASF (Badische Anilin and Soda-Fabrik) has sought to construct a vast chemical plant on the South Carolina coast, only to have given up this site area under pressure from local esthetic and other environmental groups.

FIGURE 50. TRANSPORTATION PATTERNS FOR CHEMICALS AND ALLIED PRODUCTS BY SOURCES, MODES, SHIPPING DISTANCES, AND DESTINATIONS

Originating area and number	Shipments (million tons)	Percent shipped by[1]:				Distance shipped (%)				Destination of shipments (percent of tonnage shipped to region)[2,3]								
		Rail	Motor carriers	Private trucks	Water	Up to 99 miles	100-299 miles	300-999 miles	1,000+ miles	New England	Middle Atlantic	East North Central	West North Central	South Atlantic	East South Central	West South Central	Mountain	Pacific
Boston area; Providence, Pawtucket, Warwick, R.I.	3.43	8.6	76.0	13.8	0.5	23.6	16.2	57.8	2.4	30.8	10.4	4.8	0.3	48.0	4.3	0.7	–	0.7
Hartford, Conn.; Bridgeport, Waterbury, New Haven, Norwalk, Stamford, Conn.; Springfield, Chicopee, Holyoke, Mass.	0.70	31.5	58.7	7.7	0.8	33.9	25.9	29.0	11.2	28.8	34.4	12.2	1.7	8.4	5.2	3.6	0.4	5.3
New York City area	0.66	2.3	75.2	14.0	0.8	27.2	35.5	26.3	11.0	15.8	38.3	10.6	4.1	22.0	1.9	3.4	1.1	2.8
Newark, N.J.; Jersey City, Paterson, Clifton, Passaic; Middlesex and Somerset counties, N.J.	4.94	18.1	63.3	15.3	0.8	43.9	22.7	23.0	10.4	8.9	52.6	10.8	3.2	14.9	1.8	2.3	1.4	4.1
Philadelphia area; Wilmington, Del. area; Trenton, N.J.	5.43	23.2	52.6	22.8	1.2	53.1	20.3	20.6	6.0	6.8	59.7	10.4	1.7	14.2	2.3	2.3	0.3	2.3
Baltimore area	2.19	31.6	40.4	16.1	11.8	42.6	31.4	22.5	3.5	5.7	38.1	14.3	1.1	36.9	0.9	1.5	0.1	1.4
Allentown, Pa.; Bethlehem, Easton, Reading, Pa.	0.35	20.9	54.4	24.7	–	48.7	24.2	19.4	7.7	10.5	57.7	13.2	0.8	8.9	1.2	3.2	–	4.5
Harrisburg, Pa.; Lancaster, York, Pa.	0.09	–	77.6	22.4	–	27.1	39.4	20.9	12.6	3.8	40.7	30.2	2.2	11.9	0.4	0.5	0.3	10.0
Syracuse, N.Y.; Utica, Rome, Albany, Troy, Schenectady, N.Y.	1.39	72.6	21.0	5.3	1.1	6.2	65.9	20.5	7.4	19.8	57.2	8.3	5.1	4.1	1.3	2.1	0.1	2.0
Buffalo, Rochester, N.Y.	2.29	66.3	15.8	14.2	–	17.7	44.9	35.6	1.8	8.9	51.4	19.4	0.5	14.4	3.7	0.6	–	1.1
Cleveland; Akron, Canton, Lorain, Elyria, Youngstown, Warren, O.; Erie, Pa.	3.37	57.4	28.6	13.5	0.1	23.6	32.7	38.9	4.8	3.2	33.6	38.5	2.6	10.5	5.0	3.2	0.6	2.8
Pittsburgh, Pa.; Wheeling, Weirton, W. Va.	3.30	46.7	21.7	6.1	25.4	23.7	44.9	29.6	1.8	4.3	37.0	15.7	2.2	35.1	3.9	0.4	0.2	1.2
Detroit; Flint, Ann Arbor, Mich.; Toledo, O. 4	1.53	14.4	83.4	2.0	–	23.0	31.1	42.7	3.2	–	–	–	–	–	–	–	–	–

FIGURE 50 (cont.)

Originating area and number	Shipments (million tons)	Percent shipped by[1]: Rail	Motor carriers	Private trucks	Water	Distance shipped (%) Up to 99 miles	100-299 miles	300-999 miles	1,000+ miles	Destination of shipments (percent of tonnage shipped to region)[2,3] New England	Middle Atlantic	East North Central	West North Central	South Atlantic	East South Central	West South Central	Mountain	Pacific
Cincinnati; Dayton, Hamilton, Middletown, Springfield, O.	1.26	25.9	69.9	3.3	–	14.3	38.9	41.4	5.4	2.6	15.2	45.1	7.2	12.7	9.3	2.6	0.4	4.9
Chicago; Gary, Hammond, East Chicago, Ill.	7.07	35.6	41.5	22.2	0.4	26.3	37.3	32.2	4.2	1.0	4.5	58.6	16.9	3.8	4.9	3.6	3.1	3.6
Milwaukee; Kenosha, Racine, Wis.	0.57	36.4	58.9	4.6	–	11.1	28.9	52.2	7.8	4.7	14.9	46.7	10.6	4.6	2.0	6.6	3.4	5.5
Minneapolis-St. Paul	0.38	17.5	54.0	27.6	–	22.0	37.6	33.6	6.8	0.2	1.3	23.9	61.7	1.3	2.5	2.7	0.9	5.5
St. Louis area	4.19	57.2	33.7	2.6	6.1	8.2	40.2	45.2	6.4	1.6	6.2	30.1	20.8	5.9	16.0	12.0	2.5	4.9
Atlanta, Ga., area[5]	0.22	40.6	58.3	0.8	–	35.3	21.3	42.4	1.0	–	–	2.3	5.9	76.2	1.7	–	8.7	0.3
Dallas-Fort Worth area	1.80	23.1	63.3	13.0	–	25.9	39.8	33.2	1.1	–	0.2	8.5	7.7	5.6	9.7	76.2	1.0	–
Houston; Beaumont, Port Arthur, Orange, Galveston, Texas City, Tex.	14.68	36.8	12.4	5.1	45.2	23.1	18.8	28.5	29.6	6.6	13.2	8.5	8.7	7.3	11.6	45.5	–	2.2
Denver	0.04	3.6	92.3	1.9	–	4.5	11.9	60.9	22.7	0.6	7.0	22.1	–	7.3	11.6	13.7	22.7	6.3
Seattle, Tacoma	0.84	47.5	29.6	1.7	16.6	50.6	32.1	12.5	4.8	–	–	0.1	0.2	0.6	–	–	13.9	85.4
San Francisco area	3.09	26.5	54.9	18.0	0.3	48.1	10.6	38.4	2.9	0.1	0.2	1.5	0.7	–	–	0.6	4.1	93.3
Los Angeles area	4.65	17.7	67.2	14.3	0.6	58.5	10.9	25.2	5.4	–	1.0	1.4	0.7	0.6	0.4	0.8	7.2	87.9

Source: U.S. Dept. of Commerce, 1967 Census of Transportation, Commodity Transportation Survey.

Notes: Figures shown are for Transportation Commodity Classification (TCC) 28, chemicals and allied products, unless otherwise noted in column one. (1) Percent shipped by air and other modes omitted, so totals do not all add to 100. In most cases, the difference is less than 1%. (2) States included in regions: NEW ENGLAND—Me., N.H., Vt., Mass., R.I., Conn.; MIDDLE ATLANTIC—N.Y., N.J., Pa.; EAST NORTH CENTRAL—O., Ind., Ill., Mich., Wis.; WEST NORTH CENTRAL—Minn., Ia., Mo., N.D., S.D., Neb., Kan.; SOUTH ATLANTIC—Del., Md., Va., W. Va., N.C., S.C., Ga., Fla.; EAST SOUTH CENTRAL—Ky., Tenn., Ala., Miss.; WEST SOUTH CENTRAL—Ark., La., Okla., Tex.; MOUNTAIN—Mont., Ida., Wyo., Colo., N.M., Ariz., Utah, Nev.; PACIFIC—Wash., Ore., Calif., Alaska, Hawaii. (3) Sampling variability was 20-29% for originating areas 6, 7, 8, 10, 18, 23, 24; it was 30-50% for areas 16, 17, 20, 22, 25. For others it was under 20%. (4) Based on TCC 282, 2821, 28211, 284, 285, 2851, 28511. (5) Based on TCC 284 only.

Source: Chemical Week, August 19, 1970, p. 64.

FIGURE 51. In most cases wildlife adjusts to man's chemical plants and other resource-producing operations, as this photograph indicates. Admittedly, the two in such close juxtaposition appear incongruous. However, given man's needs and the limited remaining areas that can be devoted to wildlife, the required security for nature's devlopment can be compatible with spatial needs for such petrochemical plants as the one shown, and it offers certain economies of land use. Courtesy Exxon Company, Houston, Texas, U.S.A.

tion only after huge outlays of additional capital; [21] still others continue to operate only after meeting recently imposed standards.[22] Some plants with pollution problems not yet controllable are literally floundering, wondering which way to go.[23]

While the general public and its crusaders have had some grounds for objecting to chemical activities and attendant wastes, it is equally clear that

---

[21] According to *Chemical Week,* August 19, 1970, the Mead Paper Company agreed to invest in pollution controls over 10 percent of a $100-million proposed Kraft paper mill in Escanaba, Michigan, before that state's Pollution Control Commission would authorize the proposed plant.

[22] The Champion Paper Company of Pasadena, Texas, invested millions of dollars in research, development, and in-plant modifications to reduce the hydrogen sulfide odors and to purify waste waters in order to keep this plant producing paper for *Time* and *Life* magazines (*Life* since has ceased publication).

[23] There are currently no economically feasible sites for new producers using chlorine, caustic soda, and mercury.

the only hope for man's being able to survive under existing and anticipated population pressures is through chemistry. Thus, for the chemical-processing industries, pollution is both an opportunity and a challenge. Society is looking in large part to the chemical industry not only to find solutions to chemical plant pollution problems but also to solve major issues as excessive flush toilet flows, auto emissions, oil spills, phosphate [24] in detergents, and, indirectly through new products and fuels, noise and odor problems as well.

Air emissions by the chemical industry are proving hardest to control. Sulfur oxides, carbon monoxide, ozone, hydrocarbons, and various particulates (such as fluoride particulates) are among the most difficult to treat. So far, filter systems, electrostatic precipitators, air or liquid vortexes, and scrubbers have been the four means of control found most feasible—outside of improved chemical processes per se. In addition, there is hope that sulfur oxides are amenable to control methods proposed and/or in testing stages.[25]

Chemical plants also are interested in using chemicals and chemical processes to convert into recycled, usable commodities the mountains of solid wastes inundating much of the so-called civilized world. Admittedly, waste contains many valuable raw materials; how to separate them into useful components is the question. To known mechanical separation processes must be added such chemically related steps as pyrolysis and partial burning techniques; also, where feasible, to these might be added catalysts and chemical reagents to aid if necessary in screening, flotation, magnetic and heavy media separation, and pure chemical treatments. All offer the chemical plants opportunities for growth and service in the future despite growing odds against their finding sites and raw materials.

Thus, it should be expected that a new breed of chemical firms will emerge to serve not only the "pollution markets" of the chemical firms but also all aspects of society's pollution problems.[26]

THE CHEMICAL INDUSTRY IN RETROSPECT AND PREVISION

Due in part to its awesome vastness, complexities, and pervasiveness, the technology of the chemical industry has become a significant target of the counter-culture(s) sweeping the United States (and much of the

---

[24] Some states and local governments passed laws banning or restricting the use of phosphates in laundry detergents in the early 1970s, but U.S. Surgeon General Jesse L. Steinfeld urged them in mid-1971 to reconsider their actions because, he said, phosphates—still harmful to water bodies—are the least of three evils. He said available substitutes are too caustic and pose a health problem.

[25] *Chemical Week*, June 17, 1970, p. 86.

[26] Nalco Chemicals, Monsanto's Enviro-Chem Division, Spurn Industries, etc.

THE GM DOUBLE-ALKALI SYSTEM

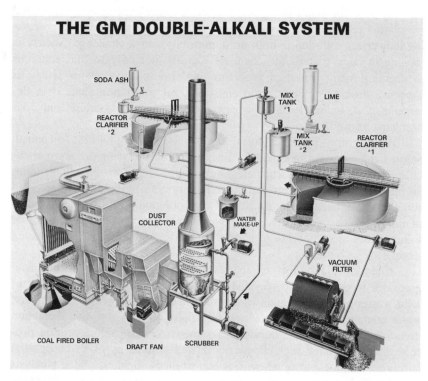

FIGURE 52. Diagram of a double alkali system used to cleanse industrial stack gases of pollutants. It is effective but adds considerably to production costs. Courtesy General Motors Corporation, Detroit, Michigan.

world). Perhaps this is true because the chemical industry en masse has failed to make man happy or solve his moral problems, let alone lead him to a utopia. However, perhaps at most, the industry is guilty of holding out hopes that were too high in that its promises of material advantages have often implied social benefits beyond the mere materials produced. Perhaps society is guilty of wishful thinking and has indulged in unreal dreams of just how far chemical technology can help man attain social goals as well as meet his material needs and wants. Perhaps the industry has been more concerned about the good that its fertilizers, low-cost papers and inks, and its plastics and fibers do for mankind, rather than about the harm caused by refuse and pollutants. If so, this is only further evidence that man, even in his highest orders of technology, is human and thus fallible. However, the chemical industry has been highly successful to date in separating and in identifying what has gone wrong in the environment and what constitutes progress in producing a growing list of useful items— and in producing these in volumes at costs that can be borne by society. Chemical technology has done much to ease man's intolerable struggle with the soil and attendant agricultural elements so as to accommodate the masses now populating the earth and still provide man with some time and energy for the arts and other cultural aspects of his earthly existence. It has even made the counter-culture possible by providing free time from drudgery and the wresting of subsistence from an otherwise stubborn, even niggardly, nature (earth). Man now has the time and energy to look about him and take inventory. Logically, a technology that despoils and takes apart the elements of nature has but to redirect that technology to put things back into order—at a cost, just as today's chemical technology has become effective only through costs in time, labor, and money.

The danger that chemical technology presents today is that chemists and chemical technology managers have made *units* of the industry *goals* in and of themselves as well as a *means of meeting man's wants or needs*. To this extent, then, society (through the counter-culture) is bringing economic, political, and social pressures to bear on the industry so that even capital investments, operating costs, manpower, and corporate growth are being manipulated in search of an equalized balance with nature.[27] Almost en masse, the industry is tackling pollution abatement, and more and more chemical firms are accepting a responsibility to test every new product for its environmental effects and compatability with health and safety considerations. Indeed, many facets of the industry are finding economic, as well as social, opportunities. That society will be expected to pay for the attendant costs is axiomatic. What it does not pay for directly as a part of materials purchased, it will finance in taxes, by which government will set standards, conduct surveillance, and enforce controls.

The environmental impact, the personalizing influences, and the technological capabilities of the chemical industry still hold some of man's highest hopes to accommodate—and even control—his growing numbers. Significantly, moral freedoms need not be subjected to the complexities and vastness of the chemical industry, for this is an industry which, by its very nature, has learned to identify, isolate, and treat problem areas so as to develop a volume flow of a controlled product. And even though its processes are highly instrumented, automated, computed, and controlled, the industry, in its dealings and interfacings with society and the environment, does not have to live by impersonalities nor with unconcern for the qualities of the earth.

That the industry is undergoing drastic change is unquestioned. A share of what previously were profits is being devoted now to social concerns—even though it means that growth is slowed as capital is siphoned off for environmental and societal considerations. New products are being released only after more careful and deliberate developmental and testing programs. Management is being broadened in the assigned scope of its re-

---

[27] "Learning to Live With Ecology," *Chemical Week,* June 16, 1971, p. 11.

sponsibilities toward ecological considerations. And cleaner production processes are being developed.

The chemical industry, as both a user of physical resources and a producer of materials, is still man's greatest hope for continued progress in his making both urban and rural life more physically acceptable, and—in light of predicted populations for tomorrow—even physically possible. The industry undoubtedly will become ever more complex, more vast, and pervasive in years ahead. Although it remains to be seen, it is expected that the industry can reestablish satisfactory environmental balances and continue to progress.

SELECTED BIBLIOGRAPHY

BACKMAN, JULES, *The Economics of the Chemical Industry*. New York: Manufacturing Chemists Association, 1970.

BERENSON, CONRAD (ed.), *The Chemical Industry: Viewpoints and Perspectives*. New York: Interscience Publishers, 1963.

CORLEY, H. M. (ed.), *Successful Commercial Chemical Development*. New York: John Wiley & Sons, Inc., 1954.

"Dow Cleans Up Pollution at No Net Cost," *Business Week,* January 1, 1972, pp. 32–35.

GIRAGOSIAN, N. H. (ed.), *Chemical Marketing Research*. New York: Reinhold Publishing Corporation, 1967.

HAPPEL, JOHN, *Chemical Process Economics*. New York: John Wiley & Sons, Inc., 1958.

HEMPEL, EDWARD, *The Economics of Chemical Industries*. New York: John Wiley & Sons, Inc., 1939.

KAHN, ALFRED E., "The Chemical Industry," *The Structure of American Industry,* ed. Walter Adams. New York: The Macmillan Company, 1963.

PICHIRALLO, JOE, "PCB's: Leaks of Toxic Substances Raise Issues of Effects, Regulation," *Science,* September 3, 1971, pp. 899–902.

PUTNAM, JOHN J., "Quicksilver and Slow Death," *National Geographic,* October, 1972, pp. 506–27.

UNITED NATIONS, INDUSTRIAL DEVELOPMENT ORGANIZATION, *Techniques of Sectoral Economic Planning: The Chemical Industries*. New York: United Nations, 1966.

SHREVE, R. NORRIS, *The Chemical Process Industries*. New York: McGraw-Hill Book Company, 1956.

YOUNG, GORDON, "Pollution, Threat to Man's Only Home," *National Geographic,* December, 1970, pp. 738–81.

TEN

RESOURCES
IN WORLD AFFAIRS

In economic and political affairs since pre-Phoenician days, mineral resources have been much like a ghost peering over the shoulders of world decision makers whenever they sat in serious deliberation—whether these decision makers were industrialists, statesmen, or *military strategists.* Strength, measured as economic wealth, political power, or *military/police might,* has long been in large measure dependent upon minerals and their availability.

Today, with the specter of hunger throughout the world, even the exercise of man's territorial imperative takes on somber overtones and begins with the control or use of minerals. Indeed, even if one calculates or assumes that acquisition and/or control of territory is inherent in the security of a nation or group, today the stewardship of that territory can endure only if key minerals are available for its continued development or exploitation. And when all other mobilization techniques fail—and sometimes even before that—nations will ask that *military strategists* take whatever measures may be necessary to ensure a country's continuing ability to mobilize those basic resources that are required to meet the needs and wants of its people. In many cases, this is tantamount to ensuring the security of that nation.

Even before the advent of industry, minerals were a powerful motivating force.[1] Salt licks, or deposits, have been the cause of struggles between men since prehistoric time; today, without guaranteed access to adequate resources of energy and raw materials, no nation can aspire to the goals of self-determination, solve the problems of material poverty of its own or other people, or exert more than a passive force for the good of mankind. Even those nations endowed with rich and productive soils cannot fully exploit such soils without certain key minerals. It is a shock to many thoughtful citizens of the United States and other civilized countries to think in terms of fighting for, or demanding access to, certain basic resources. Such action is sometimes deemed immoral. This is true even if these resources are critical to the security and the welfare of the nation concerned. And when the need for such essential minerals or other basic resources is not understood, the general public often rises in indignation and objects to what the country may be doing in the name of some ideology or to protect its territorial imperative.

Some provocative questions can be posed: Did the United States fight in South Vietnam to protect its interest in the tin deposits of Southeast Asia? Did the United States fight in Korea in order to maintain access to the tungsten deposits there? How long would the Western nations of the world refrain from actively involving themselves in a hot war in the Middle East if their interests in the oil supply of that area were seriously threatened? Is the United States the only country that mobilizes its forces in order to assure itself of overseas sources of minerals and other basic resources? Or did the Russians forceably suppress the 1956 Hungarian revolution in order to maintain control over the vast and impressive bauxite deposits of that nation? Did both Germany and Japan undertake World War II with the acquisition of strategic minerals in mind? Turning to a more general line of questioning, we might ask: What roles do minerals play in the military/police actions of the world? Will nations actually engage in warfare to protect or to gain mineral deposits? Or are these deposits incidental in the larger and everlasting struggle to protect or to spread ideologies? Or do nations fight to guard that which they feel is "sacred and right"?

With these questions in mind, we might consider the examples of tin, tungsten, the U.S.S.R., Germany and World War II, and Japan and the Pacific Basin. Many other examples could be included, but these five

---

[1] Many history books make some fleeting reference, often parenthetically, to the importance of minerals or other basic resources in various major world conflicts. John Parke Young, *The International Economy* (New York: The Ronald Press Company, 1963), pp. 16–21, for example, notes the role that mineral and other resource wealth played in the Crusades and much later in the exploration and colonization of the New World—from the time of Columbus to the Spanish conquistadores.

are representative and, in the interest of brevity, will serve to illustrate the point.

THE EXAMPLE OF TIN

In the early 1970s, certain widely known and publicized proponents of immediate and unconditional U.S. withdrawal from Vietnam, together with advocates of more vigorous action against poverty at home, publicly announced that the United States was in Vietnam fighting for, of all things, *tin*. Their argument usually concluded with this question: "And what mother, wife, or sister wants her son, husband, or brother dying for tin?" The applause that this question commonly elicited indicated how widely held is the belief that tin is a cheap, almost worthless commodity, certainly not a substance worth fighting to obtain. Yet, without this vital metal, how can any nation release manpower from drudgery, through the substitution of machinery, and thus enable its people to wage effective battles to eliminate forms of poverty, to remove massive slums, to construct housing in depressed areas, to build schools and libraries, and to construct factories to provide more employment? This question, in turn, calls for a closer consideration of the many qualities of tin and an examination of its role in modern technology.

Tin, a silvery white metal, possesses an unusual combination of properties. It is nontoxic, fuses easily, has an extremely high degree of malleability, resists corrosion, and alloys readily with other metals. Figure 53 indicates the uses of tin during the earlier, critical Vietnam war years. Tinplate, a declining application of tin, is by far the largest category of use. This category is followed by solder, bronze and brass, and babbitt, in that order, and numerous other listed applications. Although glass, enamels, and plastics have been utilized as welcome, lower-cost—and in many cases adequate—substitutes for certain uses of tin, no satisfactory substitutes have been found to date for tin's place in solder, bronze and brass, or babbitt.

Most critical with regard to babbitt [2] (a rare, antifriction metal, absolutely essential to the manufacture of cast liners—unless one can consider costly silver a practical substitute), tin is a vital metal in terms of U.S. survival as a nation. Without it, ball or roller bearings,[3] which make possible machinery for defense and machinery to fight poverty, would be

---

[2] Babbitt is about four-fifths tin alloyed with antimony and copper.

[3] Anyone who questions the vital role that these bearings play in the functioning of a nation needs only to recall that some of the very first Allied targets selected for saturation-type bombing during World War II were the German ball-bearing factories. If these could have been destroyed, the war would have ended much sooner.

FIGURE 53a. CONSUMPTION OF PRIMARY TIN IN THE UNITED STATES BY FINISHED PRODUCTS

(long tons, tin content)

Product	1954–58 (average)	1959	1960	1961	1962	1963
Alloys (miscellaneous)	345	309	260	300	322	290
Babbitt	2,388	2,157	1,841	1,744	2,186	2,225
Bar tin	1,101	1,174	894	1,165	1,439	1,580
Bronze and brass	3,941	3,868	3,350	3,168	3,959	4,128
Chemicals including tin oxide	631	790	648	674	824	1,088
Collapsible tubes and foil	830	930	788	939	1,010	992
Pipe and tubing	103	79	35	31	30	28
Solder	9,664	7,046	6,660	7,598	12,349	12,856
Terne metal	167	58	132	51	166	298
Tinning	2,304	2,057	1,996	2,035	2,180	2,142
Tinplate	32,504	25,275	33,238	31,185	28,708	28,351
Type metal	129	129	98	96	104	116
White metal	1,183	1,764	1,452	1,190	1,215	1,044
Other	140	197	138	112	110	71
Total	55,430	45,833	51,530	50,288	54,602	55,209

Source: U.S. Department of the Interior, Bureau of Mines, *Mineral Facts and Problems,* Bulletin 630 (Washington, D. C.: Government Printing Office, 1965), p. 967. These figures cover the earlier years of the Vietnam war, important to the above discussion; similar tables were not included in the 1970 edition (Bulletin 650).

impossible. Prices of a gamut of machinery, from automobiles and airplanes to agricultural and industrial equipment, could be dictated by the power that controls tin supplies.

The dominance of Malaysia as a source of tin is clear when the data of Figure 54 are analyzed. Nearly 85 percent of the supply of new tin comes directly from Malaysia—which lies only 250 miles or so across the narrow Gulf of Siam from Vietnam—and much of the remaining 15 percent also originated in Malaysia and has merely arrived in the United States via the non-Malaysian nations listed in Figure 54. The United States has met about one-twentieth of its requirements with more-expensive Bolivian tin, but at present this is far from being a satisfactory substitute. Complete U.S. dependence on Bolivian tin would supply America's current rate of consumption from known deposits for only nine years or less.

Thus, the vital and critical nature of the Vietnam war takes on

FIGURE 53b. CONSUMPTION OF SECONDARY TIN IN THE UNITED STATES BY FINISHED PRODUCTS

(long tons, tin content)

Product	1954–58 (average)	1959	1960	1961	1962	1963
Alloys (miscellaneous)	167	138	141	120	106	144
Babbitt	1,890	1,981	1,780	1,794	1,477	1,439
Bar tin	143	243	216	108	110	88
Bronze and brass	13,492	13,241	11,986	13,025	12,428	11,784
Chemicals including tin oxide	932	1,043	1,284	1,415	1,486	1,350
Collapsible tubes and foil	75	113	127	59	79	72
Pipe and tubing	47	40	43	28	14	33
Solder	9,822	12,986	11,618	10,436	7,220	6,739
Terne metal	191	242	337	167	182	263
Tinning	63	74	39	41	59	55
Type metal	1,340	1,263	1,333	1,193	1,212	986
White metal	109	142	90	124	85	95
Other	57	34	36	41	25	46
Total	28,328	31,540	29,030	28,551	24,483	23,094

Source: U.S. Department of the Interior, Bureau of Mines, *Mineral Facts and Problems,* Bulletin 630 (Washington, D.C.: Government Printing Office, 1965), p. 967.

altogether different hues when considered in terms of whether the United States can solve or overcome its domestic poverty, protect itself, and even exercise its territorial imperatives without Malaysian tin. It is argued by some American critics that Southeast Asia is a local problem for Asians to solve, and that the United States should "mind its own business." These critics claim that once South Asians decide their own future, the United States then can purchase its necessary minerals from them in the open market. There is no reason to believe that, if the future were decided in favor of communism, the Communists would be any more willing to sell vital minerals to Americans later than they are today. Communist nations also need these nonrenewable resources for future industrial and economic development. Thus the United States fought long and hard in Southeast Asia to keep the area "free"—free to furnish the U.S. requirements of strategic metals and other basic resources that it cannot acquire in sufficiently large quantities elsewhere. In that sense, the United States *was* "minding its own business" by protecting its interests in Southeast Asia. The 1973 U.S. withdrawal will make interesting history!

FIGURE 54. TIN IMPORTED FOR CONSUMPTION IN THE UNITED STATES, BY COUNTRIES

(Long tons)

Country	1954–58 (average)	1959	1960	1961	1962	1963
Belgium-	5,316	705	1,601	680	1,826	383
Luxembourg	139	325	939	1,672	1,850	1,867
Congo (Leopoldville & Ruanda Urandi)	334	850	336	4	——	103
Indonesia	187	200	550	150	50	1,023
Malaysia	38,994	22,404	29,521	32,955	34,808	36,410
Netherlands	7,778	2,820	432	55	——	25
Nigeria	——	——	——	544	1,176	2,066
United Kingdom	4,894	15,693	5,924	2,810	1,346	1,590
Other Countries	420	581	235	1,023	345	134
Total	58,062	43,578	39,538	39,893	41,401	43,601

Source: U.S. Department of the Interior, Bureau of Mines, *Mineral Facts and Problems,* Bulletin 630 (Washington, D.C.: Government Printing Office, 1965), p. 967.

THE EXAMPLE OF TUNGSTEN

With the advent of the nuclear and space era, tungsten—and its availability in the Free World—became a problem of awesome proportions to industrial and governmental decision makers. There was the specter of foreseeable domestic deposits becoming exhausted before 1980,[4] yet this metal—because it has the highest melting point of either tool or structure metals—is vital to continued national progress in terms of meeting U.S. industrial, nuclear, and space requirements. Figure 55 shows the world's tungsten reserves in 1954, the general picture of tungsten sources that prevailed during the period the United States was most actively involved in Korea.

It is not surprising that the United States, with an appetite for nearly 50 percent of the Free World's tungsten production, selected the 38th parallel as the boundary between North and South Korea, because, although it is not a good military boundary in terms of terrain, nor even a good political boundary in terms of history, it is just far enough north to include

---

[4] U.S. Department of the Interior, Bureau of Mines, *Mineral Facts and Problems,* Bulletin 630 (Washington, D.C.: Government Printing Office, 1965), p. 1005.

FIGURE 55. WORLD TUNGSTEN RESERVES

(Estimated units of tungsten trioxide in measured, indicated, and inferred, ore in 1954)

Country	Thousand short-ton units WO_3	Country	Thousand short-ton units WO_3
Argentina	500	Mexico	100
Australia	1,600	Nigeria	small
Bolivia	5,500	Peru	550
Brazil	2,500	Portugal	2,000
Burma	4,800	Southern Rhodesia	100
Canada	1,000	Spain	650
Mainland China	134,500	Sweden	small
France	150	Tanganyika	small
Cambodia	300	Thailand	500
Japan	100	United Kingdom	400
Korea	7,000	U.S.S.R.	1,700
Malaysia	1,400	United States	9,000

Source: U.S. Department of the Interior, Bureau of Mines, *Mineral Facts and Problems,* Bulletin 630 (Washington, D.C.: Government Printing Office, 1965), p. 1001.

the Free World's largest wolframite [5] mine—just *barely* far enough north. To suggest that the selection of the 38th parallel—such an unlikely, difficult-to-defend boundary—was only *coincidental* with the location of the tungsten mine either would be naive or would suggest that American political and military planners were derelict in their assigned duties. And, since the time of the Panmunjon talks, it is doubtful that subsequent technological advancements in metallurgy have altered or decreased the keen interest evidenced in South Korean tungsten—especially in light of China's world market output and price manipulation, made possible by its relatively abundant tungsten ore deposits. Indeed, in light of China's activity throughout most of the 1960s, the only stability given the tungsten industry has been provided by energetic and expensive efforts to develop and maintain both U.S. domestic output and South Korean production. Thus, the Korean conflict and U.S. maintenance of troops in that country are explained, at least in part, by mineral considerations.

---

[5] Wolframite is a mineral that is a primary source of tungsten, which in turn is used in such varied applications as high-speed cutting tools, magnets, lathes, razor blades, knives, hacksaws, chisels, files, large guns, armor plate, and armor-piercing shells.

Perhaps the most flagrant example of possible danger to a nation's industries and its people caused by lack of knowledge *or consideration* of resource importance was the decisions of President Franklin D. Roosevelt at the Yalta Conference following World War II. At Yalta, President Roosevelt, evidently without adequate technical support or advice of one of his staff members (Alger Hiss, later convicted of perjury)—and without adequate knowledge or appreciation of mineral resources—met with Premier Joseph Stalin of the U.S.S.R. to divide between the two countries the spoils of World War II.

Included among Roosevelt's concessions to Stalin (which consisted of most of central and eastern Europe) were the Joachiminthal pitchblende mines of Czechoslovakia (along with German prisoners to work the mines) and the bauxite deposits of Hungary—the main source of all of Europe's aluminum prior to World War II. These two minerals alone made Yalta one of the most significant international conferences in all of the world's history. The pitchblende of Joachiminthal made it possible for the U.S.S.R. to catch up in the atomic nuclear race without the expense and time that would have been necessary had it been forced to rely entirely on its domestic betafite ores or other forms of radioactive sands as sources of uranium. Because of pitchblende, is it surprising that Czechoslovakia was not allowed to consolidate its forces to organize a serious revolt?

Similarly, as the United States had demonstrated an ability and capacity to produce more than 1 million planes a year, this, in a relative sense, made the aluminum-poor U.S.S.R. a have-not nation in terms of air power. Thus, the U.S.S.R. was given the mineral (aluminum) means of overtaking America in this vital area. It was not unexpected, therefore, that the Hungarians, suffering under the oppression of a demanding U.S.S.R. five-year plan imposed on them, attempted a revolt that was decisively crushed by more than 35 heavily armored U.S.S.R. divisions. In this action some of the most brutal fighting took place in the bauxite mining and aluminum processing districts.[6]

Other examples of the U.S.S.R.'s using force to obtain minerals (or, to gain settlements in which mineral resources were a primary consideration) include its acquisition of the Pechenga nickel mines in what was formerly northern Finland as a part of the 1940 settlement of the Russo-

---

[6] Whether this fighting in the vicinity of bauxite mines and aluminum plants was intentional or by chance may be debated, but that the U.S.S.R. sent its greatest concentration of troops to these areas and that most of the areas' minerals still move to the U.S.S.R. is not debatable. For example, see Laszlo Zsoldos, "Economic Integration of Hungary into the Soviet Bloc" (Columbus, Ohio: Bureau of Business Research, 1963), p. 107.

Finnish war,[7] and its incorporation after World War II of all of Sakhalin Island for its oil, not to mention its past and current efforts at fomenting strife in the oil-rich Near East [8] or in the pitchblende-rich African Congo.

The foregoing U.S. and U.S.S.R. mineral cases show clearly that military intervention is not limited to any one side in the struggle for survival among nations as they compete for access to vital minerals. These discussions are not in any manner a moral justification of military force by an industrial nation. However, the cases show well that nations do indeed resort to violence when their sources of vital minerals are endangered.

GERMANY AND WORLD WAR II

World War II might well be a classic illustration of how a country can lack sufficient basic resources to feed its designs of power and to satisfy its real wants and needs. Often Adolph Hitler found it necessary to translate Germany's needs for basic resources first into Nazi ideological terms and then, secondly, into terms of space, or *lebensraum*. For example: the coal-rich Saar Valley was a subject of political struggle between France and Germany dating from World War I. The decision to govern the Saar Basin by a League of Nations commission in 1918 satisfied neither Germany nor the Saar inhabitants, who were primarily German. After the 1935 Saar plebiscite (a vote that some historians believe was strongly influenced by Hitler), this valuable industrial area was returned to Germany. Germany virtually fought the second World War with Saar coal, using it to make synthetic rubber and—utilizing the hydrogenation process [9]—gasoline and other "petroleum-type" products. The next territory that Hitler set his eye on was the Erzgebirge, the Sudeten lands of Czechoslovakia, a German-speaking area that, it was argued emotionally, was actually more German than Czech; but, *incidentally,* at that time it was also the location of one of the world's largest known pitchblende deposits. And Hitler's scientists, who were already working on the atomic bomb, needed pitchblende and heavy water. Consequently, these two basic resource needs were given early consideration by Hitler as he began his plan of world conquest. So the Sudeten lands fell to Germany and, along with them, uranium-rich pitchblende. Hitler also attacked Norway, ostensibly for more than one reason; perhaps he sought submarine berths or lairs from which to attack the North Atlantic shipping and sealanes, and perhaps, also, he had in mind the heavy-

---

[7] Clifford H. MacFadden et al., *Atlas of World Affairs* (New York: Thomas Y. Crowell Company, 1946), pp. 86, 91.

[8] *U. S. News & World Report,* June 19, 1947, pp. 38–40.

[9] Max W. Ball, *This Fascinating Oil Business* (New York: The Bobbs-Merrill Company, 1940), p. 209.

water plant at Narvik. In addition to the copper mines of Yugoslavia and Finland, there were those of *Norway*—and German industry had suffered greatly during World War I because of its deficiency in copper. Then came the most grandiose plan of all; after Hitler had swept England off the Continent [10] and had overrun France for all practical purposes, he turned his eyes to the heartland of the world—the "Soviet Heartland." [11]

The reason for Hitler's attention to this area was that Germany's militarists and strategists, particularly General Haushofer (the "high priest of German geopolitikers"), regarded economic self-sufficiency as one precept of German *geopolitik*. This precept included a recognized need for economic control of basic resources and their required and related extractive industries. In this regard, the agricultural potential of the Ukraine and the rest of the "Soviet Heartland," and the occurrence there of rich coal, iron ore, limestone, nickel, petroleum, copper, and manganese deposits, made this area a vital target of conquest.

JAPAN AND THE PACIFIC BASIN

Minerals played an equally major role in Japan's moves before and during World War II.[12] Japan was receiving 90 percent of its oil from the United States, the Caribbean, and the East Indies in 1941, and when Franklin Roosevelt froze shipments of U. S. oil to Japan in that year, the Imperial Military Headquarters had to move aggressively in order to seek sufficient oil to reach the distant points marked on the Imperial chart. The U. S. oil-shipment freeze was also probably a major factor in turning the eyes of Japanese war lords from Siberia toward Southeast Asia.[13]

Sumatra and Borneo held the petroleum Japan needed, and northwest Malaya and the Philippines had the iron ore (Japan had taken Manchuria earlier to satisfy its coal requirements but did not have sufficient iron ore

---

[10] England was a thorn in Hitler's side, but its minerals were not vital enough to warrant the expenditure of the men required to capture it; England could primarily offer coal, and Hitler already had taken over the coal of the Saar.

[11] The "Heartland" extends from the Volga River eastward into Siberia, and from the Arctic Sea southward to the plateau and upland of Iran and Afghanistan.

[12] William M. McGovern, *Strategic Intelligence and the Shape of Tomorrow* (Chicago: Henry Regnery Company, 1961), pp. 34–35; Herbert Feis, "The Road to Pearl Harbor," *Readings in American History,* II, Glyndon G. Van Deusen and Herbert J. Bass, eds. (New York: The Macmillan Company, 1963), pp. 389, 407–408.

[13] Feis, op. cit., p. 407, believes the Japanese timetable to attack Pearl Harbor was advanced considerably because of its limited store of oil after the U.S. freeze on oil shipments.

to meet its demand for steel). Indonesia and the Philippines had chrome and manganese; the Celebes had nickel; Malaya, tin and rubber; Indonesia, bauxite for aluminum; and the islands of Nauru and Oceia, phosphates for artificial fertilizer.

It is interesting to note that Communist China was in almost an identical position in the 1960s—insofar as vital minerals were concerned—as Japan was in the late 1930s, before the beginning of open Japanese hostilities.[14]

THE PROBLEM IS WORLDWIDE AND TIMELY

As with the Phoenicians in an early era, and as with Japan and Germany in this century, mineral resources have been, are, and will continue to be of primary concern to every country and to every individual whose goal is national development and/or power. There is little doubt that in Germany, Hitler's campaigns—along with other considerations—were designed to obtain heavy water from Norway; aluminum from Hungary; pitchblende, iron, and coal from Poland and Czechoslovakia; and nickel, manganese, and oil from the Ukraine. Likewise, there is no doubt that Japan's aggression in the Pacific was strongly resource-oriented—and that the same is true today for China's interest in Malaysia and Indonesia. Certainly there are other considerations, but the need for mineral resources is there, and not all nations are capable of, nor can they afford, *economic* penetration of an area for the purpose of securing raw materials, such as Japan is doing in Alaska, Australia, and even Continental United States. (Japan is seeking a replacement for Manchuria's rich mineral deposits, taken from Japan during World War II by the U.S.S.R., then returned to China only after much of Japan's mining and other industrial equipment had been delivered to the U.S.S.R.'s Komsomolsk coal and iron ore areas north of Khabarovsk.)

True, the United States and most nations have, where possible, made economic and political arrangements for obtaining minerals (as illustrated by U. S. and Netherlands activity in Venezuela); but many of the mining areas opened by U. S. funds are now no longer available to this nation on an economic or political basis. For example, Cuba, Mexico, and even America's friend, the Philippines, limit foreign ownership. What alternative resource will the United States then have, once the sources of key minerals are closed, especially in those areas where U. S. economic and political efforts have been tried and found wanting? And, unless the United States

---

[14] McGovern, op. cit., pp. 149–50.

is to decline as a world power—as Great Britain has done—minerals must continue to be available to U. S. industries at an economic price that America can afford to pay.[15]

The discussion in this chapter does not paint a very optimistic picture of peace on earth. Prospects that the world will forge within this century a permanent and lasting peace—free of political conflicts and confrontations over minerals—are dim. It is not a question of moral issues, but of national survival! If there is any faint hope that peace can be found in time, probably it will come about through some overriding power that is worldwide in scope and not limited by national boundaries and national needs. One future possibility is the development of the world corporation—a movement that is so significant in its potential (but also fraught with dangers) that it has been made the subject of the next chapter.

SELECTED BIBLIOGRAPHY

ECKEL, EDWIN C., *Coal, Iron and War; A Study in Industrialism, Past and Future.* New York: Henry Holt and Company, 1920.

FEIS, HERBERT, *The Road to Pearl Harbor.* Princeton, N.J.: Princeton University Press, 1950.

HODGKINS, JORDAN A., *Soviet Power: Energy Resources, Production and Potentials.* Englewood Cliffs, N.J.: Prentice-Hall, Inc., 1961.

LEITH, C. K., *World Minerals and World Politics.* New York: McGraw-Hill Book Company, Inc., 1931.

LEITH, C. K., J. W. FURNESS, and CLEONA LEWIS, *World Minerals and World Peace.* Washington, D.C.: The Brookings Institution, 1943.

LOVERING, T. S., *Minerals in World Affairs.* New York: Prentice-Hall, Inc., 1943.

McDIVITT, JAMES F., *Minerals and Men.* Baltimore: The Johns Hopkins Press, 1965.

McGOVERN, WILLIAM M., *Strategic Intelligence and the Shape of Tomorrow.* Chicago: Henry Regnery Company, 1961.

MENDELSSOHN, PETER, *Design for Aggression.* New York: Harper & Brothers Publishers, 1946.

---

[15] It is not a question of obtaining minerals to help ensure industrial profits (which are seemingly abhorred by the "antiestablishment" elements in American society). The reader is reminded that industrial profits contribute to national income and furnish other economic benefits; the industries also contribute to national defense, furnish employment, aid economic development, and help alleviate poverty at home.

MOUZON, OLIN T., *Resources and Industries of the United States.* New York: Appleton-Century-Crofts, 1966.

PARK, CHARLES F., JR., *Affluence in Jeopardy.* San Francisco: Freeman, Cooper and Company, 1968.

PEARCY, G. ETZEL, "Geopolitics and Foreign Relations," *The Department of State Bulletin,* L, No. 1288, March, 1964, pp. 318–30.

SHIMKIN, DEMITRI B., *Minerals, A Key to Soviet Power.* Cambridge, Mass.: Harvard University Press, 1953.

U.S. DEPARTMENT OF THE INTERIOR, BUREAU OF MINES, *Mineral Facts and Problems.* Washington, D.C.: Government Printing Office, 1970.

ELEVEN

THE WORLD CORPORATION OR SUPRANATIONAL COMPANY

The world corporation, or supranational company, appears to be emerging as the dominant phenomenon evolving out of man's scramble for basic resources. At present, trends point to multinational corporations as the ultimate arrangement of the "firm." However, logic suggests that the multinational corporation is nothing more or less than a corporate form of colonialism. Once this point is recognized, it follows that the ultimate is truly a worldwide corporation or global supranational company—not yet feasible given the existing ideological schisms.[1] Yet, that the multinational firm *has* arrived and is a potent force in resource management, even on a worldwide scale, cannot be denied.

FORCES PRODUCING MULTINATIONAL CORPORATIONS

Conditions precipitating the multinational corporations of today and the world supranational companies of tomorrow are both clear and subtle.

---

[1] The element *multi* is of Latin origin, meaning "many"; so a multinational corporation is one with offices and/or subsidiaries and operations in various nations. *Supra,* meaning "above," is akin to *super* but emphasizes location or position; thus a supranational corporation is beyond or outside the authority of a national government. Apparently, the term *multinational corporation* was first used in a 1958 speech by David Lilienthal.

Usually interrelated, the forces or causes are easier detailed than generalized for analytical reasons. Some of the leading causes include the following:

1. Control of basic raw materials for industrial use.
2. Environmental restrictions in the original "home" country.
3. Assemblage of widespread undertakings under one management, producing the necessary economic clout to compete with powerful national firms of such countries as Japan, France, or Italy, or the huge giant corporations of the United States.
4. Inexorable, exponential growth of demand for basic raw materials in all parts of the world.
5. Inflationary rises in prices of what already is increasingly becoming relatively scarce materials.
6. Growing interdependence of nations for raw materials.
7. Intense current "push" to commit all known and potential raw materials.
8. Need (even though not widely enunciated as yet) to push back the frontiers of resource management and technology—perhaps beginning with fusion—lest man's appetite for raw materials outrun nature's supply of basic building blocks (ores, arable soils, etc.).
9. Erosion of "home nation" advantages because of rising wages and raging inflation.
10. "Home nation" restrictions on the employment of foreign workers.
11. Pressures to diversify overseas in order to level off or hedge local, regional, or national economic fluctuations.
12. Desire to gain entrance to protected markets.
13. Necessity to reduce certain transportation costs by producing locally.
14. Exigency of taking advantage of an excess of one or more currencies.
15. Incentive to acquire or take advantage of firms, wherever located, with low price-to-earnings ratios.
16. Advantage of gaining technologies or patent rights.

The chief deterrents to a truly global pattern of world supranational companies are the:

1. Rise of nationalism.
2. Adversity of ideologies.
3. Fear of such companies by the world's political dictators.
4. Apprehension among many people that giant multinational companies (such as Mitsubishi of Japan or General Motors of the United States) will grow even larger because "to those who have, more will be given" as a result of their greater experience and resources.
5. Enmities, antipathies, and fears for—or of—certain peoples.

6. Spotty performance of multinationals, with more favorable performance centered in the already "have" nations.[2]

7. Controls on foreign investments.

8. Fears that the multinational corporations stifle, rather than stimulate, trade.

This last point is worthy of comment. That there are forces causing nations to look beyond their borders for raw materials is not new; but there are serious concerns, especially in the United States, England, and other once-rich nations, that the multinational corporations are barriers to trade. In brief, there is a belief that U.S. firms have gone overseas in the past to set up plants and to transplant technology. It was hoped that this would stimulate trade, and this seemed to be the case for a while. Now, many peoples have reached—or, are reaching—levels of self-sufficiencies and are competing for the world's limited raw materials. The reassuring favorable U.S. trade levels existing from the Civil War until the middle 1960s have vanished within a decade, and our once overwhelming technological (trade secret) advantages are almost gone. In a nation that once was confident that global conglomerates promised answers to world differences, one now finds strong trade-union opposition and serious management doubt in the long-range view.[3] Some economists also are reacting hesitantly because of the potential for supranational corporations of the future to return capitalism to the unregulated, uncontrolled conditions of the 1800s. Already some corporate empires wield more clout than some governments, and the forecast is a world order, run out of corporate offices, too powerful for national controls.

THE SITUATION TODAY IN TERMS OF HOPES AND PROMISES OF WORLD CORPORATIONS

At present, there is no firm expectation that supranational corporations will become a fact any time soon; rather, the present multinational-firm pattern seems to be in jeopardy in many countries.[4] South American nations speak of expropriations, Canada voices opposition to U.S. domination of its markets, and the Common Market thinks in terms of divestiture.

---

[2] See "Annual Survey of Internal Corporate Performance: 1972," *Business Week,* July 7, 1973, pp. 60–65.

[3] Numerous articles in the *AFL-CIO American Federalist* have expressed labor union concern. One article (July, 1972) says "once proud countries are losing the power to shape their own destinies, to guide their economies, to collect their taxes, to lift up their people [because] they are increasingly at the mercy of stateless, soulless, anonymous multinational corporations."

[4] Libya and Chile are two nations expropriating the assets of national firms. Even Chile's reaction to and takeover from a communist system has not resulted in quick promises to return Chile's industry to foreign interests.

Whether all of this is only a temporary stumble in the long run is not possible to ascertain at this point.

As already noted, key minerals that are located behind *restricting* boundaries and are controlled by *hostile* ideologies and/or nations take on a new light and, indeed, become part of a long-range struggle for national survival—especially in the case of such gigantic nations as the United States. If such a struggle is to be successful, it must be supported by the industrial facets of U.S. national existence, and these, in turn, can exist only if the requisite key mineral resource building blocks continue to be available. What are the alternatives? At best, slow decline; and, at the worst (because of the "breadbasket" nature of our nation), a loss of territory, and slavery. In any event, this country's freedom to select courses of action, individually and as a nation, will disappear. How "cheap" is the tin? What is the "real" worth of a wolframite? Does the emerging world corporation offer possible solutions to the problems of obtaining resources or of equalizing resource distribution?

The world corporation movement as an alternative to international military and police action remains one of the world's great hopes in man's constant struggle to allocate resources more perfectly. This hope is held out despite the potential disadvantages threatened by such a movement.

The idea of international trade, of course, is not new. What is new is the emergence during the 1960s of modern corporations as world entities— as world powers. The shift—actually begun about 1950—was away from international trade (manufacture in one nation and sales to many others) and over to international production (manufacture *and* sale in each major market).

The flexibility and economic power of many world corporations exceed the strength of most nations. For example, General Motors ranked 18th in 1967 among the world's entities in terms of gross product (G.N.P. for nations)—the Netherlands was 17th. In fact, of the world's 40 largest G.N.P. entities, seven were corporate enterprises in 1967. And it is expected that soon at least 15 of the top 40 will be corporations.

Consider the power of world corporations: it may well have been that Ford's decision to locate its major Common Market automobile production plant in Belgium rather than (as had been planned) in France caused President DeGaulle to "step down." Perhaps it was not Ford's judgment alone that determined DeGaulle's course of action; but, when it was combined with GM's decision to locate a 5000-employee plant in Antwerp (instead of Alsace) and Phillips Petroleum's decision to locate a polyethylene plant in Belgium (rather than in Bordeaux), the total forces resulted in pressures greater than even Charles DeGaulle could withstand during the height of his presidency.

Further evidence of the vitality wielded by modern global corporations is found in the fact that some nations have nationalized certain facets of their industries only to have them purchased by a world corporation—e.g., FRIONOR of Norway, Nestle of Switzerland, etc.

Today, it is estimated that there are some 1200 world corporations. Some 800 are American in origin; some 300 are West European; and Japan alone headquarters some 60 international firms. Even before the rapid inflationary period of the mid-1970s, U.S. investments abroad were estimated at $60 billion; annual goods and services of these firms exceeded $100 billion, with know-how constituting a major share. That is, the licensing of techniques and processes and the sale of patents constituted close to 50 percent of the value of such goods and services.

The impact of these global corporations is felt throughout the world.[5] Mergers are occurring almost as a worldwide epidemic, but they are especially prevalent in countries such as Sweden and Australia, which must mass their internal and external economic strength in order to compete.

Divided loyalties are producing interesting trends toward a world citizenry. Regarding certain global corporations, loyalties seem to be waxing increasingly strong toward the international corporation and away from the nation and state. This is especially noticeable in the Western European Common Market and on the east and west coasts of the United States.

The big differences between peoples are seen now in: (1) availability of managerial talent, (2) technological know-how, (3) worker productivity, (4) education levels (e.g., Japan), and (5) value systems, rather than in raw materials from mines, farms, and forests—as was the case when Strausz-Hupe wrote his classic on geopolitics.[6]

The global corporations are still referred to often as *American* multinational, or *Japanese* multinational, corporations; but increasingly they are losing their national identities, as their managements and their stockholders are becoming as multinational as their production and marketing operations. Some corporations of U.S. origin have cut their American moorings and have begun to drift as it were on the high seas of international waters. While economists have theorized about "comparative advantage" of one nation over another,[7] global corporations have come to practice their own form of

---

[5] Companies of foreign origin (Lever Brothers, Norelco, Shell, Toyota and Datsun, British Petroleum) are as familiar to Americans as U.S.-organized corporations (General Motors, Goodyear, Coca-Cola, Singer, Eastman Kodak, National Cash Register, International Business Machines, General Electric, Woolworth, Colgate-Palmolive, Gillette, Heinz, and the oil companies) are familiar to people abroad.

[6] Robert Strausz-Hupe, *Geopolitics, The Struggle for Space and Power* (New York: G. P. Putnam's Sons, 1942).

[7] The concept of comparative advantage holds simply that a nation should specialize in the manufacturing and marketing of those goods in which it is comparatively most efficient (or has the least comparative disadvantage) and import those products in which it has the lowest efficiency.

comparative advantage. With capital, innovation, technology, management know-how, equipment, etc., the highly mobile worldwide corporations have been able to work their own comparative advantages—in one country as opposed to another—in taxes, labor costs, subsidies, and protected markets. It is not possible to discuss all of these finer points here; but they are very real and very practical.

The world corporations, in their computers, even have their own language.

World corporations find expanded opportunities in international agreements such as the World Bank, the Nuclear Nonproliferation Agreement, Intelsat, and Inter-sputnik.

The global corporation makes it possible for Japan to reach out and secure the basic resources that it needs—peacefully, rather than by force of arms, as was the case when it took Manchuria.

Japan invested more in Alaska in 1970 than did the United States. Japan buys American logs and coal away from the U.S. users. In turn, the United States controls 30 percent of the European car market, 85 percent of its computer markets, etc. At the same time, Japan also is investing in Australian and Canadian mines and Indonesian oil fields, mines, farms, and forests; it has invested in many South American countries and reached agreements with the U.S.S.R. and China. Japan's international economic ventures have, through that country's unique unification of finance and production, become simply arms and avenues of national policies.

The role of banking interests, too, has become worldwide in scope. For example, on the day that President Kennedy was assassinated, and on the day that Robert Kennedy was shot, a telephone call from New York to Zurich set up stabilizing funds that some individuals feared might be needed to shore up the United States economy. Today, the economies, including fiscal systems of all Free-World economies, are interdependent.

Although space does not permit a discussion of it here, the U.S.S.R. and China, too, are moving more and more toward exchanges with the world corporations on the international scene (some of the cars in the U.S.S.R. use British engines; and Fiat, Olivetti, and Renault and other world corporations are already doing business in the U.S.S.R.; also, China has invited American-based companies to help search for oil in the offshore waters of the "awakening giant"). Even the management revolution that apparently is now under way in the U.S.S.R.—if success is judged by profits, rather than by ideology—may well have been affected, at least partly, by worldwide pressures evolving out of the global corporation movement.

Thus, in brief, it now appears that the "Grand Global Resource-Oriented Schemes" of Haushofer, Mackinder, and Strausz-Hupe are more nearly embodied in the world corporation movement, rather than in nations or states per se (recent activities of the United States in South Korea and Vietnam notwithstanding).

Out of the resource- (and labor-) based world corporation movement, it is becoming clear that, as the technocrats of the global corporations take over, there may well develop greater differences between professional groups and economic classes than between national or political lines. Producers of many mineral, forest, or farm commodities—and bankers, too, throughout the world—may well have more in common than two citizens of a single nation. Similarly, chemists have their international languages (and interests), as do mathematicians, physicists, medical doctors, and other professional disciplines. The impact of these basic resource producers and professional groups on national borders, offshore limits, nuclear treaties, international communications, and communication systems may well be the bases for the great dynamics of our time; and the world corporation trend may make it possible for nations to tend more toward domestic issues, rather than prepare so much for war.[8] The geopolitical facts of national concern may well be taken care of by world corporations.

Making global corporations into useful world citizens, to serve mankind's needs and wants, is the task of all individuals. These corporations may well be the hope and promise of a means to allocate resources on a worldwide scale—without nations resorting to wars or threats of war.

SELECTED BIBLIOGRAPHY

BEHRMAN, JACK N., *National Interests and the Multinational Enterprise.* Englewood Cliffs, N.J.: Prentice-Hall, Inc., 1970.

BROOKE, MICHAEL Z., and H. LEE REMMERS, *The Strategy of Multinational Enterprise.* New York: American Elsevier Publishing Company, Inc., 1970.

KINDLEBERGER, CHARLES P. (ed.), *The International Corporation.* Cambridge, Mass.: The M.I.T. Press, 1970.

---

[8] During the decade of the 1960s, investment of U.S. companies abroad increased 146 percent, and sales of foreign factories owned by U.S. companies virtually matched that figure (*U.S. News & World Report,* July 19, 1971, pp. 38–39). Some authorities are predicting that the multinational companies will have a global influence by the 1980s as great as all but the very largest nations, and already they are becoming a major factor in international banking and finance. British historian Arnold Toynbee predicts that the time will come when some island in the world will become "a kind of Vatican City as a seat for the world's multinational corporations," where huge firms can have their own bases of operations without interference from even the largest governments (ibid., p. 41). If that day arrives, we shall see the supranational corporation as a reality!

MARTYN, HOWE, *Multinational Business Management*. Lexington, Mass.: D. C. Heath and Company, 1970.

"On The Way: Companies More Powerful Than Nations," *U.S. News & World Report*, July 19, 1971, pp. 38–41.

PENROSE, EDITH T., *The Large International Firm in Developing Countries*. Cambridge, Mass.: The M.I.T. Press, 1968.

ROLFE, SIDNEY E., and WALTER DAMM (eds.), *The Multinational Corporation in the World Economy*. New York: Frederick A. Praeger, Publishers, 1970.

SALERA, VIRGIL, *Multinational Business*. Boston: Houghton Mifflin Co., 1969.

WILKINS, MIRA, *The Emergence of Multinational Enterprise*. Cambridge, Mass.: Harvard University Press, 1970.

TWELVE

THE INTERIM PERIOD
FOR RESOURCES

In the first 11 chapters, the character of resources was shown, on the one hand, as being timeless and unchanging; yet, on the other hand, resources was described as an extremely dynamic concept. The latter interpretation is vividly illustrated by the worldwide fuel crisis that surfaced so dramatically in the 1970s. It was a crisis brought on by, among short-term factors, the finite nature (including localized occurrence) of fossil fuels—a nonrenewable fund-type resource. As the production of fossil fuels failed to keep pace with seemingly ever-growing demands, man turned flailingly in all directions in an attempt to escape his dilemma—a dilemma resulting not from an absolute consumption of all fossil fuels, but from the adverse environmental effects of the burning of fossil fuels and the prospects that fusion (the ultimate fuel) was less than 20 or 30 years away. This is a period less than sufficient to depreciate the costs of *traditional* power plants at *traditional* cost ratios. Meanwhile, intermediate suggestions included geothermal, solar, and wind sources of energy, wider use of water power, and many types of chemical reactions.

Solutions usually imply far more than economic considerations alone. Most fuel policies have long been administered politically, and, with the specter of fuelless winters and resultant hardships, the issue became truly a moral/psychological one. There was also the constant specter of a possible military/police application to force interim solutions globally.

Once fusion becomes feasible as a source of energy, and the transition to its widespread use is made, the world will enter an entirely new resources era—one in which man will more nearly be able to control (perhaps even shape) environments of his own choosing. Even in such an era, there will be problems of priorities and, conceivably, even "where to set the world's thermostat."

The first part of this text dealt primarily with the theoretical aspects of resource development. In Chapters One through Four, the indispensability of resources to man's culture and social achievement was set forth. The purpose of these four chapters was threefold:

1. The authors have sought to make it abundantly clear that man is inexorably bound up in resources—that resources affect all that he does, including even his values and value systems. And, in this regard, man is at the resources crossroads—concerning fuels, water, air, metals, and other basics to satisfactory living patterns. Man must decide which way to turn, which road or roads to take. The struggle is on, and battle lines are drawn. Vested interests are arrayed against the newly emerging industrializing people. Conservationists are aligned against preservationists. Both, in turn, are aligned against the exploiter. Alarmists are crying out against the complacent. In fact, the hue and cry is so great that the struggle alone promises to consume prodigious quantities of paper and human energies through courts and legislative halls. It is even possible that society may be sinking in a sea of rules and regulations that are whipsawing the patience of man by demanding applications to open a mine or a plant, with attendant processing delays, etc., until the snowballing effect seemingly serves to reinforce the waste and abandon with which man has been using scarce resources.

   Resources—the product of a tripartite interaction of nature, man, and culture—can be either created or destroyed by a society. On the one hand, technology can significantly extend the utility of man's resources; but its impact can be damaging to nature if not applied carefully. On the other hand, the point at which the various environmental commissions, with their elaborate sensor devices—including satellites, watershed, and other surface monitorings, and on and on—become countereffective may be agonizingly near. The result could be a collapse in material values as we now know them and a loss of mobility and, in turn, time and place utility. Man *is* at the crossroads!

2. The nature of resources was considered in these chapters and found to be sometimes fickle and sometimes steadfast, with the nonrenewable resources unrelenting in their requirements for: (a) administered prices, (b) constant exploration, (c) stockpiling, (d) new mining techniques by which to reach ever less accessible sources, (e) new transportation by which to reach ever more distant deposits, (f) new processes by which to claim ores increasingly less concentrated by nature, and (g) new or better ways by which man allocates his resources.

3. From the foregoing, a need for ever wiser resource-related decision-making processes evolves. The resource concepts presented are fundamental if man is to learn how to manage his resources. Even, or especially, with the advent of fusion power becoming a practical energy source, wise resource management will be critical—if man is to survive or escape devastating wars or widespread servitude. Thus, the ultimate goal of this text is to provide the rubric for those in industry or government who are, or would be, managers of resources. And, for students of resources, the text is intended to disseminate further the invaluable principles and ideas set forth by Erich Zimmermann, build on them, add to them, and present all of them in terms of present and future resources patterns and problems (as envisioned in the early 1970s).

Chapters Five through Eleven developed selected resource problems of particular importance at this time. These are the *Zeitgeist* problems of today.

Water (Chapter Five) was noted as existing in abundance but horribly abused by man. Yet, as a "flow resource," it can be—and is being—renewed. Sections of Lake Erie are showing improvement, as are such once-polluted streams as the Ohio River. In the latter case, it was noted that a new *level* of government, the Ohio River Commission, has been created between the state and federal levels to facilitate the establishment, policing, and enforcement of uniformly acceptable standards among the various states in the Ohio watershed. In this regard, even such poisoned water bodies as Lake St. Clair—once laden with, and seemingly dead from, mercury and other industrial wastes—is again showing more of the blue sparkle that made it a renowned recreation area. Even such vile liquid flows of sewage, chemical waste, and industrial garbage as the Houston Ship Channel are showing that some of man's worst pollution trends are *not* irreversible.

Man also is learning much about aquifers; and, through the use of spreading weirs, recharge wells, dams, and sumps, he is no longer rushing water to the sea as quickly as possible. Wide areas of pavement and roofs and vast tillage systems consisting of literally millions of miles of clay underground drainage pipes are now being used to collect waters for both surface and underground storage. Also, along the Long Island and California coasts, recharge wells into which fresh water is forced are creating effective dams of fresh water that are repulsing salt water encroachments that have so seriously affected fresh water supplies along these coasts and that remain as serious problems around Galveston Island and elsewhere. Although much remains to be done, man now understands a great deal of the technology needed to deal with the water cycle and to maintain it as a healthy closed system, salutary in all of its open segments.

Similarly, man understands the technology that permits the near maximization of gravity's power in the water cycle. Remaining to be more fully developed are the means of storing energy realized in peak flow seasons for use in off or slack water seasons. In this regard, reservoir construction has done much; still, better electrical storage devices are needed if India and other monsoon areas are to capitalize fully on the energy potentials of "running water."

Also pointed up and highlighted in the text is man's turning to the seas for resources. He not only is turning to the seas for such traditional uses as transportation and food, but also now is seeking out vast freshwater springs, minerals and ways to live under—as well as on—the water. He will learn more of ocean rivers or currents and tidal ranges in his search for resources. Man is beginning to learn about inner space, as well as about outer space. Indeed, the role of the seas in man's scheme of resources has not really changed since Sir Walter Raleigh made his seemingly eternally true statement that "whoever commands the seas . . . commands the riches of the world."

It is now evident that, even though man may have tremendous work ahead if he is to manage the earth's water cycle, his understanding—given the necessary investment and the will to act—suggests that he can treat as a renewable resource the water upon which he is so dependent. Perhaps the real key to man's comprehension of his water problems came as a

FIGURE 56. Our small world, as seen from the moon. Can anyone doubt the fact that we live in a closed system, with its finite limitations?

result of a space age realization that the planet earth *is* a closed system and that six-billion-plus humans are disrupting the system established by nature.

In the chapter "Land: The Renewable Resource" (Chapter Six), the various meanings of land were presented. It was noted that land means *different things* to *different people*. Land was seen as the first of the great building blocks that man, early in his history, discovered could be destroyed by over-grazing, improper cultivation, careless fires, and other abuses. Although man often does not agree on land use (for example, housing v. farming, cattle v. sheep grazing, plowing v. pasturing, mining v. forest, grass v. forest, etc.), he is able to measure acceptable intensities of land use that will not allow degradation of the soil by eroding agents of wind, water saltation, and gravity. Man has learned to rebuild soil on once-denuded areas. By applying proper fertilizers and the use of ground cover vegetation, he has returned to rich productivity such vast areas as the once impoverished red and yellow lateritic soils of southeastern United States.

It was in regard to land that man first developed such land-use schemes as rural zoning and public forests—for a multiplicity of uses, including timber growth, watershed control, recreation, wildlife protection, and preservation. Land use became the first major resource of concern to man. It has long been the cause of the battle between conservationists and preservationists. Finally, it was noted that "land" transcends economic implications alone, to encompass pride, security, confidence, landscape, beauty, and even religious commitments. In the consideration of all resources, no other single resource affects man as markedly as *land;* seemingly his values and entire value system hinge on land and its ownership. From the great schisms of the communist system at the one pole to the pure, free-enterprise system at the other, land, problems of ownership, and benefits from its productivity have involved arguments among nations, states, families, friends, and neighbors. Land and attitudes toward land have constituted fundamental differences among peoples. The "territorial imperative" is so strong in man that almost all conflicts—including religious and ideological wars, or wars over minerals, timbers, or defense postures—are related to land, and, in time, "land" becomes a Hungary, Korea, Vietnam, Sinai, or one of the other battlegrounds.

Although water may be the "essential" resource, land is the key resource and one that caused the famous World War II prediction that "he who rules the Heartland rules the world"—a statement so imaginative and so powerful that Hitler (through his advisor, General Karl Haushofer) turned to the east to seize the vast land resources of the Soviet Ukraine, steppes, and plains. The fact that U.S.S.R. leadership recognized the same values in its Heartland produced the world's most costly battle—Stalingrad. The fact that the North American continent possesses even greater extents of good, arable land holds promise of great opportunities equalled only by the dangers of its being coveted by other nations.

In the chapter "Air: The Ubiquitous But Troubled Resource" (Chapter Seven), air appears to have gone through the same steps of public concern as water. Long considered infinite—an image literally shattered by the automobile age—air now is seen as *definitely finite*. Here, as with water, public awakening has produced concern and brought widespread corrective actions. Even recently-emerging industrial nations such as Japan, surrounded by millions of square miles of ocean, recognize the implications of their industrial activities, and certain areas with unusual combinations of climatic influence suffer more than others. Cities such as Los Angeles, Denver, Tokyo, and Houston are now at work combatting pollution, while some areas such as Pittsburgh and St. Louis are past the most adverse periods of their severest pollution and provide evidence that man can, if he only will, control his technology.

Much remains to be done, but air pollution boards are established in industrialized nations, standards are set, monitoring systems are being implemented, and enforcement has begun. Measures to prevent air pollution—as with water pollution—are costly. Combined, the measures will add much to worldwide inflationary pressures. And the question of whether standards of living will fall becomes secondary to the realization that, without these measures, man and his civilizations would be destroyed.

In the chapter "Minerals as Basic Stepping Stones to Civilizations and Social Achievement" (Chapter Eight), the dependence of man's affluence on minerals was shown as central. Significant aspects of minerals also encompass their limiting characteristics, including: (1) their finite nature under today's technologies, (2) their limited occurrence, (3) the constant requirements for further exploration, (4) the need for stockpiling, and (5) the concept of administered prices. Today, as never before, man needs fusion to create a breakthrough in his drive to bring affluence to all mankind—to erase poverty. In fact, there is evidence right now that, rather than man's providing affluence, just the opposite seems to be taking place. Mineral limitations, in terms of both geography and geology, are forcing the seekers of mineral wealth to go deeper and farther—thereby using up even more minerals to beget minerals. Obviously the effects are cumulative with a snowballing result, further stoking worldwide fires of inflation.

Real shortages of many minerals—especially in the areas of fuel for energy development and the rationing of scarce space-heating fuels, gasoline for automobiles, and kerosene for jet aircraft—are already a reality. The many nations that have oil and gas have organized globally to maximize their opportunities, while the "have not" nations are seeking means to keep prices within reason and are being forced to seek an elusive self-sufficiency. The latter case includes the United States.

Shortages and an ever-growing need to reuse scrap materials—particularly in the case of iron, alloys, and aluminum—are forcing changes in freight rate structures in favor of the movement of scrap, rather than ore concentrates from the mine. This changing freight structure includes new routes, terminal facilities, market areas, and laws. The goal is not only the prevention of accumulation of litter or relief of pressure on garbage dumps and landfills, but also the saving of dollars that go for (outbound) payments for foreign ores. More than 60 percent of the iron ore used in the United States and almost all of the bauxite (aluminum ore) are now imported. Thus, reuse may well become an absolute necessity. At any rate, *reuse* considerations are currently one of the main areas of dynamics in mineral development and *use*.

New technologies are emerging at an unprecedented rate. Under way are efforts to find techniques to exploit economically oil-rich shales, ever-lower grades of ores (e.g., copper, molybdenum, etc.) and research drives to find substitutes for tin, copper, and other equally dear metals. At the same time, man is learning alternate means within the industrial processes so as to eliminate the need to use known dangerous minerals such as mercury, asbestos, and radium.

Current and lasting problems regarding mineral development include:

1. How to effect wider uses of acceptable substitutes (such as glass for aluminum in cookware) in a free society and still retain consumer choice; and
2. How to find adequate capital outlay to implement new manufacturing technologies in the face of already heavy fixed investments.

Progress may be slower than what is acceptable to many persons in society, yet so rapid as to be financially disastrous to others. But this latter consideration should not be taken lightly, as it often means lost jobs or painful dislocations—and even the demise or distress of entire cities or towns.

There is no evidence, however, that man's use and continued development of minerals will be limited by technology. Indeed, there is ample evidence to suggest that minerals from the sea or distant lands may be more costly than would applications of technology to the concentration of domestic deposits. And, it is especially in regard to technologies (flotation, centrifics, chemistry-reagents, and catalysts) that hopes are high that minerals will continue to be available in adequate quantities in the interim period before "fusion."

The entirety of Chapter Nine was devoted to "The Chemical Industry:

User and Builder of Resources." An understanding of the resource aspects of this particular industrial type is essential to an appreciation of the axiom cited by Erich Zimmermann that "resources are not—they become." Chemical processors, while some of the worst polluters of water, air, and land, are also the hope that technology can be controlled or that substitutes for minerals and products from forest, farm, and sea can be synthesized.

The chemical industry is painted generally as having the following characteristics: (1) possessing keen competition (although some segments of the industry are oligopolistic and certain economists will dispute this) in terms of costs, raw materials, processes, products, and national or world markets, (2) experiencing rapid change in products and markets, (3) demanding high research and development investments, (4) undergoing high rates of obsolescence and depreciation, (5) requiring multistage, interlocking plant processes, (6) having high capital investment per worker, (7) needing price stability, and (8) being largely water oriented—whether for transportation, plant processes, or effluent.

It is seen, in conclusion, that even though the chemical industry is notable as an environmental offender and is prodigious in its demands for, and use of, basic physical resources, it is still man's greatest hope for holding back the tide of poverty that will engulf man if chemical technology and industry are not adequately available to feed, house, and clothe the world's burgeoning peoples.

"Resources in World Affairs" is the subject of Chapter Ten. World political and industrial leaders have long been forced to consider minerals, land, and water as decision-making factors. In this triumvirate, minerals are king. With the right kind of minerals in sufficient volume, man can create productive combinations of soil and water or, if necessary, seize them by force. Even before the advent of modern industry, man fought over minerals at salt licks. Whether seemingly immoral or not, any nation that would remain strong and a viable factor in the world's decision-making processes must first ensure that it has access to essential minerals with which to protect itself or to take the offensive. If a nation would remain strong, there is no alternative to its having access to minerals of many kinds, including tin, bauxite (aluminum), iron, wolframite (tungsten), and others. In fact, most governments publish lists of those minerals considered to be strategic, critical, and essential to an economy.

That military force still is a means of a nation's garnering minerals and other resources has been made abundantly clear in recent decades by the violent reaction of the U.S.S.R. to the 1956 Hungarian revolt, whereby the Soviet Union ensured the continued availability of bauxite from which to produce aluminum and, in turn, airplanes in a near all-out effort to "catch up" with the 110,000-plane annual capacity attained by the United States during World War II. In the 1951 Korean conflict, tungsten played a key role because this metal was needed to produce jet engines—critical in the worldwide changeover from reciprocating engines to jets. Even though difficult to prove or disprove, considerations of tin must have been in the minds of those believing in the so-called "domino theory" of Southeast Asian countries as destined to fall, one by one, under communist forms of government. Even the Mid-East wars between Israel and Arabs include considerations of oil as well as of arable land and living space. Minerals still sit at the council tables of man, and their "voices" are given keen consideration.

Clearly nations have fought for minerals. Supposedly the initial undertaking to secure needed minerals is economic in nature. If this approach fails, then political means are sought. If these fail, moral/psychological persuasion is tried. If none of these measures produces the needed mineral, there may be a resort to police or military measures. To avoid war in this day and age, the world is likely to try such an economic/political organization as the giant global company, which knows no national boundaries.

Chapter Eleven, "The World Corporation or Supranational Company," was included to give emphasis to man's need to garner resources by means other than war. Although the movement's history is too brief for one to predict with accuracy, it still could be a hope of better things to come for more of the world's people. To some, the supranational company is but another form of colonialism. Yet in many ways it serves to spread affluence by creating jobs and disbursing profit benefits more widely, thereby (at least to some degree) sidestepping a need to use force. Many multinational firms are reporting impressive profits. Others are not faring well. The supranational company could be the next logical step beyond the current multinational organization.

The chief forces militating against the global corporation are also the seeds of strong nationalism. Even with a supposedly "fair price," the loss of jobs in previously labor-oriented nations to out-of-country plants, and transportation considerations, combine with cultural differences (especially in terms of language, values, and value systems) to cause certain individuals to "Buy American" or "Buy Swedish," etc. The resistance comes from many directions—unions, communities, etc. Many nations do not allow consumers to elect where an item is made, or they strew embargoes, tariffs, and/or red tape in the paths of existing and would-be world corporations. Perhaps the fear of "seizure," as exemplified in Libya, Iran, Mexico, Chile, and a long list of other countries, is the greatest deterrent to an even more widespread growth and acceptance of the global corporation concept. The supranational company of the future undeniably offers hope of reducing dangers of war, broadening markets, and decreasing poverty; but whether it can equalize resource allocations remains to be proven because—although it *can* accomplish this—there is the question of whether man has the patience to "truly test" it. Globally, it appears at this time to be a still-distant possibility.

In summary and conclusion, this text theorizes that there is not now a place for the prophets of doom—foretelling man's demise because of the finite nature of resources. Rather, there is every reason to believe that man is becoming master of his technologies and will be able to weather the resource storms bound to occur before the "age of fusion" arrives. Once fusion becomes a reality, the resources field is likely to become an entirely new "ball game." The already dynamic nature of resource development will gain unbelievable impetus.

What the text purports to show is that the management of resources is vital to man's progress. Indeed, man's future civilizations and social achievements hinge on how well he handles his resource problems.

For this reason, it is argued that more and more educational effort needs to be directed toward the development of more knowledge about resources and toward the dissemination of resource concepts, axioms, understanding, interpretations, and appreciations. To that end, this book has been compiled, written, and dedicated.

INDEX